# Re-use—The Art and Politics of Integration and Anxiety

# Re-use—The Art and Politics of Integration and Anxiety

EDITED BY
# JULIA A. B. HEGEWALD
# SUBRATA K. MITRA

**⊗SAGE** www.sagepublications.com

Los Angeles • London • New Delhi • Singapore • Washington DC

*First published in 2012 by*

**SAGE Publications India Pvt Ltd**
B1/I-1 Mohan Cooperative Industrial Area
Mathura Road, New Delhi 110 044, India
*www.sagepub.in*

**SAGE Publications Inc**
2455 Teller Road
Thousand Oaks, California 91320, USA

**SAGE Publications Ltd**
1 Oliver's Yard
55 City Road
London EC1Y 1SP, United Kingdom

**SAGE Publications Asia-Pacific Pte Ltd**
33 Pekin Street
#02-01 Far East Square
Singapore 048763

Published by Vivek Mehra for SAGE Publications India Pvt Ltd, typeset in 10/13 pt Palatino by Diligent Typesetter, Delhi and printed at Chaman Enterprises, New Delhi.

**Library of Congress Cataloging-in-Publication Data**
Re-use—the art and politics of integration and anxiety/edited by Julia A.B. Hegewald and Subrata K. Mitra.
     p. cm.
   Includes bibliographical references and index.
   1. Historic preservation—India.   2. Politics and culture—India.   3. Social change—South Asia.   4. Historic preservation—Political aspects—India.   5. Historic buildings—Conservation and restoration—India.   6. Historic buildings—Remodeling for other use—India.   7. Architecture—Conservation and restoration—India.   8. Art and state—India.   9. India—Cultural policy.   10. India—Religious life and customs.   I. Hegewald, Julia A. B.   II. Mitra, Subrata Kumar, 1949–   III. Title: Re-use.

| DS419.R48 | 363.6'90954—dc23 | 2011 | 2011051202 |

**ISBN:** 978-81-321-0655-5 (HB)

**The SAGE Team:** Gayeti Singh, Arpita Dasgupta, and Rajinder Kaur

*The editors dedicate this book to*
*the countless generations of anonymous re-users in South Asia*
*who have striven to put the infinite into the finite,*

*whose creative efforts have kept alive the past linked to the present,*
*and who have contributed to bridging the worlds of re-use and scholarship.*

*Thank you for choosing a SAGE product! If you have any comment, observation or feedback, I would like to personally hear from you. Please write to me at* <u>contactceo@sagepub.in</u>

—Vivek Mehra, Managing Director and CEO,
SAGE Publications India Pvt Ltd, New Delhi

**Bulk Sales**

SAGE India offers special discounts for purchase of books in bulk. We also make available special imprints and excerpts from our books on demand.

For orders and enquiries, write to us at

*Marketing Department*
*SAGE Publications India Pvt Ltd*
*B1/I-1, Mohan Cooperative Industrial Area*
*Mathura Road, Post Bag 7*
*New Delhi 110044, India*
E-mail us at <u>marketing@sagepub.in</u>

*Get to know more about SAGE, be invited to SAGE events, get on our mailing list. Write today to* <u>marketing@sagepub.in</u>

*This book is also available as an e-book.*

————ॐ————

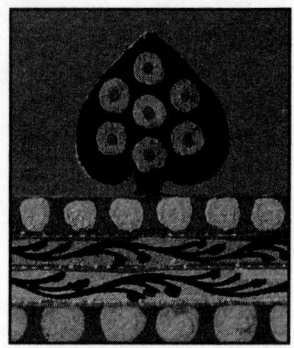

# CONTENTS

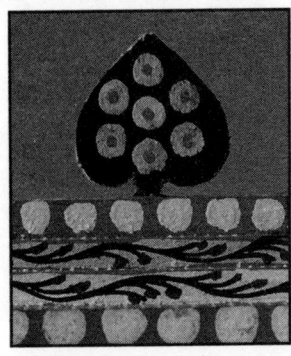

# LIST OF PLATES

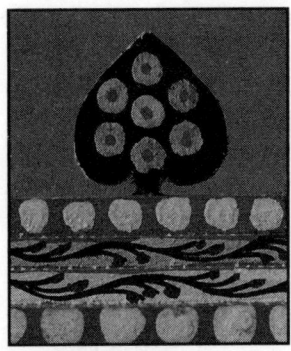

# PREFACE

The idea of this volume first took shape in course of a lively discussion on 're-use in art and politics' at a panel that we organised on the occasion of the Twentieth European Conference on Modern South Asian Studies (ECMSAS) in Manchester, UK, in July 2008. The aim of the panel was to critically engage with the concept of 're-use' and bring together specialists working in a number of disciplines in the humanities and the social sciences, and to engage with the diversity of re-use in the wider region of South Asia and beyond. The discussion, during and after the panel, convinced us that there was a need for a platform to sustain a debate on this vital aspect of life in South Asia. We also felt the need to balance the coverage of the two dimensions of re-use—the visual and religious, and the social and political—and invited five more specialists to join us for the publication. The final shape that the text has taken is itself evidence of the re-use of the initial presentations, enriched through engaging conversations with colleagues from a number of fields, in different locations and on the sidelines of several conferences. In this sense, the book is a testimony to a collaborative effort among the authors, editors, critics and students spread across Europe, South Asia and the United States.

\* \* \* \*

Most of all, the volume represents the sustained intellectual engagement of the authors and editors with the fascinating world of South Asia, a region whose visual and religious lives are constantly enriched by the social, political and economic process in a reciprocal interaction. The result is the emergence of a civilisation which, even as it is caught in the process of rapid change, nevertheless retains its links with the past, based on hybrid forms, categories, rituals, processes and institutions that conflate the past and the present.

The volume also marks a point of departure for the two editors who have been engaged in a regular dialogue on aspects of re-use since 2006. To our great good fortune, serendipity has joined design. In autumn 2007, Julia Hegewald started teaching a course on re-use in South Asian art and architecture to her final year BA students in Art History and Visual Studies at the University of Manchester. Following this, early in 2008, Subrata Mitra became the co-ordinator of the area A—Governance and Administration, in the interdisciplinary Cluster of Excellence, 'Asia and Europe in a Global Context: Shifting Asymmetries in Cultural Flows' at Heidelberg University, Germany. These contexts opened up access to lively discussions with engaged students, and to new colleagues, ideas and conferences, addressed to cultural and conceptual flow.

We hope that the theoretical background provided in this volume will position the term 're-use' more firmly within a network of interrelated alternative terms, and that the diversity of papers from a number of regions and periods in South Asia will stimulate further debate and research contributions to the area. We are delighted to have found such a diversity of viewpoints articulated in the scholarly papers, but any views and opinions expressed in the chapters are those of individual authors and do not necessarily represent the views and opinions of the editors.

* * * *

We take this pleasant opportunity to thank our co-authors who have responded to our incessant queries with exemplary alacrity, often on issues that were far outside their basic disciplines, because that is germane to the nature of this interdisciplinary book and its transdisciplinary approach. We would like to thank the audience at the panel in Manchester and the many colleagues who engaged with us in lively and often controversial debates (which have given us the desire and the ability to put this volume together), and in understanding both the potential and the limits of the term re-use.

We are grateful to several friends who have helped in many valuable ways: Irene Martin-Alvarez, who as student assistant, contributed to the smooth running of the panel in July 2008; Lion König who rendered valuable help in his double capacity as co-author and research assistant and Prasanna Nayak who helped collect the sacred artefacts of Lord Jagannatha. We would like to thank Professor Ulf Hegewald, who made photos of our Jagannatha objects and reworked the large number of photographic illustrations for this volume. We would also like to express our gratitude to the German Research Foundation (DFG), who provided valuable financial support to Julia Hegewald through the Emmy Noether Programme and to Subrata Mitra through the Cluster of Excellence. This has made it possible to organise the panel in Manchester, invite some of the speakers and to hold a number of editorial meetings in Germany and in the UK between 2008 and 2010. A fortuitous meeting with Dr Sugata Ghosh,

Vice President (Commissioning) with SAGE Publications India Pvt Ltd, at the Manchester panel started a conversation that led to a contract; we thank him for his trust in this highly experimental project and for his assistance and encouragement through the long process of turning ideas into text.

* * * *

Finally, the chapters of this book introduce the reader to different forms of re-use—some successful and others less so—and illustrate recurring themes and patterns in the history of re-use, which give tangible form to the theory of re-use presented in this book. The aim of this collection of essays, however, is not simply to present an accumulation of instances of re-use from a number of contexts, but to generate and sustain a new approach, which seeks the evidence of continuity, hybridity and indigeneity in the rich and diverse life of the region. In putting these chapters together, it is our hope to have provided a platform for scholars and students of South Asian life to take these issues further.

JULIA A. B. HEGEWALD
and SUBRATA K. MITRA
July 2010

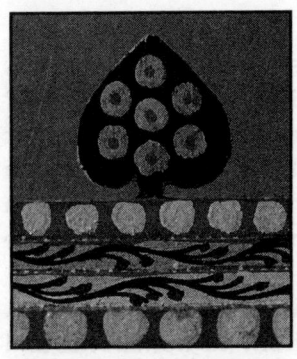

*Chapter 1*

# ART AND POLITICS

## THE DIALECTICS OF DUALITY, AFFINITY AND CONFLUENCE

### BY JULIA A. B. HEGEWALD AND SUBRATA K. MITRA

This book offers a novel approach to the relationship of the past and the present in terms of the concept and theory of 're-use', and illustrates its main argument through several case studies in art and architecture, ritual, modes of worship, institutions and national icons. It joins the growing field of transcultural flow and social change with three principal aims. First, it introduces the theory of re-use as an important heuristic tool in analysing and interpreting cultural and political changes and the transnational flow of ideas, concepts and objects. Second, it contributes to the transdisciplinary debate between traditionally clearly delineated disciplines—here the humanities, and social sciences in particular. In the third place, with regards to these two debates, it provides a regional focus on South Asia, which constitutes an exceptionally fertile area for re-use studies and for the bridging of disciplinary boundaries.

## THE PUZZLE

Why do old forms and practices persist, not merely as decorative appendages but as liminal, hybrid and functional manifestations, in the midst of the new? The presence of 'outdated pomp' in royal and presidential processions, archaic manners and rituals in contemporary settings, sacred objects and symbols in modern public buildings or lingering vestiges of vanquished civilisations in the holy shrines and palaces of the victors have been documented in a wide variety of scholarly works.[1] The meeting of opposites—for example, the modern and the traditional—is not always a scene for peaceful accommodation. However, as the case studies of this volume—drawn from the humanities and the social sciences—show, dualities are sometimes overcome through converging affinities, leading to the creation of novel and innovative hybrid forms. The fact that the fault lines marked by conflicts of belief, ritual, power, status or race sometimes get transformed into overlapping or hybrid categories— flexible enough to generate intellectual and artistic coherence underpinning a new political order—is a testimony to the agency of those who are able and willing to see the affinity that might underpin duality and difference, and who generate the momentum for confluence where unending war or conflict might have appeared inevitable.

The concept of duality of the modern and the traditional characterises many disciplines—most particularly the social sciences—that deal with the theme of the 'discontinuity' that marks the modern world apart from the traditional. The notion of modernity dwelt upon by the great Enlightenment thinkers, like Condorcet, present the idea of progress in the form of a necessary break with the pre-modern past. The Marxist theory of revolution is the epitome of this approach.[2]

The humanities have been less drastically affected by the basic idea of a paradigmatic break between the past and the present, or a necessary duality of facts and values. However, the modern art movement also saw itself as a break with the past and this has been reflected in arthistorical research. It is striking that

---

[1] See Rudolph & Rudolph (1967), Asher & Metcalf (1994), Davis (1999), Eaton (2000), Hegewald (2006a; 2006b; 2007; 2009; forthcoming), Hegewald & Mitra (2008) and Tillotson (1990) just to name a few. For more details on the available literature, see Chapter 2 in this volume.

[2] As Rudolph and Rudolph (1967: 3) comment:

> The idea of dialectical conflict denigrates the past in its assumption that 'theses' will be consumed in the fires of revolutionary change. Building on such assumptions, theorists of social change in new nations have found a dichotomy between tradition and modernity. Useless and valueless, tradition has been relegated to a historical trash heap. Modernity will be realized when tradition has been destroyed and superseded.

although artists argued that the 'old' and 'traditional' was outdated and gone, art historians continued to focus on the 'classical' periods and for a long time did not see the links with and the merit of the more recent material. As we shall see in the section on 'Re-use as a Bridge between the Disciplines', the field of economic development and cultural change has been dominated mostly by the social sciences that have acquired, in this process, hegemony over the way we imagine the past and the imperative of replacing it with the present. The following three sections will briefly introduce the three main underlying themes of this book, regarding the contested relationship of the past and the present.

## The Concept and Theory of Re-use[3]

'Re-use' essentially refers to using an item again. This can be an object, an edifice, building materials, a style, a law, a concept, a form of governance, an idea or anything else. It is a deliberate and selective process in which existing elements are borrowed and taken out of their former surroundings to be applied to a fresh context. For this to happen, a disruption and break has to happen, favouring a confrontation with something new. Re-use does not imitate and replicate; it is a creative combination of old and novel elements, which aims to take the item or concept further.

The individual chapters in this book examine different forms of re-use in South Asian art and architecture, in jewellery, in dance-theatre, in politics, the creation of states and in religions. These introduce the concept of re-use of tangible objects—such as statues, architectural spaces and forms of governance—and of less concrete items—such as motifs, styles and beliefs. Instead of treating artistic, religious and political developments as linear evolutions, the chapters in this book encourage its readers to think of them more as continuous modification of the past, and a periodic return to earlier forms. These can be indigenous as well as non-local elements, which have entered the scene through transnational, transreligious or transcultural exchanges to form composite constructs.

Such changes are brought about through borrowing, appropriation and assimilation, both enforced and voluntary. The various milieus which favour the creation of such hybrid cultural artefacts, religions and forms of politics are war and conquest, trade and travel, and potentially any other form of social interaction which creates an encounter with the 'other'.

Nevertheless, as will be argued in more detail in Chapter 2, re-use is not inevitable, but brought about through agency. Cultures and people who re-use

---

[3] Re-use, as a theoretical concept, is discussed in more detail and greater depth in the following chapter in this volume.

have a specific motive and aim. A particularly beautiful style or image can be re-used out of aesthetic reasons or a motif can be applied in varying frameworks and with diverse connotations over the time of its existence. The annexation and re-use of a sacred or symbolic item can express political messages about domination and power and can play an important role in generating legitimacy for the latest ruling elite. A significant aspect of re-use is that it is discerning and choosy and that whereas some elements are adopted and filled with a new significance, others get deprived and emptied of meaning or even destroyed.

When conquering groups appropriate the sacred sites, buildings and statues or the political control centres and symbols of those who have lost power—to transform them into objects and institutions which serve their own purposes—they leave a trail of anxiety and loss, which, at first, can only be remedied by memory or denial. History has shown, however, that re-use as a compromise in which not all is lost but enough is retained to establish a connection with the past, can lead to hybridity, to assimilation and finally to integration.

The following chapter on the theory of re-use examines alternative terms, such as 'hybridity', 'indigenisation', 'syncretism', 'pluralism' and others, which are used alongside and instead of the term 're-use'. Yet, the following chapter—and this volume as a whole—argues in favour of the particular strength and validity of the term 're-use'.

## Re-use as a Bridge between the Disciplines

The humanities, generally more closely associated with traditional and conservative seats of learning, are regularly still seen as largely 'text-based studies', using primary sources, which are concerned more with the past than with the present. Some consider that they are dealing with too diverse contexts[4] and with non-measurable entities. With the establishment of new social science subjects, especially during the 1950s and 1960s, well over one-third of all academics today are based in the social sciences. These are judged to provide quantitative and verifiable data through opinion polls and surveys, which indicate change and relate to the present. Critics of this approach accuse social scientists of basing their conclusions merely on 'opinions'. On the other hand, a similar critique has been lodged against the reading of texts in the humanities,

---

[4] This leads to a situation where material from one source or area can rarely be applied to another. This has been contrasted with surveys in the social sciences where identical sets of questions are applied to a large number of contexts, producing comparable data.

which can be regarded as subjective interpretations.[5] In fact, these are discussions about methods and about what counts as legitimate knowledge or valid evidence.

Contrasting with these allegations and old categorisations is that the division between the two disciplines is a modern phenomenon. Scholarship at the University of Bologna (eleventh century), the oldest university in the world, combined the subject of law with the arts.[6] When working together 'across the divide', one realises how artificial this separation is and how porous and ambivalent the borders are.[7] Changes taking place at present have led to an often more ethnographical and less text-based approach in the humanities and an appreciation of non-statistical dimensions in social science scholarship.[8] In this volume, specialists from the humanities and the social sciences have applied one and the same method—the theory of re-use—and have judged it to be a fruitful tool in examining data from a wide diversity of contexts.

## Re-use and the Region of South Asia

The concept of re-use and the debate between the disciplines are, in this volume, examined in the context of South Asia. The choice of this particular region as exceptionally well suited with regards to the discussion of these issues, derives from the fact that it is home to well over one-fifth of the world's population and is a region celebrated for its diversity literally in all areas of life.

In South Asia, there is incomparable cultural and stylistic, linguistic, ethnic, religious and political diversity, just to name a few. India is the birthplace of four major world religions: Hinduism, Buddhism, Jainism and Sikhism. In addition, it possesses communities of considerable size professing to all other world faiths. India prides itself on unity in diversity, as a country where despite many

---

[5] The humanities are aware of the multiple 'readings' of texts. Based on mediaeval practice—and this is still reflected in the modern context of the Holy Scripture of the Roman Catholic Church—a text has four senses. The main two are the literal (or historical) and the spiritual. The latter consists of the allegorical, the moral (tropological) and the anagogical readings. See the *Catechism of the Catholic Church* (CCC 115–119), for instance, on the webpage of the United States Conference of Catholic Bishops.

[6] In addition, students also read subjects which nowadays would be categorised as natural or medical sciences. See the official webpage of the University of Bologna.

[7] In some universities, history is considered a subject belonging to the humanities and elsewhere to the social sciences. The same applies to anthropology, archaeology and linguistics.

[8] The 'Research Network on Love', based in the School of Social Sciences at the University of Manchester, recruited staff from the humanities as the issues raised and the data provided by participants in interviews (largely on emotions) was often not measurable in traditional forms and required experts offering alternative tools.

approaches and views, democracy prevails. South Asia's history is marked by invasions and the settlement of new ethnic groups, which have produced composite cultures with many shared traditions and beliefs. Notwithstanding, it is a region which has strong local traditions and identities which, for the most part, are not perceived as antagonistic to the larger whole. During colonial rule, an involuntary confrontation with Western culture and political institutions left many scars but made India stronger and more diverse. Located strategically between the western Asian states and the Far East, it has been crossed by networks of trade routes and has communicated through ocean trade with cultures in remote quarters of the world.

These issues illustrate both the potential for as well as the actual amount of re-use that has and is taking place throughout the region. The contributions in this volume draw on a wide variety of geographical areas, subjects and periods, reaching from temples constructed during the early centuries of the common era, via the colonial and Independence periods, to the present day.

## RE-USE IN SOUTH ASIA: ART AND POLITICS

Within the larger context of the humanities and the social sciences, this volume stresses the close link between and the subtle interrelatedness of culture and politics.[9] It agrees with recent scholarship which does not consider culture as a totally separate and autonomous domain which is independent of and isolated from social and political life.[10] It acknowledges that culture and politics are changeable and that they influence one another. However, this does not mean that in a specific place and time, what constitutes culture and politics cannot be defined.[11] Even though they have constituent areas which are more adaptable and allow subtle variations on a theme, politics and art both have a firm structure, which is largely predetermined through their past. The modern state in India builds on elements drawn from its British, Mughal and Hindu predecessors (Mitra 2012).

This volume brings together scholarly contributions that focus on specific historical examples of appropriation, selective transformation, conquest, conversion and other forms of the re-use of doctrines, designs, buildings, institutions, forms of government laws, practices and rituals. After a theoretical introduction to the

---

[9] The contributions by Hegewald and Mitra, Nayak, and also Mitra and König in this volume focus specifically on the connection between art and politics. This plays a major part in the contribution by Lorenzetti, and indirectly in many of the other chapters too.

[10] This has been argued by the Canadian political philosopher James Tully (1995). A debate on these issues can be found in Kompridis (2005: 318–43).

[11] It does not mean that culture and politics have no structure and are entirely fluid and unbound as described by Kompridis (2005: 319).

concept, philosophy, motifs and limitations of re-use in Chapter 2 by Julia A. B. Hegewald, the book introduces twelve examples of re-use, taken from a vast variety of contexts in South Asia. The first six contributions focus more closely—although never exclusively—on re-use in the arts and the latter six more clearly on politics. Fascinating are the many references in the first set of chapters to political meanings, and to culture and tradition in the latter. This illustrates the ability of the concept of re-use to bridge the divide between the disciplines.

## Re-use Applied in the Humanities

The first chapter by Julia A. B. Hegewald and Subrata K. Mitra—creating a microcosmic representation of the whole volume—brings together re-use studies from the humanities and the social sciences, and combines cultural and political re-use within one chapter. At the start of the chapter, Hegewald analyses three art historical instances of the re-use of Jaina temples by the Vira-Shaiva (Lingayat) community in northern Karnataka. All three illustrate forcible appropriations of sacred places and statues, but illustrate different approaches and intentions.

In the former Jaina temple at Hallur, it is largely the architectural structure—treated by the latest owners as an empty shell—which has been filled with new functions. A number of the Jina (Jaina teacher) sculptures inside as well as on the outside of the temple display features of desecration and mutilation but they have not been entirely destroyed. This suggests that the figures are likely to have been preserved to emphasise the triumph of the Vira-Shaivas over the former Jaina elite to act as symbols of victory.

In the second example from Adargunchi, the temple structure appears to have been of lesser importance. In this instance, the large statue of an enlightened Jaina teacher inside the sanctum was the foremost object of re-use. The sacred icon has been reconsecrated and treated as a figural portrayal of Shiva, locally called Doddappa. At both sites, the Jainas have been excluded from their former sacred sites.

At Kagvad, the circumstances are different. Despite the fact that the Vira-Shaivas have taken over the main temple area on the ground floor and have appropriated some former Jaina images, the Jainas still venerate their principal icons inside the same edifice. This is done in subterranean chambers underneath the temple. The latter situation illustrates the chance for integration which can be found in re-use, but also the power—here mainly religious—which new groups gain through such appropriations.

In the case study of the cult of Jagannatha by Mitra in this chapter, the analysis of the origin and evolution of a regional belief system in Orissa—within a time frame of about a thousand years—helps us understand the crucial role of religion in generating political order and legitimacy. For a political order to be legitimate, secular authority has to be firmly embedded in a moral order that encompasses the whole spectrum of the society, stretching from the holders of power to its helpless subjects. The morality of such authority might derive from multiple sources, including sacred beliefs, as also the visible benefits of social and economic transactions and institutional arrangements that encapsulate the sacred.

The chapter shows how, starting with the Aryan invaders of Orissa who appropriated Jagannatha—initially, a tribal totem—every successive invasion has seen the virtue in accommodating the cult within its larger structure of authority. This encapsulation has led to a certain measure of synthesis and the proliferation of hybrid practices, some of which can be seen in the analysis of ritual, practice, iconography and ancillary to sacred and social customs. This polymorphous moral order produced a limited measure of tolerance even for the foreigner (*yavana*s), as long as their beliefs could be accommodated within the plural pantheon and multitude of social practices, rituals and customs at local and regional levels. Jagannatha, the result of the synthesis of a tribal form and Aryan worship, became the subject of re-use during successive regimes of Muslims, British colonial rule and finally, the secular, post-Independence state.

Spread over several centuries and located in two different regional contexts, the joint essay by Hegewald and Mitra indicates a pan-Indian process of re-use, with a comparative frame, where culture and politics interpenetrate and lead to the emergence of hybrid forms that, in course of time, acquire the veneration of society.

\* \* \* \*

The contribution by the historian of art and architecture, George Michell, which follows, continues the theme of temple architecture in South India, but focuses on Hindu edifices. Michell stresses that there is evidence for the re-use of building techniques and styles throughout the Indian subcontinent, especially in the art of temple building.[12] In this contribution, he focuses on the city of Kumbakonam and the surrounding area of the Kaveri River Delta in Tamil Nadu.

The chapter commences by examining the re-use of architectural forms, first established under the Chola rulers in the eighth and ninth centuries, exemplified by the Nageshvara Temple at Kumbakonam. Michell illustrates how certain formal elements—predominantly components of the elevation and the carved decorations of this early style—lend themselves particularly well to novel

---

[12] Although the editors of this volume propagate the term 're-use' to describe the adaptation and remodelling of earlier elements or styles (as outlined in more detail in Chapter 2), Michell uses a variety of terms, such as 're-use', 're-invention', 're-orchestration', 'revival', 'retro', 'retrograde' and 'resuscitation' to refer to similar practices.

applications and further developments in different environments. Elements which were used on a small scale in earlier periods were capable of being enlarged and applied on a monumental scale during later periods, as can be seen in the eleventh-century Chola temples at Thanjavur and Gangaikondacholapuram. In other words, due to certain formal aspects, the Chola style was particularly well suited to being re-used.

However, also the political associations connected with this artistic style contributed to a desire to re-use it strategically. The dynastic style of the Cholas gave visual expression to a powerful state and was therefore consciously revived, re-used and extended under the following Vijayanagara and Nayaka rulers (from fourteenth to eighteenth centuries), who evidently recognised its political and regional significance. Michell analyses in meticulous detail examples of what he calls the 'Neo-Chola' style. He argues that it is the dialogue between the Chola and the re-used Neo-Chola style which lies at the core of architectural developments in the city of Kumbakonam.

As is typical of re-use more generally, former elements were not simply imitated and copied but integrated into a new framework, aiming to improve on the earlier style and creating something novel. In this particular case study, however, Michell also shows that there are instances where the re-use of features associated with the imperial Chola style by later rulers created monuments—especially sanctuaries (*vimanas*) and gateway towers (*gopuras*)—which constitute such close copies of the earlier style that it is sometimes difficult to distinguish them from the Chola originals. He concludes that this confusion "seems to have been the intention: to remake the city's architectural image in the imperial Chola mode".

It appears that the later Vijayanagara and Nayaka dynasties intended to provide themselves with a strong regal identity and with dynastic continuity in the form of architectural structures 'pretending' to be Chola in style. This aimed at connecting themselves, as Michell suggests, with a "perhaps more glorious era", and granted them the necessary legitimacy for ruling the region.

\* \* \* \*

Contributing from his expertise as a curator of fine and decorative arts, Nick Barnard moves our attention from monumental temple structures to the applied arts. His chapter focuses on nineteenth-century jewellery designs, both Indian and European, and illustrates how, with changing attitudes towards precious ornaments, different forms of re-use were applied. His story of re-use starts with the British looting of valuable objects in contexts of war, such as the capture of Tipu Sultan's treasure in 1799 and the appropriation of the Koh-i-Noor diamond during the annexation of the Punjab in 1849. Barnard illustrates that during this period, very little of the plundered jewellery survived in its original form. Falling into the category of 'recycling'—which will be explained in the following chapter—jewellery was broken down into its raw materials, the gold molten down and its constituent elements sold off simply for financial gains. In this crudest way of re-use, the journey of the raw materials is difficult to trace.

Those pieces which were not broken up entirely were, in most circumstances, still altered to adapt them to the tastes of their new owners. Frequently, this involved the resetting and recutting of the stones. By and large, the European clientele admired the costly gems but not so much the Indian-style decorations, leading to the removal of the stones and their resetting in European-made jewellery. In this form, the ornaments became 'wearable' but lost their Indian character. Just like the breaking down of the jewellery into its basic materials for monetary gains, this constitutes a relatively unsophisticated form of re-use where items are only re-used for their value but do not involve the transfer of cultural associations and motifs.[13]

Contrasting with this tendency are important royal ornaments, which held a particular political and symbolic significance, such as the Koh-i-Noor or the Timur Ruby, which although changed by their colonial owners, were purposely made to retain their Indian character. These were objects of financial and aesthetic appreciation, but more so, they were understood as symbols of power and British imperial control.

It was only after the Great Exhibition of 1851, at which displays of Indian jewellery were prominently presented and admired, that the public started to appreciate Indian-style ornaments in their original and more indigenous form. Initially, these foreign ornaments concerned only an elite group of society, predominantly collectors, assembling curiosities and design reformers, interested in improving the quality of British design and public taste.

Nonetheless, soon after, the impact of these extraordinary exhibits were also felt in other areas. Princess Alexandra received Indian jewellery as her wedding gift and the paintings of several Pre-Raphaelite painters, such as Dante Gabriel Rossetti, depicting Indian-style jewellery as items of exotic beauty.[14] This reflected a new awareness of and interest in Indian jewellery, which helped to prepare the ground for its later success in fashion, where it was turned into an affordable and desirable accessory for the British public. During the Aesthetic Movement, with its interest in handmade jewellery, Liberty's in London started stocking traditional Indian as well as Indian-inspired jewellery towards the end of the nineteenth century.

---

[13] It is fascinating to observe that Barnard demonstrates that people at the time were aware of the ethical questions relating to such destructive re-use. This is expressed in Wilkie Collins' novel *The Moonstone* (2007), which narrates the tragedy that affected all those who owned a precious stone removed by force from a statue enshrined in the temple at Somnathpur.

[14] This illustrates an interesting case of 're-use' by representing an object and by 're-using' it in a different medium—in this instance, painting.

Besides, Barnard also examines the re-use of European jewellery design forms in India, which became widespread during the mid-nineteenth century. The ornaments were largely produced by Indian jewellers who at first targeted the European expatriate community in India. Increasingly, however, wealthy Indians and royalty turned to wearing Westernised forms of jewellery, which again constituted hybrid forms. Traditional Indian techniques and motifs were employed in ornaments made for the European market and often reveal subtle transformations of traditional Indian ornaments for Western purposes. These pieces of jewellery, and those produced by European jewellers who established workshops in India, show intriguing materialisations of the re-use of shapes and techniques in a seemingly limitless exchange between Europe and South Asia.

\* \* \* \*

The fact that re-use plays a crucial role in all forms of the arts becomes clear in the next chapter by Katrin Binder, a researcher and practitioner of Yakshagana. This is a form of dance-theatre, performed throughout the coastal region of Karnataka. Binder focuses on re-use of content and form in historical and modern texts underlying the plays. The performances follow what she calls a 'play-text' (*prasanga*) consisting largely of a combination of poems, set in a variety of metres and songs. Their contents are enacted in dance and elaborated upon through improvised dialogues.

In the past, the texts providing the storyline for the performances were primarily based on religious stories, such as the Sanskrit epics, the *Purana*s and *bhakti* literature. The Sanskrit sources were translated into the local vernacular, usually Kannada (but from the 1950s, also Tulu), which as Binder argues, constitutes a first level of re-use. However, even though they remain close to the basic story, over time the texts were more closely adapted to local situations. Patrons could emerge in the disguise of heroes in the plots and the composer's preferred deity could be given particular importance.[15]

As outlined by Binder, the Yakshagana poets used a kind of copy-and-paste method and directly re-used poignant metaphors, entire phrases and long verses from the sacred source texts, merely replacing individual words to adapt them to the rhythm and metre of the play. In addition to the re-use of general content, and of actual wordings and vocabulary, compositional form and metres were re-used from Sanskrit sources. This refers to the poetic metre, the *raga–tala* combinations, used in the Yakshagana plays. Here, a 'basic' metre, intended for a simple recitation, has been re-used and adapted to be sung. This has been modified to meet the performative needs of a musical style of presentation

---

[15] The adaptation of Sanskrit literature continues to the present day and those plots which nowadays make reference to Sanskritic sources are referred to as 'old' *prasanga*s (play-texts).

and its associated aesthetic considerations. In this instance, the textual sources have been used as a kind of blueprint matrix, as Binder explains, for the creative adaptation of the material.

This shows that re-use and the integration of elements from earlier traditions were achieved on a number of levels. Through this manifold and creative re-use of earlier literary forms from other contexts, combining poetry and song in a single performance, led to the creation of the distinct Yakshagana style as an independent literary genre.

Nowadays, writers and poets of Yakshagana plays integrate elements from diverse backgrounds, for example, local oral narratives, legends, stories about historical characters and events, elements from novels, television serials and modern cinema. It appears that Yakshagana had never been as popular and prolific as it is at present, providing a firmly rooted cultural identity to the inhabitants of the region and acquiring the status of the most important performing arts form of the entire state of Karnataka. The temptation to use this popularity commercially has, to a certain extent, altered the meaning of this ancient art and raised questions about a possible decline in quality.[16]

However, not Yakshagana alone re-uses its surrounding culture and history. Yakshagana itself and its characteristic idioms too have been re-used by performers of other forms of performing arts and by the local theatre. Today, Yakshagana drama is preformed not only in Kannada, but also in Tulu, spoken in the southern area of the coastal region. This challenges the dominant role of Kannada as the official regional language. In addition, it questions the authority of *brahminical* culture, as Tulu Yakshagana habitually makes references to folk traditions and divinities. By creating a distinct form of Yakshagana for the Tulu-speaking community, its theatre is supporting the creation of an independent regional identity, which is part of a larger tradition but still distinct.

Even the Basel missionaries, Herrmann Mögling (1811–81) and Ferdinand Kittel (1832–1903), re-used the Yakshagana style to teach biblical stories. The aim was to communicate the Christian message more effectively by packaging it in a locally understood literary form. Re-use has changed but also guaranteed the survival of this traditional dramatic genre for over four centuries, and today, Yakshagana is employed as a means to keep local 'tradition' and 'Indian culture' alive.

\* \* \* \*

Continuing the link with the modern period, the chapter by the art historian Tiziana Lorenzetti examines the re-use of Western modernist as well as

---

[16] These are concerns which are also shared in the chapter by Prasanna Nayak on modern folk art in Orissa, later in this volume.

of indigenous traditional motifs and pictorial techniques in Indian painting dating largely from the early twentieth century. Lorenzetti commences by illustrating the strong influence which Western artistic traditions, and particularly certain painters, such as Wassily Kandinsky, had on Indian art. The author stresses that there is a sharing of formal methods, colours and thought patterns underlying the creative work.

Although the two major art schools at that time—the J. J. School of Art in Bombay (1857) and the Kala Bhavana at Shantiniketan (1919)—provoked an engagement with modern Western art, Lorenzetti stresses that they propagated an appreciation and commitment towards indigenous Indian artistic traditions too. According to her, the aim was to create "a meaningful artistic dialogue between the past and the present" and an environment where "tradition and modernity were not postulated as necessary adversaries, but as mutually complementary phenomena".

The engagement with local traditions played an even stronger role in the Bengal School, where folk and village arts were promulgated as the main inspiration for and source of a modern art movement in India which was non-European in character. This return to and re-use of local popular art reflected the political atmosphere at the time, which was nationalist in ideology and strove towards Indian Independence. In a way, a similar liberation, yet in artistic terms, was the objective in the return to local popular arts. The art movement in Shantiniketan turned towards classical Indian themes, such as religious myths and village life for their subject matter and towards the *pattacitra* tradition (paintings on cloth) and the style of Kalighat painting in terms of techniques. An interest in indigenous art forms, and the creation and support of handicrafts and cottage industries became an expression of the artists' identity, authenticity, national spirit and modernity; it not only expressed but also supported an evolving national ethos.

The prime example of this new 'Bengali folk' style is Jamini Roy, who has inspired generations of artists. Similarly, the classical Thanjavur and the Brahmari styles of painting were and are still re-used during the twenty-first century. In the latter style, re-use is constituted by the combination of a traditional painting technique, which has been applied to another context, characterised by a wider colour repertoire made possible through the availability of synthetic pigments today.

It is fascinating to observe that the rhythm of the line work of the contemporary Brahmari paintings seem to mirror the kinetic forms developed in European avant-garde art, which provided such a vital source for re-use in earlier contemporary Indian art.[17] However, as Lorenzetti points out, despite the fact that the

---

[17] This illustrates the cyclic nature of re-use and tradition, which will be picked out as a central theme in the following chapter on the theory of re-use.

paintings look modern, they are "quintessentially Indian" and this and other types of modern Indian art contributed actively—through the re-use of ancient autochthonous forms and styles—to the creation of a pictorial, and in extension of a political (national), identity for the newly independent India.

* * * *

The following contribution by Prasanna K. Nayak, an anthropologist, connects the group of chapters on art and architecture at the start of this collection and those to follow, which focus more on political issues. Like Lorenzetti, Nayak examines modern instances, in his case the re-use of tribal motifs and the production of tribal-style arts. As he outlines, this is largely done by non-tribals for political purposes and monetary gains.

Through the public display of tribal artefacts in offices, at state celebrations and at political rallies, government and local parties aim to invest themselves with a certain aura of authenticity, indigeneity and a legitimacy to represent the people of Orissa. In the past, the legitimacy of the king depended on his official acknowledgement of tribal cultural beliefs and practices and, in return, on tribal sanctions and blessings. Although contemporary governments wish to appear modern and progressive, at the same time, they aim to suggest a deep-rootedness in the culture and tribal past of the state and to imply an unbroken continuity of local rule. This clearly shows the strong connection between, what Nayak calls, the politics of art and the art of politics.

In addition, there is a marked increase in art exhibitions, cottage industry centres of tribal arts and local dance and drama performances organised by government, non-government and private agencies. Whereas Nayak applauds the attention paid to tribal culture and the support provided to preserving some of its traditions, he questions the authenticity of these recent artefacts, outfits and performances.

Oriya art is largely ritual art and consists of signs and symbols, each of which have a specific associated meaning. The folk artists are not considered to be secular artists and ordinary mortals. They are believed to be endowed with special qualities and regarded as practitioners of sacred ceremonies. Traditional art production has to follow strict rules and any dereliction from these guidelines is deemed to adversely affect the artist and his community. Therefore, genuine practitioners of tribal cultural art would not produce sacred artefacts or perform ritual dances and religious theatre in a non-ritualised environment for party-political, their own or somebody else's financial gain.

Today's creators of imitation tribal artefacts have simply been trained to cheaply re-use and reproduce patterns and objects for a mass market. Nayak equates these production centres with factories whose main incentive is to generate profit, from which authentic tribal artists have been excluded.[18] Additionally, he questions the intentions of the supporters and organisers of such centres and events. Whilst preserving tribal art on the surface, politically and financially oriented productions and performances deprive this traditional art form of its most precious aspect: its ritual value. Only the outer shell, the aesthetic or visual expression of the original piece, is re-used. Through this, the traditional shamanic and ritual significance of the art are in danger of being overlaid with new meanings. According to Nayak, such practices impose "versions and images of the past on tribals which are cut off from their roots". The idea that the present changes our view of the past is a recurrent theme in many chapters in this volume.

For the tribals, this art is a visual expression of their cultural identity. Contrasting with this, the cheap modern reproductions and imitations take on a supra-regional and, in many cases, even a global implication, where a localised tribal art is meant to compete with Indian art from other areas. This can also be seen in instances where the local ritual art of specific tribes are sold as simplified representatives of a much more general 'golden past', as examples of India's exotic character and its stagnation in the past—a colonial and long-outdated perception.

Indian culture has survived because of its re-use of the past, the continuity of designs and practices and their reinvestment with fresh meanings. However, this chapter illustrates a different level of aggression towards and an anxiety felt by Oriya tribals. In this chapter, we do not hear about the appropriation of their sacred sites or statues but about the re-use of their motifs and practices by people who are insensitive in their re-use to the original significance and values of these sacred items. Although, on the surface, this might temporarily help the tribal arts to survive, Nayak warns that in the long run, this kind of re-use is in danger of destroying tribal art because maybe too little of the essential elements of this form of art has survived in its faint modern shadow.

## Re-use in Social and Political Studies

The first group of six chapters have drawn their examples primarily from an arts background, but have shown that artistic re-use can convey religious and

---

[18] Nayak has a valid point when he describes the changed significance of art in a ritual and in a political or commercial context. However, it is important to remember that a pure and original form of any cultural expression rarely existed and that what retrospectively appears to be pure in fact often represents a mixture of long-forgotten ingredients and meanings (see Chapter 2). With regards to the 'traditional authenticity' of Mingei, Japanese folk crafts, for instance, Kikuchi shows that Mingei in fact is a hybrid construct (1997: 343–54).

political messages as well, particularly those relating to power relations. These issues play an even more focal role in the following collection of six chapters, which examine the interpenetration of politics, culture and society. Re-use helps us answer two questions of great consequence to the comparative analysis of decolonisation and the success of post-colonial democracy which underpins many of the more explicitly political of the chapters that follow.

Four processes which have deeply affected the structure of power have generated the necessary, but not sufficient, conditions for the dialectics of the modern and the traditional to play itself out. These include British colonial rule that affected the ascriptive boundaries in which social groups are ensconced; the impact of these changes on the culture and status of the twice-born *varnas*, which then spread to the *shudra* castes, and beyond them, to minority religions; westernisation which brought in the concept of equality and fundamentally affected the concept of personhood in Indian society; and finally, legislations and modern institutions that led to secularisation and, in the process, dismantled ritual barriers to status and occupation. Some of these processes that had preceded India's Independence in 1947 facilitated the relatively smooth transfer of power from British colonial rule to an independent Indian state.

* * * *

The chapter by Clemens Spiess addresses the ease with which the political leaders of the Indian National Congress moved in to the positions of power previously occupied by British colonial rulers, and India's success in establishing a democratic government in contrast to the majority of post-colonial states. His main argument consists in the elaboration of the long process of engagement of the Indian National Congress, which led the anti-colonial movement against British rule, stretching over a period of over six decades prior to Independence in 1947. The engagement took the form of both its resistance to alien rule and the participation of Congressmen and women in elections to various positions in local and regional governments. The British rulers started setting up these elaborate sets of representative institutions in order to meet the growing demand for participation. The consequence of this dual process of collaboration and competition between the British Raj and the Indian society was the emergence of modern political institutions that were British in form but at least partly Indian in content.

Spiess describes this as a process of "'indigenisation' whereby parties and parliamentarianism acquired local roots and adapted to indigenous conditions while retaining their canonical form and featuring institutional continuity". In opting for institutional continuity—Spiess describes this rhetorically as "The Empire is dead; Long live Westminster"—leaders in post-colonial India made a strategic choice to retain the institutions of parliamentary democracy. In the process of being 'used' by Indians, these had acquired local roots in the form of the conflation of the Indian social structure and the social basis of political parties, which are crucial to the functioning of parliamentary politics. The process of induction of these hybrid institutions into the Constitution of the new republic was not always smooth or free of controversy. We learn from the deliberations of the Constituent Assembly the many objections against the continued presence of alien forms within the organic law of a new, independent nation. Spiess shows how the process of conflation of the British and the Indian, and the induction of these hybrid forms into the agenda for the governance of independent India, came incrementally, one step at a time. As early as 1928, the *Nehru Report*, formulating the future Constitution of India, had pointed out that the interaction of Indian society and the British form of governance had produced "a new form, one of acculturation to the Indian way of thinking". As evidence of this thinking, he quotes from the report: "[W]hat India wants and what Britain has undertaken to give her, is nothing else than Responsible Government [and] the assimilated tradition of England has become the basis of Indian thought" (AICC 1928: 6–7).

In the event, what India finally chose had striking differences with the original model. India's form of parliamentary government had more of an emphasis on executive leadership than parliamentary accountability. Instead of parliamentary sovereignty, India opted for a form of countervailing forces where the power of the national parliament was limited, on the one hand, by the written Constitution with the Supreme Court as the watchdog of this form of separation of powers. On the other hand, in India's federal form of government, the powers of the central government, howsoever generous to central leadership, were still limited by those allocated to the regional governments. Indians, Spiess points out, were modifying the original model even whilst re-using it. The political condition—turmoil caused by the Partition of British India into two hostile neighbours, with violent repercussion for the minorities in both countries, leading to millions of refugees criss-crossing the subcontinent—was a main reason for the concentration of power in the hands of the central executive. Spiess argues that a second consideration came from pragmatic considerations of power, for the "more flexible, but too permissive" Westminster parliamentary form gave the Congress leadership a greater room to manoeuvre than the more rigid American form of separation of powers. The fact that the flexibility of the Westminster model and the national reach of the Congress party could deliver power easily into the hands of the Congress elite was certainly among the calculations for the strategic mix of the two systems of rule.

The choice of re-using the Westminster form of parliamentary government with a strongly pronounced Indian content was both contingent on the context and opportunistic by the way of the political pragmatism that was the hallmark of the Congress party. In the event, this original choice produced a form of governance that has stayed the course over the past sixty years. The reasons for its stability are the second major contribution of this chapter. The institutional arrangement of the new Republic produced the requisite space for the policies of nation building, economic development and political order. Most important of all, the Indian model—composite in many ways—produced a fortuitous solution to the hubris of Jawaharlal Nehru, the all-powerful Prime Minister and the committed democrat, and Rajendra Prasad, the President who was both a competent administrator and a compliant politician. The pattern of the relationship of these two early leaders set the mould for the successive generations. This has increasingly led to the transfusion of non-parliamentary norms and values into the parliamentary arena such as the buying and selling of votes and other forms of corruption. The results have produced a mixed fortune for the Westminster model on alien soil. On the one hand, the induction of India's cultural diversity into the political arena—thanks to the interpenetration of the social structure and the electoral system and party competition—a multicultural state has steadily taken the place of the monocultural politics, which is the bane of many post-colonial states. On the other hand, organic solidarities, re-using social networks as electoral alliances, have sometimes led to vicious inter-community conflicts, negating the tolerant ideals of India's secular democracy, and enhancing the anxiety of India's minorities.

\* \* \* \*

Like Clemens Spiess, Jivanta Schöttli also approaches the theme of transition from colonial rule to post-colonial democracy, and the role of re-use in facilitating this shift, but more from the angle of agency than that of structure. Whereas Spiess selects the structure of the political system—in this case, the Westminster model of parliamentary democracy and the party system as the main basis of his argument—the agency and leadership that underpinned the process of transition are her main conceptual windows. Her chapter focuses on the life and times of Jawaharlal Nehru. Aristocratic and privileged by birth, educated in England, Jawahrlal Nehru initially came to high office through the support of his father Motilal Nehru—the president of the Congress party and an influential link to the emerging Indian elite—and Mahatma Gandhi who was to remain Nehru's vital link to Indian tradition and the Indian masses. His subsequent rise was an evidence of his capacity and ambition—a fact that helps us appreciate his decisive voice in guiding the political course of India during the formative years of Independence.

Nehru belonged to a generation of leaders for whom politics was more than a mere pursuit of power. India, for these statesmen, was making a painful transition from the past to the future, and politics was to be the platform for the creation of the new out of the old. The articulation of these visions often took the shape of sharp debates and copious writing. Besides his charged domestic political agenda, international travel and organisational involvement with the Congress party, Nehru—who saw himself as a man of letters—wrote at length about history, current problems and about his vision of the future. Of this rich output, Schöttli has selected the *Discovery of India* (1946) as the main source of Nehru's understanding of Indian history, tradition and, as he puts it, his quest for the 'spirit of India'.

Nehru's understanding of modernity is underpinned by a dialogue with the past because his vision of the future and his project of nation and state building were firmly anchored within one, overall framework. The modern, independent state, and the public sphere that would be kept clear of private issues such as religion, language and community, would be the bedrock on which a democratic political system, complete with mass representation and a democratic constitution, was to be erected.

The state is a central theme because Nehru sought to deny the importance of other sources of collective identity, such as the role of culture and religion. These he regarded as divisive rather than as unifying forces. His committment to modernity led him to believe in science, technology, social reform and economic planning. "The mould of Nehru's state is European, or more precisely British, and in fact, ironically, represented great continuity with some of the dominant colonial practices and priorities." In the final analysis, then, "Nehru acted as a central agent in the transfer of an essentially Western 'social imaginary' into the Indian context".

The *Discovery of India* demonstrates Nehru's firm belief that continuity with the past brings legitimacy for the present, and that it is this continuity and the genealogy of the state that stretches back all the way to the Classical Age that imbues the modern state in India with its resilience. Nehru, the quintessential purveyor of modernity in terms of its three key rubrics—the modern economy, the public sphere and popular sovereignty—needed, nevertheless, a continuity with the past for its legitimacy. This paradox points in the direction of a central dilemma in Nehru and his genre of re-use of the past. How can one reject the past if one also needs the past to legitimise the present? The re-used past, masquerading as the modern, thus conceals a deep insecurity about the self at its core. Nehru holds on to the modern vessel by the way of its institutional veneer and filled it in as and when the need arose. No doubt, Nehru himself was a hybrid, "a queer mixture of the East and West, out of place everywhere, at home nowhere" as he put it in his *An Autobiography* (Nehru 1953: 597), but the social imaginary which he embodied did not carry a strongly indigenous imprint.

\* \* \* \*

Thierry diContanzo introduces the issue of the public sphere to the discourse on the transition from colonial rule to post-colonial governance. The columns of the media—in this case, a daily newspaper—are seen as the public platform for the articulation of opinions about the shape of things to be. The origin, use and re-use of the idea of Pakistan—a vision for a land of the pure, future homeland for South Asia's Muslims—is the main link of the chapter to the book as a whole. The concept of Pakistan emerged out of a process that brought together the ambitious, the opportunist and the true believers in the Islamic cause under one banner. The idea of Pakistan and the nature of the state to emerge from it are the fulcrum around which the debate in the columns and editorials of the *Star of India*, the daily newspaper that diCostanzo has chosen for deeper analysis, raged.

This chapter covers the period from the early 1930s, when the independence of British India had started appearing to be real, leading to intense jockeying for power among the competing political forces of colonial India, to the Partition of India in August 1947. This period corresponds roughly to the lifespan of a daily paper called the *Star of India*, an Indian Muslim daily newspaper from Calcutta. The paper belonged to an upper-middle class group of wealthy Muslims living in Calcutta or in its economic hinterland. The group was in favour of a certain selective economic protectionism but was also open to outside influences—especially British and American, not so much Islamic. Together with Lahore and Delhi, Calcutta was one of the three main centres of Indian Muslim journalism. In the context of the 1930s—the Indian press as a whole was undergoing massive commercialisation—the *Star of India* wished to provide advice and respond to the needs of a well-to-do readership at a time when Indian society was going through social, economic and political upheaval. The daily offered the possibility for Muslims to experience a new and proud sense of community through the vision of a common language, history and culture in its columns.

When the *Star of India* was created in 1932, it supported a moderate anti-colonial line and wished to offer a different product from the pro-regime and the pro-Congress press. In formulating the concept of Pakistan and giving it a specific twist depending on the interest of the author, the debate was tapping into two main sources of knowledge and categories, namely, mainstream Indian nationalism and Islam. The idea of Pakistan and its historical sub-meanings, diCostanzo asserts, are therefore a re-use of two pre-existing intellectual traditions. The strategic selection and deletion of these ideas in the construction of Pakistan in the print media are analysed with an eye on the context and the specific situation of the authors of these scripts.

The chapter examines the whole range of opinion from Indian anti-colonial nationalism and the Indian Muslim idea of Pakistan to a purely Islamic state to be carved out of British India as a homeland for South Asian Muslims. The new political entity was intended to cater to the moral and religious needs of the purveyors of these opinions. In the process, we learn what was re-used from Indian nationalism in the idea of Pakistan and what was rejected, and why the idea of Pakistan as a branch of unitary Indian nationalism eventually failed. The author concludes that 'Pakistan' has, in the end, produced less integration and more anxiety concerning the future of Muslims in South Asia.

The visions of the future and the shapes the struggle for the rights of Muslims—of which a Muslim homeland was the most extreme expression— show different degrees of the re-use of Islam and the core values of Indian nationalism. They were formulated out of a need to resist what many saw as Gandhi's unitary nationalism. The essay joins the argument of Jivanta Schöttli with regard to Nehru's adaption of liberal institutionalism to Indian conditions. Re-use, which is generally agency-driven, nevertheless, is deeply influenced by the structural constraints within which agents operate. For a long time, the *Star of India* viewed the failure of that federal idea as being due to the opposition of one man only, Gandhi—it must be noted that Nehru was rarely criticised and that the *Star of India* sometimes endorsed the creation of a 'genuine' Indian nationalism on the lines of the model developed by Nehru. It rejected the Gandhian project of an inherent Hindu identity for Indian Muslims and all other minorities.

Ironically, the newspaper, having first served merely as a forum for the articulation, analysis and composition of the idea of Pakistan, eventually became its champion. As a final twist to this irony, when the concept of Pakistan became a reality, the *Star of India*, which had in the meantime moved on from being a forum of debate to a partisan advocate, no longer at home in its native Calcutta, moved to Karachi where it went through a metamorphosis, and re-emerged under the name of *The Star*. The chapter explains how and why the integration of the elements advocating Pakistan—land of the pure, under the banner of Jinnah—also remained a source of anxiety, leading eventually to its break-up and the emergence of Bangladesh. What emerged from this shrinking of the state, having reinforced the re-used Islamic core of the state in a smaller but more coherent territory, still remained the cause of residual anxiety, as one can notice from the shimmering ethnic discontent at the margins of the state of Pakistan.

\* \* \* \*

The chapter by Edward A. Rodrigues is the first in the volume which focuses more specifically on religious issues, namely the re-use of the Buddhist religion (*dharma* or *dhamma*) by the social reformer and leader of the Dalit movement, B. R. Ambedkar, in the 1950s. Ambedkar was not a religious but a political leader who fought for social justice and equality for the outcastes, Scheduled

Castes or Dalits, in India. He aimed to create a social structure based on inclusive norms and practices to provide Dalits with dignity and social rights and to protect them against caste oppression.

Ambedkar had attempted to achieve this through the creation and connection with a number of political associations and parties. For instance, he closely engaged with Marxist Communism but in the end rejected it as unsuitable for the Dalit cause as India's communists in early-twentieth-century Bombay were, as Rodrigues explains, largely upper-caste Hindus unconcerned with caste discrimination. Ambedkar concluded that within the ancient framework of Hindu caste society, equality could not be achieved and hence his decision to take outcaste Hindus outside the realms of the Hindu faith and caste system.

In his role as the spokesperson, Ambedkar approached a number of religious leaders in India. However, in the end, only Buddhism and Sikhism remained amongst his possible candidates for re-use. Rodrigues informs us that Islam and Christianity were rejected as they found their origin outside of South Asia. Ambedkar did not wish to take Dalits outside the fold of Indian civilisation and did not aim to widen the cleft between Dalits and Hindus.

Ambedkar had been interested in Buddhism from an early age; he had read about this ancient religion, met some of its religious leaders and visited a number of Buddhist countries. He considered it a fundamental part of the Indian civilisation and a moral religion in which the concept of equality was valued. Strictly religious issues did not play a major role. The re-use of Buddhism in the political struggle for Dalit emancipation was a strictly intellectual exercise.

The central concern was to provide the Dalits with a new identity, which was separated from the memory and stigma of untouchability, and with a place in an inclusive social system. As in India one's social position is tightly linked up with one's religion, Ambedkar created a new religion although his principal intention was political and social. As Rodrigues explains, Ambedkar "was convinced that Buddhism could be re-used to ensure its continuing relevance for modern times". It is imperative that he did not 'use' or 'join' an existing Buddhist community in Asia but that he 're-used' aspects of Buddhism to create his own new form of this faith. In this, he re-used elements which could be appropriated in the search for a changed and enhanced identity for the Dalits, and he rejected those—for example, rituals and beliefs—which appeared too close to the religion they were aiming to leave behind.

Ambedkar's wish was to create a religion of empowerment which was active and progressive. He argued for a return to the Buddha's own core teachings, into which he interpreted modernist values of morality, justice, equality and rationality. This was not a quest for the establishment of an authentic form of

Buddhism but a social strife out of social exclusion. In the creation of Navoyana Buddhism, Ambedkar combined certain aspects of the ancient teachings of the Buddha with modern political ideas. He did not simply preach the return to an ancient ideal tradition, but an engagement with the modern world on the basis of ancient morals and principles. This constitutes an interpretation of Buddhism, which sees it exclusively as a means of Dalit emancipation and liberation.

In 1956, Ambedkar and an estimated 500,000 of his followers formally converted to his new form of Navoyana Buddhism. They considered it to be a "vehicle of social transformation for both Dalits and non-Dalits", as Rodrigues tells us, since hierarchical structuring and exclusion was not just a problem of the Dalits. Even though the re-use of Buddhism did not solve all the problems of the Dalits of India, it is a poignant example of the re-use of an ancient faith system for modern political and social emancipation. Remarkably, many Buddhist converts did not entirely abandon their Hindu roots and engaged in a re-use of Hindu elements in the new form of Navoyana Buddhism as well, illustrating the never-ending circular movements of re-use.

\* \* \* \*

The next religion which has been examined in the context of re-use is Jainism. Sabine Scholz investigates the re-use and reformulation of ancient Jaina concepts in the contemporary British and North American Jaina diaspora. She focuses on the creation of organisations targeting young Jainas and non-Jainas in the West by exposing them to debates and discussions in English on general ethical and moral living, and not with doctrinal sermons in Indian languages. The first organisation of this type, founded in Britain in 1987, was the Young Jains UK. This served as a model for a similar association in America, known as the Young Jains of America, in 1991.

It is fascinating that from the West, the concept of the youth organisation returned in a reverse flow along the path which Jaina migrants had taken to reach the West. In many instances, this was via East Africa and in subsequent years, the Young Jains Nairobi was established. Similar groups followed in Australia and Singapore. Finally, what had commenced in the diaspora, among second- and third-generation young professionals, returned to the country of origin of this ancient religion in 2005, when the Young Jains of India were formed.

Among the Jaina organisations founded by immigrant Jainas in the diaspora, the concept of the so-called Jain way of life became a central notion, which circles around three core principles, the so-called three A's of Jainism. These are *ahimsa* (non-harming), *aparigraha* (non-possession) and *anekantavada* (non–one-sidedness).

*Ahimsa* is the primary moral precept of all Jainas. It forms the focus of the first vow an ascetic takes on his way to initiation but is equally important for lay practitioners. It is closely connected with the concept of vegetarianism. Whereas in its traditional framework, *ahimsa* was seen as a means for individual spiritual progress, in its re-used form in a modern and Westernised context, it is portrayed as a solution for the world's problems and the creation of peace.

The vow of *aparigraha* consists in the encouragement of a feeling of nonattachment and the voluntary limitation of one's own possessions and needs. Relating to male Digambara ascetics, this takes the extreme form of rejecting all clothing and wandering naked. Re-used by modern Jainism, this ancient religious concept takes on a wider and often ecologically oriented angle. Reinterpreted as 'non-possessiveness', *aparigraha* becomes an influential instrument for a responsible approach to the environment, the saving of natural resources, and the establishment of justice and fairness in the world.

*Anekantavada*, the third concept, is the philosophy of many viewpoints. According to this, reality is manifold, dependent on many variants and cannot be described in an unconditional statement. This position has been used to classify other religions and philosophical systems as one-sided (*ekantavada*) and as lacking the comprehensiveness of the Jaina view of reality (*anekanta*). Through its belief in non–one-sidedness, Jainism can absorb other religious and philosophical systems as partial truths and integrate them (or re-use them) in what in their eyes is a more wide-ranging and all-embracing system. In its modern interpretation, and under the new disguise of 'intellectual *ahimsa*', its meaning has been turned upside down. Almost reversing its original traditional understanding, it is now taken to refer to tolerance towards other opinions and respect for all religions.

The creation of the 'Jain way of life' and the 'three As' reflect a branding and marketing approach, typical of North America where these were first formulated. In the Western diaspora, ancient Jaina principles have been taken out of their traditional framework and been filled with different connotations, which represent Jainism as a universal way of life and not as a specific Indian religion with rituals and the need for formal conversion. The latter aspect is one which so far has been more closely associated with Buddhism. However, this chapter identifies Jainas as tremendously creative re-users on multiple levels, as a religious community distinct from other faiths but tightly intertwined with them and as practitioners with a strong capability to survive by adapting to the demands of an ever-changing world.

* * * *

The joint chapter by Subrata K. Mitra and Lion König examines and compares re-use in the creation and recreation of the cultural symbols and icons of the state: Marianne and Bharat Mata. By comparing the two, it relates issues observed in India to developments in a similar context in France—outside the immediate regional South Asian focus of this volume.[19] This shows that issues raised in this publication are not unique to South Asian countries.

The authors describe the icons as the foci which communicate a sense of unity and coherence to an idea which is far more complex than what the simple images reveal. They are easier to comprehend than long treatises and more persuasive as they appeal both to reason and emotions. They can bridge language barriers without translation because of their power of visualisation. In most examples, not just one but various 'candidates for iconisation' were available and considered, indicating the element of choice we have encountered already in many of the chapters. The authors stress that the entire process of artistic production of a national allegory is deeply political—and in the situation of India, intensely religious. Despite the essential element of choice, the authors outline that both invention and coincidence come into play when images are used as part of nation building.

In order to function effectively, the icons need to contain an element of the past, something the people can relate to, which provides continuity. This is more problematic than one might expect—as is eloquently shown by the authors—because by choosing a representative image or an episode of the past, one legitimises and establishes one version of history. It is this version which will be standardised through the icon and will be remembered.

With regards to the French national allegory, two types of representations prevail: that of the revolutionary, forceful and martial Marianne—celebrated by Eugene Delacroix in 1831—and that of the nurturing mother—popularised in the famous painting by Honoré Daumier in 1848. Other paintings and statues of Marianne, to be found in French public buildings and in cities throughout the Republic, are less ideological. Her image adorned the old Franc banknotes and coins and these days, it is found on Euro coins minted in France. Even though her name and associated values survive very much unaltered, newly elected Presidents have their publicity machines choose new contemporary illustrations of Marianne, embodied by famous actresses, fashion models, and recently by a woman of Moroccan descent to advertise the modern multiethnic France—and thereby re-using an old concept.

There are many parallels but also many differences in the Indian case of Bharat Mata. National icons are created during times of struggle and the united struggle for the freedom and rights of a nation. In India, religion played a

---

[19] This contribution also refers to the national allegories of other states, such as Germany's Germania, the United States of America's Uncle Sam and Britain's two national icons, John Bull and Britannia. During the early years of Tony Blair's time as Prime Minister in the 1990s, Britannia was reinvented by the spin doctors of New Labour. In her new disguise, the term 'Cool Britannia' was primarily associated with British fashion culture, art, trendy magazines and a fast-changing lifestyle.

catalytic role in the fight for Independence, something not to be encountered in the French Revolution where the church stood against the nascent nation. This led to the creation of Marianne—a secular 'goddess'. Much less is known about the birth of India's national allegory and this chapter offers a commendable step in illuminating her history and multivalent meanings. Fascinating similarities with regard to the French case are the dual links with the mother figure and the warrior goddess, already encountered in the European example. The name Bharat Mata (Mother India) draws our attention to her view as a motherly type, derived from a long history of mother goddesses, although she is less commonly depicted in her nurturing mothering form. Most delineations draw upon and directly re-use the imagery of warrior goddesses, such as Kali and Durga.

It appears that Bharat Mata is a later form of a regional movement in Bengal, which created Banga Mata (Mother Bengal). In the nationalist visualisation of the fight for Independence, Bharat Mata with her lions is frequently associated with other re-used elements, such as the Ashoka pillar, the addorsed lions and the wheel, all symbolising the first unified greater Indian Empire. We do not only encounter re-use of previous symbols and historical and religious imagery in the creation of the icon of Bharat Mata. In the 1980s, Bharat Mata was re-used in Madras to create a local figure of national identity, Tamilttay (Mother Tamil), indicating the limitations of one image to represent the whole of India with its diverse communities and faith groups.

This problem is further illustrated by the authors in their discussion of the dispute roused by the painting entitled 'Bharat Mata' by the modern Indian Muslim painter M. F. Husain (1915–2011). Today, the national allegory of Bharat Mata is being re-used by the Hindutva movement. In this context, the goddess has also been connected with and superimposed onto a map of undivided India (Akhand Bharat) creating Hindu-nationalist cartography. These depictions are referred to as 'bodyscapes' or personalised maps in which body and map fuse or where the body replaces the map. This is not the first time that maps have been employed to symbolise the Indian motherland. In the 1930s, this was used to produce a neutral, less Hindu-centric image of this diverse nation. However, the contour of the homeland alone appears to have been too abstract to gain popularity with the nation and represents an unsuccessful case of re-use of the concept of sacred geography.

Mitra and König conclude that to look for the 'real' Bharat Mata misses the point. There is no genuine pure form which was re-used in this national allegory and there is no indisputable authentic Mother India. As the authors state: "images were re-used and modified according to the needs of their times. Both Marianne and Bharat Mata created integration as well as disintegration and anxiety." Re-use offers variety and choice, leading to the creation of tradition and an ever-changing cultural development.

## CONCLUSION

Re-use is a bridge between the humanities and the social sciences, for it helps understand affinities among the many aspects of post-colonial life that the mechanical difference between the two major disciplinary areas projects in terms of disconnected dimensions. This volume, with contributions from the humanities and the social sciences, illustrates that through re-use, the past is generally in attendance in the present and that we need to understand changes that have taken place to measure as well as to interpret our world today in the light of the past.

On the whole, the chapters coming from across a broad spectrum of disciplines help us put the dualities such as parochial–universal, sacred–profane and art–science in context of the world as heuristic devices that help appreciate the diversity and inner contradictions of modernity and tradition in the phenomenal world, and follow their dialectical interactions that lead to the evolution of new forms. We learn from the chapters that the linkage between tradition and modernity is continuous rather than dichotomous.[20]

What matters in the final analysis, however, is how one connects with the past. The memory of the past is necessary but not sufficient. The courage and sense of risk to rework and reformulate it as a better alternative compared to those that are given is indispensable to successful re-use. Such has, indeed, been the case with the examples—of Nehru, Ambedkar, the proponents of Pakistan in the columns of the *Star of India* and the young Jaina advocates of *anekantavada*, to name just a few—that we have seen in this book. The Rudolphs, commenting on Gandhi, the arch re-user, say:

> He [Gandhi] did not return unselfconsciously to wallow in the nostalgia of the familiar and the comfortable, the truths of sentiment unleavened by those of conscience and the mind. Gandhi experienced and knew other alternatives.... Gandhi's return to that path, the path of home truths, grew out of his discomfort with the alternatives he tried, with his sense that he could not be himself by following them.... Through an alien cultural experience, he won the freedom to choose, rather than be possessed by, the familiar, to reformulate and transform home truths.(Rudolph & Rudolph 1967: 247)

---

[20] Rudolph and Rudolph comment:

> If tradition and modernity are seen as continuous rather than separated by an abyss, if they are dialectically rather than dichotomously related and if internal variations are attended to and taken seriously, then those sectors of traditional society that contain or express potentialities for change from dominant norms and structures become critical for understanding the nature and processes of modernization. (1967: 10)

The example of Gandhi's 'experiments with truth' shows how one might derive new meanings from old truths. But it called for considerable skill in mass mobilisation, institutional analysis, visualisation and theatrics, but above all, great courage, entrepreneurship and discipline. For the potential re-user, the last named are the key catalysts, without which the potential for re-use stops short of becoming actual.[21]

## BIBLIOGRAPHY

## Secondary Sources

All India Congress Committee (AICC), 1928, *The Report of the All-Parties Conference*, Part I. AICC, Allahabad.

Asher, Catherine B. & Thomas R. Metcalf (eds), 1994, *Perceptions of South Asia's Visual Past*. American Institute of Indian Studies, New Delhi; Swadharma Swarajya Sangha, Madras; and Oxford & IBH Publishing, New Delhi, Bombay and Calcutta.

Collins, Wilkie, 2007, *The Moonstone*. Oneworld Classics, Richmond.

Davis, Richard H., 1999 [1997], *Lives of Indian Images*. Motilal Banarsidass Publishers, Delhi.

Eaton, Richard M., 2000, "Temple Desecration and Indo-Muslim States". In: David Gilmartin & Bruce B. Lawrence (eds), *Beyond Turk and Hindu: Rethinking Religious Identities in Islamicate South Asia*. University Press of Florida, Gainsville, pp. 246–81.

Hegewald, Julia A. B., 2006a, "From Shiva to Parshvanatha: The Appropriation of a Hindu Temple for Jaina Worship". In: Catherine Jarrige and Vincent Lefèvre (eds), *South Asian Archaeology 2001*, 2 vols., Editions Recherches sur les Civilisations, Paris, pp. 517–23.

———, 2006b, "Architectural, Sculptural and Religious Change: A New Interpretation of the Jaina Temples at Khajuraho". In: P. Flügel (ed.), *Studies in Jaina History and Culture: Disputes and Dialogues*, Routledge Advances in Jaina Studies, Vol. 1. Routledge, London and New York, pp. 401–18.

———, 2007, "Domes, Tombs and Minarets: Islamic Influences on Jaina Architecture". In: Adam Hardy (ed.), *The Temple in South Asia*, Volume 2 of the proceedings of the 18th conference of the European Association of South Asian Archaeologists, London 2005. British Association for South Asian Studies and the British Academy, London, pp. 179–90.

---

[21] "When he [Gandhi] turned to satyagraha and ahimsa, he revived the traditional view of courage, a view that carried with it commitments to non-violence, self-suffering, and self-restraint, qualities Englishmen had perceived differently and identified with cowardice" (Rudolph & Rudolph 1967: 248). Nehru writes of Gandhi and India: "He had instilled courage and manhood in her people;... courage is the one sure foundation of character, he had said; without courage there is no morality, no religion, no love" (Nehru 1960: 12 as cited in Rudolph & Rudolph 1967: 248).

Hegewald, Julia A. B., 2009, *Jaina Temple Architecture in India: The Development of a Distinct Language in Space and Ritual*. Monographien zur Indischen Archäologie. Kunst und Philologie, Band 19, Herausgeber Stiftung Ernst Waldschmidt, G+H-Verlag, Berlin.

———, forthcoming, "Building Citizenship: The Agency of Public Buildings and Urban Planning in the Making of the Indian Citizen". In: Subrata K. Mitra (ed.), *Citizenship in South Asia*. Samskriti Publishers, New Delhi.

Hegewald, Julia A. B. & Subrata K. Mitra, 2008, "Jagannatha Compared: The Politics of Appropriation, Re-use and Regional State Traditions in India". *Heidelberg Papers in South Asian and Comparative Politics* (HPSACP). No. 36, pp. 1–37. Available at http://archiv.ub.uni-heidelberg.de/volltextserver/frontdoor.php?source_opus=8015.

Kikuchi, Yuko, 1997, "Hybridity and the Oriental Orientalism of 'Mingei' Theory". *Journal of Design History*. Vol. 10, no. 4 (Special issue *Craft, Culture and Identity*), pp. 343–54.

Kompridis, Nikolas, 2005 (June), "Normativizing Hybridity/Neutralizing Culture". *Political Theory*. Vol. 33, no. 3, pp. 318–43.

Mitra, Subrata K., 2012, "From Comparitive Politics to Cultural Flow: The Hybrid State and the Resilience of the Political System in India", in Philip Stockhammer (ed.), *Conceptualizing Cultural Hybradization: A Tramsdisciplinary Approach*, pp. 107–30. Heidelberg: Springer.

Nehru, Jawaharlal, 1953, *An Autobiography*. Penguin India, Delhi.

———, 1960, *Freedom from Fear: Reflections on the Personality and Teachings of Gandhi*. Delhi.

Rudolph, Lloyd I. & Susanne Hoeber Rudolph, 1967, *The Modernity of Tradition: Political Development in India*. The University of Chicago Press, Chicago.

Tillotson, Giles H. R., 1990, "Delhi: The Axis of Empire". In: Giles H. R. Tillotson (ed.), *Mughal India, Architectural Guides for Travellers*. Viking, London, pp. 27–69.

Tully, James, 1995, *Strange Multiplicity: Constitutionalism in the Age of Diversity*. Cambridge University Press, Cambridge and New York.

## Internet Sources

The University of Bologna. Available at http://www.eng.unibo.it/PortaleEn/Students/User+guide+to+Campus+Branches/User+Guide+to+Bologna/history.htm (accessed on 27 June 2010).

United States Conference of Catholic Bishops, *The Catechism of the Catholic Church*. Available at http://www.usccb.org/catechism/text/ (accessed on 27 June 2010).

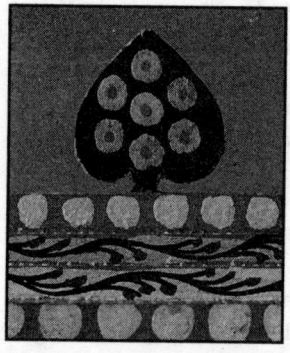

*Chapter 2*

# TOWARDS A THEORY OF RE-USE

## RUIN, RETRO AND FAKE VERSUS IMPROVEMENT, INNOVATION AND INTEGRATION

### BY JULIA A. B. HEGEWALD

Traditionally, the aim of academic research and scholarship has been to order and classify the world into clearly delineated categories and to describe cultures and political systems as unique, stable and largely homogenous entities. Since the 1980s, a general movement taking greater interest in diversity, the mixed and the subtly in-between, has won attention and significance, especially in postmodern analytical debates. This approach recognises that reality is much more complex than previously outlined.[1] It acknowledges the impact historical,

---

[1] In the area of art history, for example, members of the International Association of Art Critics publicly conceded in 1978 that Impressionism was not the only style in France during the second half of the nineteenth century and that Modernism was not a single but a conglomerate of styles. They agreed that more nuanced differentiations and more diverse views in the valuation of works of art by art historians and art critics were needed (College Art Association 1980: 377).

political and religious changes and global influences have had on cultures, examines the interpenetration of nations, styles and concepts, and illustrates the transnational and global flow of ideas in different directions. The questioning of fixed regional borders and the acknowledgement of the interconnectedness of cultures have also provoked a certain crossing and dissolution of traditional disciplinary boundaries between individual subjects and between the humanities and the social sciences in particular. The present publication contributes to this debate by exploring the concept of 're-use' in the context of the wider region of South Asia.[2] Through the phenomenon of re-use, new elements become available to cultures and favour renewal and innovation. By acknowledging this theory and by working with it, we hope to penetrate into new levels of cultural and political analysis and understanding.

## THE THEORY OF RE-USE

'Re-use' basically describes the act of using an item more than once. If one performs a search on the worldwide web for the term, most entries obtained relate to the environmentally friendly re-use or recycling of raw materials and organic waste. Surprisingly, many issues raised in this area can be transferred and applied to our study of re-use in South Asian culture and politics.

As will be shown in the various examples considered in this book, there are different forms of re-use. In the literature relating to environmental awareness and ecologically sound re-use, an important category is so-called conventional re-use. This relates to a situation where an item is used again to fulfil the same function as before. This can be a milk bottle, which after it has been cleaned, is refilled and used as a container for milk again, or a Jaina temple, which after it has been temporarily abandoned, is reconsecrated by the Jaina community.[3] In both cases, the item—re-used bottle or temple—is used in precisely the same manner as before. In addition, there is what is generally referred to as 'new-life re-use', in which an item is used another time but for a different purpose. In this instance, the washed milk bottle now performs a changed function as a vase for

---

[2] There are a number of notable studies which have examined cultural hybridity and conceptual flow in South Asia. Amongst these are: Asher and Metcalf (1994), Cohn (1996), Davis (1993, 1999), Eaton (2000), Hillenbrand (1988), Tartakov and Dehejia (1984), Trainor (1992) and Wagoner (1996). A more detailed study of re-use in South Asian art and architecture is under preparation by the author.

[3] This mere interruption in the use of a site or building with no altered function is frequently difficult to prove. As nothing has changed, one can only know about such re-use from historical sources of some kind. Possibly, some additions have been made after the re-consecration, but these are not necessarily linked to the act of re-use.

flowers, an act also referred to as 're-purposing'. Transferred to our architectural examples, the temple would either be used as a place of worship by another religious group or be adapted to a different function, such as a school or police station (see Plate 2.1). A third major form of re-use, deduced from the eco-literature, is known as 'recycling'. This describes the breaking down of an item into its raw materials, which are used to create a new and usually an entirely unrelated object. In this instance, the milk bottle would be crushed and transformed, for example, into fibreglass used for loft and roof insulations. Transferred to the context of South Asian temples, this would refer to the dismantling of temple structures and the re-use of the building materials, especially the stone, to raise a novel structure (see Plate 2.2, top).[4] Nick Barnard, in this volume, draws an interesting distinction between what he describes as artistic re-use and meaningless recycling. In his chapter on Indian and European jewellery, he states:

> It may be debated whether the use of materials to supply the production of British ornaments, in instances such as Captain Cochrane's Seringapatam brooch as well as the royal jewels, is a case of mere recycling rather than meaningful re-use. [....] However, important stones such as the Koh-i-Noor [....] were an essential tool of rulership in India, both for their symbolism and their value. [....] The significance of the Koh-i-Noor's appropriation for the symbolic head of the British imperial polity is obvious, and goes beyond mere recycling. [....] This supports the view that the employment in such an overtly political context of important royal gems was a case of meaningful re-use, and that this was done with some awareness of their political and—sometimes—of their historical and aesthetic value.

This statement further illustrates that the differentiation between re-use and recycling can also lie in the intentions and sensitivities which have or have not been expressed with regards to the creation of composites.

Whereas in the eco-area, recycling generally has positive connotations, the breaking up and 're-cycling' of art and religious objects has, for most of us, negative associations.[5] This study places a particular emphasis on the emotions connected with re-use in culture and politics. In this area, memory plays a notable role. During the process of re-use, certain elements and meanings get lost and this can create anxiety in those whose objects have been 're-purposed'. However, in the long run, the incorporation of elements from the past in the

---

[4] In the area of statues, metal figures—particularly those made of precious metals such as gold, silver and bronze—are melted down to be used for new religious objects or for more material items, such as jewellery or armoury.

[5] This has partly to do with Western approaches to the preservation of objects and monuments, which try to conserve an archaic and ideal version of the past, devoid of later additions. In South Asia, one is generally more open towards 'improving' on the past and making use of the latest materials and gadgets to 'beautify' temples. Despite this, there is a clear difference between a religious community dismantling their own temple to build a more modern replica of it and another religious group tearing down the sacred structures of a different faith to use the material for the glorification of their own religion.

present creates a certain continuity and can actively contribute to integration (see Plate 2.2).

* * * *

'Conventional re-use' undoubtedly is the form of re-use which is least interesting for our enquiry, as it simply describes a disruption in use but no real change. Much more significant, both culturally and politically, is when an item is re-employed by different people, in a changed framework or environment, when it fulfils a new purpose or when it has been filled with altered implications and values (new-life re-use). In art historical terms, this may relate to the re-occupation of a space or the re-dedication of an image and cannot be described as a 'neutral' act any longer (see Plate 2.3). Such behaviour clearly has wider implications and is likely to convey religious and political messages to the new as well as to the previous users.

Although, as we have pointed out above, especially the taking apart of an item or a concept to form an entirely novel object or theory (recycling) can have negative connotations, acts of re-use are not always linked to aggression. In some instances, people have used the re-use of a style to prevent aggression, following the principle of mimicry (see Plate 2.4) (Hegewald 2007, 2009). Cultures themselves constantly make reference to and re-use aspects of their own past to shape the present and the future in ways which provide cultural cohesion and an awareness of tradition. Besides, people come into contact with different cultures, fashions, new beliefs and ideas and voluntarily absorb aspects (see Plate 2.5). Innovative media are discovered or developed in which certain 'old' forms do not make sense and need to be adapted.[6]

The contributions combined in this publication focus on the region of South Asia. This is an area which is particularly rich in re-use, as it represents the cradle of many newborn faiths—which engaged with existing religions, ventured out and were re-used by surrounding cultures—and because it is an area which has been invaded and crossed by merchant routes, exposing its own people and those entering along these arteries of conquest and trade, to new and different concepts and cultural practices. Re-use, however, is a phenomenon which happens everywhere in the world.[7] This is further illustrated in the final chapter by

---

[6] For instance, early cave architecture in India initially imitated wooden forms in stone but then freed itself to become a more independent architectural expression. With the introduction of paper, the format of earlier palm leaf manuscripts changed as the new medium offered the opportunity to depart from the elongated narrow format of the palm leaf used for centuries before.

[7] Especially well-known examples are the Dome of the Rock in Jerusalem and the Babri Masjid in Ayodhya. For further details on these sites, see Hegewald and Mitra (2008: 2). However, also major museums, which display objects in a different environment and give them a new meaning—in many cases a change from religious use to aesthetic appreciation—are centres of re-use. Reflecting this notion, John Berendt in his novel *The City of Falling Angels* calls the Louvre "the single greatest monument to organized theft in the history of art" (2006: 398).

Mitra and König, which opens the debate wider by looking beyond the regional limits of South Asia by comparing approaches to the re-use of national allegories in India and France.

## COMMON THEMES IN RE-USE

An especially interesting area of re-use studies is the continuity of religious sites. Mircea Eliade (1907–86), as a leading interpreter of religious experience, has made a considerable contribution to this subject. Eliade's central theory is that *hierophanies* (manifestations of the sacred)[8] form the basis of religion and divide the human experience of reality into two main areas: the sacred and the profane (Eliade 1987: 10–13). Sacred space and time are qualitatively fundamentally different in nature from profane space and time. Sacred places in our world are sites where the sacred has broken through the hierarchical levels and spheres of the cosmos and has made communication with the sacred possible (Eliade 1987: 20–24). Eliade argues that as such channels to the sacred remain open, they can be used by other religious groups who have taken over a sanctified place. Another term used to describe sites of special significance, which have attracted the attention of other religions and people, is the Latin expression *genius loci* (spirit of the place). This can be the protective spirit of a place or in a wider sense, the distinctive atmosphere of a location.

Whether it is connected to religious ideas about communication with the sacred or more simply the special character or aura of a place, invading groups and followers of new religions all over the world have been attracted to the sacred sites and places of worship of previous populations or religious groups (see Plate 2.6). A variety of reasons can be offered to explain this. It might be that, as Eliade argued, communication with the divine is favoured at places where a break in the levels of the religious cosmos has already occurred. Following the spirit of the *genius loci*, the atmosphere of a specific site—which can, for instance, be shaped by striking landscape features, such as mountain peaks, groves, the confluence of rivers or caves—might have constituted locales, which over generations, attracted different peoples (see Plate 2.7). However, more overtly political issues too might have played a role in some instances. It is a strong statement of conquest and occupation to annex the sacred locations

---

[8] This term, coined by Eliade, combines the elements *hieros* (sacred, holy) with *epiphaneia* (appearance) (Eliade 1987: 11). This more general 'appearance' or 'manifestation of the sacred' (*hierophany*) stands out against the more restrictive term *theophany* (an appearance of god), to indicate a less theistic and more inclusive approach to religions.

of a conquered people and to replace their gods with those of the invaders. On a more practical level, the re-use of already existing edifices sped up the process of establishing the latest ruling and religious elites. In addition to saving time, it saved money, as no new building materials had to be produced and transported (see Plate 2.8).[9]

Annexations often happen during times of political, religious or military conflict. During such unstable periods, sacred sites can be deserted or newly established rulers and religious authorities aim at asserting and confirming their recently acquired powers. However, in some instances, changes in the denomination of religious buildings have happened relatively peacefully by the adoption of deserted and decaying structures and their conversion to the requirements of a different faith or people (Hegewald 2006a, 2006b). The occupation of an already existing building and its transformation can again accelerate the process of establishing novel religious sites or centres of governance in deserted and war-swept regions.[10] For the same reason, edifices have been dismantled and their constituent elements have been re-used as material for the construction of new places of worship or other kinds of buildings. It is important to remember, however, that all these cases do not only constitute economical and speedy approaches to building but that, in addition, they can bear strong religious and political messages. The destruction and re-appropriation of sacred spaces and images—but also of government headquarters or national symbols—can imply a lack of respect for the religion, culture and rulers of forcibly subdued local cults.

Another very potent area for re-use is travel. Leisure travel and tourism are relatively recent phenomena, but the overland and sea routes of merchants and the converging paths of pilgrims have spanned long distances and connected distant continents and people since millennia. Before television and the internet enabled the exchange of ideas and knowledge of faraway countries, pilgrimage and trade took believers and merchants out of their known surroundings and exposed them to different political systems and laws, new and distinct religious and philosophical concepts, artistic styles, music and foreign cuisines. In addition, artists travelled along these routes as well and continued to practice the style of their home region, at times, in faraway places (see Plate 2.9). In many cases—as, for instance, in the posts

---

[9] Concrete examples of the continuity of religious sites in South Asia have been discussed in Hegewald and Mitra (2008: 3) and in Hegewald (forthcoming).

[10] The Jainas, for instance, absorbed a number of damaged and deserted structures at Khajuraho in Madhya Pradesh and converted these to their own ritual use (Hegewald 2006a, 2006b and Hegewald & Mitra 2008: 15–22).

along the so-called Silk Route—trade and the propagation of religion (in this instance, Buddhism) went hand-in-hand. A religion such as Buddhism, which actively seeks to expand, inevitably overlaps with earlier religions and traditions and brings about tensions in addition to assimilation and intermixing. In a way, the expansion of Buddhism far beyond the limits of its original region of influence and the survival of this faith to the present day has been explained through its ability to adapt and absorb local traditions and to tolerate and absorb some of the former beliefs and practises of its most recent followers without violating its own ethical precepts and religious structure (see Plate 2.10).

The issue of 'survival' is a further critical aspect of re-use, which can be encountered in a number of ways. Invading forces might bring destruction and a termination to the reign of rulers, forms of government and the dominance of religions. Through the re-use and adaptation of certain buildings or statues, selected institutions or rights, some elements of the previous culture might survive. Quoting from Walter Benjamin, Subrata K. Mitra and Lion König in this volume remind us that "it is the victors who tell the story", as it is the victorious who have the power to decide what is retained and re-used and what is lost and forgotten. The fact that the past influences the present is well known, however, as the two authors continue to stress, "important point here is to recognise that the present influences the past; for what we recognise in an unspecific past as definite depends on who we are and what we want to achieve through our recounting of the past". On the other side, suppressed cultures too re-use objects. Initially, this might be done for the purpose of survival, but ultimately this can aid the construction of a fresh identity and the transformation of victimhood into agency. As has been described above, Buddhism appears to have survived outside India due to its ability to integrate and adapt, but it did not survive in its country of origin. This is a phenomenon which also Katrin Binder in this volume illustrates in connection with the Yakshagana theatre tradition. She states:

> [...] some of the changes [in Yakshagana theatre] are so profound that one has to ask where Yakshagana stops and a new genre emerges. In all, Yakshagana successfully employs re-use to evade its potential sidelining into an endangered species of entertainment, overshadowed by cinema and home TV. It thus actively transforms its role as a potential victim into an assertion of its popularity—using cinema scripts as well as using TV broadcasts of performances for its own ends.

In other contexts, the introduction of revolutionary media, such as cinema and television, safeguard the survival of stories, for instance, the great Indian epics, which traditionally were sung by bards and performed by troupes, but which nowadays many children in India will primarily know from television adaptations.

## ALTERNATIVE TERMS TO DESCRIBE SIMILAR PROCESSES

Articles on associated subjects, and also some authors in this publication, use a number of other terms to describe partial aspects or issues relating in some way to the concept of re-use examined in this book. The following section aims to introduce the reader to the meanings and connotations of some of these terms and provides reasons for the editors' preference to employ the term 're-use'.[11]

The alternative term which has probably received the largest amount of publicity and attention, as it has been employed by the anthropologist and critical theorist Homi K. Bhabha (b. 1949)—and subsequently more widely in popular culture—is 'hybridity'. Hybridity or hybridisation refers to the mixing of different ingredients, and the term hybrid refers to something which is composite or heterogenic in nature. Bhabha sees this as a positive phenomenon, which contributes to the creation of what he calls a 'Third Space' (Bhabha 1994: 37). Originally, the term derives from the biological sciences where it implies a certain level of randomness and coincidence. Pollen fly and create unintentional and accidental hybrids. Despite its beginnings in biological sciences, and the awareness of some that coincidence is not a major issue when examining cultural hybridity, the term has widely been applied and continues to be used in the cultural realm.[12] Due to its strongly biological connotations and the importance of the element of conscious choice and intention in cultural and political change, the editors prefer the term 're-use'. Werbner cites a number of examples where the expression 'intentional hybrid' has been employed in order to remedy this deficiency (2001: 136). Whereas the fashionable term 'hybridity' is generally seen as a metaphor to describe cultural and political processes (Kapchan & Strong 1999: 239; Stross 1999; Tomlinson 2006; Dorst 1999), the term re-use is less oblique and more immediately describes actual practice.

Another term which has commonly been employed is 'indigenisation'.[13] The term is predominantly used in the social sciences, such as the political sciences (and here, above all, in research on citizenship), in ethnography and in

---

[11] This short introduction does not lay claim to providing a comprehensive summary of all the nuances of these individual terms and the many debates relating to them. The literature on hybridity and globalisation alone is vast and diverse and combines contributions from practically all scientific disciplines. The reasoning in this section primarily aims to illuminate the editors' choice for the term 're-use'.

[12] For the origin of the term in biological sciences, see Stross (1999) and Kapchan & Strong (1999). Stross draws two important differentiations: biological hybrids involve only two parents whereas culturally hybrid creations can have many 'parents'; while a genetic inheritance cannot be influenced, cultural 'inheritance' is based on choices (Stross 1999: 264–65).

[13] See, for instance, the chapter by Spiess in this volume.

anthropology, although this term too is applied in biological literature.[14] Similar to the previously discussed term hybridity, indigenisation is more limited as a word than the neutral re-use. Indigenisation implies that new elements are being introduced to a situation which is perceived as 'indigenous' and 'native'—implying that this is relatively closed and pure—and that the external elements, which are seen as the 'other', lose their purity and clarity by being coloured by an indigenous culture.[15] Even though there are some situations where this is what happens, re-use as a term is much wider and acknowledges the fact that what may be perceived as 'indigenous' and 'original' by some has, in many cases, been altered and influenced by generations of re-use and has rarely developed in complete isolation.

Also, fashionable in popular culture and writings, although originating from sociology and the social sciences more generally, is the term 'globalisation'. This term too has been used to describe and explain complex composite realities. However, as phenomena rarely are truly 'global'—meaning uniform across contexts and forming to a single uniform and homogeneous culture (Tomlinson 2006: 571)—the corrupted form 'glocalisation' is now often preferred.[16] Glocalisation pays more attention to the particular and the distinctive and refers to the global interacting with the local, to describe phenomena, which we in this publication call re-use.[17] Katrin Binder in this volume illustrates this central point by stating: "Re-use as theory explicitly takes cognisance of motivations and contexts." Still, the term globalisation continues to be used to describe an international network of communication, trade and transport, which connects people all around the world. Through modern information technology, individuals worldwide have the chance to obtain information on other cultures much more easily. To a certain extent, it confronts people with the 'other' and stimulates borrowing and re-use. However, neither globalisation nor glocalisation describe or explain what really happens. Why are some inspired by and react to certain aspects they are confronted with and not to others? Why when exposed

---

[14] Related terms are 'acculturation' (or 'mimicry') and 'interculturation' (Munasinghe 2006). In the biological sciences, the use of the term indigenisation can, for instance, relate to the indigeneity of amino acids in fossils (Macko & Engel 1991).

[15] See, for instance, the study by Merlan (2009).

[16] The new discursive category of 'glocalisation' was formulated by Robertson (1995: 28). An alternative preferred by some authors is the form 'local/global'. See, for instance, Meduri (2008: 304). On the issue of resistance to globalisation, see also O'Connor (2002).

[17] Ritzer defines glocalisation as the "interpenetration of the global and the local, resulting in unique outcomes in different geographic areas" (2003: 193). Making the opposite point, there are interesting cases where, for instance, Evangelical Christians in Thailand aim to minimise localisation and syncretism and propagate the upholding of a framework of teachings and values which are universal and shared by its members worldwide (Zehner 2005). This raises the more general issues of how much variation and localisation a religion—or in extension, a form of government or a style—can afford to remain orthodox or true to its values.

to the same data do inhabitants in a number of localities react to it differently?[18] In a way, globalisation and its variants simply describe a modern phenomenon and not a reaction to it. One may go one step further and question how modern an experience globalisation really is. Silk travelled along trade routes from the Far East to mediaeval courts, the Indus Civilisation traded with Arabia, and Gujarati textiles have been excavated at Fustat in Egypt and in Indonesia (Barnes 1998). Our idea that past societies were tightly delineated communities, unaware of the world beyond the limits of their own kingdom or framed locality, is an outdated perception. Re-use happened long before globalisation was named and favoured through air travel and the worldwide net (see Plates 2.5, 2.9 and 2.10).

Whereas hybridity, indigeneity and globalisation are fashionable jargon, associated with ideological frameworks and sets of values, there is a whole series of more descriptive terms which are not as loaded with meaning and which have been used to describe similar phenomena. Originating from a background in the natural sciences are the terms 'diffusion' and 'symbiosis'. The concept of diffusion, which comes from the physical sciences, again describes a random act. This is the spread of items or ideas from an area of high concentration to one of lower intensity. While the spread of Buddhism, democracy or Marxism, an artistic style, cultural artefacts (Theunissen, Grave & Bailey 2000) or of a specific culture (Kirk 1975: 19) can be described as diffusions, this provides us with no information on the dynamics and the agents involved in this. Whereas patterns of diffusion in physics can be carefully predicted and calculated, cultural diffusion does not follow strictly predictable rules. In physics, diffusion happens naturally, through spontaneous movement or natural influences such as thermal changes. The term excludes the element of the human actor or agent, who is so important when it comes to re-use.[19] Diffusion in water is known by the specialist term 'osmosis' and, interestingly, this specific form of diffusion has been absorbed as well, especially into popular language. Pop culture is full of references to the term 'cultural osmosis' and is therefore regularly used by university students when writing about re-use.[20] Like so many before, the alternative term symbiosis originates in biological research. It describes a close

---

[18] Tomlinson describes this by saying "the global distribution of the cultural goods of a dominant culture has no predictable linear consequences [...] cultural appropriation always involves adaptation and generates new particularities" (2006: 571–72).

[19] A further term, which was coined by the anthropologist and ethnologist Claude Lévi-Strauss, is the French 'bricolage'. Lévi-Strauss applied this term to what he described as arbitrary combinations of myth motifs (Kapchan & Strong 1999: 240).

[20] In fact, when used in popular and pop culture, the term cultural osmosis actually has a different meaning. In these contexts, it is taken to describe a phenomenon where without having experienced something oneself, one knows about it by being part of a culture or scene, as if by osmosis. For more information, see http://everything2.com/title/cultural+osmosis.

interaction between several species or organisms. In many instances, both creatures profit from this relationship and as such reflect a mutual connection. In addition, there are associations where one benefits but the other remains unaffected (commensal) or where one profits but at the expense of the other (parasitic). In a way, these are valuable questions also to ask with regards to our cultural and political re-use examples in South Asia, but the term symbiosis is only helpful with regards to some re-use cases.

Two terms more closely connected with the study of religions are 'syncretism' and 'pluralism'. Syncretism literally means 'Cretan federation' and refers to the practice of Cretan cities to unite and reconcile their differences when faced by an external enemy.[21] By extension, it is today mainly used to mean to 'combine' and describes the reconciliation, merging and unity of different (often conflicting) belief systems. Siv Ellen Kraft describes syncretism as "the politics of religious synthesis" and anti-syncretism as "attempts to protect religious boundaries" (2002: 142). Religious syncretism allows for an inclusive approach to other faiths and cultures and constitutes a blending of belief systems or traditions. A crucial issue in syncretism, however, is the will or intention to strike alliances and to integrate.[22] Whereas random occurrences too could be described as leading to syncretism, one would not describe the destructive annexation of a temple or the stealing of a sacred statue as a syncretic deed. Although the lasting consequence of re-use frequently is integration, not all acts of re-use can be called syncretism. The second term, pluralism, is a more neutral expression, describing a diversity of views or approaches as opposed to one single interpretation. In the area of South Asian studies, however, it is nowadays closely associated with the 'Pluralism Project' focusing on religious diversity in the United States of America.[23] Religious pluralism refers to the acceptance of other faiths and is often closely linked

---

[21] For a detailed discussion of the meaning and the varied associations of the term syncretism, see Stewart (1999) and *Webster's Third New International Dictionary of the English Language* (1993: 2319). Despite its prominent use in religious discourse, the term syncretism has been applied in the description of religious architecture too (Gates 1984) and even Fascist architecture (von Henneberg 1996), just to name two examples from outside the area of religious studies.

[22] Mentioned above has been the anti-syncretic focus of evangelical Christianity, illustrated by the example of Thailand, which focuses on the preservation of 'essential truths' and the 'integrity' of evangelical core values (Zehner 2005).

[23] Since 1991, the Pluralism Project at Harvard University examines America's changing religious landscape, which increasingly has become multicultural and multireligious (See http://pluralism.org/). Ideas derived from this project have been taken to India, where the historical situation, however, is very different (Guha 1997). Without denying its general importance, more recent scholarship has questioned the theoretical basis of the project (Machacek 2003).

to the concept of ecumenism.[24] However, in addition to religious pluralism, there is cultural pluralism (Watson 1980), political pluralism (Park & Shin 2006) and pluralism in a number of other areas.[25] Pluralism simply describes diversity and choice. This does not necessarily involve the continuity of certain features, the interlinking of different aspects, and their changing function over time, which are implied in the term re-use.[26]

Another set of terms which acts as an alternative for the word re-use comes from the history of art and architecture. There is 'eclecticism', denoting an approach which does not exclusively draw from a single style or paradigm but which combines several distinct ideas, theories and styles (see Plate 2.11).[27] Eclectics have been criticised for a lack of consistency even though in actual fact most historical buildings which have been enlarged during several periods, have continued to be used by changing rulers and have been adapted to new functions, and are inevitably eclectic. The styles of entire periods, such as the historicism of the nineteenth century, have been classified as eclectic (de Sola-Morales 1987). However, eclecticism is "an almost universal phenomenon" (Meeks 1953: 15). Alongside its use in the area of architecture, the term has been applied in the fine and decorative arts (Meeks 1950), in the history of ideas (Kelley 2001), in music (Middleton & Beebe 2002) as well as in cultural studies more generally.[28] Useful for our reflections on terminology is that authors writing on eclecticism are often conscious of and sensitive to the element of selectivity

---

[24] The chapter by Sabine Scholz on the re-use of ancient concepts in modern Jainism in the Western diaspora in this volume touches on this issue. It illustrates the reinterpretation of the concept of *anekantavada* (non–one-sidedness) to express intra-religious pluralism and tolerance towards other denominations. However, as Scholz shows clearly, this was not the original meaning intended by the term.

[25] Cultural pluralism refers to the coexistence of different cultural trends within a country or region. Often, it is used to describe a situation where alongside a major culture, minority traditions retain their cultural identity and interact and influence mainstream traditions. By political pluralism, it is meant that in a democracy, power is not held by one person only but that it lies with a number of institutions. In addition, it describes the coexistence of discrete political systems or separate political parties. Some studies in the natural sciences refer to so-called medical pluralism, illustrating the fact that cultural and political studies have not only re-used terminology from the natural and medical sciences but also the other way round.

[26] In rare cases, even the religious term 'transfiguration' has been used to describe cultural change, as can be seen in the article by Meduri on the 'transfiguration' of Indian dance in the diaspora (2008). Literally, transfiguration relates to the temporary transformation of a person into a divine being and is closely associated with the transfiguration of Christ. A more impartial term might be more helpful when dealing with world cultures.

[27] The creation of good architecture, as well as the formulation of good architectural history, requires methodological eclecticism, as has been pointed out by Carpo (2005).

[28] The chapter by Nick Barnard in this volume examines eclecticism in South Asian and European jewellery. A fascinating study of eclectic cultures in Europe is that of the Asante Empire by McCaskie (1972).

when it comes to the combining of elements (McCaskie 1972: 44–45; Lyman 1988). This is an element which is of utmost importance in re-use. Re-use, however, makes it clearer which is the main context and which is a new or re-used element entering the scene, whilst the basic term eclecticism treats all combined elements equally and does not establish structural hierarchies.

Art historians employ terms such as: revival (see Plates 2.12),[29] reinvention, retrospective, retrograde (or simply retro), relaunch, reorchestration and even resuscitation, a term clearly borrowed from the area of medicine.[30] In a way, these alternative words probably come closest to the term re-use as all as a group refer to the return to something already existing or from the past, which is brought alive in a different place or period. However, all of them, to a certain extent—and particularly the term retro—have fairly negative connotations.[31] They refer to an idealised situation or shape in the past, and an attempt to return to this state or form arousing feelings of nostalgia. In many instances, we can encounter an idealising of the past in re-use cases as well—see, for instance, the contributions by Katrin Binder and the joint contribution by Subrata K. Mitra and Lion König in this volume. The term re-use, however, is more impartial and unemotional, and it refers to the creation of something new out of an idealised past. In this sense, it is more akin to the term 'reform'. The word reform, however, is predominantly used when dealing with ideologies and religions, but not when referring to objects. Additionally, a reform always aims—or at least pretends—to improve. Whereas the long-term effect of re-use frequently is to improve—at least in those instances where the best is chosen to create something enhanced and superior—in the short-term, however, the annexation of temples and images of another group causes distress and can only from the side of the victors be seen as a change for the better.[32]

Therefore, the term re-use is preferred and presented in this publication as the most suitable, adaptable and unbiased term, explaining the largest number of possible re-use cases. The discussion has shown how many situations

---

[29] The term revival is particularly closely associated with architectural styles, such as the late eighteenth and early nineteenth centuries' Greek Revival (for example, in the United States), the Gothic Revival around the same time (for example, in Britain) and the late nineteenth-century Romanesque Revival (for example, in Scotland), which have been analysed in the relevant literature. However, the term is also intimately connected with the revival of religions, such as the so-called Islamic revival.

[30] The use of this diversity of terms can, for instance, be seen in the chapter on south Indian temple architecture by George Michell in this volume.

[31] The term retro is closely connected with the establishment of retro brands. These are relaunched historical brands with often only superficially updated features, which primarily aim at commercial gains and not at a serious engagement with the past. They basically constitute a marketing tactic (Brown, Kozinets & Sherry 2003).

[32] There are other more specialised terms, which have only been applied in specific disciplines. For instance, 'intertextuality' relates to the juxtaposition of different texts in literary studies.

constitute re-use, how complex and diverse re-use cases are, and have so far focused on disassociating itself from alternative terms used alongside or instead of it. The term re-use has a history too but the implications which are associated with it in the present publication go beyond its previous remit. So far, the word has—in addition to its use in the eco-area outlined before—mainly been used in art history. Here it is employed in situations where there is continuity of sacred sites (Wallace 2003), where edifices have been re-used (Cavanagh & Mee 1978; Hegewald 2006a, 2006b; Hegewald & Mitra 2008), where the building materials of previous structures have been re-employed to raise new structures (Allen, Rose & Fulford 2003, March 2004) or where styles have been re-used strategically (Hegewald 2009) (see Plate 2.4).[33] Re-use contains an earlier existing element, which is taken out of its previous context and it contributes to the creation of something distinct and novel in the present. This complex item can last as it contains an important element from the past and therefore constitutes continuity and contributes to the further establishment of tradition. As such, despite containing an element of the past, re-use looks forwards and not backwards. It does not represent an end but a new beginning.

## TOWARDS A DEFITION OF RE-USE: FROM ART HISTORY TO UNIVERSALITY

The question whether art—a new style or the work of a young innovative artist—is a continuation of something already existent or something entirely novel has been a central question in art historical debates. To a large extent, Western artists become famous and their works highly rated, because the rhetoric surrounding their personalities and their oeuvres portrays them as the creators of something new and unique. On the other hand, artists have continuously re-used earlier styles, genres and motifs. Indeed, the term 'motif' describes a re-used pattern, image or theme. Some of the most successful artists of the twentieth century have clearly integrated non-local elements into their works. Pablo Picasso drew inspirations from African art and a large number of painters, such as Vincent van Gogh, Claude Monet, Camille Pissaro and Gustav Klimt were

---

[33] Furthermore, the term re-use appears in biology, wildlife and medical literature, but to a lesser extent than those words discussed previously. In art history, there are also a number of studies which focus on re-use but do not necessarily name it by using this specific term. See footnote 2 in this chapter for a number of references. There is a small collection of papers by Aitken (2009), Kasdorf (2009), Patel (2009), Sears (2009) focusing on re-use in an Islamic context in an issue of *Archives of Asian Art* (Vol. 59) . Although the introductory essay (Patel 2009a) outlines to a certain extent the history of this approach in the available literature, it does not engage with the theory of re-use or with the reasons for choosing this term.

influenced by Japanese arts, specifically *ukiyo-e* woodblock prints. Nevertheless, these artists created new, original and unique works of art. Notwithstanding, the desire to disguise and mystify one's sources of re-use is still widespread amongst artists.[34]

Reflections on re-use in the fine arts open up an even deeper discussion about the place and value of the 'original' and the 'copy' in art historical discourse.[35] This involves identifications of forgeries, which are pretending to be authentic works in order to rectify high prices, but also masterful copies of certain famous paintings, which had their rightful place at least at certain points in the past.[36] In instances where paintings have been overpainted many times or a Romanesque church that has been adorned with trappings during the Baroque, the question arises, which is the authentic layer that should be preserved?[37] In the modern printing world with high quality reproductions, which do not pretend to be originals but as they are photographs or scans of the original, they nevertheless have a certain authority and link to the masterpiece, causing the debate about authentic and inauthentic artworks to be widened further. It becomes quickly apparent that there are many degrees of differentiation between the two dichotomous extremes of original and forgery. Important is the conclusion which at least some art historians have reached, namely that "Original and copy are not well-defined terms: not only because they are linked by intermediaries [...] but because they contaminate one another by forming a cycle that repeats through history" (Elkins 1993: 114).

This quote points its finger directly at the aspect of this debate, which is of significance for our examination of re-use. It is significant that in re-use too there rarely is one authentic and unique original which has been re-used, may this be an artwork, a religion or a form of government. As Mitra and König

---

[34] The artist Wolfgang Laib (b. 1950) has directly re-used the shapes of Islamic graves in his sculptural forms. The titles of these works do not reveal his source (Laib 1988) and it is only when one examines his sculptures before the background of a later publication of photographs taken by the artist on his travels (Laib 2002) that he indirectly reveals his inspirations. Few people in the West would know about such picturesque objects in foreign countries and take them for purely original artistic conceptions by the artist. On the other hand, the artistic transformation of these forms makes them into something distinct which, one can argue, is original to Laib.

[35] Art historians tend to classify works of art as originals when they possess one or more of the following three properties: originality, primacy and uniqueness (Elkins 1993: 114).

[36] Usually, such copies do not aim to be photorealistic (strict copies) and do not mechanically copy 'line by line' (Duncum 1988: 203). They make direct reference to a celebrated painting but at the same time create a new and—at least to a certain extent—an independent work or art. This approach was, for example, supported by the Baroque academies. See, for instance, the seventeenth-century copy of *The Virgin with the Family of the Burgomaster Jacob Meyer*, originally painted by Hans Holbein the Younger in Max J. Friedländer (1941: plates A and B).

[37] The early Russian icon known as the *Virgin of Vladimir* has been overpainted at least five times in the past seven centuries (Elkins 1993: 114).

point out in their contribution in this volume, the "question, whether there is such a thing as 'the real' Bharat Mata continues to be open". Re-use is not primarily about the identification of a 'genuine pure form' (Mitra & König in this volume), which may once have existed but more about a recognition that things are continuously changing and reacting to one another. The creation of new religions can often, at least partially, be seen as a reaction to existing local faiths and when such a recent belief system travelled to other countries, it took with it idiosyncrasies of its country of origin, which then reacted to and absorbed local features as well.

Another crucial issue raised in the quote from Elkins above (1993: 114) is the question whether at all and, if so, then how to judge copies or mixtures which are created through re-use and hybridisation. Elkins appears to use the term 'contamination' rhetorically, but this is an issue which has been greatly debated. A number of authors (Stewart 1999: 42; Tomlinson 2006: 572) quote from an essay by Salman Rushdie in which the writer explains that his novel:

> *The Satanic Verses* celebrates hybridity, impurity, intermingling, the transformation that comes from new and unexpected combinations [...] I rejoice in mongrelization and fear the absolutism of the Pure. Mélange, hotch-potch, a bit of this and a bit of that is *how newness enters the world*. [...] *The Satanic Verses* is [...] a love song to our mongrel selves. (Rushdie 1990: 4)[38]

Rushdie is obviously in favour of creative mixing but he clearly is playing with feelings of discomfort, which are traditionally associated with impure mixtures. Human beings like to divide and organise, to classify and to assess items either as pure and true or as subforms and corruptions. The question is whether such categories exist out there in nature or whether they are socially and culturally constructed (Stross 1999: 255). This critical approach to something which obviously is not a pure form seems to derive from the original use of the term 'hybridisation' in the areas of biology and racial mixing (or segregation). As a consequence, Tomlinson concludes that the "absolutism of the pure", as Rushdie called it in his essay, "is the main political thrust of all metaphors of cultural mixture: that they undermine the more dangerous myths of origin, lineage, and, above all, purity" (2006: 572). In this volume, the chapter

---

[38] Stross mentions a number of other pejorative terms, which have been employed to describe hybrids, such as 'half-breed', 'half-caste', 'mutt' and 'mutation' (1999: 254, 264). This is an issue which Kapchan and Strong write about in detail. Quoting Victor Turner, they use terms such as 'contaminated', 'promiscuous' and 'impure' (Kapchan & Strong 1999: 239). The issues of purity and impurity in connection with hybridity and creolisation form the focus of the article by Munasinghe (2002). Also, in the area of biology, value-based statements are employed when referring to hybrids. See, for instance, Huskins (1929: 399) for the use of the term 'abnormal' as an equivalent of something 'of hybrid nature'.

by George Michell gains a new significance. He describes how, contrasting with fears about diluting one's lineage through re-use, the re-use of a formerly established style can provide a young dynasty with an 'architectural' lineage and through re-using styles loaded with connotations can create a 'pure origin' which did not in fact exist. In this context, the study by Bender and Cadge (2006) is of particular concern. It indicates that religious conflicts and the movement of religious traditions into new environments does not necessarily threaten and dilute them but can have the opposite effect of strengthening and reshaping their borders.

Stross goes one step further in describing 'hybrid cycles', in which after some time has passed, a hybrid or re-used composite form becomes so accepted and established that it is considered homogenous and pure again. Transformed in this way, it can be re-used and coupled with other elements to help generate other kinds of re-use in the future (1999: 255, 265–66). In a way, this is what Elkins describes in the context of art history in his article entitled "From Origin to Copy and Back Again" (1993) and particularly in the quote above, where he refers to "forming a cycle that repeats through history" (Elkins 1993: 114).[39] Also, a number of contributions in this volume (for example, Mitra & König; Rodrigues) refer to this non-linear process of re-use. In addition, this issue illustrates that we are dealing with notions of perception and artificial classification and not with proven realities. Everything out in the world relates to other items and continuously absorbs from and relates to its environment.

What is harder to define than the theory of re-use are the limits of this concept.[40] Have we got a clearly defined category or is everything we do re-use? Can there ever be anything entirely new?[41] Starting with the last question, one has to stress that we are all aware that there have been clear innovations, that groundbreaking styles and innovative motifs have been created. This, however, does not necessarily mean that no aspect of them has existed before or has been re-used in their formation. For instance, the birth of the Abstract Art Movement, towards the end of the nineteenth century in Europe, was a novel and revolutionary

---

[39] In a different context, this cyclical nature of re-use and hybridity has been discussed in Kikuchi (1997: 344).

[40] Werbner encounters the same problem when defining the limits of hybridity in the environment of rural Berber communities in the High Atlas Mountains of Morocco. She illustrates that whereas some hybridisation and a venturing into liminal spaces can revitalise a community, some Islamic reformists do not approve of such social renewal and regard it as an attack on the sacred (2001: 141–42, 143–49). On the limits of hybridity, see also Dorst (1999).

[41] These questions arose primarily in conversations held by the two editors with Prof Dr Hans Harder in Heidelberg in April 2007 and with colleagues during our panel on the European Conference on Modern South Asian Studies in Manchester in July 2008.

development. But this does not mean that it did not employ known symbols or that nobody before had used abstraction in art. As a consequence, some prefer simply to call re-use 'continuity'.[42] However, might this not be too easy a way out? Is really everything possible and no classification achievable? If this was the case, should we not simply stop examining art history, religions and political changes as all is simply continuity and happens naturally?

There is considerable room for disagreement here. We understand our world in categories. Countries have borders even if these can change over time, political parties have names although their manifestoes might resemble one another, architectural styles have been categorised despite the fact that they might be revived in later centuries, religions have been named, though such terms and 'isms' are today questioned. Human beings make sense of their surroundings by ordering and systematising their surroundings and by understanding items in separate and specific frameworks. Even though these contexts might be culturally and socially created, they are perceived as realities. There is a way, which lies between the two extremes of traditional classifications, which allowed for no hybrids and the postmodern angst that no categories at all can be applied. Re-use crosses perceived and to a certain extent culturally conditioned boundaries and generates items which are composite and—at least for a while—are perceived as being heterogeneous in origin and composition. This does not question the validity of forms and styles but allows for the celebration of the heterogeneous, which does not easily fit into boxes.

Another essential point is that there is structure in all this change. The fact that cultures are not static but continuously developing entities does not mean that everything about them is changeable and constantly in flux. In most instances, cultural change happens slowly, selectively and usually only alters a comparatively small area of a large- and long-established pool of cultural practices. It is not enough for two different cultures simply 'to meet' for hybridity or for re-use to occur. Werbner stresses the importance of critical consciousness in the encounter between discrete cultures when she says: "A key issue is that of reflexivity within, as well as in the encounter between cultures" (2001: 149) and the examples of the anti-syncretic Christians in Thailand and the orthodox Muslims in Morocco have shown that the blending of religious and cultural traits can at times be consciously suppressed. In some instances, such as in invasions and political takeovers, it is important to consider the more general questions of politics, economy and power relations, and not just the element of personal preference. However, power changes and inequality does not provide the only motor to make re-use happen and it is not the neutral 'masses' which

---

[42] Here I refer, for instance, to a personal conversation with Dr Christina Luczanitz in Heidelberg in April 2007. This idea has been discussed in Wallace (2003).

we so often hear about who effect change, but it is individuals making choices and taking actions.

**\* \* \* \***

Re-use is a conscious and selective process in which existing elements are borrowed or salvaged and taken out of their former environment in order to be applied to a new context, or they are left within their old milieu but filled with new meanings, or they get manipulated and react to new external influences.[43] This also includes resistance to certain new elements. For this to happen, a disruption or change has to take place, favouring a confrontation with something different. Re-use generally takes advantage of opportunities created by new situations, may this be warfare and conquest, trade and commerce, travel and pilgrimage, social and political changes, development of innovative and unknown materials and media through inventions or the exposure to other cultures and religions. Re-use is not imitation and therefore not concerned with creating forgeries. It is a creative combination of old and new elements, which aims to re-elaborate, improve and carry further an idea, a style, an institution or a concept.

One crucial aspect for an item or act to classify as re-use is the continuity of something already present. Another one is the focal element of agency. Re-use does not just happen because it represents continuity or because in biology hybrids occur from time to time. Re-use only materialises when agents and actors make it happen. It involves an active deed, there needs to be a reason for why something is re-used and based on this motivation or aim, people make strategic choices about what to re-use and what not to re-use, what to destroy and what to simply deprive of any use and value (Hegewald & Mitra in this volume). Those items which are re-used have to be filled with a new significance, with novel functions. In this sense, re-use is conscious and self-conscious. It aims to combine the best to create something innovative and more lasting. How these re-used items are perceived by various audiences depends on their relationship with the individual items that have been fused. Re-use can create anxiety and it can contribute to integration.[44] Items and concepts which

---

[43] The selective nature of what we call re-use in this chapter has also been stressed in the article by Winslow (2003) with regards to potters in Sri Lanka. Winslow uses the more general term hybridity, which at least in its original form does not imply agency.

[44] Werbner (2001: 150) writes in this context:

> Whether cultural hybridity is generative and fertilizing depends on how its varied audiences interpret it. For some multiculturalism, cultural borrowings and mixings, constitute an attack on their felt subjectivity. In a world in which local people feel their culture to be under threat from globalization Western cultural forces or from incoming stranger migrants, interruptive hybridity may be experienced not as revitalizing and fun, but as threatening a prior social order and morality.

are based on re-use often persist longer because they establish continuity and involve different groups of society. In this context, it is fascinating to observe that even biological hybrids of plants (hybrid corn, for instance) have shown to be more resilient (Whaley 1950: 10).

## CONCLUDING THOUGHTS

With the collection of essays presented in this volume, it is intended to widen and to deepen the debate on 'hybridity', questions of 'globalisation', 'indigeneity' and other terms proposed by scholars from a number of scientific areas. This publication propositions the term 're-use' as the clearest and most helpful in many situations. However, following Tomlinson's mistrust of pure theory, which he judges as always provisional,[45] more than defending a single term, it has been hoped to widen the debate on cultural and political re-use, contribute a focus on South Asia to the discussion and illustrate the value gained when artificial boundaries that separate the wider disciplines of the humanities and social sciences are creatively and positively subverted.

## PHOTO CREDIT

All photographs reproduced in this chapter are by Julia A. B. Hegewald.

## BIBLIOGRAPHY

### Secondary Sources

Aitken, Molly Emma, 2009, "Parataxis and the Practice of Reuse, from Mughal Margins to Mir Kalan Khan". *Archives of Asian Art*. Vol. 59, pp. 81–103.

Asher, Catherine B. & Thomas R. Metcalf (eds), 1994, *Perceptions of South Asia's Visual Past*. American Institute of Indian Studies, New Delhi; Swadharma Swarajya Sangha, Madras; and Oxford & IBH Publishing, New Delhi.

---

[45] Tomlinson (2006: 572) writes: "A pure theory sounds to me like a rather dangerous instrument, something that brooks no dispute, something indeed, that should not fall into wrong hands. I prefer to think of theories as always provisional, as modest heuristic entities encouraging dialogue."

Allen, J. R. L., E. J. Rose & M. G. Fulford, 2003, "Re-use of Roman Stone in the Reedham Area of East Norforlk: Intimations of a Possible 'Lost' Roman Fort". *Britannia*. Vol. 34, pp. 129–41.

Barnes, Ruth, 1998, "Indian Trade Textiles: Sources and Transmissions of Designs". In: Jessica Hallett & Conceição Amaral (eds), *Cultures of the Indian Ocean*. Exhibition catalogue, Commissão Nacional para as Comemorações dos Descobrimentos Portuguese and Instituto Portugués de Museus, Lisbon, pp. 230–42.

Bender, Courtney & Wendy Cadge, 2006 (Autumn), "Constructing Buddhism(s): Inter-religious Dialogue and Religious Hybridity". *Sociology of Religion*. Vol. 67, no. 3, pp. 229–47.

Berendt, John, 2006 [2005], *The City of Falling Angels*. Penguin Books, New York.

Bhabha, Homi, 1994, *The Location of Culture*. Routldege, London.

Brown, Stephen, Robert V. Kozinets & John F. Sherry, 2003 (July), "Teaching Old Brands New Tricks: Retro Branding and the Revival of Brand Meaning". *The Journal of Marketing*. Vol. 67, no. 3, pp. 19–33.

Cavanagh, W. & C. Mee, 1978, "The Re-use of Earlier Tombs in the LH IIIC Period". *The Annual of the British School of Athens*. Vol. 73, pp. 31–44.

Carpo, Mario, 2005 (December), "Architecture: Theory, Interdisciplinarity, and Methodological Eclecticism". *Journal of the Society of Architectural Historians*. Vol. 64, no. 4, pp. 425–27.

Cohn, Bernhard S., 1996, "The Transformation of Objects into Artifacts, Antiquities, and Art in Nineteenth-century India". In: Bernhard S. Cohen (ed.), *Colonialism and its Forms of Knowledge: The British in India*. Princeton University Press, New Jersey, pp. 76–105.

College Art Association, 1980 (Autumn–Winter), "Pluralism in Art and in Art Criticism". *Art Journal*. Vol. 40, no. 1/2 (Special edition *Modernism, Revisionism, Pluralism, and Post-Modernism*), pp. 377–79.

Davis, Richard H., 1993 (February), "Indian Art Objects as Loot". *The Journal of Asian Studies*. Vol. 52, no. 1, pp. 22–48.

———, 1999 [1997], *Lives of Indian Images*. Motilal Banarsidass Publishers, Delhi.

Dorst, John D., 1999 (Summer), "Which Came First, the Chicken Device or the Textual Egg? Documentary Film and the Limits of the Hybrid Metaphor". *The Journal of American Folklore*. Vol. 112, no. 445 (Special edition *Theorizing the Hybrid*), pp. 268–81.

Duncum, Paul, 1988 (Summer), "To Copy or Not to Copy: A Review". *Studies in Art Education*. Vol. 29, no. 4, pp. 203–10.

Eaton, Richard M., 2000, "Temple Desecration and Indo-Muslim States". In: David Gilmartin & Bruce B. Lawrence (eds), *Beyond Turk and Hindu: Rethinking Religious Identities in Islamicate South Asia*. University Press of Florida, Gainsville, pp. 246–81.

Eliade, Mircea, 1987 [1957], *The Sacred and the Profane: The Nature of Religion—The Significance of Religious Myth, Symbolism, and Ritual within Life and Culture*. A Harvest/HBJ Book, Harcourt Brace Jovanovich Publishers, San Diego, New York and London.

Elkins, James, 1993, "From Original to Copy and Back Again". *British Journal of Aesthetics*. Vol. 33, no. 2, pp. 113–20.

Friedländer, Max J., 1941 (May), "Artistic Quality: Original and Copy". *The Burlington Magazine for Connoisseurs*. Vol. 78, no. 458, pp. 143–51.

Gates, Marie-Henriette, 1984 (September), "Duras-Europos: A Fortress of Syro-Mesopotamian Art". *The Biblical Archaeologist*. Vol. 47, no. 3, pp. 166–81.

Guha, Sumit, 1997 (November 8–14), "Cultural and Religious Pluralism in India and the US". *Economic and Political Weekly*. Vol. 32, no. 44/45, pp. 2851–53.

Hegewald, Julia A. B., 2006a, "From Shiva to Parshvanatha: The Appropriation of a Hindu Temple for Jaina Worship". In: Catherine Jarrige and Vincent Lefèvre (eds), *South Asian Archaeology 2001*, 2 vols, Editions Recherches sur les Civilisations, Paris. pp. 517–23.

———, 2006b, "Architectural, Sculptural and Religious Change: A New Interpretation of the Jaina Temples at Khajuraho". In: P. Flügel (ed.), *Studies in Jaina History and Culture: Disputes and Dialogues*, Routledge Advances in Jaina Studies Vol. 1. Routledge, London and New York, pp. 401–18.

———, 2007, "Domes, Tombs and Minarets: Islamic Influences on Jaina Architecture". In: Adam Hardy (ed.), *The Temple in South Asia*, Volume 2 of the proceedings of the 18th conference of the European Association of South Asian Archaeologists, London 2005. British Association for South Asian Studies and the British Academy, London, pp. 179–90.

———, 2009, "Jaina Temple Architecture in India from the Fifteenth and Later Centuries: Stylistic, Religious and Political Meanings". In: Anke Fissabre & Caroline Helmenstein (eds), *Festschrift: Jan Pieper zum 65. Geburtstag—Von seinen Schülern, Freunden und Kollegen*. Gesammelt und zusammengestellt am Lehrstuhl für Baugeschichte der RWTH Aachen, Eigenverlag, pp. 67–88.

———, forthcoming, "Building Citizenship: The Agency of Public Buildings and Urban Planning in the Making of the Indian Citizen". In: Subrata K. Mitra (ed.), *Citizenship in South Asia*. Samskriti Publishers, New Delhi.

Hegewald, Julia A. B. & Subrata K. Mitra, 2008, "Jagannatha Compared: The Politics of Appropriation, Re-use and Regional State Traditions in India". *Heidelberg Papers in South Asian and Comparative Politics (HPSACP)*. No. 36, pp. 1–37. Available at http://archiv.ub.uni-heidelberg.de/volltextserver/frontdoor.php?source_opus=8015 (accessed on 28 June 2011).

von Henneberg, Krystyna, 1996 (April), "Imperial Uncertainties: Architectural Syncretism and Improvisation in Fascist Colonial Libya". *Journal of Contemporary History*. Vol. 31, no. 2 (Special edition *Aesthetics of Fascism*), pp. 373–95.

Hillenbrand, Robert, 1988, "Political Symbolism in Early Indo-Islamic Mosque Architecture: The Case of Ajmir". *Iran*. Vol. XXVI, pp. 105–17.

Huskins, C. Leonard, 1929 (April), "Criteria of Hybridity". *Science*. New Series. Vol. 69, no. 1789, pp. 399–400.

Kapchan, Deborah A. & Pauline Turner Strong, 1999 (Summer), "Theorizing the Hybrid". *The Journal of American Folklore*. Vol. 112, no. 445 (Special edition *Theorizing the Hybrid*), pp. 239–53.

Kasdorf, Katherine E., 2009, "Translating Sacred Space in Bijapur: The Mosques of Karim al-Din and Khwaja Jahan". *Archives of Asian Art*. Vol. 59, pp. 57–80.

Kelley, Donald R., 2001 (October), "Eclecticism and the History of Ideas". *Journal of the History of Ideas*. Vol. 62, no. 4, pp. 577–92.

Kikuchi, Yuko, 1997, "Hybridity and the Oriental Orientalism of 'Mingei' Theory". *Journal of Design History*. Vol. 10, no. 4 (Special edition *Craft, Culture and Identity*), pp. 343–54.

Kirk, William, 1975 (March), "The Role of India in the Diffusion of Early Cultures". *The Geographical Journal*. Vol. 41, no. 1, pp. 19–34.

Kraft, Siv Ellen, 2002, "'To Mix or Not to Mix: Syncretism/Anti-syncretism in the History of Theosophy". *Numen*. Vol. 49, no. 2, pp. 142–77.

Laib, Wolfgang, 1988, *Wolfgang Laib*. Edition Galerie Buchmann, Basel.

———, 2002, *Die Neun Planeten: Oder wie die Zusammenhänge auch sein könnten—The Nine Planets: Or How the Interrelationships Also Could Be*. Museum Folkwang Essen, Hatje Cantz, Ostfildern-Ruit.

Lyman Thomas, W., 1988, "The Politics of Selective Eclecticism: Monastic Architecture, Pilgrimage Churches, and 'Resistance to Cluny'". *Gesta*. Vol. 27, no. 1/2 (Special edition *Current Studies on Cluny*), pp. 83–92.

Machacek, David W., 2003 (Summer), "The Problem of Pluralism". *Sociology of Religion*. Vol. 64, no. 2, pp. 145–61.

Macko, Stephan A. & Michael H. Engel, 1991 (September 30), "Assessment of Indigeneity in Fossil Organic Matter: Amino Acids and Stable Isotopes". *Philosophical Transactions: Biological Sciences*. Vol. 333, no. 1268 (Special edition *Molecules Through Time: Fossil Molecules and Biochemical Systematics*), pp. 367–74.

McCaskie, T. C., 1972 (January), "Innovational Eclecticism: The Asante Empire and Europe in the Nineteenth Century". *Comparative Studies in Society and History*. Vol. 14, no. 1, pp. 30–45.

March, Chrystelle, 2004, "La Réutilisation des Éléments d'Architecture du Temple Haut du Sanctuaire de Zeus à Gerasa à la Période Byzantine". *Syria*. T. 81, pp. 147–75.

Meduri, Avanthi, 2008, "The Transfiguration of Indian/Asian Dance in the United Kingdom: Contemporary *Bharatanatyam* in Global Contexts". *Asian Theatre Journal*. Vol. 25, no. 2, pp. 298–328.

Meeks, C. L., 1950 (September), "Picturesque Eclecticism". *The Art Bulletin*. Vol. 32, no. 3, pp. 226–35.

———, 1953 (December), "Creative Eclecticism". *Journal of the Society of Architectural Historians*. Vol. 12, no. 4, pp. 15–18.

Merlan, Francesca, 2009, "Indigeneity: Global and Local". *Current Anthropology*. Vol. 50, no. 3, pp. 303–33.

Middleton, Jason & Roger Beebe, 2002 (May), "The Racial Politics of Hybridity and 'Neo-Eclecticism' in Contemporary Popular Music". *Popular Music*. Vol. 21, no. 2, pp. 159–72.

Munasinghe, Viranjini, 2002 (August), "Nationalism in Hybrid Spaces: The Production of Impurity out of Purity". *American Ethnologist*. Vol. 29, no. 3, pp. 663–92.

———, 2006, "Claims to Purity in Theory and Culture: Pitfalls and Promises". *American Ethnologist*. Vol. 33, no. 4, pp. 588–92.

O'Connor, Alan, 2002 (March), "Local Scenes and Dangerous Crossroads: Punk and Theories of Cultural Hybridity". *Popular Music*. Vol. 21, no. 2, pp. 225–36.

Park, Chong-Min & Doh Chull Shin, 2006 (May–June), "Do Asian Values Deter Popular Support for Democracy in South Korea?". *Asian Survey*. Vol. 46, no. 3, pp. 341–61.

Patel, Alka, 2009a, "The Historiography of Reuse in South Asia". *Archives of Asian Art*. Vol. 59, pp. 1–5.

———, 2009b, "Expanding the Ghurid Architectural Corpus East of the Indus: The Jageshvara Temple at Sadadi, Rajasthan". *Archives of Asian Art*. Vol. 59, pp. 33–56.

Ritzer, George, 2003 (September), "Rethinking Globalization: Glocalization/Grobalization and Something/Nothing". *Sociological Theory*. Vol. 21, no. 3, pp. 193–209.

Robertson, Roland, 1995, "Glocalization: Time–Space and Homogeneity–Heterogeneity". In: Mike Featherstone, Scott M. Lash & Roland Robertson (eds), *Global Modernities*. SAGE Publications, London, pp. 25–68.

Rushdie, Salman, 1990, *In Good Faith*. Granta, London.

Sears, Tamara I., 2009, "Fortified *Matha*s and Fortress Mosques: The Transformation and Reuse of Hindu Monastic Sites in the Thirteenth and Fourteenth Centuries". *Archives of Asian Art*. Vol. 59, pp. 7–31.

de Sola-Morales, Ignasi, 1987, "The Origins of Modern Eclecticism: The Theories of Architecture in Early Nineteenth Century France". *Perspecta*. Vol. 23, pp. 120–33.

Stewart, Charles, 1999 (Autumn), "Syncretism and Its Synonyms: Reflections on Cultural Mixture". *Diacritics*. Vol. 29, no. 3, pp. 40–62.

Stross, Brian, 1999 (Summer), "The Hybrid Metaphor: From Biology to Culture". *The Journal of American Folklore*. Vol. 112, no. 445 (Special edition *Theorizing the Hybrid*), pp. 254–67.

Tartakov, Gary Michael & Vidya Dehejia, 1984, "Sharing, Intrusion, and Influence: The Mahisasuramardini Imagery of the Calukyas and the Pallavas". *Artibus Asiae*. Vol. 45, no. 4, pp. 287–345.

Theunissen, Robert, Peter Grave & Graham Bailey, 2000 (June), "Doubts on Diffusion: Challenging the Assumed Indian Origin of Iron Age Agate and Carnelian Beads in Southeast Asia". *World Archaeology*. Vol. 32, no. 1 (Special edition *Archaeology in Southeast Asia*), pp. 84–105.

Tomlinson, John, 2006 (November), "Mixed Metaphors: Commentary". *American Ethnologist*. Vol. 33, no. 4, pp. 571–72.

Trainor, Kevin M., 1992 (June), "When Is a Theft Not a Theft? Relic Theft and the Cult of the Buddha's Relics in Sri Lanka". *Numen*. Vol. 39, fasc. 1, pp. 1–26.

Wagoner, Phillip B., 1996, "'Sultan among Hindu Kings': Dress, Titles, and the Islamicization of Hindu Culture at Vijayanagara". *The Journal of Asian Studies*. Vol. 55, no. 4, pp. 851–80.

Wallace, Saro, 2003, "The Perpetuated Past: Re-use or Continuity in Material Culture and the Structuring of Identity in Early Iron Age Crete". *The Annual of the British School at Athens*. Vol. 98, pp. 251–77.

Watson, J. K. P., 1980 (June), "Education and Cultural Pluralism in South East Asia, with Special Reference to Peninsular Malaysia". *Comparative Education*. Vol. 16, no. 2, pp. 139–58.

*Webster's Third New International Dictionary of the English Language* (unabridged). 1993 [1961], Philip Babcock Gove (editor-in-chief), Könemann, Cologne.

Werbner, Pnina, 2001 (March), "The Limits of Cultural Hybridity: On Ritual Monsters, Poetic License and Contested Postcolonial Purifications". *The Journal of the Royal Anthropological Institute*. Vol. 7, no. 1, pp. 133–52.

Whaley, W. Gordon, 1950 (January), "The Gift of Hybridity". *The Scientific Monthly*. Vol. 70, no. 1, pp. 10–18.

Winslow, Deborah, 2003 (February), "Potters' Progress: Hybridity and Accumulative Change in Rural Sri Lanka". *The Journal of Asian Studies*. Vol. 62, no. 1, pp. 43–70.

Zehner, Edwin, 2005 (Summer), "Orthodox Hybridities: Anti-Syncretism and Localization in the Evangelical Christianity of Thailand". *Anthropological Quarterly*. Vol. 78, no. 3, pp. 585–617.

## Internet Sources

The Pluralism Project at Harvard University: Available at http://pluralism.org/ (accessed on 19 June 2010).

Everything2, Cultural Osmosis: Available at http://everything2.com/title/cultural+osmosis (accessed on 19 June 2010).

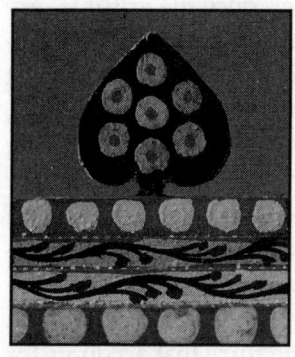

## Chapter 3

# THE PAST IN THE PRESENT

## TEMPLE CONVERSIONS IN KARNATAKA AND APPROPRIATION AND RE-USE IN ORISSA

### BY JULIA A. B. HEGEWALD AND SUBRATA K. MITRA

### INTRODUCTION

Centres of pilgrimage in india are often replete with rituals, temples and customary practices which have a certain 'family resemblance'.[1] Some might display features of 'invented traditions',[2] while others might appear to be largely local

---

[1] Empirical research involving measurement of phenomena routinely assumes that "categories are logical bounded entities, membership in which is defined by an item's possession of a simple set of criteria features, in which all instances possessing the criteria attributes have a full and equal degree of membership" (Rosch & Mervis 1975: 573–74). Though widely apart in terms of geography, language, culture and time, we suggest that temple conversion and appropriation of subaltern icons share a 'family resemblance' and as such, belong to the phenomenon of re-use.

[2] The term 'invented tradition' is used in a broad, but not imprecise sense. It includes both 'traditions' actually invented, constructed and formally instituted and those emerging in a less easily traceable manner within a brief and dateable period—a matter of a few years perhaps—and establishing themselves with great rapidity (Hobsbawm 1996: 1).

in character. Often, experts and lay devotees alike might think of them as unique and specific to the area where they are located. However, once the artful fakery intended to give the object an appearance of timelessness is scraped off, some distinguishing features of these structures that connect their past with their present form reveal themselves. One finds in them a conflation of elements from the past, added to the contingencies of the present, in a manner that coheres well, giving them the appearance of a unified structure with a central logic. A shared myth on the part of the community that underpins them, a secondary set of social and political institutions that constitute a protective ring around them and a hierarchy of functionaries and rituals that constitute their administrative core complete the constellation of these bodies. Strategic re-use of the past to make the present more potent, relevant, rooted and legitimate is the driving force that accounts for the emergence, resilience and generality of these hybrid structures. Despite their diversity and putative idiosyncrasy, the political and cultural dynamic that goes into the making of these customs, rituals, cults and beliefs has a general pattern to it.

The chapter draws material from two different regions and illustrates two major forms of re-use. Based on the comparative accounts of Jaina temples from Karnataka in South India, which have been converted by the Vira-Shaiva community[3] and the cult of Jagannatha in Orissa, East India, the chapter examines the processes of the re-use of sacred sites and venerated objects and the use of such hybrid entities, which give an enduring character to India's regional traditions. The first section analyses the physical takeover of temple buildings and sacred statues, which, treated as hollow shells by their new owners, have been filled with new meanings. The second section illustrates the re-use of tribal gods by Oriya kings, and the survival of this distinct and composite cult under Muslim and colonial rule through its appropriation and adoption for different political functions. On the basis of this comparative understanding of the regional narratives, the chapter seeks to show that such re-appropriations which cause anxiety can also create an opportunity for integration.

## TEMPLE CONVERSIONS IN KARNATAKA

The following three case studies from northern Karnataka—from the sites of Hallur, Adargunchi and Kagvad—will illustrate different levels of re-use

---

[3] The Vira-Shaivas are by many regarded as a Shaiva sect which was reformed by Basava, also known as Basavanna, in the twelfth century. Although some scholars, such as Prof. Jogan Shankar from the University of Bangalore (private conversation in February 2006) argue that there is a difference between Vira-Shaivism and Lingayatism, these have usually been treated as two terms to describe one faith. This is the line taken in this article.

of initially Jaina architectural structures and venerated sculptures by the Vira-Shaiva community. They will demonstrate that acts of appropriation cause anxiety for those deprived of their holy places and revered objects, but that—in the long run—they can constitute a chance for integration—both major themes of this book.[4] The three examples are representative of distinct approaches to the appropriation of sacred space and holy imagery. Of particular concern in these three situations will be items which were re-used and which were not. Were the items destroyed, neglected or filled with new functions and values? Which intentions lay behind the physical changes undertaken by the new users, and how do these convey contrasting messages? The latter questions are of crucial importance for the mutual coexistence of different people and faiths within a diverse and multireligious society of the kind present in India.

## Re-using Sacred Architecture at Hallur

The first temple example comes from the village of Hallur in the Dharwar district of northern Karnataka. The Megudi Temple at Hallur was constructed as a place of Digambara Jaina worship between the seventh and the ninth centuries CE (see Plate 3.1).[5] It appears that during the twelfth century, it was converted for Vira-Shaiva ritual use.[6] The temple consists of a large closed hall, a small vestibule (*antarala*) and an image chamber (*garbha-griha*) surrounded by an internal circumambulation path (*pradakshina-patha*). Typical of Jaina temple constructions, it was conceived as a double-storeyed edifice with shrines on two superimposed floor levels. This allowed the temple to house a number of sacred statues and objects for veneration.[7]

---

[4] The authors do not condone acts of aggression. They acknowledge that appropriations—due to the pragmatic fact that they save time and money for conquerors and can make strong religious and political statements—have widely happened in the past and continue to take place particularly during times of aggression and change. Although, initially, those who have been dispossessed will not be able to consider this as anything else than a deprivation and injustice, history has shown that such appropriations have in many cases led to hybridisations and in the long-term to the integration of cultures and religions.

[5] Due to its close resemblance to the Meguti Temple at Aihole (CE 634), the Hallur Jaina temple has been dated by some scholars to the second half of the seventh century (Srinivasan 1974: 197). According to Mankodi (1975: 205, 211–13) and the records of the American Institute of Indian Studies at Gurgaon, the structure has been assigned to the late eighth century (AIIS Neg. no. A 21.36 and A 21.38). However, Meister and Dhaky (1986: 146–47) and Suresh (2003: 109) argue for a construction date during the late ninth century, which seems very late.

[6] From the early twelfth century, the Vira-Shaiva community substantially gained in influence—particularly in the northern area of Karnataka—and appropriated many Jaina shrines.

[7] It is a typical characteristic of Jaina temple architecture throughout India to display complex spatial layouts which are typified by the presence of multiple and usually interconnected shrine rooms on the horizontal and on various superimposed vertical levels. For a detailed discussion of these issues, see Hegewald (2009, 2001).

For our examination of re-use, the sculptural programme associated with the Hallur temple is particularly interesting. A free-standing icon of a Jina,[8] which is likely to have once been installed on a pedestal in one of the two superimposed sanctums, has been positioned on the floor in the closed hall (see Plate 3.2). Its placing on the bare floor clearly signals its desecration by the new Vira-Shaiva re-users of the space. The Jina rests against one of the pillars in the central aisle, close to the entrance of the temple. In this position, in a well-lit section of the temple and on the main access route to the *grabha-griha*, it is passed and seen by anybody entering the temple. As such, it conveys a strong message of intrusion and desecration and would cause great anxiety for Jaina devotees who would have been used to venerating this as one of the most sacred objects of the temple before its conversion. Therefore, it was a stronger religious and political message to keep the image inside the temple than to remove it entirely.

The figure is that of a seated Jina, sheltered underneath a triple parasol, flanked by two attendants. Which of the twenty-four Jinas is represented cannot be ascertained at this stage as no symbol of recognition (*lanchana*) has been preserved. Following Shaiva practice, and reflecting the new dedication of the temple and its associated statues, sacred white ash has been applied to its surface. The treatment of this sculpture presents the starkest assertion by the new religious group. It is the most explicit violation of the deposed Jaina faith and makes the strongest statement about conversion and annexation of this temple.

Otherwise, the Jaina imagery inside the temple has been preserved intact. This includes a central seated Jina, located on the lintel leading into the sanctum (*lalata-bimba*) on the ground floor. Also unaltered are sculpted representations of the attendants of the Jina, his *yaksha* and *yakshi*. These have been carved on the external sides of the image chamber, in the sections leading into the internal ambulatory. The two depictions are in varying degrees of completion, indicating that the temple was unfinished at the time of its appropriation. Nowadays, the *garbha-griha* contains a *linga*, the phallic symbol of the god Shiva. A sculpted representation of the god's vehicle (*vahana*), the bull Nandi, has been positioned in the vestibule and is facing the abstract emblem of Shiva. This signals the conversion of the temple to the Lingayat religion.[9]

By contrast, the upper shrine of the temple has been emptied and is no longer in ritual use (see Plate 3.3). Orthodox Vira-Shaivism rejects temple worship, the offering of sacrifices and the practice of pilgrimage (Padoux 1987: 12). This is

---

[8] 'Jina' means 'conqueror' or 'spiritual victor'. It is a descriptive term used to refer to the twenty-four enlightened teachers of the Jaina religion. Other words habitually used to refer to the Jinas are *tirthankara*, *arhat* and *kevalin*.

[9] There is no agreement on whether Vira-Shaivism should be regarded as a sub-sect of Hinduism, as a distinct religious group, or as a caste. McCormack (1963: 59–71) and Michael (1983: 310) in particular have written about this question.

based on the view that the inner experience and development of the individual is more significant than external rites (Michael 1983: 310). According to Vira-Shaiva teachings, the human body is regarded as the true temple (Bowker 1999: 581).[10] As a consequence, Lingayat temples follow a very reduced temple ritual, making additional image chambers, which are so typical of Jaina temple structures, entirely superfluous.

The sculptures adorning the external walls of the Meguti Temple at Hallur have largely been preserved as well. These consist of a group of eight tall standing Jaina icons. These are raised on small pedestals and convey the impression of merging with the architecture in the form of figural pilasters. Following Digambara practice, the images are nude and unadorned. There are four representations of the twenty-third Jina Parshvanatha, easily recognised by the cobra hood above his head, and four of Gommateshvara—Rishabhanatha's enlightened son.[11] At the front of the temple are two depictions of the Jina Parshvanatha. Positioned on the long exterior sides of the hall—east and west—a central statue of this Jina is flanked by standing figures of the ascetic Gommateshvara. Whereas the six images on the long walls have remained unscathed, those flanking the entrance to the temple look as if they have been mutilated.[12] The statue to the west has been deprived of one of its arms and the one to the east has been defaced.[13] In these two sculptures, the expression of victory and the forcible appropriation of the site by Vira-Shaivas appears to have found further expression. As a consequence, a worshipper approaching the temple will instantly realise that this temple has been converted. However, this also signals not an uncontrolled destruction but strategic planning in the damaging of certain key icons. The figures carved out of the stone of the temple wall have not been removed or destroyed to such an extent that they cannot be recognised as Jaina images any longer. Besides, no attempt has been made by the new occupiers of the temple to convert or appropriate the statues to reflect representations more fitting for their specific mythology or religious system.[14]

---

[10] The religious reformer Basava taught that no temples are necessary in order to worship god, and that no one needs to renounce worldly life in order to be a religious person (Leslie 1998: 242).

[11] Gommateshvara is alternatively known as Gommata or Bahubali.

[12] This has also been highlighted by Meister and Dhaky (1986: 147) and by Suresh (2003: 110).

[13] The defacing of a ritual statue is a poignant gesture. It is known from Islamic instances of the desecration of sculptures as well. Targeted were usually the faces or heads (decapitation) and the breasts of female representations. The removing of an arm, as can be seen in the second figure, is less common.

[14] With respect to Vira-Shaivism, in which the *linga*—the phallic symbol of the god Shiva—forms the single focus of veneration, this would admittedly have been difficult, but the next two case studies illustrate that this too was done in a Lingayat context. Also in connection with other religious groups, such reinterpretations of sculptures are well known and can regularly be observed at converted sites. Particularly frequent throughout India is the re-interpretation of former images of the Jina Parshvanatha as representations of the Hindu god Vishnu-Narayana, which is favoured by the shared association of both characters with a hooded snake (see Plate 2.3).

One has to assume that the Vira-Shaivas appropriating the temple used two methods to degrade the until-then-powerful local Jaina elite. The approach applied to the main sacred image and the statues flanking the door was to actively desecrate and mutilate them. The second approach, which is more subtle but no less powerful, was to retain the original Jaina identity of the temple, to remind the deposed community that once this was their sacred site but that it has been annexed. There is no attempt here to cover up the act of appropriation.[15] On the contrary, the fact that the Jaina identity of the temple has purposely been preserved with the sculptures of the Jinas displayed like trophies on the outside of the temple conveys a very powerful message. The main area of the temple was re-used and filled with new meaning by providing the space for a limited Lingayat ritual, but no alternative function was attributed to the upper chamber. This shows that re-use is always a selective act in which people choose to retain certain elements and to reject others in order to create something distinct.

The discrete approach in this re-used temple structure might be explained by the fact that Vira-Shaivism, in its radically reformed structure, represented a new movement, which took this specific form only in the mid-twelfth century, shortly before the likely conversion of this specific temple. The new religion swept over the south of India because of its immediate appeal to the population. This seems largely to have been based on its propagation of social reforms, such as the rejection of caste differentiation.[16] To use ancient temple constructions and their annexation to argue for continuity or legitimacy at a certain site was therefore not an option. On the contrary, the aim was to demonstrate the strength and vigour of this modern movement, and to document its rapid expansion and proliferation throughout large parts of the Deccan and surrounding areas. In this respect, the preservation of Jaina imagery on recently absorbed temple structures was employed as a sign of victory, as a reminder that the Lingayats had been triumphant and that they had terminated the long dominance of the Jaina elite in the region. Moreover, although Lingayats erected representations of Shiva's bull Nandi and generally depict certain minor divinities, the *linga* is their sole object of worship.[17] Therefore, the re-appropriation or reinterpretation of annexed sculptures was—at least in the beginning and for orthodox Lingayats—not really a valid option.

---

[15] See the analysis of the conversion of a former Hindu temple at Khajuraho through the Jaina community for an example where the aim was to entirely conceal the act of annexation (Hegewald 2006a, 2006b; Hegewald & Mitra 2008: 15–22).

[16] Early Jainism too acted as a reform movement which acted against the injustices of caste hierarchy and challenged the established Hindu social system. In practice, however, caste differentiation survived in Jainism through the creation of distinct Jaina castes and the continued membership of certain castes of traders in particular.

[17] The *Vacana-shastra-sara* and the *Ganabhashya-ratna-male* condemn the veneration of Shiva in any other form than that of the abstract *linga* (Nandimath 1979: 34, 147–48).

However, it is also important to consider the available choices and the cost–benefit calculations made by the re-users. Whilst the Lingayat faith does not provide an immediate incentive to construct temples, the new converts were traditionally used to temple worship and to sacred structures as centres for the expression of their beliefs. The reformed movement, however, had no particularly sacred sites of their own yet and did not encourage the development of such pilgrimage centres. Viewed in this light, the conversion of existing structures acquires a further dimension of expression.[18]

## The Re-use of a Religious Icon at Adargunchi

The second site, which will be discussed in less detail as it reflects many of the issues raised in connection with the temple at Hallur, adds a new aspect to our investigation into the re-use of sacred places in northern Karnataka. This revolves around the question of the re-use and reidentification of sacred images.[19] The temple under discussion is these days known as the Doddappa Temple in Adargunchi village in the Dharwar district of Karnataka.[20] According to local accounts, Basava himself, during his time as treasurer of the then assassinated King Bijjala, took refuge in Adargunchi and villages in the surrounding area after the murder (Parthasarathy 2002: 59). Up to the present day, the area remains a stronghold of the Lingayats.

The Doddappa Temple is faced by a small platform with foot imprints (*padukas*) and is raised on a terrace, reached via a broad set of steps at the front (see Plate 3.4). The temple has a wide porch (*ardha-mandapa*) connected to a pillared hall. This larger *mandapa* is open towards the porch, but has closed sides.[21] Through a doorway with beautifully adorned carved sides and lintels, one reaches an *antarala* and consequently the shrine. Today, the *garbha-griha* has been clad with modern white glazed tiles. Those behind the icon are decorated to create a frame around it and other individual tiles depict Hindu gods and

---

[18] Research conducted in winter 2009 by Dr Tiziana Lorenzetti as member of the interdisciplinary Emmy Noether Project on Jainism in Karnataka, now based at the University of Bonn, has shown that during the past twenty to thirty years, Vira-Shaivas have started constructing temple structures of their own. This material will be published in the forthcoming team publication by Hegewald, provisionally entitled *Distinction and Dialogue: Jaina Art, History and Culture in Karnataka*.

[19] In the previous situation, the statues had been re-used in so far that they had either been kept inside the temple but desecrated or they had been preserved on the outside but been mutilated in parts. In the second instance, the issue of the renaming, re-dedication and re-consecration of statues will be broached.

[20] In the limited available literature, Adargunchi can alternatively be spelled Adagunchi.

[21] This style of a semi-enclosed hall is typical of south India. For a discussion of this form of half-enclosed hall, see Hegewald (2009: 502).

goddesses. The sanctum has a side entrance to the right. The image chamber houses a massive stone statue of a Jina, measuring about three metres in height. In the corner opposite the side entrance is a Shiva *linga* raised on a high *yoni* pedestal (see Plate 3.5). Outside the side entrance is a small stone Nandi facing the *linga*. Although the Jina and the door frame are ancient vestiges, probably dating from around the tenth or eleventh centuries, the temple as a whole has been rebuilt extensively and represents a replacement structure from a relatively recent date. As substantial sections of the temple have been plastered, tiled and covered with thick layers of paint, a more detailed examination of the structure would be necessary to provide further details.

The account in the Dharwar district gazetteer—of which the first English translation was produced in 1995 (Parthasarathy 2002)—offers a confusing picture with regards to the temple. However, this exemplifies the situation surrounding many re-used temples where the past and the present as well as religious denominations and associations get easily tangled. The short paragraph in the gazetteer describes the temple as follows:

> The Doddappa temple, a Jaina Basadi at the entrance of the village, is venerated by people of all castes. This entirely modern temple consists of a garbhagriha, an *antarala*, and a[n] *ardhamandapa*. It houses an approximately eight ft. tall image of a Tirthankara seated *in padmasana* posture. The lion-seat, upon which the Tirthankara's image is placed, has an unpolished inscription of four lines containing details of its installation.[22] The attractive carvings upon the door-frame of the *antarala* of this temple hold our attention. (Parthasarathy 2002: 784)

The presence of the colossal stone statue of the seated Tirthankara clearly indicates the original denomination of the temple as Jaina. This is an issue which also the Jaina community in the area is still very aware of.[23] However, when the author visited the village in 2007, the temple was firmly in Vira-Shaiva hands. It is possible that the phrase above, describing it as a temple which "is venerated by people of all castes", is an indirect way to refer to its Lingayat denomination as a religion which welcomed people of all castes. The description in the gazetteer identifies the temple as a modern construction. On this basis, we may infer that the temple was either destroyed during the Vira-Shaiva takeover, was already damaged or was replaced to beautify the temple or to increase its Lingayat connotations after the annexation.[24] In

[22] Unfortunately, no transcript of the inscription was available to the authors.
[23] Sabine Scholz, research assistant to Julia A. B. Hegewald in the Emmy Noether research group on Jainism in Karnataka, was taken to the temple by representatives of the local Jaina community in 2005.
[24] It is a relatively common occurrence throughout South Asia for religious communities to tear down their own temples in order to replace them with new constructions. Contrasting with our Western romanticisation of the past, in Asia, these can be regarded as cleaner and better by some.

this instance, it seems that despite the fact that both temple and image were initially taken control of, the primary object of re-use was the statue of the Jina.

At Adargunchi, the icon was not taken down from its pedestal and desecrated, as at Hallur—which due to its enormous size and its associated weight would admittedly have been very difficult. An option would have been to destroy it, as has been done in other places. However, in this case, it was appropriated for Vira-Shaiva ritual use. The depiction of the seated Jina, again without *lanchana*, cannot be identified.[25] It is a striking sculpture, due to its disproportional size (about three metres in height) and its black polished stone, which is not common for statues in the region. Owing to these unusual features, it would have been well known and would have represented an important revered item in the sacred geography of temples and pilgrimage sites of the Jainas in the area. To appropriate such a rare sacred figure was therefore a powerful act, demonstrating the new strength of the reformed Shaivas. This might have been the reason why the Vira-Shaivas decided at Adargunchi to appropriate the image and to convert it into an object of their own veneration.

As at Hallur—where, however, the desecrated statue is not venerated—its religious transformation has been indicated by painting prominent parallel white lines onto the forehead, the lower and the upper arms, the shoulders, the chest, the belly, the legs and the inherent stone pedestal of the sculpture (see Plate 3.5). Here, they have been applied in permanent paint. The sacred symbols serve as the conclusive evidence of the appropriation and re-use of the icon of the vanquished faith. Additionally, it is regularly draped with fresh flower garlands, which is a tradition in Hindu temples, but is not practised in connection with Digambara statues of the fully enlightened Jinas.[26] Although according to an orthodox interpretation of Vira-Shaiva doctrine, a re-used Jaina depiction can only have had very little religious significance, it would have been cultivated as a sign of domination and control. However, it is fascinating to observe that even though Vira-Shaiva doctrine recommends the sole veneration of the *linga*, this image illustrates that there are ways in which existing statutes of other religions too could be absorbed. At Adargunchi, the Jina icon has been re-named and is referred to as 'Doddappa', meaning paternal uncle in the local Kannada

---

[25] The statue might have been a depiction of the twenty-fourth Jina, Mahavira (http://www.jaintirths.com/karnataka/dharwar.htm).

[26] Digambara images of the Jinas are undressed and undecorated, reflecting the Digambara conviction that the Jinas lived the tenet of non-possession to the final consequence by rejecting all clothing. In this area they contrast with the Shvetambaras, whose monks wear simple white garments and whose statues are dressed and frequently adorned. By decorating or clothing a Digambara statue, these become unfit for Digambara veneration, which equals their desecration. For further information, see Hegewald (2009: 72–74).

language.[27] Locally, no information was available about the specific meaning of Doddappa, who does not appear to have a specific significance in a Vira-Shaiva context.[28]

In addition to the figural representation, the venerated foot imprints raised on a small platform at the front of the temple have also been converted into sacred Vira-Shaiva footprints. In order to state this clearly, they have been marked with the same white lines as the Jina, as well as with red dots to mark the toes and the ball of the foot (see Plate 3.6).[29] However, in order to further reaffirm the new Vira-Shaiva message, a *linga* too has been enshrined in the image chamber, next to the former Jaina statue. This reconfirms the present religious denomination of the temple and caters to more orthodox tastes.

It is fascinating that by entering the temple from the side, whose entrance is faced by a Nandi representation, the devotee enters a much more straightforward Vira-Shaiva temple where the large Tirthankara is merely passed on the side. This approach to the temple offers a much more conventional vision of the religion in which *linga*s are venerated—if not as sole then at least as focal objects of devotion. This second entrance to the temple expresses a less confrontational approach towards the Jainas. It seems that the *linga*, the side entrance and the Nandi were added later in the development of the temple, at a time when the Vira-Shaivas were more established in the region, were less antagonistic and had started to integrate.

## Syncretic Use of Space at Kagvad

The third example combines the two approaches examined so far: the re-use of a temple structure and the re-use of captured statues. Whereas at Hallur and

---

[27] See, for instance, the study on "Modes of Address in Kannada: A Sociolinguistic Study of Language Use in Mysore District" by L. Manjulakshmi. Available at http://www.languageinindia.com/sep2004/manjulakshitermsofaddress1.html. This form of 'appropriation through elevation' is comparable to the transformation of a tribal icon to a high Hindu god in the Orissan case of Jagannatha. This process of elevation can be seen in the sacred nomenclature—Jagannatha (Lord of the Universe), Patitapabana (Deliverer of the Fallen) and Chakadola (the All-Seeing-Eye)—used for the purpose.

[28] It is interesting that there is a further Doddappa Temple at Hemavati in the Anantapur district of Andhra Pradesh, which is dedicated to Shiva and where Doddappa is treated as an epithet of Shiva. It is striking that a ninth-century inscription on a pillar in the temple complex, records a grant of land made to a Jaina temple (*basadi*), possibly indicating a takeover and rededication similar to the one at Adargunchi (http://www.whatisindia.com/inscriptions/south_indian_inscriptions/volume_9/nolamba_pallavas.html).

[29] In the subcontinent, foot imprints play a significant role in a Jaina, a Buddhist and a Vaishnava temple environment. They generally are less common in a Shaiva or a Vira-Shaiva context, although Basava's wooden slippers are venerated at many sites. See, for instance, the example from Kagvad discussed later in this chapter.

Adargunchi, there was an unmistakable termination of Jaina veneration and a re-use of the architecture and the images by the Vira-Shaivas only, the final instance from Karnataka illustrates that there are also cases where although temple and icons have been taken over, Vira-Shaivas and Jainas today perform their rituals alongside one another in separate areas of one and the same temple structure.

The third temple, again originally a Jaina structure, is located at Kagvad in the Belgaum district of Karnataka. Due to what appears to have been a series of conquests and annexations, resulting in continuous alterations and restoration campaigns, it is difficult to date the structure precisely. According to local tradition, the temple was targeted during the period of Muslim invasions. In order to protect the sacred and precious sculptures of the temple, two large stone statues of the Tirthankaras were removed—probably from the main image chamber on the ground floor—and relocated to chambers dug into the earth deep below the temple. These are reached by narrow passageways, access to which was initially carefully hidden. Even nowadays, there is no prominent doorway marking the access to these subterranean chambers and the stairs have not been widened (see Plate 3.7).[30] No information was available at the site with regards to the question whether the lower floor levels existed prior to the threat of invasions in the region or whether they were only excavated at this point. It is common for Jaina temples throughout the subcontinent to have chambers below the main level of access and in many circumstances these have been used to hide precious icons during unstable political times and to protect them from desecration and theft.[31] It is unusual that the temple at Kagvad has two accessible underground floors with Jaina depictions installed and venerated on both of them.[32] On the floor positioned one storey below is a shrine housing an image of Parshvanatha (see Plate 3.8) and one further level down reveals a chamber dedicated to the Jina Shantinatha.

It appears that during the time of Islamic invasions in the area, intruders targeted the temple, possibly looted some of its most precious images and caused the Jainas themselves to remove the two largest and most important statues of the Jinas to secure subterranean locations below the temple. The Muslims do not

---

[30] At Adargunchi, the underground image chambers are relatively difficult to reach. Access is provided through small openings and along narrow passageways, which are not high enough to allow a person to walk upright. Nevertheless, as was documented during fieldwork in February 2007, the sacred icons are actively venerated on a daily basis.

[31] The monograph by Hegewald (2009) analyses a large number of temples where statues were hidden underground. In many instances, they remain enshrined in their subterranean places up to the present day. There are also documented examples, where the sculpture on the ground floor was not properly installed according to ritual conventions but used to divert attention from the sacred representations kept below the ground (Jain 1963: 128).

[32] Even though subterranean chambers to provide cool accommodation for travelling ascetic teachers in the summer heat are often found on several levels below the ground, image chambers are in most temples found only on one underground floor level.

seem to have used the sacred space of the temple for their own prayers, though there are examples in the region where this was the case.[33] At least according to local lore, the vacated ground floor level was taken over by the Lingayats, who profited from the chaos and destruction left behind by the invasions.

The Lingayats re-used the architectural space and at the same time annexed the remaining small Jaina statues, which are now lined up on a stepped pedestal in the central space of the Vira-Shaiva temple.[34] The majority of these are bronzes, representing attendants of the Jinas, so-called *yaksha*s and *yakshi*s. The Yaksha Brahmadeva amongst these rides a horse and there are further sculptures of bronze horses and elephants.[35] A small stone representation of a four-faced Jina (*caturmukha*) has been prominently placed in their middle. The main objects of veneration in the present Lingayat shrine are two converted stone Jaina *kshetrapala*s, guardians of the sacred temple complex (see Plate 3.9). The black stone images have been dabbed with sandalwood paste, adorned with *tilaka* markings, been crowned, surrounded by metal frames and adorned with spiky reflecting metal plates, which dramatically mirror the light of the surrounding candles. The three-pronged spikes are clear allusions to Shiva's trident (*trishula*) and—despite the fact that there is a Jina represented behind one of the *kshetrapala*s—leave no doubt about the new dedication of the statues. These have been re-interpreted as figural depictions of the god Shiva. Flower offerings and bronze miniature representations of Basava's wooden slippers, which are widely venerated by Vira-Shaivas, further support the altered meaning of the sculptures.

This is the situation at Kagvad in the early twenty-first century.[36] The ground floor is a Vira-Shaiva temple and the statues worshipped inside are the former Jaina icons. On two superimposed levels below the ground, the new Lingayat users allowed the continuous veneration of the main sacred Jaina images.[37] It is

---

[33] The large open pillared hall of the Aratranbat Gudi Hindu temple at Bankapur near Hangal in Karnataka was used as an Islamic prayer hall by the new Muslim community. In Andhra Pradesh, in the so-called Deval Masjid or Pattar Masjid, in the fort of Bodhan, a Muslim prayer hall was accommodated inside a former Jaina temple. The Jaina origin is still apparent from its name and from a series of Jina figures on the pillars of the hall. For further details, see Desai (1957: 102), Jawaharlal (2002: figs. 33, 34) and Hegewald (2007).

[34] An illustration has been published in Hegewald and Mitra (2008: Plate 11).

[35] For a detailed discussion of the importance of Brahmadeva for Jainas in Karnataka, see Hegewald (2011).

[36] Members of the Emmy Noether Research Group (DFG) on Jainism in Karnataka under the guidance of Julia A. B. Hegewald carried out fieldwork at the site in 2005 and 2007.

[37] As appropriations are such sensitive issues, it was impossible to gain any further details on the exact sequence of events. In order to allow for a peaceful coexistence of Jainas and Vira-Shaivas at the site, it is the Muslims who are these days exclusively blamed for the destruction at the site, and the two indigenous religious groups unite against a shared concept of an 'enemy'. Despite this, it is noteworthy how much Jaina temple architecture in India absorbed Islamic decorative features and planning ideas (see Plate 2.4). For further details, see Hegewald (2007).

unclear when the dual use of the temple commenced, but today the two groups worship harmoniously alongside one another. At Kagvad, a complex multi-layered structure constitutes a multireligious temple building. To use the term syncretic might go too far to describe worship at the site, as it is not the same statues in one and the same sanctum, which are venerated by different groups. However, the structure as a whole represents a building, which in syncretic fashion accommodates worship and ritual by two different—and in the past not always amicable—religious groups.

## THE CULT OF JAGANNATHA (ORISSA)

Jagannatha is a Hindu deity of tribal origin. The cult of Jagannatha—a cluster of rituals, practices and institutions, centred around the belief in the divinity of Jagannatha (literally, the Lord of the Universe)—is the second regional study that underpins this chapter. The conflation of tribal customs and high Hindu beliefs that one finds in this cult illustrates the process of re-use, which has come about through an effective, though surreptitious, interpenetration of sacred beliefs, social practices and the political process over the course of the past centuries in the regional context of Orissa. Orissa is unusual compared to the north, west and central parts of India with regard to inter-community conflicts whose relative absence in this region is explained by specialists and lay devotees in terms of the integrative ability of the shared belief in Jagannatha Mahaprabhu.[38]

The cult of Jagannatha is acclaimed as the key reference point in the sacred geography of Orissa.[39] It draws on a network of temples and local religious practices, of which the temple of Jagannatha in Puri is the epicentre (see Plate 3.10). However, the cult is by no means exclusive to this temple town but is spread throughout Orissa and other holy places in India in the form of replica temples.[40] In the analysis that follows, we account for the origin and evolution

---

[38] Mahaprabhu—the chief of gods—is another variation on the theme of the Lord of the Universe. The relative absence of anti-Muslim riots in Orissa in sharp contrast to northern, western and central India is significant. However, in view of the spate of recent anti-Christian violence in Orissa that has taken place in the western hill districts; this calls for further comparative analysis.

[39] The concept refers to the linkage between space and belief. For a depiction of the concepts of modern maps and religious maps, see Gole (1989). A religious map of Puri, the site of the Jagannatha Temple, is depicted under the concept of *sankhakshetra*, which describes the town in the shape of a conch shell. See Mitra (1997: 100).

[40] Architectural evidence for the linkages between the Jagannatha Temple at Puri and the Oriya temple architecture as a part of the evolution of a regional style between the ninth and the thirteenth centuries, see Donaldson (1987).

of the cult and its linkage with popular consciousness in the region in four parts. The first refers to the origin of the cult, based on myth, memory and history. The second focuses on the iconography of Jagannatha, and draws on the body, symbols and rituals associated with the god. The third part analyses the role of political power in the process of re-use, drawing on institutions, taxation and the search for legitimacy on the part of the rulers of Orissa, stretching from the original Hindu founders of the temple of Jagannatha all the way to the post-Independence State of Orissa. Finally, in the fourth section, we analyse the links between the society and re-use based on custom, gender, class and religion. The illustrations of popular consciousness are drawn from anecdotes and mythological narratives whereas the themes of structure and agency are drawn from post-Independence legislation and institutional arrangements.[41]

## Origin: The Myth, Memory and History

The simultaneous presence of high Hindu rituals, and priests and practices of tribal origin within the mode of worship of Lord Jagannatha is a salient feature of the cult. Several versions of the origin of this practice are available (Mishra 1984; Eschmann et al. 1986). One version suggests that the king of Puri, which is referred to as *Purusottamakshetra* or *Srikshetra*, wishing to extend his authority over the tribes of western Orissa,

> [...] deputed his Brahmin priest Vidyapati to negotiate with the king of the *Shavara* tribe. Vidyapati was not well received. He then agreed to marry the daughter of the Shavara king, Lalita, and, [...] was then shown the place where the Shavaras worshipped *Jagannatha*. After this, the king of Puri went to the forest, assured the Shavaras that their mode of worship would be preserved [...] and the Shavaras agreed to the wooden gods being carried to *Purusottama Kshetra*. From that time, the image of Purusottama is made out of the same wood as the Shavaras were worshipping. The Shavaras were called the *Daitya*. Accordingly, the offsprings of Vidyapati and Lalita were called *Daitya-pati* or Daitapati. These Daityapatis have the exclusive right to take care of the Lord when the latter falls sick just before the car festival [...] [in their customary fashion]. (Mishra 1984: 2)

The myth of origin, as it has come down over the generations, is also the basis of current practice—down to the minute details of ritual, the actual renewal

---

[41] The analysis below draws on some primary sources in Oriya (Panda 1979) and secondary sources by Oriya authors (Das & Mahaptra 1979; Mishra 1984; Panda & Panigrahi 1984) as well as the German–Indian team of Eschmann, Kulke and Tripathi (1986).

of the wooden deities from the same manner as of yore—and as such, give a customary basis to the original re-use of the tribal god by its Aryan appropriators. However, the myth of origin does not appear to have left the trail of bitterness and anxiety that we have seen in the memories of the Vira-Shaiva acquisition of the Jaina places of worship. Instead, the act of appropriation appears to have been conducive to the integration of the particular section of tribals with the Aryans.

## Iconography: Body, Symbol and Rituals

The cult of Jagannatha symbolises the regional tradition of 'tribal-Hindu continuum'. Commenting on this synthesis of the Hindu symbols of *sankha*, *chakra*, *gada* and *padma* with tribal totemic features, Eschmann et al. suggest:

> The archaic iconography of the cult images on the one hand and their highest Hindu iconology—on the other, as well as the existence of former tribals (*daitas*) and Vedic Brahmins amongst its priests, are by no means an antithesis, but a splendid regional synthesis, of the local and the all-Indian tradition. (Eschmann et al. 1986: XV) (see Plate 3.11)

The conflation and appropriation we find in the body of the god is reflected in the architectural style of the temple as well, for the temple permits other:

> [...] religious cults in India to come freely and offer prayer in their own manner. The *Vaisnavas* regard Jagannatha as *Vishnu*, the *Shaktas* offer their prayer in *Shakti Mandira*. They regard Jagannatha as *Bhairava* and Bimala as *Bhairabi*. This was in response to the great popular movement of *Tantrika Buddhism* of Western Orissa. Some of the greatest religious leaders who preached and propagated this form of *Vajrayana Tantrik Buddhism* were from the untouchable class and the hill tribes. But when this Vajrayana movement became popular, Jagannatha of Puri as the *Buddhabatara* became amenable to being worshipped as *Bhairava* of the *Tantra* cult, and as usual caste consideration did not stand in the way. The *Shaivas* and the *Ganapatiyas* etc. regard Jagannatha as their, own specific deity. The process of synthesis and cultural integration continues and enlarges throughout the ages in this great shrine of Puri. (Mishra 1984: 9)

## Re-use and Power: Institutions, Taxation and Legitimacy

The Jagannatha cult thus provides a good example of what Embree has described as *incorporation through encapsulation*—a method through which a niche is found for different faiths within an overall structure of harmonious social practices, recognised and protected by the custom of the land.[42] The distinction that Embree draws is between toleration, a Western liberal concept, and encapsulation, which is equivalent to communal accommodation achieved through a form of social 'trench warfare', the result of centuries of conflict between invading Muslims and India's regional and local traditions, and the consequent re-use through hybridisation.

The concept of *rashtradevata*, a key instrument of legitimation of power through the integration of sacred belief and secular power, is an important element of Orissa's regional state tradition.[43] The rituals surrounding a *rashtradevata* become a historical repository of the residues of successive empires, and a symbol of synthesis and continuity. The importance of Jagannatha as Orissa's *rashtradevata* and the instrumental role of the cult in the legitimation of royal authority in Orissa can be seen from the consecration of the Gajapati king of Puri as the Calanti Vishnu (the moving Vishnu), the institution of Pandas, and the religious economy of the Jagannatha Temple. Thus, the ensemble of priests and royal temple policy helped in the formation and consolidation of the mediaeval Hindu kingdoms of Orissa. Royal patronage of Hinduised tribal deities and the construction of huge temples legitimised royal power on the Hindu–tribal frontiers and encapsulated tribal communities within Hindu society.

> In Orissa, this development culminated in the construction of the present temple at Puri after 1135 A D. and the dedication of the whole Orissan empire to its deity Jaganath ('Lord of the Universe') in 1230 A.D., under whose overlordship (*samrajya*) and orders the Hindu Rajas of Orissa pretended to rule their *praja*. (Eschmann et al. 1986: xvi)

---

[42] At no point is Indian thought more alien to Western thought than in its assertion that there are many levels of truth, which gives to Indian civilization the characteristic that has been mistakenly understood as toleration. What follows from the assertion is not toleration; rather, all truths, all social practices, can be encapsulated within the society as long as there is willingness to accept the premise on which the encapsulation is based (Embree 1990: 30).

[43] Mishra (1984: XII) refers to the local belief that,

> [...] each *Rashtra* (kingdom) was protected by a deity that was considered to be its supreme authority. The deity was installed in the capital and members of the royal family used to worship him. If the deity had originally been installed by some aboriginal tribes, it was patronised by the kings who allowed these tribal people to continue their services in the temple in some form or other. The result is that, many deities in Orissa up to the present times continue to be worshipped by the tribal people although they have been accepted in the aryanised form as the presiding deities (*Rashtradevata*) of particular kingdoms long since. (Mishra 1984: XII)

The devotion to the cult, actively promoted by the Hindu rulers, became a method of gaining legitimacy from the population divided—vertically by class and caste—and horizontally by the Hindu–tribal divide.[44] The Pandas, the priestly order of Puri and the Gajapati king played complementary roles within the Jagannatha cult. The king, ruling as the first *sevak* (servant) of Jagannatha, could count on the loyalty of ordinary people, tribals and feudatory rulers.

The method of legitimation of power by according due respect to holy places and sacred symbols, and thus incorporating them within the structure of existing secular power perfected by the Gajapati kings appears to have survived the decline of the Hindu Gajapati kings during the successive centuries as Orissa was conquered successively by Muslim, Maratha and eventually, British rulers. This explains how the cult survived the Muslim invasion. Kulke explains this in terms of the:

> […] collusion between the Mughal Subahdar of Cuttack and the Gajapati, both of whom were driven respectively by the lucrative pilgrim tax and the determination to protect the dignity of the gods under trying circumstances. As a consequence, despite the conquest of Khurda, no disturbance of the Jagannatha cult is known nor do we hear anything about the flight of priests from Puri. (Kulke in Eschmann et al. 1986: 333–34)

Kulke suggests that this 'economic toleration' of Hindu holy places by the Muslim functionary (a not unusual practice by cash-hungry rulers):

> … must have been the reason why Aurangzeb, by a new decree in 1692 explicitly ordered the destruction of the Jagannatha temple. But Divyasimha Deva, the then Raja of Khurda met the Subahdar and agreed with him to arrange a pretended destruction under his own supervision. After what were probably some minor demolitions, a faked image of Jagannatha was sent to Aurangzeb and the main

---

[44] Kulke summarises the role of ritual in the legitimation of royal authority—examples of re-use of local and lower order symbols by higher level authorities that we have examined above—in early statecraft as follows:

> The acknowledgement of the dominant autochthonous deities as tutelary deities by the early Hinduised chiefs and Hindu rajas, above all, aimed at the consolidation of the newly established sub-regional power *within* the nuclear areas. The function of this early religious policy thus seems to have been mainly the *vertical* (internal) legitimation for the establishment of a hierarchically structured Hindu kingship in a more egalitarian tribal society. This function [....] bridged the gulf between the folk and the elite. Legitimation of royal power of the regional Hindu kingdoms, on the other hand, seems to have striven mainly for its horizontal recognition by equivalent rivals and potential rioters amongst the feudatories [....] fulfilled by the political architecture of the huge imperial temples with its egalitarian court-cult and its new centralised ritual structures. (Kulke in Eschmann et al. 1986: 136–37)

gate of the temple was closed. But the daily rituals of the cult were continued by some priests who entered the temple through a secret side door in the southern temple wall. Aurangzeb was again informed about this situation in Puri. He recalled the Subahdar and sent a high officer as an examiner to Puri. But according to an Oriya chronicle, the Raja of Khurda accomplished a masterstroke and managed to bribe even him—or as the chronicle paraphrased it 'he won him as a friend'—with a gift of 30,000 rupees. Till the death of Aurangzeb in 1707 A.D., the temple of Jagannatha was officially closed, but the cult continued to such an extent that several rajas visited the temple and performed their traditional royal rituals covertly. Only a few months after Aurangzeb's death in 1707 A.D., the doors of the temple were forcibly opened by a minister of Khurda and the chiefs of the eighteen Gadajata states, and the cult was renewed in its previous greatness. *It is obvious that all this could happen only with the toleration of the Muslim Subahdar in Cuttack.* (Kulke in Eschmann et al. 1986: 334, emphasis added)

According to Mishra (1984: 63), the British maintained the practice of economic toleration and political protection, very much for the same reason when they took power in Orissa in 1803. Lord Wellesley had issued instructions to Colonel Campbell, the Officer Commanding the British troops in Orissa, that on his arrival at Puri,

[...] he should take every possible precaution to preserve the respect due to the Pagoda and to the religious beliefs of the Brahmanas and the pilgrims. He should also assure the priests that they would not be required to pay any revenue or tribute to the British government which they had not been paying to the Mahrattas and they would be duly protected in the exercise of their religious views. (Mishra 1984: 63)

One has to admire the master stroke of British statecraft, for in one stroke, it achieved the double objective of colonial rule: how to honour local custom and make a quick penny in the process!

The British also codified the basic structure of an administrative system for the temple. When direct administration proved to be inconvenient, they resorted to indirect rule. Mishra (1984: 64) informs us that a *paricha* (keeper of records) was kept in charge of the management of the temple and, in 1805, the Collector was authorised to receive applications from the *paricha* in connection with the administration of the temple. This does not appear to have been popular with the Anglican Missionaries in London who bitterly criticised the government for taking an interest in the temple of Jagannatha. The government, therefore, decided to give up the direct supervision of the 'idolatrous rites' in the temple. By the Regulation IV of 1806 the superintendence was transferred to an assembly of three *pandits* nominated by the Collector of Pilgrims taxes and appointed by the government. The pilgrims tax, which was temporarily suspended in 1803, was revived in 1806 and a Collector of Pilgrims taxes was appointed by the government. For the purpose of levying the pilgrims tax, a classification of pilgrims into three categories was made. The temple contributed handsomely to the cash flow of the East India Company, the sum:

> [...] varying from half to one lakh rupees. When the Pilgrims tax, yielding a net amount of five thousand nine hundred and fifty five pounds to the East India Company was seen by missionaries as a State sanction of idolatry, the Company abolished the Pilgrims tax and vested the Raja of Puri with full authority in regard to the management of the temple and its properties by act X of 1840. (Mishra 1984: 65)

After Independence, a new act, the Puri Shri Jagannatha Temple (Administration) Act, 1952 (subsequently amended in 1954) was made "to provide for better Administration and Governance of Shri Jagannatha Temple at Puri and its Endowments" (Mitra 1997: 110). Its preamble described it as an Act to provide for the Administration of the Jagannatha Temple and its endowments by "the consolidation of the rights and duties of Sevaks, Pujaris and such other persons connected with Seva, Puja and management thereof". The Act and the Report on the Record of Rights compiled by the government show that "the temple is a public and not a private temple". The Raja of Puri, the former Raja of Khurda, in whom the superintendence was vested in 1840 "for the time being" acts as a trustee. "The Temple remained in the eyes of the law a public institution endowed by the state government with the Raja of Khurda as the Trustee with all the obligations and the Rights of a Trustee."[45]

By the general superintendence vested in it, the state government was in the same position as the Maharajas of Orissa before the advent of the Mughals, and it was similar to the situation during the Maratha period and the early years of the British rule in Orissa. The administrative structure of the temple indicates a complex blending of customary temple institutions and those set up by the modern state. The main institutions as prescribed by the Act are the Shri Jagannatha Temple Managing Committee, the office of the Administrator and the Shri Jagannatha Temple Fund.

Under the new administrative structure, the Raja of Puri has lost his former position as superintendent of the temple. Although he is the chairman of the Committee, he has no right to force the Committee to act in his interest. The other eleven members of the Committee are directly or indirectly controlled by the state government. The recent position of the Raja of Puri has, consequently, a more ritual character. The ritual importance of the Raja of Puri gains by his

---

[45] Presler (1987) has shown the evolution of another regional tradition using a similar model. The Record of Rights Report is an attempt to give a formal shape to the customary practices governing modes of worship and their material compensation through offerings of pilgrims and other incomes of the temple.

being the successor of the Gajapatis of Orissa. By this quality, he is the first (and the foremost) *sevaka* of Jagannatha, and accordingly he holds the highest rank in the hierarchy of the ritual organisation of the temple. He also receives the biggest share of the *bhoga* (sacred offerings) as remuneration for his service, in addition to his monthly salary as chairman of the Committee. The temple itself is regarded as a public institution. "The Administrator and every person authorised by him or the Committee while acting, under any of the provision of this Act, be deemed to be public servants, within the meaning of section 21 of the Indian Penal Code" (Hein 1986: 445).

The political control, which the government has over the temple is further reinforced through economic control. The convergence of the two sources of control is brought about by several Zamindari Abolition Acts after 1947. In lieu of the revenues drawn from this landed property, the temple is now receiving a fixed amount of payment, which makes the temple very much dependent on the government of Orissa, restoring in a way the situation which existed under the powerful kings of the former Orissa empire. An analysis of the budgetary position of receipts and expenditures of the Jagannatha temple shows a chronic deficit, made good by the government through annual grants.

## Transcending Hierarchy through Re-use:
## Caste, Gender and Religion

Within the cult of Jagannatha, sections of Hindu society formerly considered untouchable have traditionally been given a position of relative dignity compared to their status in other parts of India. The practice dates back to the arrival of Chaitanyadeva, the Vaishnava mystic in Puri in the fifteenth century. Mishra (1984: 3–4) provides the narrative of Dasia Bauri, an untouchable, whose piety has given him an enduring place in the devotional songs associated with Jagannatha. The custom grew at Puri around the same time that higher caste people should dine together with the untouchables if *mahaprasad*—offerings to Lord Jagannatha—is served. In this mode, Jagannatha appears as the Patitapabana the 'purifier and redeemer of the down-trodden'. Other evidence of the social integration of untouchables through mythological bonds based on the Jagannatha cult include the ritual of *chherapanhara*—where the king of Puri sweeps the ground in front of the chariots at the time of the car festival. Yet another instance is the Oriya poet Sarala Das, a *shudra*, who rendered the *Mahabharata* into Oriya. The first Oriya writer to undertake this task, Sarala Das, was accorded the title 'Shudramuni'.

Yet another form of re-use is the accommodation of the subaltern status of women within the patriarchy, but in a form that is imbued with dignity. Mishra

(1984) suggests that the Jagannatha cult has helped moderate the extremes of gender domination in Oriya society through the myth of goddess Laxmi's visit to an untouchable woman. In this episode, Goddess Laxmi, who was moved by the devotion of an untouchable woman, went into her house, "made herself visible [...] to the devoted woman and granted all prosperity to her" but, as a consequence, was:

> [...] denied admission to the temple by Lord *Jagannatha* at the instance of Lord Balaram (the elder brother of *Jagannatha*). But Goddess Laxmi refused to submit [...] When she [Laxmi] lived away from her husband and his brother, both the brothers suffered a great deal of miseries. (Mishra 1984: 5)

And Laxmi was invited back to the temple, her prestige enhanced. Having stood her ground, Laxmi established the double principle—of the dignity of women, whether goddess or untouchable—and of deliverance through devotion. Both principles, opposed to the inequality of caste and gender, are integral to Vaishnavism and strongly associated with Puri and Jagannatha. The assimilation of custom and belief from lower orders to high Hinduism without questioning the latter's hegemony can be seen as a successful case of re-use.

Another key feature of the Jagannatha cult is the incorporation of Islamic sacred beliefs within Hindu rituals and social practices. The quintessential story is that of Salabega—the:

> [...] offspring of a Muslim *subedar* of Cuttack and a brahmin woman [...] who learnt from his mother a great deal about [...] [and subsequently] became a great devotee of Jagannatha [...] The prayer verses composed by him are sung [...] in mass prayers and inside temples. Both the Hindus and Muslims claimed his body when he died. Then there was a compromise and his body was buried by the side of the Chariot-route of Lord Jagannatha at Puri so that his spirit could see Jagannatha every year during the Car Festival. (Mishra 1984: 8)

Other instances of local practices that combined Hindu and Muslim rituals include Satyanarayan Puja where Hindus and Muslims share the offering known as *siriniprasada*, offered to God, referred to as Satyanarayan by Hindus and Satyapira by Muslims (Mishra 1984: 9).

The close link between the vernacular Oriya medium and the cult of Jagannatha provided a helpful backdrop to the growth of Oriya regional nationalism. In Oriya literature, during the sixteenth and the eighteenth centuries, Jagannatha figures in a prominent way. Many mediaeval authors, for example, paid their homage to Jagannatha in *janana*s and *bhajana*s, narrative poems in vernacular Oriya with a religious theme. With the onset of British rule in 1803, native resistance to Bengali officials working under the East India Company found a natural ally in the Oriya language movement and strengthened the aspiration for political autonomy, leading to the Paika rebellion of 1817. One of the first acts of the leaders of the rebellion was to march on Puri and to try to induce Mukunda Deva, the Raja of Khurda/ Puri and the custodian of the Jagannatha Temple, to accept the leadership of the rebellion. The priests of the Jagannatha Temple gave the rebellion their support by declaring publicly that British rule would end in Orissa, which added to the morale of the Paikas. These historical events provided a link between Jagannatha and the emergence of Oriya nationalism.

Another enduring link between Jagannatha, the Oriya identity and regional nationalism was provided by modern Oriya literature by Ramasahkar Roy, one of the pioneers in this field, who introduced the theme of nationalism into Oriya literature perhaps for the first time through his play *Kanci Kaberi* (1880–81), in which a prominent role was assigned to Jagannatha as the defender of Oriya interests against her enemies. This continues to be a popular theme for poets, playwrights, authors of books for children and school text books in Orissa. The link between the cult of Jagannatha and the post-Independence elite who were the key actors of the government and politics of Orissa was provided by the fact that many of them hailed from the Sasan villages (land grant village, mostly to Brahmin priests), gifted to priests of Jagannatha who had the task of maintaining the ritual and management of temple property.

> The traditional intellectual elite of Orissa, the Sasan Brahmins of the Puri district, were able to retain their influence in the administration of the province after Independence because their traditional training emphasised qualities like literacy and the knowledge of statecraft. [...] The relatively moderate material base most of the Sasana Brahmins were able to retain (a few acres of land and the community fund of the village) could however be utilised to retain those civilisational privileges (professional training) which had always been the material base of their excessive elitism. The centre of its application shifted away from the Jangannath temple to the secular administration in Bhubaneswar and the new professions. (Pfeffer 1986: 437)

In Orissa, the process of double accommodation—of competing sacred beliefs among themselves—and the ensemble of sacred beliefs by secular power has continued in spite of the changes of political rule. Historical evidence from Orissa shows that the British conquerors of Orissa quickly understood the nature of sacred geography and continued the 'normal' practice of providing protection to Jagannatha. The British obviously understood the political value of religious patronage, in view of the fact that the vigorous protest from Christian missionaries, horrified at this lenient treatment of the heathen 'Juggernaut' merely caused them to resort to the subterfuge of maintaining the practice through the Raja of Khurda, a Hindu intermediary whose ritual position as the chief *sevaka* (servant) of Jagannatha was thus reinforced through the patronage of the colonial state.

The government of Orissa has continued the British practice of recruiting the good offices of Lord Jagannatha for the legitimacy of the post-Independence government based on popular rule. As our analysis of the administrative structure of the temple shows, the King of Puri, the 'moving Vishnu' is the crucial hinge between sacred beliefs and secular power. At least during the peak periods of the major festivals, he provides a physical link between the temporal and the moral orders. Chakadola—the unblinking, all-seeing-eyes of the three deities—adorn public buildings, government publications and social occasions. In more recent times, the Jagannatha Temple administration, a part and parcel of the government of Orissa, has started distributing the sacred objects from the chariot to the believer as much as to those with more secular intentions, putatively to promote Oriya culture, but quite likely, also with an eye to enhancing the legitimacy of the regional state (see Plate 3.12).

Finally, in Orissa, instead of destruction and large-scale conversion, what one finds is hybridisation, consecrated in the name of the Patitapabana, like the ocean that washes the shores of the holy site of the main temple of Jagannatha, taking in all the impurities of the world and rendering them back restored. The interesting point here is the stability of the practice of re-use and accommodation through the ages, first innovated by the conquering Aryan invaders of Orissa from the south and then put into practice by every successive ruler, including, ultimately, the secular state of Orissa. Jagannatha—a folk deity, administered by a public committee with public funds—has found his way to the hearts and minds of his devotees, calendars and wedding invitations—and the inner architecture of public buildings where the unblinking eyes of the Lord of the Universe keep a fixed gaze on civil servants and supplicants going on with their daily transactions.[46]

Under the surface of this plausible picture of the cult of Jagannatha as the great dissolvent that conflates social division and generates a general re-use of Hindu religious categories for social integration, however, there lurks, nevertheless, a subterranean layer of anxiety. Exclusive reliance on sacred sources commented on by authors who are themselves of upper-caste origin has its own

---

[46] The wheel comes a full circle with the transformation of Jagannatha—the tribal totem to a folk deity of the twenty-first century—by the way of poster art.

In India, life, art and religion are one. The process of creating a work of art is also an act of worship, one though which the invisible manifests as the visible, and the artist who 'invokes' the image gives form to the formless, seeking to discover the unknown through the known. (Mukherjee 1987: 4)

limitation as a guide to social practice. As such, it is helpful here to look at some evidence from the lowest level of Oriya society in the form of a narrative, from Muli, the untouchable protagonist of Freeman's *Untouchable*:

> She [Muli's mother] went to Puri every two years or so to visit Lord Jagannatha, but she never went inside the temple. I myself went into the outer compound of the Jagannatha temple for the first time only in 1970. *I didn't go into the inner room*; I have never seen anybody of my caste enter the temple compound before this time. (Freeman 1979: 124, emphasis added)

Clearly, the testimony of Muli, the untouchable protagonist of this ethnographic account of everyday life in Orissa, alerts us to the limits of egalitarianism in Oriya society. But, in conjunction with the folk narrative, one can see in the access to Jagannatha both a benchmark of the spread of social equality and an integrative mechanism that can draw ritually distant sections of society together, even though such socially conflating moments might remain confined to the annual car festival or the ritual *chherapanhara*. The Lion gate (*simhadwara*) of the Lord of the Universe, many of whose servants are members of the secular state of India, nevertheless remains closed to the non-Hindu and to the 'former' untouchables.[47]

## CONCLUSION: MEMORY, RE-USE AND THE PUBLIC SPHERE

We learn from Hobsbawm that:

> Invented tradition is taken to mean a set of practices, normally governed by overtly or tacitly accepted rules and of a ritual or symbolic nature, which seek to inculcate certain values and norms of behaviour by repetition, which automatically implies continuity with the past. In fact, where possible, they normally attempt to establish continuity with a suitable historic past. (Hobsbawm 1996: 1)

The examples of re-use and state-formation in changing societies analysed in this chapter are not, in this sense, entirely 'invented'. They are socially constructed through chronologies, textual sources and secondary institutions. They show the dynamic among different religious groups, and between the state and religion, in an inter-generational timeframe. They examine how the moral economy of religion and the institutions of the state accommodate one another through appropriation and institutionalisation of the products of theft,

---

[47] The Untouchability Offences Act makes the use of the word untouchable without the prefix 'former' criminally actionable.

plunder and re-use. The process is not always elegant or peaceful and the generations—of 'losers', 'winners' and 'post-re-use elites'—might have very different kinds of memories of the salient events that mark any takeover. Re-use may integrate, but not without its residue of the desire for revenge, or anxiety about the inevitable resistance from the progeny of the vanquished.

In the section on Vira-Shaiva re-use in Karnataka, the first example of the converted Jaina temple at Hallur illustrates the conscious re-use of an edifice by an incoming religious group. It shows the conscious preservation of the edifice, even of building elements which are no longer in use, and the safeguarding of apparent Jaina imagery on the inside and outside of the temple, in order to emphasise the forcible expropriation and conversion of the temple by the Vira-Shaivas. In this instance, although some figures have partially been mutilated or desecrated, others have been left unscathed but have not been given a new religious significance. This is different at Adargunchi where the prominent statue and its associated foot imprints appear to have been the main object of attraction for the Lingayats. Both cases advertise the forcible appropriation of temple and icons and appear to utilise these as political statements causing anxiety and feelings of loss and suppression in the deposed local Jaina elite. In the temple at Kagvad, sacred space is—despite the partial destruction and annexation of the shrine and of some sculptures—nowadays shared by Jainas and Vira-Shaivas alike. Here, the act of disturbance is blamed on the Muslims and this might offer both parties the opportunity for a peaceful and relatively balanced coexistence and a move towards syncretism and integration. The latter example illustrates the coexistence of religious practices and the opportunity that lies in the theory of re-use. It offers a compromise in which people do not have to lose everything, but where enough of the past can be preserved in order to transform it into something new, which continues a link with the past. The existence of the past in the present guarantees the survival and the durability of the structures, statues and to a certain extent the rituals of the overpowered, parts of which are given a fresh lease of life in the new practices.

The case of Orissa helps us raise the crucial issues of religion and political legitimacy in the context of India's regional traditions. These general issues can be formulated as follows. For political order to be legitimate, it has to be firmly embedded in a moral order that encompasses the whole of the society. The morality of such authority might derive from a diversity of sources, including the idea that sacred beliefs underpin secular power, as well as from the visible benefits of social and economic transactions where most people enjoy some small improvement in their standard of living. Some sections of society may adhere strongly to magical beliefs in the power of the supernatural, beliefs which would often include a deity of fear and love, holding the society together through ritual and punishment. The political universe of pre-Muslim India was composed of a hierarchy of divine beings, competing and collaborating to produce a moral order which reinforced the temporal authority of the actual power holder. As we learn from Embree (1990), this polymorphous moral order produced a limited measure of tolerance for the *yavana*, as long as their beliefs could be accommodated within the plural pantheon and multitude of social practices, ritual and custom at local and regional levels.

This form of dynamic encapsulation, as we see in the case study of Orissa, and from south India, survived the arrival of Islam, in the course of which some new objects of devotion, social practices and political customs were added to the regional and local repertoire. Compared to the north, where Islam was politically victorious earlier and held power longer and where the Muslim social order was constantly reinforced with fresh waves of invaders, the encounter between Islam and local religion in other parts of India was sporadic, relatively static and more of a war of slow attrition than a brilliant blitz. This moral 'trench warfare'[48] in the south and the east where the armies of Islam confronted local and regional Hinduism over extensive unfortified terrain, and over long periods of settlement, produced no clear 'winners', as neither side commanded overwhelming force with which either could destroy the other. What emerged from this stalemated conflict, instead, was a philosophy of 'live and let live', celebrated in shared rituals, saints and holy places, numerous enough to make the point. Apart from the sporadic acts of vandalism and desecration that broke out during periods of imperial instability, the 'normal' state of political management of holy places produced curious cases of Muslim rulers who protected Hindu shrines, with an eye, no doubt, on the lucrative pilgrim tax. The same scenario—clash-conflation–re-use—has reproduced itself in the cases of the Shavara–Aryan, Jaina–Vira-Shaiva, upper caste–untouchable and the ubiquitous gender conflicts.

Re-use theory helps us question two flawed constructions of modern India. The first, is an idealistic view, in which eternal India presents Indian culture as a fixed, undifferentiated essence, accessible only to a learned elite which must be protected from any source of internal impurity or external contamination. Thanks to the discoveries of research driven by re-use, we know the amount of cultural borrowing that has gone into making India what she is today—a vibrant, diverse and interlocked society—which has the inner resources to sustain democracy and integrate globally without necessarily losing its own identity and specificity. Though the examples in this chapter are chosen from Indic religions, re-use as a phenomenon is not specific to India. The destruction or forcible conversion of sacred edifices sanctified by one religious group

---

[48] The analogy is from Axelrod (1984), who shows how recursive, stalemated conflict in close proximity might produce implicit cooperation among enemies.

through the followers of new or incoming faiths is a recognised phenomenon in the history of architecture.[49]

The second view of India—thanks to the political and intellectual efforts of generations of modernists—which has defined life as the sum total of interests, cast in a 'modern' design fabricated in the West. The hiatus between this elite-driven, desiccated post-war concept of universal modernity and the Indian masses has ushered a motley crowd of essentialists, revivalists and traditionalists to India's public sphere (Mitra 1990, 1991). The empirical research that underpins this article shows that the 'modern' is often the most recent tranche of a process of continuous evolution that connects it to the 'traditional'. The conflict and conflation of the material, and the symbolic, is the driving force behind this process of rejection, selection, re-use and incorporation. What passes for the 'modern' in India—namely, constitutional structures and institutional arrangements inspired by modern values, rational economic planning and modern buildings designed by Western architects—can ignore the symbolic links to Indian tradition and culture only at their peril. Nor is this typical only of India. The resilience of religious rituals in the 'materialist West', the recrudescence of the Orthodox Church in post-Soviet Russia and the re-used Ashoka Chakra in the Indian flag are reminiscent of the generality of the re-use of ideas and symbols.

India's regional traditions, on which more field research is needed, might provide the basis for the creation of an institutional structure for the accommodation of sacred beliefs to the secular authority of the national state. From this perspective, the roots of the present crisis of legitimacy go back to the manner in which the secular principle was enshrined within the constitution and the spirit in which it was implemented in practice. From the beginning, despite the end of foreign colonial rule, no consistent attempts were made to derive the principle of government from local and regional cultural and political traditions in India. The result, as Inden (1990: 197) reminds us, was a:

> [...] nation-state that remains, ontologically and politically inaccessible to its own citizens. Its government continues to be just like its immediate British Indian ancestor, merely a neutral enforcer of unity on a morselised society, continually in danger of being pulled apart by 'centrifugal forces'. In contrast to this 'secular'

---

[49] A prominent example is the Dome of the Rock in Jerusalem. It was constructed on the site of a pagan temple, which then was claimed as a place of worship by the Jews, and consequently converted by the Muslims into a mosque. Similarly, in the church of San Clemente in Rome, three layers of occupation, spanning almost twenty centuries, and combining elements of a classical mithraeum, an early Christian basilica and a mediaeval Church, have been preserved one above the other (Ercoli, Belford & Mitchell 1995: 185–97; Guidobaldi & Lawlor 1990).

nation-state, which has come under growing strain from its inability to accommodate the legitimate role of sacred beliefs in Indian politics, the regional tradition of Orissa where sacred beliefs and secular power were conflated and linked to social practice, provides a model that has historically withstood the challenge of communal conflict.

Finally, ritual, art and symbol—the essential ingredients of re-use—are the only chance that mortal men have to identify with forces larger and more enduring than their limited lives. Furthermore, symbols are much more amenable to the creation of enduring bonds, unlike mortar, cement, land, power and other components of material desires, buildings and liberal political institutions. The re-use of selected elements from the past makes it possible for us to live with the knowledge of the inevitability of death. The examples of re-use and the vital dynamic links between the past and the present discussed in this chapter show that in theory, if not always in life, the symbolic can balance the material, and that one can straddle across the divide of time, space and power.[50]

## PHOTO CREDIT

Photos 3.1 to 3.10 are by Julia A. B. Hegewald and the photos for Plates 3.11 and 3.12 were taken by Ulf Hegewald.

---

[50] Having said as much, we must also take into account the fact that the empirical examples that the chapter is based on are all from India and that might create the impression, as V. S. Naipaul argues, that "Indian history telescopes easily" (Naipaul 1977: 4). Naipaul terms it "An Old Equilibrium", and continues:

> Sometimes, old India, the old, eternal India many Indians like to talk about, does seem just to go on. During the last war some British soldiers, who were training in chemical warfare, were stationed in the far South of the country, near a thousand-year-old Hindu temple. The temple had a pet crocodile. The soldiers, understandably, shot the crocodile. They also in some way—perhaps by their presence alone—defiled the temple. Soon, however, the soldiers went away and the British left India altogether. Now, more than thirty years after that defilement, and in another season of emergency, the temple has been renovated and a new statue of the temple deity is being installed. (Naipaul 1977: 13)

> Re-use is not unique to the Indian civilisation and there are general processes at work. In the Indian context, they take the shapes desribed in this chapter, in Chapter 2 and in the diverse contributions in this book.

# BIBLIOGRAPHY

## Secondary Sources

Axelrod, Rober, 1984, *The Evolution of Cooperation*. Penguin, London.

Bowker, John (ed.), 1999 [1997], *The Oxford Dictionary of World Religions*. Oxford University Press, Oxford and New York.

Das, K. B. & L. K. Mahapatra, 1979, *Folklore of Orissa*. National Book Trust of India, New Delhi.

Desai, P. B., 1957, *Jainism in South India—and Some Jaina Epigraphs*. Gulabchand Hirachand Doshi, Jaina Samskriti Samrakshaka Sangha, Sholapur.

Donaldson, Thomas, 1987, *Hindu Temple Art of Orissa*, Vol. 1–3. E. J. Brill, Leiden.

Embree, Ainslie, 1990, *Utopias in Conflict: Religion and Nationalism in Modern India*. University of California Press, Berkeley.

Ercoli, Olivia, Ros Belford & Roberta Mitchell, 1995 [1993], *Rom*. Dorling Kindersley Limited, London; and Reise-und Verkehrsverlag, Berlin.

Eschmann, Annecharlotte, Hermann Kulke & Gaya Charan Tripathi (eds), 1986, *The Cult of Jagannath and the Regional Tradition of Orissa*. Manohar, Delhi.

Freeman, James, 1979, *Untouchable: An Indian Life History*. George Allen & Unwin, London.

Gole, Susan, 1989, *Indian Maps and Plans*. Manohar, Delhi.

Guidobaldi, Federico & Paul O. P. Lawlor, 1990, *The Basilica and the Archaeological Area of San Clemente in Rome: A Guide to the Three Levels with Ground Plans*. Apud S. Clementem, Rome.

Hein, E., 1986, "Temple, Town and Hinterland: The Present Network of Religious Economy". In: Annecharlotte Eschmann, Hermann Kulke & Gaya Charan Tripathi (eds), *The Cult of Jagannath and the Regional Tradition of Orissa*. Manohar, Delhi, pp. 439–68.

Hegewald, Julia A. B., 2001, "Multi-shrined Complexes: The Ordering of Space in Jaina Temple Architecture". *South Asian Studies*. Vol. 17, pp. 77–96.

———, 2006a, "From Shiva to Parshvanatha: The Appropriation of a Hindu Temple for Jaina Worship". In: Catherine Jarrige and Vincent Lefèvre (eds), *South Asian Archaeology 2001*, 2 vols, Editions Recherches sur les Civilisations, Paris. pp. 517–23.

———, 2006b, "Architectural, Sculptural and Religious Change: A New Interpretation of the Jaina Temples at Khajuraho". In: P. Flügel (ed.), *Studies in Jaina History and Culture: Disputes and Dialogues*, Routledge Advances in Jaina Studies Vol. 1. Routledge, London and New York, pp. 401–18.

———, 2007, "Domes, Tombs and Minarets: Islamic Influences on Jaina Architecture". In: Adam Hardy (ed.), *The Temple in South Asia*, Volume 2 of the proceedings of the 18th conference of the European Association of South Asian Archaeologists, London 2005. British Association for South Asian Studies and the British Academy, London, pp. 179–90.

Hegewald, Julia A. B., 2009, *Jaina Temple Architecture in India: The Development of a Distinct Language in Space and Ritual*. Monographien zur Indischen Archäologie, Kunst und Philologie, Band 19, Herausgeber Stiftung Ernst Waldschmidt, G+H-Verlag, Berlin.

———, 2011, "Sacred Symbols, Enlightened Beings and Temple Guardians: The Display of Holy Elements on Pillars in Jaina Temple Complexes in Karnataka". In: Julia A. B. Hegewald (ed.), *The Jaina Heritage: Distinction, Decline and Resilience*, pp.134–60. Heidelberg Series in South Asian Studies Vol. II, Samskriti Publishers, Delhi.

Hegewald, Julia A. B. & Subrata K. Mitra, 2008, "Jagannatha Compared: The Politics of Appropriation, Re-use and Regional State Traditions in India". *Heidelberg Papers in South Asian and Comparative Politics (HPSACP)*. No. 36, pp. 1–37. Available at http://archiv.ub.uni-heidelberg.de/volltextserver/frontdoor.php?source_opus=8015

Hobsbawm, Eric, 1996 [1983], "Introduction: Inventing Traditions". In: Eric Hobsbawm & Terence Ranger (eds), *The Invention of Tradition*. Cambridge University Press, Cambridge, pp. 1–14.

Inden, Ronald, 1990, *Imagining India*. University of Chicago Press, Chicago.

Jain, KailashChand, 1963, *Jainism in Rajasthan*. Gulabchand Hirachand Doshi, Sholapur.

Jawaharlal, G., 2002, *Jaina Monuments of Andhra*. Sharada Publishing House, Delhi.

Leslie, Julia, 1998, "Understanding Basava: History, Hagiography and a Modern Kannada Drama". *Bulletin of the School of Oriental and African Studies*. Vol. 61, no. 2, pp. 228–61.

Mankodi, Kirit, 1975, "A Rastrakuta Temple at Hallur in Bijapur District". In: U. P. Shah & M. A. Dhaky (eds), *Aspects of Jaina Art and Architecture*, Gujarat State Committee for the Celebration of 2500th Anniversary of Bhagvan Mahavira Nirvana. L. D. Institute of Indology, Ahmedabad, pp. 205–14 and plates 1–11.

McCormack, William, 1963 (January–June), "Lingayats as a Sect". *The Journal of the Royal Anthropological Institute of Great Britain and Ireland*. Vol. 93, no. 1, pp. 59–71.

Meister, Michael & M. A. Dhaky (eds), 1986, *Encyclopaedia of Indian Temple Architecture: South India—Upper Dravidadesha (Early Phase, A. D. 550–1075)*, 2 vols. American Institute of Indian Studies, New Delhi and University of Pennsylvania Press, Philadelphia.

Michael, R. Blake, 1983 (February), "Foundation Myths of the Two Denominations of Virashaivism: *Viraktas* and *Gurusthalins*". *The Journal of Asian Studies*. Vol. 42, no. 2, pp. 309–22.

Mishra, K. C., 1984, *The Cult of Jagannath*. Firma K. L. Mukhopadhyaya, Calcutta.

Mitra, Subrata K. (ed.), 1990, *The Post-colonial State in Asia: The Dialectics of Politics and Culture*. Wheatsheaf, Milton Keynes.

———, 1991, "Desecularising the State: Religion and Politics in India after Independence". *Comparative Studies in Society and History*. Vol. 33, no. 4, pp. 755–77.

———, 1997, "Religion, Region and Identity: Sacred Beliefs and Secular Power in a Regional State Tradition of India". In: Noel O' Sullivan (ed.), *Aspects of India: Essays on Indian Politics and Culture*. Ajanta, Delhi, pp. 87–128.

Mukherjee, Priya, 1987, *Pathway Icons: The Wayside Art of India*. Thames and Hudson, London.

Nandimath, S. C., 1979, *A Handbook of Virashaivism*. Motilal Banarsidass, Delhi, Varanasi and Patna.

Naipaul, V. S., 1977, *India: A Wounded Civilization*. Penguin Books, London.

Panda, Bhagawan, 1979, *Ordisara Dharma* [in Oriya]. Grahtha Mandira, Cuttack.

Panda, Daityari & Sarat Chandra Panigrahi, 1984, *The Cult and Culture of Lord Jagannath*. Rashtrabhasha Samavaya Prakashan, Cuttack.

Padoux, André, 1987, "Virashaivas". In: Mircea Eliade (ed.), *The Encyclopedia of Religion*, Vol. 13. Macmillan Publishing Company, New York; and Colier Macmillan Publishers, London, pp. 12–13.

Parthasarathy, T. A. (chief ed.), 2002 [1995], *Gazetteer of India: Karnataka State Gazetteer—Dharwad District (Including Gadag and Haveri Districts)*, (Rev. ed.). Government of Karnataka, Bangalore.

Presler, Franklin, 1987, *Religion under Bureaucracy: Policy and Administration of Temples in South India*. Cambridge University Press, Cambridge.

Pfeffer, Gerog, 1986, "Puri's Vedic Brahmins: Continuity and Change in Their Traditional Institutions". In: Annecharlotte Eschmann, Hermann Kulke & Gaya Charan Tripathi (eds), *The Cult of Jagannath and the Regional Tradition of Orissa*. Manohar, Delhi, pp. 421–37.

Rosch, Eleanor & Carolyn B. Mervis, 1975, "Family Resemblances: Studies in the Internal Structure of Categories". *Cognitive Psychology*. Vol. 7, pp. 557–78.

Srinivasan, K. R., 1974, "Monuments & Sculpture A. D. 600 To 1000: The Deccan". In: A. Ghosh (ed.), *Jaina Art and Architecture*, Vol. I. Bharatiya Jnanpith, New Delhi, pp. 184–201.

Suresh, K. M., 2003, *Temples of Karnataka (Ground Plans and Elevations)*, 2 Vols. Bharatiya Kala Prakashan, Delhi.


## Internet Sources


Jain Tirthas, Dharwar, Karnataka. Available at http://www.jaintirths.com/karnataka/dharwar.htm (accessed on 14 June 2010).

L. Manjulakshmi, 2004 (September), "Modes of Address in Kannada: A Sociolinguistic Study of Language Use in Mysore District". *Language in India*. Vol. 4, p. 9. Available at http://www.languageinindia.com/sep2004/manjulakshitermsofaddress1.html (accessed on 14 June 2010).

The Indian Analyst, "South Indian Inscriptions: Miscellaneous Inscriptions in Kannada". Volume IX, part 1, Nolamba-Pallavas. Available at http://www.whatisindia.com/inscriptions/south_indian_inscriptions/volume_9/nolamba_pallavas.html (accessed on 26 June 2010).

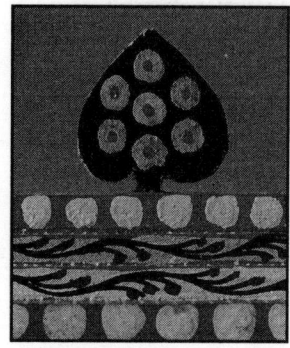

*Chapter 4*

# CHOLA AND NEO-CHOLA TEMPLE ARCHITECTURE IN AND AROUND KUMBAKONAM, TAMIL NADU[1]

## BY GEORGE MICHELL

Any account of the re-uses of the past in Indian culture must acknowledge the country's vivid and varied architectural traditions. Revivals of building techniques and practices occurred in almost all regions of India during the last two millennia, especially in temple architecture, where conservative priestly rites guaranteed the preservation and, where necessary, the resuscitation of older forms for sanctuaries that accommodated images and emblems of worship. This does not mean that temple architecture, whether Hindu or Jaina, was always retrograde in design. Revivalist sanctuaries are often combined with subsidiary structures that are innovative in terms of building form and technique as well as sculptural and painted decoration.

---

[1] This article is based on a paper presented at a symposium on Kumbakonam held at the British Museum, London, in June 1996.

This combination of older and newer typologies is particularly striking in Tamil Nadu, a zone characterised by a continuity in building practice that spans the careers of successive ruling dynasties over a period of more than 1,000 years. Nowhere is this better seen than in the development and subsequent revival of Chola religious architecture, as represented by the religious monuments in and around the city of Kumbakonam in the heart of the Kaveri River Delta. Perhaps the most striking feature of the many Hindu temples here is the coherence of a building tradition that extends from the ascendancy of the Cholas in the eighth to ninth centuries to the era of Maratha domination in the seventeenth to eighteenth centuries. As will be outlined below, the Chola paradigm was consciously resuscitated under the later Vijayanagara (fourteenth to sixteenth centuries) and Nayaka rulers (seventeenth to eighteenth centuries) to create monumental, revivalist mode temples in a style that is here termed Neo-Chola. It is the relationship between Chola and Neo-Chola styles that lies at the core of architectural developments at Kumbakonam. While there is no claim that Kumbakonam's temples manifest radically variant tendencies to those elsewhere in the Tamil zone during these centuries, the discussion here is restricted to examples within the city and its immediate vicinity. Building projects at Kumbakonam reflect the status of the city as a leading economic, cultural and religious centre, rather than a ceremonial seat of regal power. This reputation has been sustained through the centuries, down to the present day.

## DEFINITIONS AND OVERALL ARCHITECTURAL DEVELOPMENT

Before considering the principal religious monuments of Kumbakonam and its environs, it is necessary first to discuss some overall features of the stylistic analysis attempted here. Consecutive phases of temple architecture in the city suggest a linear progression from the announcement of the architectural paradigm under the early Cholas to its revival and extension under the Nayakas. From the very beginning, the term 'Chola' assumes a double meaning since it refers to both a dynasty and a style; a third meaning, which alludes to a specific geographical zone, is also implied. The heartland of the Chola kingdom and its architecture is the Kaveri Delta, an area dominated in earlier centuries, as today, by Kumbakonam. From its very inception in the ninth century, the Chola style was imbued with political and regional associations. The more or less continuous evolution of the Chola style under the patronage of successive dynasties confirms its sustained meaning as an appropriate hallmark of the dynasty, as well as its homeland, the Kaveri Delta. The fact that the Chola idiom became widespread throughout the Tamil country, and even beyond, is a testament to the diffusion of Chola political and cultural influence.

Certain formal aspects of Chola architecture seem to have made this idiom particularly appropriate for a dynastic style. The basic combination of elevational components, yet to be described, rendered the Chola idiom capable of repetition and enlargement, thereby allowing a dramatic increase in scale. Comparing the small-sized shrines of the late ninth century with the grandiose complexes of the twelfth and thirteenth centuries makes this process of augmentation strikingly clear. Architectural development parallels the progression of the Cholas from local chiefs to forceful rulers commanding a substantial tract of south India. The imperial potential of the Chola style is convincingly realised in the great towered sanctuaries, or *vimana*s, of royal temples at Thanjavur and Gangaikondacholapuram,[2] as well as in the quartet of imposing towered gateways, or *gopura*s, at Chidambaram,[3] all on the fringes of the Kaveri zone. That such majestic structures were fully capable of giving visual expression to regal ambitions must have been apparent in later times, judging from the widespread adoption of the Chola style under Vijayanagara and their Nayaka successors. Both these lines of rulers seem to have recognised the political and regional resonances of the Neo-Chola style. After all, the Nayakas of Thanjavur, rulers of Kumbakonam, became masters of exactly the same heartland as that of the Cholas. The Nayakas were evidently interested in the architectural achievements of their forbearers, and they did not hesitate to make substantial repairs and extensions to the great monuments at Thanjavur and Gangaikondacholapuram.

That this imitative Neo-Chola mode becomes the dominant mode of later projects is obvious in the sixteenth and seventeenth century *vimana*s and *gopura*s which crowd the core of Kumbakonam, as well as lesser sites in the vicinity. Neo-Chola architecture in the city is most conspicuous in the *gopura*s with which all of the important religious foundations were furnished. Such towered gates replicate, and even surpass, the ample dimensions of *gopura*s such as those at Chidambaram already mentioned. Furthermore, these *gopura*s are formally arranged so as to emphasise the axial configuration of the religious monument, generally with alignments of elements coordinated with the sanctuary housing the principal divinity. Sculptural embellishment also follows Chola precedent, especially on the *vimana*s. Sometimes the imitative mode is so successful that it is extremely difficult to distinguish later copies from earlier originals. Indeed, this seems to have been the intention: to remake the city's architectural image in the imperial Chola mode.

---

[2] The Brihadishvara Temple at Thanjavur dates from 1010 CE and the temple of the same name at Gangaikondacholapuram was constructed in the mid-eleventh century.

[3] The Nataraja Temple at Chidambaram substantially dates from the twelfth and thirteenth centuries but also contains later additions.

However, it is important to acknowledge at the outset that Vijayanagara and Nayaka architecture is not entirely retrograde. Certain aspects of temples are characterised by innovation, none more so than the spacious columned halls, or *mandapa*s, that precede the most significant sanctuaries. The transformation of granite stone supports into complex piers with cut-out colonettes and fully carved beasts and figures is one of the outstanding artistic contributions of the Vijayanagara period. Though ultimately deriving from earlier practice, the sculptural elaboration of columnar forms far surpasses Chola antecedents. This forward-looking aspect of later temples is best represented at Kumbakonam in the outer *mandapa* of the Ramasvami Temple, one of Govinda Dikshita's principal architectural contributions to the city.

## THE PARADIGM ANNOUNCED: EARLY CHOLA TEMPLES

Religious architecture at Kumbakonam opens with the Nageshvara Temple (see Plate 4.1), a short distance north-west of the Mahamakam Tank. This monument is amply supplied with Chola epigraphs, the earliest of which dates back to 886 CE, during the reign of Aditya I (r. 871–907). It is this temple that serves as the prototype for all developments to follow, both in the city and in its immediate hinterland; for this reason, it is worth describing it at some length. The *vimana* of the Nageshvara Temple, together with its attached antechamber and four-columned *mandapa*, all aligned on an east–west axis, present a delicately worked, pink granite exterior. Walls are raised on an *adhishthana*, or basement sequence, running uninterruptedly around the building. This superimposes petalled frieze, part-octagonal element and miniature blocks carved with legendary scenes both beneath and above a projecting band. Walls are articulated by full-height pilasters with projecting capitals and flattish brackets. Angled struts carved as dancing figures and musicians are placed above the capitals on the *vimana*. Sculpture niches are framed by secondary pilasters with split-shafts and capitals supporting delicate relief pediments, with *makara*s, or aquatic beasts, at the ends and miniature figures in part-circular frames in the middle. Central niches projecting prominently from three sides of the *vimana* accommodate diverse deities and an unidentified royal donor, perhaps Aditya himself. These divine and human personalities are flanked by attendant sages and maidens in turning and twisted postures. The figures are all carved in the most refined Chola manner, with subtly modelled bodies and jewelled costumes, and gentle facial expressions. The walls are overhung by curved eaves interrupted by foliated *kudu*s, or horseshoe-shaped blind arches, positioned over the pilasters. A frieze of *yali*s, or leonine beasts, marks the ends of the roof slabs. The pyramidal tower that rises above displays prominent corner *kuta*s and central *shala*s, domical and vaulted model roof forms, respectively, on two diminishing, superimposed storeys. The tower is crowned with a *kuta* roof with prominent *kudu* motifs on four sides, and a *kalasha*, or pot-like finial.

That this sophisticated idiom was not limited to Kumbakonam is demonstrated at Pullamangai, an insignificant village some twenty kilometres west of the city. The Brahmapurishvara Temple here, which dates from about 910 CE during the reign of Parantaka I (r. 907–954), displays many of the characteristics observed in the Nageshvara Temple, though with certain variations. The *adhishthana* at Pullamangai introduces the frieze of *yalis*, known previously only in the cornice. The animals here are sensitively modelled; so, too, the blocks with legendary scenes placed on either side of the projecting band. The *vimana* walls at Pullamangai present triple projections on each side framed by full-height pilasters, extending up to the cornice. Fully evolved intermediate projections of lesser height are created by pairs of secondary split-pilasters. These are topped with their own sequence of brackets, curving eaves and enlarged *kudu*s inserted into the cornice that runs around the top of the walls. The tower repeats the scheme of the Nageshvara Temple, except that the central *shala*s on both storeys are projected forward to achieve a more three-dimensional effect. The increased decorative tendency of early Chola art is seen in the fanciful scrollwork that embellishes *adhishthana* and cornice elements, as well as pilaster shafts. The basic iconographic programme established at the Nageshvara Temple is repeated here, but accessory figures are reduced to relief carvings on the wall surfaces in between the pilasters. Prominent features of the sculptural decor are the brackets fashioned as dancers positioned beneath the cornice and fully carved seated *gana*s, or dwarfish imps, placed on the roof of the attached *mandapa*.

Several much smaller and simpler structures in the Kumbakonam area show that this refined architectural style was not sustained during the later tenth and the eleventh centuries. This is illustrated by the west-facing Suryanarayana and *linga* subshrines in the courtyard of the Nageshvara complex, the former preserving an epigraph mentioning Rajaraja I (r. 985–1012), as well as the *gopura* in the east wall of the same enclosure. Undecorated *adhishthana* sequences and pilastered walls in these subshrines and *gopura* display nothing of the stylistic sophistication noted in the Nageshvara and Brahmapurishvara *vimana*s, suggesting a decline in resources and artistic standards in and around Kumbakonam. This, evidently, was not the case at centres which benefitted from the presence of the king and court, as at Thanjavur and Gangaikondacholapuram, where majestic monuments of unprecedented height were erected by Rajaraja I and his successor Rajendra (r. 1012–44) in the first two decades of the eleventh century. However, these projects fall outside the scope of the present discussion, which is confined to Kumbakonam and its immediate environs.

## THE PARADIGM DEVELOPED: LATER CHOLA TEMPLES

Kumbakonam's importance seems to have revived markedly after the middle of the twelfth century, judging from the richly embellished monuments commissioned by the late Chola rulers on the peripheries of the city. This is best shown by the Airavateshvara Temple (see Plate 4.2) erected by Rajaraja II (r. 1146–72) in 1166 at the royal residence of Rajarajapuram, now Darasuram, two kilometres south-west of Kumbakonam's centre. Not only the site, but also the temple deity, originally bore the name of the patron, Rajarajeshvara. The monument survives as the masterpiece of the late Chola style, surpassing earlier achievements at Thanjavur and Gangaikondacholapuram in the quality of its sculpted decor, while making no attempt to rival monuments at those sites in extent or height. A somewhat detailed description of the Airavateshvara Temple is appropriate because it is here that many of the architectural elements that will become essential attributes of the Neo-Chola style first make an appearance in Kumbakonam.

The *vimana* of the Airavateshvara Temple consists of a square sanctuary entered from the east through a columned antechamber and a vestibule, the latter with doorways on the north and south. The vestibule opens directly into a spacious *mandapa* with thirty columns. A doorway on the east gives access to a larger *mandapa*, with five-bayed openings on the east and south and a nine-bayed porch projecting outwards on the south reached by double flight of steps. The temple, together with the small south-facing Chandeshvara subshrine, stands in the middle of a rectangular court surrounded by colonnades. An entrance gate is placed in the middle of the east wall of the enclosure, beyond which are a small Nandi pavilion and an altar. About 100 metres further east stands a large and unfinished *gopura*. A related monument is the Daivanayaki Amman Temple a short distance to the north.

Typical late Chola features are observed throughout the Airavateshvara Temple. The *adhishthana* carried around the *vimana* and attached *mandapa*s is raised on a plinth with a frieze of *yali*s surmounting a curving cornice and panels of dancing *gana*s. The *adhishthana*, which rises on a flowing petalled moulding, has a fluted part-circular element in the middle, topped with a frieze of *yali*s and a sequence of relief panels illustrating the stories of all the sixty-three Nayanmars. The *vimana* walls have five projections on each of three sides, each framed by a pair of pilasters with part-circular or part-octagonal shafts and prominent double capitals with projecting square elements. The central and outermost projections are wider so as to accommodate secondary pairs of split-pilasters framing sculpture niches. They are headed by relief pediments with flowing ornament on the sides or miniature eaves and elongated *shala*s in the middle. Carved icons in the middle of three sides of the *vimana* include diverse aspects of Shiva. The niche housing an image of Dakshinamurti in the middle of the south *vimana* wall was once preceded by a small pavilion, of which only the lower storey still stands. The intermediate recesses, four on each side, are occupied by single pilasters standing in pots. Flattish pilasters rising upon the pots are capped with eaves and *kudu*s. The pyramidal tower over the *vimana* displays four diminishing storeys, each with the usual complement of corner *kuta*s, central *shala* and intermediate *kudu*s rising on short pilastered walls. Further, *kudu*s decorate the capping hemispherical roof, much embellished with plasterwork in later times.

The elevational treatment of the remainder of the Airavateshvara complex displays typically late Chola features. The *mandapa* walls are dominated by niches formed from pairs of split-pilasters projecting away from the walls, carried on independent and varying sequences of *adhishthana* mouldings. The pilasters carry fully modelled sequences of eaves, *yali* friezes and deeply cut *kudu*s, the last set into the cornice that terminates the walls. These projections alternate with simple recesses flanked by split-pilasters and headed by shallow foliated pediments. Significant variations are noted at the southern porch. The *adhishthana* here displays miniature niches topped with both *shala*s and *kudu*s. Staircases are flanked by elaborate balustrades with flowing tops, terminating in striding elephants. Fully-modelled wheels next to richly bridled prancing horses decorate the adjacent plinth. Peripheral porch columns have seated *yali*s at the bases, with prominent square capitals projecting from the tops. Columns inside the porch show superimposed architectural facades, with miniature figures framed by pilasters and eaves in shallow relief. Elsewhere, columns have triple blocks enlivened with fanciful scrollwork containing miniature figures. Variations are noted on the five-bayed opening on the east face of the outer *mandapa*. Columns here have shallow square colonettes with seated *yali*s at the base attached to the main shafts. Brackets take *pushpapottika* forms, with characteristic curving petalled ends. The coffered ceilings within the *mandapa* are characterised by deeply cut lotus medallions.

Many elements of the Airavateshvara Temple's main unit are repeated in the surrounding colonnades. Perforated *jali* screens with geometric patterns are added between the supports in the north-west gallery of the compound. The Chandeshvara subshrine is a modest structure with a two-storeyed tower, capped with a hemispherical roof. A large *shala* elevated on a pilastered wall crowns the east gate. An incomplete and dilapidated *gopura* stands to the east of the complex (see Plate 4.3). This presents superimposed *adhishthana*s, the lower series distinguished by projecting niches resembling those on the *mandapa* walls of the main temple. The walls above display shallow niches set in pilastered projections of unequal width distributed in symmetrical formation, four on either side of the central passageway. Pilasters standing in pots fill the intervening recesses. Nothing survives of the multi-storeyed brick tower; possibly it was never added.

The *vimana* and attached *mandapa* of the nearby Amman Temple at Darasuram is also raised on an ornate plinth. This has carved panels, interrupted by miniature niches headed by *shalas* and *kudus*. Wall projections on a plain *adhishthana* are framed by pilasters rising from the heads of standing *yalis* modelled in relief. The rectangular sanctuary is roofed with a tower showing prominent projections in the middle of the long sides. These create a cruciform shape that is carried up into the capping *shala* roof.

This somewhat lengthy description of the Airavateshvara Temple and its neighbouring monument is justified by the influence of its architectural design and sculptural treatment on succeeding temples of the late Chola period. Like the Airavateshvara Temple, the relatively modest Somanatha Temple at Palaiyaru is also ascribed to the period of Rajaraja II. Though Palaiyaru is now only an obscure village, eight kilometres south of Kumbakonam, epigraphical sources indicate that it was once a favoured residence of the Chola kings. The Somanatha Temple stands on a plinth with double friezes of *yalis* and unadorned panels, with shallow projections in the middle of each side. This contrasts with the *adhishthana*, which echoes the multiple projections and recesses of the walls. Central projections in the middle of the *vimana* and antechamber walls show slight variations in the sequence of mouldings, though the ribbed curving moulding is retained throughout. Multi-faceted pilasters standing in pots with similarly ribbed sides occupy the recesses between the wall projections. As at Darasuram, the outer *mandapa* of the Somanatha Temple is entered through a porch that projects outwards on the south. Here, too, the plinth and *adhishthana* are adorned with relief representations of elephants, wheels and prancing horses. An unusual feature is the raised stone tray, probably for libations, that runs along this side of the porch. The complex in which the Somanatha Temple stands is entered on the east through a small *gopura* of the usual design. More impressive is the detached gate which stands a short distance further east. Though not as large as that associated with the Airavateshvara Temple, this example is better preserved, showing clearly the double *adhishthana* and the array of wall niches on either side of the central passageway. The multi-storeyed brick tower, now disintegrating, is capped with the characteristic *shala* roof.

The next phase of temple architecture in and around Kumbakonam coincides with the rule of Kulottunga III (r. 1178–1218), last of the truly powerful Chola rulers. The unassuming dimensions of the late Chola style are revealed in the *mandapa* extensions to the Nageshvara unit and in the modest Banapurishvara Temple, known in the inscriptions as Somanatha, which stands in the northeastern quarter of the city. The Banapurishvara Temple repeats the basic double-*mandapa* scheme of the Darasuram monument. Both *mandapas* are entered from the south, through simple doorways; subshrines protrude from the north walls. The plain treatment of the *vimana* and *mandapa* walls is of little interest, except for the pairs of split-pilasters carrying shallow foliated pediments. Deeper niches in the middle of the *vimana* and antechamber walls are capped with the usual eaves and *shala*s. The niche housing the Dakshinamurti icon on the southern wall of the *vimana* is concealed by a pavilion with its own pilasters, eaves and miniature roof, a device first noted at Darasuram. Single pilasters standing in pots are restricted to the recesses on the *vimana* walls.

That Kulottunga III was also capable of sponsoring large-scale projects is illustrated in the Kampahareshvara Temple erected in 1212 at Tribhuvanam, six kilometres north-east of Kumbakonam. As at Darasuram, this comprises an east–west alignment of *vimana*, antechamber, vestibule with transverse entries and twin *mandapa*s of spacious proportions. The outer hall is entered through a nine-columned porch that protrudes from the south wall. The Kampahareshvara Temple is obviously modelled on the Airavateshvara Temple. The plinth is elaborately treated, with friezes of *yali*s framing panels of *yali*s or dancers interrupted by small *shala*-headed niches. The *adhishthana* superimposes a ribbed circular element, a frieze of *yali*s and panels of stylised foliate motifs. Secondary niches headed by fully modelled eaves and *shala*s or *kudu*s alternate with those capped with shallow foliation, the latter appearing only on the *mandapa* walls. The *shala*-headed niches on the *vimana* walls, occasionally framing *jali* windows rather than carved icons, are provided with their own variant *adhishthana* series. The tower which soars upwards over the *vimana* creates a six-storeyed steep pyramid with a slightly concave profile, attaining an impressive height of more than forty metres. Parapet elements headed by *kuta*s and *shala*s at each level are effectively integrated into the overall upward sweep of the tower. Variations are noted on the south porch of the outer *mandapa*. The *adhishthana* here presents a line of miniature dancers in front of which are larger, three-dimensional attendants. The balustrade flanking the single surviving staircase is an elaborate composition with flowing sides and a *yali* accompanied by miniature warriors. The badly damaged horse attached to the extreme southern end of the east face of the plinth suggests that the porch was once provided with wheels and horses, as at Darasuram. The porch columns of the Kampahareshvara Temple have shafts with superimposed architectural facades to which are attached slender pilasters. They are overhung by double-curved eaves.

The outer gate of the Tribhuvanam complex is perhaps the finest example in the Kumbakonam area of the *gopura* type evolved in the late Chola era. The lower granite portions consist of two superimposed storeys, each complete with *adhishthana*, pilastered niches and overhanging eaves. The lower wall series alternates secondary niches with *yali* pilasters headed by eaves and deeply set *kudu*s with those showing split-pilasters and shallow foliated pediments. The upper series resembles more closely the *vimana* walls of the same monument in the use of well-articulated pilastered projections. Secondary niches containing sculpted icons are positioned in both the projections and recesses. The pyramidal brick and plaster tower that rises over is capped with the usual *shala* roof.

The Nataraja hall in the intermediate enclosure of the Nageshvara complex at Kumbakonam, though undated, cannot be far removed in time from the foundation of the Kampahareshvara Temple. Only the basement of this structure is assigned to the late Chola era, but this exhibits the typical three-dimensional carved wheels and life-size prancing horses. Large-scale striding elephants flanking the original access steps on the south side of the hall are now encased in a later domed porch with plaster replicas of the same animals on the outside. Little is left of the original plinth of the monument; the *adhishthana* is mostly a replacement. There are, however, traces of a stone tray complete with a spout running along the south side of building.

The last of the late Chola structures of Kumbakonam to be considered here is the core shrine of the Sarangapani Temple in the middle of the city (see Plate 4.4). This enigmatic structure is difficult to date because a substantial part of its fabric was entirely remodelled at later times. A further problem is that there are no primary records from the Chola era; the earliest inscription dates only from the Vijayanagara period. Even so, the resemblance of the lower portions of the Sarangapani *vimana* and adjoining *mandapa* to other projects of the reign of Kulottunga III described here suggests that the monument was probably founded in the first decades of the thirteenth century, quite possibly during the reign of the same royal sponsor.

The rectangular east-facing sanctuary of the Sarangapani Temple adjoins a square hall with twelve columns, entered at different times of the year from doorways at the two western corners. The lower portions of the building are entirely Chola in date, though there is evidence of modifications in the *mandapa* portion. The plinth consists of the usual arrangement of *yali* friezes both beneath and above panels of dancing figures and overhanging eaves. This scheme is interrupted on the north and south sides of the *mandapa* by miniature pilastered niches headed by eaves and *shala*s. The plinth here is partly obscured by fully modelled pairs of wheels with elephants as well as prancing horses. The clumsy jointing between the animals and the plinth mouldings suggests that these sculpted elements may have been reset when the building was renovated. A presumably original feature is the long tray with spouts at the ends on the east side of the *mandapa*, partly concealing the plinth. This is supported on a line of small, but fully modelled, musicians, warriors and animals, all of obviously Chola workmanship. The *adhishthana*, which is set well back, presents a petalled course, a fluted curving central section and a frieze of *yali*s at the top. Triple projections are seen on the shorter (north and south) walls of the sanctuary, with five such projections on the longer (west) wall. Similar niches project away from the walls of the *mandapa*, the last with a pierced stone screen in the middle. All these portions of the building were substantially repaired and/or replaced during the post-Chola phase. Further traces of Chola period construction within the Sarangapani complex are seen in the Lakshmi subshrine to the south-west of the main unit. Though substantially rebuilt in later times, the original Chola period plinth is still visible on the exterior. This consists of a lotus moulding, panels with fully modelled female dancers, overhanging cornice and *yali* frieze. The *adhishthana* is only partly original, as is evident in the crudely assembled blocks.

Virtually no evidence for temple building exists in the Kumbakonam area in the later decades of the thirteenth century. This is hardly surprising since these years coincided with the decline of Chola power and the invasion of the Kaveri Delta by the Hoysalas from the north-west and the Pandyas from the south.

## THE PARADIGM REVIVED: VIJAYANAGARA PERIOD TEMPLES

As elsewhere in south India, temple building in and around Kumbakonam was virtually brought to a complete stop with the conquest of south India by the Delhi army at the beginning of the fourteenth century. It was not until the 1370s, by which time the Tamil zone had come under the sway of the Vijayanagara kings and their commanders, that temples began to be repaired, extended and re-consecrated for worship. Recovery evidently took time, judging from the modestly scaled and simply furnished structures belonging to the fourteenth and fifteenth centuries; only by the sixteenth century did religious architecture once again begin to rival the achievements of the preceding Cholas. However, the Kumbakonam temples preserved only isolated signs of constructional activity under Vijayanagara. A single grant dated 1385 inscribed on the wall of the Sarangapani *mandapa* is of interest since it is the first-known record mentioning the name of the city as Kumbakonam; yet the grant in no way implies any actual construction.

A more instructive clue to building activity at Kumbakonam during Vijayanagara times is the epigraph (dated 1505) engraved onto a pilaster attached to the *vimana* walls of the Chakrapani Temple. This is the earliest available record for the monument, which is here tentatively assigned to the fifteenth century. The core sanctuary of the monument is elevated on a small rise at the northern end of the principal bazaar street that serves as the commercial heart of the city. The original *vimana*, approached through later colonnades and *mandapas*, is essentially early Chola in style. This close resemblance to ninth and tenth century architecture is possibly the first manifestation of the revival of the Chola idiom that was to become the hallmark of later religious architecture. The Chakrapani *vimana* is best compared to the original unit of the Nageshvara Temple. Indeed, it is about the same size as that of the Nageshvara, being little less than six metres square and is built of the same finely worked, pink granite. The *adhishthana* is the same as that of the Nageshvara Temple, except that a rounded element, divided into narrow facets on the central projections, replaces the part-octagon. The wall pilasters above have part-sixteen-sided shafts enlivened with delicate petalled ornament. The two-storeyed tower, though much altered in later times, is essentially the same as that as the Nageshvara Temple. Another *vimana* to be noted here is that belonging to the Someshvara Temple, standing in a walled compound immediately south of the Sarangapani Temple. The Someshvara Temple repeats the features of the Chakrapani Temple and probably also belongs to the first phase of Chola revivalism under Vijayanagara in the fifteenth century.

Further testimony of temple-building activity at Kumbakonam at this time is provided by a record on the Kumbheshvara Temple, the principal Shaiva place of worship in the middle of the city. A grant of the local Vijayanagara governor dated 1554 is incised on the *adhishthana* of the *mandapa* attached to the focal *linga* shrine of the complex. However, the considerable rebuilding of the monument during later centuries prevents any reliable chronological interpretation. What seems most likely is that the plinth, *adhishthana* and lower parts of the *mandapa* walls, including those *adhishthana* blocks inscribed with the historical record, are genuine Vijayanagara period constructions, possibly of the first half of the sixteenth century. Clear joints distinguish these portions of the structure from the upper parts of the *mandapa* walls and virtually all of the remaining fabric of the adjoining shrine and antechamber, which are clearly later replacements. The Vijayanagara plinth shows a bottom lotus moulding and upper cornice, while the *adhishthana* has a central curved element. Little can be made out of the Vijayanagara walls except the pilaster bases. What is immediately apparent is that this is a modest and unadorned idiom, closer in spirit to the early Chola manner than the elaborations of the eleventh and twelfth centuries. For a resuscitation of the more architecturally and artistically challenging style of late Chola temples, it is necessary to turn to the later constructional projects of the Nayakas.

## TRIUMPH OF THE NEO-CHOLA PARADIGM: NAYAKA TEMPLES

In spite of the substantial building works in and around Kumbakonam during Chola and Vijayanagara times, such as those already noted, much of what now can be observed of the building fabric of the city, its monumental architecture and art, and even of its educational institutions and religious practices are, in fact, a product of a much later period. The Nayakas of Thanjavur, originally governors under Vijayanagara, emerged as independent rulers of the Kaveri Delta region in the second half of the sixteenth century, remaining in power until they were dislodged by the Marathas in 1674.

It is the Nayakas who must be credited with reviving, and to some extent re-inventing, earlier modes in architectural and religious practice. A key figure in what was in effect the aesthetic, cultural and mythological reorchestration of Kumbakonam was Govinda Dikshita. The career of this determined and capable minister who served under both Achyutappa Nayaka (r. 1564–1600) and Raghunatha Nayaka (r. 1600–1645) in the last years of the sixteenth century and the first decades of the seventeenth century is detailed in the *Sahityarat-nakara*, a biography written by his own son. The great constructional projects at Kumbakonam associated with Govinda Dikshita include the foundation of the entirely new Ramasvami Temple, the erection of a set of sixteen matching pavilions on the bank of the Mahamakam Tank and the expansion of the Kumbheshvara and Nageshvara complexes. Further indications of this figure's sponsorship are seen at the nearby Pattisvaram and Naccharyarkoil. While it does not appear that Govinda Dikshita actually resided at Kumbakonam for any substantial period, his personality pervades the history of Kumbakonam more than any Nayaka regal figure. The benefactions of this minister transformed the city into the dense agglomerate of commercial arteries, residential developments, educational institutions and magnificent religious complexes that survive to this day. Govinda Dikshita's sculpted hall of the Ramasvami Temple and Mahamakam Tank pavilions must be ranked as the outstanding artistic achievements of the Nayaka era at Kumbakonam. The impetus to build on a grand scale seems to have outlasted Govinda Dikshita, thanks to the sustained prosperity of the Kaveri Delta region and the lively involvement of lesser figures. The large temples at Kumbakonam offer evidence of continuous expansion throughout the Nayaka period and even later.

Both revivalist and innovative approaches are discovered in the Ramasvami Temple, founded in 1620 according to the *Sahityaratnakara* (see Plates 4.5–4.7). Facing directly north on to the principal bazaar street of Kumbakonam, this complex shows evidence of coordinated planning. The core *vimana* and its adjoining antechamber and twin *mandapa*s of increasing size, all aligned on a south–north axis, stand in the middle of a colonnaded courtyard. A modestly scaled *gopura* on the north gives access to the outer enclosure. The space between this *gopura* and the larger example which serves as the principal entrance to the Ramasvami Temple is mostly occupied by a grandly scaled *mandapa*. This was probably added in the years immediately after the temple's establishment and then subsequently somewhat altered.

The main unit of the Ramasvami Temple emulates the essential features of the early Chola idiom. The plinth on which the building is elevated has the characteristic *yali* frieze above a curved cornice, while the *adhishthana* displays alternating sequences of mouldings including a petalled base and multifaceted central element. Wall pilasters with miniature *adhishthana* mouldings at their bases have part-octagonal or part-sixteen-sided shafts. Niches in the middle of the central pilastered wall projections have pairs of split-pilasters headed by eaves and *shalas*. Secondary niches are distinguished by shallow foliated pediments containing diminutive figures. The five-storeyed tower rising over the sanctuary, punctuated by prominent central *shalas*, is topped with a hemispherical roof. All these features are familiar from Chola architecture; so, too, the stunted *pushpapottika* brackets of the interior columns. While there are no original sculpted icons set into the wall niches, the sanctuary accommodates an impressive set of almost life-size carvings of Rama, Lakshmana and Sita.

The inner *gopura* of the Ramasvami Temple, which serves as a link between the two compounds, repeats the same *adhishthana* series and wall niches of the *vimana*. The outer *gopura*, however, presents the more usual double-storeyed scheme, with duplicated *adhishthanas* and pilastered walls. The upper wall series introduces single pilasters standing in pots in the recesses. Niches on the first and third wall projections on either side of the central passageway are headed by eaves and raised *kudus*. The tower displays the conventional sequence of corner *kutas*, central *shalas* and intermediate *kudus* on four storeys, capped with an enlarged *shala*. Seated lions and *pushpapottika* brackets carry the lintels within the passageway. The outer *mandapa* has two broad corridors meeting at a spacious central intersection. The lack of symmetry in the numbers of columns is partly explained by the walled extension that projects outwards to the west. The walls here show the usual division of *adhishthana* and pilastered bays, regularly broken by simple *jali* screens. The peripheral supports on the open north and east sides of the *mandapa* are distinguished by rearing horses and *yalis*. Four additional columns with carved figures are inserted into the space between the northern row and the outer entrance, thereby achieving a continuous roofed area linking the two *gopuras*. Supports lining the wider central aisles as well as the southernmost aisle are distinguished by pilastered niche extensions accommodating carved figures. The piers defining the central crossing have their core shafts almost totally obscured by triple-pilastered niche extensions. Column shafts have fully developed *pushpapottika* brackets. They carry additional brackets, some fashioned as seated lions, in order to raise the ceilings over the central aisles. All these features are typical of late Vijayanagara and Nayaka architecture and owe little to Chola precedent. This part of the Ramasvami Temple cannot, therefore, be characterised as Neo-Chola; rather, it embodies the innovative tendencies of the Nayaka architecture.

Among the other works at Kumbakonam associated with Govinda Dikshita are the sixteen pavilions distributed around the stepped banks of the somewhat irregular, quadrilateral Mahamakam Tank. The example near the north-west corner of the tank is the only one with sixteen columns, the four central supports being raised on a square dais. According to the relief carvings on the interior beams and ceiling, this pavilion was intended as a setting for the celebrated *tulupurusha* ceremony, in which the ruler sat on a balance to be weighed against bags of gold and other treasure. Column shafts here have triple blocks, many treated as flattish architectural facades complete with pilasters and eaves framing carvings of attendants and divinities. They are separated by polygonal or rounded sections framed by cut-out colonettes. Seated lions beneath the corner shafts protrude from between the colonettes. This columnar scheme derives from Chola prototypes, such as those seen at Darasuram. The small shrines with pyramidal roofs that abut the Mahamakam pavilions are later additions.

Additions to the Sarangapani Temple are perhaps the most elaborate of all Nayaka period projects at Kumbakonam. Unfortunately, no historical data is available to date this part of the building with any certainty. The lower portions of the main unit, ascribed here to the late Chola era, have already been described. Here, it is necessary to concentrate on the upper portions, especially the walls of the *vimana* and *mandapa*, and the interior columns and ceiling, all of which belong to the seventeenth century remodelling of the monument. Many of the elements used here imitate late Chola architecture and are thus revivalist in style. Five projections on the end (west) *vimana* wall show single pilasters standing in pots in the intervening recesses and a sculpture niche set into the more prominent central projection. Three projections on the side (north and south) *vimana* walls have sculpture niches set into the central projection and the two flanking recesses; single pilasters in pots do not appear here. The treatment of the pilaster shafts, capitals and stunted *pushpapottika* brackets all conform to Chola precedent. So, too, the split-pilasters with part-circular shafts, the capping eaves and *shalas* that frame the sculpture niches and the fluted flattish pots with tasselled bands which support the single pilasters. The walls are overhung by decorated eaves, the undersides of which have fully articulated ribs and rafters. Sculpted icons set into the niches, including Narasimha, Krishna and Vishnu in diverse aspects, are more obviously Nayaka in style than the architectural decor.

The treatment of the walls of the Sarangapani unit introduces several variant features typical of the Nayaka era. The pilasters, which create the prominent projections, four on the each of three sides, show miniature architectural facades at the base of their shafts. Split-pilasters framing deep niches carry eaves with curving petalled surfaces and cut-out ribs headed by the usual *shalas*. These elements are reduced in depth over the intermediate shallow wall niches. Small figures of sages and worshippers are cut onto the lower wall blocks between the pilasters. Of particular interest is the treatment of the front (east) *mandapa* wall, which has triple *jalis* framed by mullions enlivened with architectural facades. These screens have contrasting designs based on circles, swastikas, projecting squares, crisscross patterns and even coiled serpents (bottom centre). While almost all these elements find their counterpart in late Chola architecture, the columns within the hall, all with shafts covered with superimposed relief facades, mingle actual Chola originals with skilful Nayaka imitations. The raised ceiling, however, is definitely seventeenth-century work. This high-relief composition is crowded with sharply delineated dancers, acrobats, warriors and *yalis*. That the Sarangapani Temple was entirely remodelled in Nayaka times is borne out by the images that receive worship within the rectangular sanctuary. They depict a colossal reclining figure of Vishnu attended by the goddesses Shridevi and Bhudevi, virtually human in size, all sculpted fully in the round. Oversized images of guardians with clubs standing just before the east wall of the *mandapa* are also of later workmanship, possibly postdating the Nayaka era.

Other portions of the Sarangapani complex assigned to the Nayaka era include the repairs to the Lakshmi shrine, the large-scaled *mandapas* of the intermediate and outer enclosures and the axial *gopuras*, especially the example with ten storeys, which serves as the principal entrance to the complex from the east (see Plate 4.8). Unlike the focal unit, these additions are generally crude in quality, showing an overall concern for grandiose effect than for quality of sculptural detail. This is apparent in the east *gopura* just noted, which relies on re-used Chola period materials for its decoration. These earlier reliefs are simply inserted, not always satisfactorily, into the plinth on which the *adhishthana* and pilastered walls rise. The walls show five projections either side of the passageway, with intervening recesses occupied by single pilasters standing in pots. Further re-used Chola carvings are seen within the passageway, and also in the columned hall of the outermost enclosure. Here stands a south-facing *mandapa*, with seven-bayed openings on the sides, each with two *yali* piers and a five-bayed opening on the north. The *mandapa* in the intermediate enclosure repeats the scheme noted in the Ramasvami Temple, complete with intersecting aisles and side walls, but at a greatly expanded scale. Unfortunately, there is little of the variety of sculpted imagery that characterises the Ramasvami Temple. Yet another aspect of the Sarangapani Temple which needs to be mentioned here is the great Pottramarai Tank located immediately to the west of the monument. This is reached through a diminutive *gopura* set into the outer walls.

The expansion of the temple complex by the addition of spacious enclosures defined by high walls and axially aligned *gopuras*, and filled with subshrines and spacious *mandapas*, becomes common in sixteenth and seventeenth century religious architecture all over the Tamil country. While a full account of Nayaka period features in the Nageshvara, Kumbheshvara and Chakrapani monuments will not be attempted here, it is worth pointing out that all of these temples exploit essentially Chola styled *vimana* types and *gopura* forms. If these architectural components may be characterised as essentially derivative, and therefore quint-essentially Neo-Chola in spirit, they contrast markedly with the more innovative treatment of the columnar elements in *mandapa*s. The supports that flank the aisle leading up to the Devi shrine in the inner enclosure of the Kumbheshvara Temple, for instance, are remarkable for their three-dimensional representations of goddesses and attendant maidens. These figures project well away from the column shafts, attesting to the virtuoso abilities of the craftsmen.

The formal and qualitative attributes of Nayaka temple architecture observed at Kumbakonam apply equally to contemporary projects throughout the Kaveri Delta region, especially at Tiruvalanjuli, Pattisvaram, Mannargudi and Tiruvidaimarudur. Here it is only possible to point out the exceptional features of the diminutive Sveta Vinayaka subshrine in the outer enclosure of the Kapardishvara Temple at Tiruvalanjuli, five kilometres west of Kumbakonam. This recalls the Nayaka additions to the Sarangapani unit in the use of ornate *jali*s set between mullions decorated with superimposed architectural facades. The appearance of wheels and two prancing horses on the plinth of the entrance porch to this structure confirms the re-emergence of late Chola motifs in the seventeenth century. The adjacent *mandapa* displays columns with polygonal shafts entirely covered with tiers of facades, exactly as in the porch columns of the Darasuram monument.

## LATER STYLISTIC DIGRESSION: MARATHA TEMPLES

The last phase of temple building in the Kumbakonam region to be described here occurs under the rule of the Marathas in the last decades of the seventeenth century and through the eighteenth century. That this was a period of dwindling economic and cultural resources is suggested by the reduction in the scale of architectural projects and the increasing preference for brick as the primary medium for construction. Neo-Chola elements are still detected in the *adhishthana* sequences, pilastered wall series and multi-storeyed towers of *vimana*s and *gopura*s, but these structures are invariably rudimentary in form and often crude in execution. Nothing survives of the exuberant carved decoration that was perfected in late Chola times and imitated so successfully by the Nayakas. In compensation, however, there is the striving for new forms and techniques, such as pointed vaults and domes in mortared brickwork.

Maratha additions to earlier temples are found in virtually all of the larger temples in and around Kumbakonam. The octagonal domed pavilions standing in the outer courts of the Kumbheshvara and Chakrapani monuments, for instance, are eighteenth century structures. So, too, the similarly domed pavilions elevated on high platforms are reached by flights of steps. These structures give access to the wooden chariots that continue to be parked outside the walls of the larger religious foundations. Another Maratha period structure is the Nataraja hall built on top of the late Chola period basement already noticed in the intermediate enclosure of the Nageshvara Temple. The Maratha structure employs fanciful windows with richly encrusted plasterwork, also a lofty octagonal dome rising high over the entrance porch. The brick arcades with lobed arches carrying pointed vaults which precede the entrance to the shrines of the Chakrapani and Someshvara temples are also assigned to this era.

Not all Maratha building projects can be dismissed as mere appendages to earlier monuments; several important shrines at Kumbakonam were also founded at this time. An example is the Kashivishvanatha Temple on the north bank of the Mahamakam Tank. The *linga* and goddess shrines, which face west and south, respectively, into a common four-columned *mandapa* present simple elevations with unadorned *adhishthana*s and pilastered walls. The pyramidal brick tower over the *linga* sanctuary is capped with a ribbed hemispherical roof of squat proportions surrounded by eight *kudu*s. A *mandapa* extension to the west leads to an intermediate *gopura*. This is preceded by a large structure with brick piers decorated with corbelled brackets carrying pointed vaults of different heights. The complex is entered through a *gopura* with a four-storeyed tower. That this *gopura* scheme was sometimes replicated entirely in brick is shown in the entryway to the adjacent Virabhadra Temple. Like the Kashivishvanatha Temple, this, too, is approached through a multi-aisled hall with brick piers and pointed vaults. A further example of the Maratha style is the nearby Periyar Math. Its entrance structure consists of a line of five lobed-arched bays, the central one higher and larger, and the end ones blind. Plaster-covered brick piers are raised on a stone plinth into which is set a Nayaka period inscription. Piers are polygonal in section, with frontal pilasters rising up between the arches. The interior is of interest for the central hexagonal dome, seemingly carried on crouching *yali*s and *pushpapottika* brackets. A relief representation of a temple facade adorns the lobed arch over the inner doorway. The gateway gives access to a court with a brick residential structure on the west.

Maratha period religious foundations are distributed along the north–south bazaar street connecting the Ramasvami and Chakrapani monuments. Among the shrines that face east onto this thoroughfare is the Gopalasvami Temple, recognised by a simple brick *gopura* devoid of any tower. A brick hall with lobed arches carrying both pointed and flat vaults leads to the stone built *mandapa* and sanctuary. The Avimukteshvara Temple on the east bank of the Mahamakam

Tank may also be mentioned here. In spite of the re-used Chola and Vijayanagara materials, including several fine carvings, this twin-shrined structure belongs to the Maratha era. Its outer walls manifest a somewhat coarsely executed sequence of mouldings. The most architecturally ambitious Maratha period religious structure in the city is the Kalahastishvara Temple. This comprises a pair of plain, granite walled shrines linked by an open *mandapa* with cross aisles defined by squat, circular pillars carrying round-headed arches (see Plate 4.9). The aisles are roofed with steeply pointed vaults that meet at a cross-vault in the middle. The aisles continue to doorways in the east and south compound walls of the temple; there are no *gopuras*. Another Maratha project worth noticing here is that dedicated to Virabhadra at Darasuram. Entered from the east through a brick built *gopura*, with plinth and pilastered walls of simple design, the temple is laid out in a sequence of two enclosures. In the middle of the outer enclosure stands a domed pavilion with eight circular pillars sheltering a Nandi image. The vaulted corridors on three sides of the courtyard employ piers with finely finished animal capitals in carved brick; to the north is a *mandapa* with a lofty pointed vault. The granite sanctuary and *mandapa* in the inner enclosures are preceded by an open brick hall with ornate brick lotus capitals.

No account of Maratha architecture at Kumbakonam would be complete without mentioning the domed pavilions standing just outside all of the major religious monuments (see Plate 4.10). Raised high on circular plinths, these pavilions generally comprise eight round columns carrying round-headed or lobed arches that are sheltered by an overhang that runs continuously around the building. The dome above is generally hemispherical. Built entirely of brick and coated with vividly painted plasterwork, such pavilions are still used for accessing the wooden chariots that continue to be pulled through the streets as part of the city's festivities. Like the vaulted halls of Maratha temples, these pavilions testify to a completely new phase in the religious architecture of the city.

## CONCLUSION

This account of architectural developments over a period of more than 1,000 years in a limited region of south India has attempted to demonstrate the role of temple styles in creating identities for a number of successive local dynasties. The Cholas may be credited with inventing, or at least perfecting, an architectural paradigm that gave visual expression to their ambitions of creating an extensive and powerful state. Their temples are unprecedented in terms of scale and architectural clarity; the larger examples may truly be characterised as truly imperial in style. It was their successors—the Vijayanagara governors and the locally based Nayakas—who consciously resuscitated this imposing mode, especially for the core sanctuaries of their religious complexes. This revivalist idiom—here termed Neo-Chola—must have been considered an appropriate device of associating newly constructed *vimana*s that housed the protective divinities of later rulers with the temples of their forerunners whose impressive monuments were everywhere visible throughout the Kaveri Delta. The same is also true of sanctuaries that were repaired and renovated by later patrons in the Chola manner, sometimes so skillfully that it is difficult to distinguish original work from later copies. While this revivalist mode was always employed for *vimana*s, the *gopura*s of Nayaka projects were also designed and executed in a Neo-Chola manner. As the most prominent architectural highpoints within the city and its surrounding landscape, such revivalist structures asserted the desire of later rulers to be associated with their Chola predecessors. Punctuated with Neo-Chola *gopura*s of ever increasing height and elaboration, Kumbakonam came to resemble an extension of an earlier, perhaps more glorious era.

This re-use of the past in temple architecture, though widespread through south India, needs to be distinguished from innovations that took place at exactly the same time in and around Kumbakonam. Vijayanagara and Nayaka religious monuments were invariably provided with *mandapa*s that roofed vast spaces between sanctuaries, subshrines and *gopura*s. The outer aisles of these halls as well as the axial aisles of their interiors were lined with complex columns. These supports assumed ornate forms that incorporated vivid, almost three-dimensional sculptures as well as multiple *pushpaottika* brackets that cantilevered outwards to carry huge stone spans. Such *mandapa*s gave expression to the virtuoso capabilities and creativity of local builders and sculptures, especially in projects supported by prominent figures of the day, such as Govinda Dikshita.

Under the Marathas, who supplanted the Nayakas, an entirely novel idiom was introduced into the Kaveri Delta. Perhaps because they had migrated from a region far to the north of the Tamil zone where Islamic building traditions had a long history, Maratha temple architecture is dominated by pointed arches, vaults and domes. Brick and mortar are the principal materials of these constructions, whether additions to earlier complexes or entirely new foundations. The preference for forms and materials previously unknown in this area may be interpreted as a means adopted by the Marathas to affirm their independence from their predecessors. Perhaps the Marathas fully realised that they could never compete with the grandiose projects of the Cholas and Nayakas; thus, they promoted a modest, though highly individual architectural idiom.

## PHOTO CREDIT

All photographs reproduced in this article are by George Michell. The plan (Plate 4.7) has been reproduced courtesy of the Cambridge Kumbakonam Project.

## BIBLIOGRAPHY

Balasubrahmanya, S. R., 1966, *Early Chola Art*, Part One. Asia Publishing House, Bombay.
——, 1971, *Early Chola Temples, Purantaka I to Rajaraja I (A.D. 907–985)*. Orient Longman, Bombay.
——, 1975, *Middle Chola Temples, Rajaraja I to Kulottunga I (A.D. 985–1070)*. Thomson Press, Faridabad.
——, 1979, *Later Chola Temples, Kulottunga I to Rajendra III (A.D. 1070–1280)*, Mudgala Trust, Faridabad.
Champakalakshmi, R., 1979, "Growth of Urban Centres in South India: Kudamukku-Palaiyarai, the Twin-City of the Cholas". *Studies in History*. Vol. 1, no. 1, pp. 1–29.
Dhaky, M. A. & Michael W. Meister (eds), 1983, *Encyclopaedia of Indian Temple Architecture: South India, Lower Dravidadesa, 200 BC–AD 1324*. École Française d'Extrème-Orient, Paris.
L'Hernault, Françoise, P. R. Srinivasan & Jacques Dumarçay, 1987, *Darasuram: Epigraphical Study*. Étude Architecturale, Étude Iconographique, École Française d'Extrème-Orient, Paris.
Mahalingam, T. V., 1967, "The Nagesvarasvami Temple, Kumbhakonam". *Journal of Indian History*. Vol. 45, no.1, pp. 1–93.
Michell, George, 1994, "Revivalism as the Imperial Mode: Architecture during the Vijayanagara Period". In: Catherine B. Asher & Thomas R. Metcalf (eds), *Perception of South Asia's Visual Past*. Oxford and IBH Publishing, New Delhi, pp. 187–97.
——, 1995, "Temple Architecture: The Tamil Zone". In: George Michell (ed.), *The New Cambridge History of India I: 6, Architecture and Art of Southern India, Vijayanagara and the Successor States*. Cambridge University Press, Cambridge, pp. 73–120.
——, (ed.), 2001, *Encyclopaedia of Temple Architecture, South India, Dravidadesa, Later Phase, A.D. 1289–1760*. American Institute of Indian Studies, New Delhi.
Nanda, Vivek, Anna Dallapiccola & George Michell, 1997, "The Ramasvami Temple, Kumbakonam". *South Asian Studies*. Vol. 13, pp. 1–15.
Pichard, Pierre, 1995, *Tanjavur Brhadisvara: An Architectural Study*. Indira Gandhi National Centre for the Arts, New Delhi.
Pichard, Pierre, Françoise L'Hernault, Françoise Boudignon & L. Thyagarajan, 1994, *Vingt Ans Après Tanjavur: Gangaikondacholapuram*, 2 vols. École Française d'Extrème-Orient, Paris.
Sarkar, H., 1974, *The Kampaharesvara Temple at Tribhuvanam*. Department of Archaeology, Government of Tamil Nadu, Madras.
Sivaramamurti, C., 1960, *The Chola Temples: Tanjavur, Gangaikondacholapuram & Darasuram*. Archaeological Survey of India, New Delhi.
Srinivasan, K. R., 1972, *Temples of South India*. National Book Trust, New Delhi.

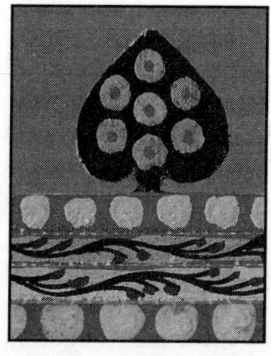

*Chapter 5*

# INDIAN JEWELLERY AND NINETEENTH-CENTURY BRITAIN

## EVOLVING PATTERNS OF RE-USE

**BY NICK BARNARD**

The ways in which Indian jewellery was re-used in nineteenth-century Britain show a complex pattern of development with several different strands emerging over time. Meanwhile, Indian jewellery was itself being influenced by European styles, posing the question of whether any circularity was involved in the process. This chapter aims to identify the different forms of re-use that occurred in this intercultural exchange of influences in the circumstances of the colonial period and the causes that brought them about, as well as examining the processes through which these different forms developed and influenced each other. The widely varying types of re-use that are presented here may also help us to consider what we mean by the term.

## EARLY FORMS OF RE-USE

The capture in 1799 of Tipu Sultan's fortress at Seringapatam by the troops of the East India Company and the death of Tipu in the battle were followed by widespread looting, halted only by hanging and flogging, but there was also an official division of the remaining spoils from Tipu's treasury as 'Prize'. This was partitioned strictly according to rank by the items' financial value (Davis 1997:153–57; Moienuddin 2000: 27). Captain Cochrane, one of the British officers, received a share including diamonds and turquoises taken from the slain Sultan's turban and, according to family records, later had these set in three necklaces and three brooches, presumably European-made, for his daughters (see Plate 5.1). These events are described in a family letter dated 18 February 1878, which accompanied a brooch set with turquoises and Golconda diamonds and acquired by the Victoria and Albert Museum (V&A), London, in 1963. It must be noted that the plant motifs on the brooch described in the letter, which are said to represent the rose, the shamrock and the thistle, do not correspond exactly to those described on the V&A brooch, which is decorated with a rose and oak leaves in the centre, surrounded by oak leaves and acorns alternating with six rosettes of turquoises each with a diamond in the centre, representing forget-me-nots—motifs suggesting enduring love.[1] The identity of the gems in the brooch as Cochrane's, although likely and typifying the treatment of jewels taken at Seringapatam, cannot therefore be conclusively proved.

Relatively little of the Seringapatam treasure survives in its original form as most of the jewels that survived the looting would have been sold for immediate financial realisation, the gold melted down and the stones reset. Pieces that were kept were usually remade. As Mohammad Moienuddin and Susan Stronge have described, most of the jewels in the portion allotted to General Harris, the Commander-in-Chief, were soon sold. The General retained one emerald necklace and one ruby necklace for his wife, which were remade within the family over time (Moienuddin 2000: 29–32; Stronge 2009: 47–54). Almost all the emeralds were recut in England, except for three drops.

Although in the eighteenth century some British soldiers and nabobs in India had adopted Indian dress and worn Indian jewellery, this ceased to be accepted in the nineteenth century. In England, stones were often removed from Indian ornaments to be reset in English-made ones. Lord Wellesley, for

---

[1] I am very grateful to Joanna Whalley and Richard Edgcumbe for their enlightening comments on the V&A brooch. There are signs that it may originally have been made as a pendant and later converted to a brooch. The 1878 letter does not discuss the source of the gold which could certainly have come from another ornament. The possibility also cannot be discounted that this brooch was remade in Paris—perhaps in association with a wedding—some years after Cochrane gave it to his daughter, using the same gems.

**Plate 2.1**
The Abaneri Kunda, Rajasthan, a water structure (ninth c. CE and later) which originally was associated with the neighbouring temple, is today used as the local police headquarters.

**Plate 2.2**

Re-used temple columns in the Quwwat-ul-Islam Masjid in Delhi, commenced in 1193 CE (top), and later pillars produced for subsequent extensions which clearly reflect the earlier examples (bottom).

**Plate 2.3**

A Jaina statue of Parshvanatha in cave no. 8 on Khandagiri Hill, Orissa, has been transformed and re-consecrated as a representation of the Hindu god Vishnu-Narayana.

**Plate 2.4**

The Shantinatha Jaina temple on Vaibhara Hill at Rajgir, Bihar, re-uses the appearance of an Islamic tomb as a means of protection and a signal of alignment.

**Plate 2.5**

The dress and attire of door guardians (*dvarapala*s) on the *torana* gateways at Sanchi (ca. first c. CE), Madhya Pradesh, reflect contacts with people of Western Asian and Greek origins.

**Plate 2.6**

A Hindu temple dedicated to the goddess Kali has been constructed immediately at the front of the entrance of the ancient Buddhist cave at Karli (second c. CE), Maharashtra.

**Plate 2.7**

View from the Jaina temples on Mount Shatrunjaya, Gujarat, towards the Islamic enclosure sacred to Angar Pir, located on the same hill.

**Plate 2.8**
After the departure of the British, the Presidents and the democratically elected parliament re-used the state buildings of the Raj in Delhi to govern the independent Republic of India.

**Plate 2.9**
The fifteenth-century wall paintings adorning the chapels of the Kumbum, a large stupa at Gyantse in Tibet, were painted by Newari artists from the Kathmandu Valley in Nepal.

**Plate 2.10**

This seven-storeyed Pagoda dating from the Goreyeo period (eleventh c. CE) in Seoul, South Korea, represents a local re-use and adaptation of the form of the Buddhist stupa originating in India.

**Plate 2.11**

Mayo College at Ajmer, Rajasthan, was designed (1875–85) in the eclectic Indo-Saracenic style.

**Plate 2.12**

The late nineteenth-century Rajabai Clocktower and University Library illustrate the Gothic revival in Bombay (left), and the stupa on Dhauli Hill (right) is an example of the modern Buddhist revival in Orissa.

**Plate 3.1**
Although the Megudi Temple at Hallur has been
converted to Vira-Shaiva use, it preserves its
former Jaina sculptures on the outside.

**Plate 3.2**
The principal Jina of the former Jaina temple at
Hallur has been taken down from its pedestal
and smeared with ashes.

**Plate 3.3**

The roof shrine of the Jaina temple at Hallur has not been given a new function by the Lingayats using the temple today.

**Plate 3.4**

Frontal view of the Doddappa Temple in Adargunchi village with the *paduka* platform and *linga* decorations adorning the porch.

**Plate 3.5**

The image chamber of the Adargunchi temple accommodates a converted statue of a Tirthankara as well as a Shiva *linga*.

**Plate 3.6**

Appropriated Jaina foot imprints have been marked with the characteristic white lines to signal their Shaiva conversion.

**Plate 3.7**

At Kagvad, a once secret passage leads to two subterranean floors below the previous Jaina temple.

**Plate 3.8**

View into the Parshvanatha shrine, one level below the ground, in which Jaina ceremonies continue at Kagvad to the present day.

**Plate 3.9**
On the ground floor at Kagvad, the former statues of Jaina *kshetrapala*s are venerated as anthropomorphic representations of Shiva.

**Plate 3.10**
The Jagannatha Temple at Puri in Orissa.

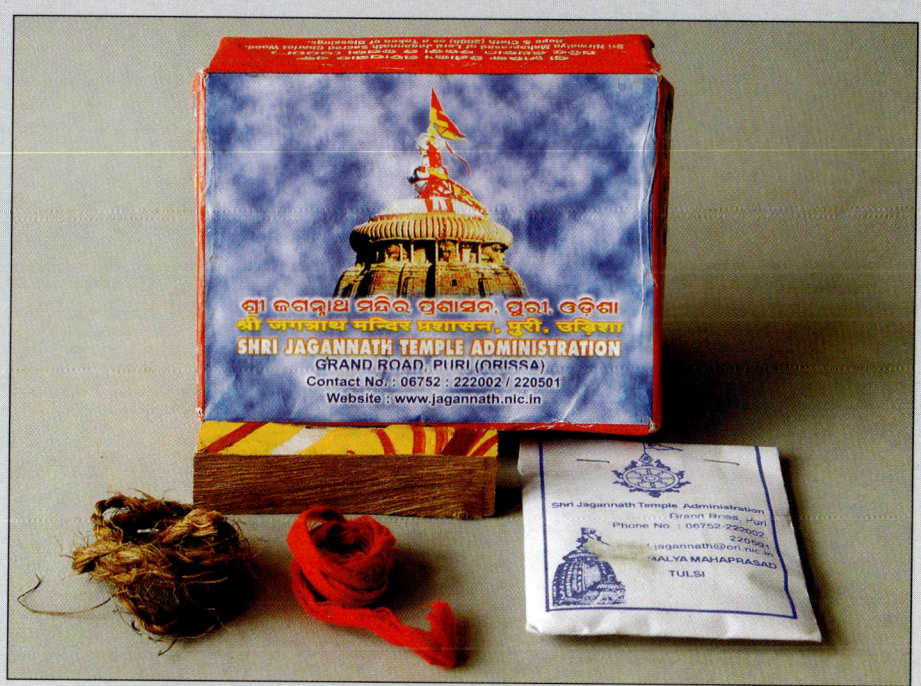

**Plate 3.11**
Jagannatha, Balabhadra and
Subhadra.

**Plate 3.12**
Sacred objects and the
secular state in Orissa.

**Plate 4.1**
Kumbakonam, Nageshvara Temple,
*vimana*, end of ninth century.

**Plate 4.2**
Darasuram, Airavateshvara Temple,
*vimana*, mid-twelfth century.

**Plate 4.3**
Darasuram, Airavateshvara Temple, unfinished *gopura*, twelfth century.

**Plate 4.4**

Kumbakonam, Sarangapani Temple, *mandapa* adjoining *vimana*, thirteenth century.

**Plate 4.5**
Kumbakonam, Ramasvami Temple, *vimana*,
early seventeenth century.

**Plate 4.6**
Kumbakonam, Ramasvami
Temple, column detail.

example, commissioned insignia from Rundell's in 1811 using mainly stones from articles given to him in India (Bury 1991: 179).

The annexation of the Punjab in 1849 was accompanied by appropriation of jewels in the Lahore Treasury by the East India Company. These included the renowned Koh-i-Noor diamond, with its centuries-old Indian and Iranian royal associations, in its enamelled gold armband. The following year, to mark the 250th anniversary of the founding of the East India Company, the Governor General of India, Lord Dalhousie, presented Queen Victoria with the Koh-i-Noor. She wore it, reset in a brooch, to the opening of the Great Exhibition of 1851 (Bury 1991: 316; Field 1987: 27–28), and lent it to the Exhibition where it drew enormous interest but also caused disappointment at its failure to glitter in the way expected. Although Indian diamonds were often faceted, Indian lapidaries carefully avoided any significant reduction in the size of the stone. In Europe, however, stones were cut down, following systems developed up to the eighteenth century, to a geometrically regular, symmetrical shape with multiple facets such as the 'brilliant cut', designed to reflect the maximum quantity of light and making the stone sparkle as much as possible, though often at the cost of half of its weight (Untracht 1997: 317). To produce the requisite lustre, and to increase its value in European terms, the Koh-i-Noor was recut after the Exhibition (*Illustrated London News* 1852: 53–4). From its original 186 carats, it lost almost 43 per cent of its weight (Balfour 1987: 15–27), changing forever the appearance of the diamond (see Plate 5.2).

* * * *

The appropriation of jewels of political and especially religious significance did not sit easily with everyone in Britain: Wilkie Collins's novel *The Moonstone*, published in 1868, when the First War of Indian Independence was quite a recent memory, describes the ill fate that befell all those who came to hold the fictitious gem, looted initially by an officer in the Mughal Emperor Aurangzeb's army from a *murti* in a temple in Somnathpur and subsequently seized by a renegade British officer at Seringapatam until its eventual return to the temple. In his preface, Collins wrote that inspiration for *The Moonstone* came from the Orlov diamond in the Russian imperial sceptre, which "was once the eye of an Indian idol" and from the Koh-i-Noor. He noted ominously that the latter was "supposed to have been one of the sacred gems of India" and that misfortune had been prophesied "to the persons who should divert it from its ancient uses" (Collins 2007: 3; Davis 1997: 153–56, 174–76). The sense of discomfort around the stone is also reflected in a tradition that misfortune would come to any male wearing the jewel, with the result that among the British royal family it has only been worn by women (Roberts 2010: 313).

* * * *

Others among the most magnificent pieces displayed in the Great Exhibition, also taken from the former Sikh treasury at Lahore, were given to the Queen. These included the enormous 'Timur Ruby' (in fact, like the three smaller stones that accompanied it, a spinel) (Stronge 1996: 5–8) and a magnificent belt of emeralds (Bury 1991: 316; Field 1987: 139; Gere & Culme 1993: 103, 124, 135; Jackson & Jaffer 2009: 28; Stronge 1999: 75, plate 80 and catalogue number 85).

Although Victoria was delighted by the "truly magnificent jewels" given to her in 1850–51, she seems to have admired the stones (most of which were not recut) rather than the ornaments they were set in. Although not all were reset, Garrard's of London were commissioned to turn some of the pieces into what were considered 'wearable ornaments', and the process continued under later royal owners (Bury 1991: 316–18). The Timur Ruby was set into a new necklace by Garrard's in 1853, which was shortly afterwards modified so that it could hold the Koh-i-Noor as an occasional alternative to the 'Ruby' (Roberts 2010: 314). Two large diamonds that had flanked the Koh-i-Noor in its armlet had, by 1859, become drop earrings to accompany a diamond necklace (Roberts 2010: 310).

It may be debated whether the use of materials to supply the production of British ornaments, in instances such as Captain Cochrane's Seringapatam brooch as well as the royal jewels, is a case of mere recycling rather than meaningful re-use. In some cases where the gemstones were reset or even recut to suit European taste and had no recognised symbolic importance, this may have some plausibility. However, important stones such as the Koh-i-Noor, which passed from ruler to ruler in a dramatic and hotly contested history involving conquest, trickery and torture, were an essential tool of rulership in India, both for their symbolism and their value. They played a vital role in the pageantry of court as signs of power in the act of *darshan* as the king's subjects beheld him (Waghorne 2009: 78–93) and the Mughal emperors and other rulers were very often depicted by their court painters holding or wearing significant ornaments. The significance of the Koh-i-Noor's appropriation for the symbolic head of the British imperial polity is obvious and goes beyond mere recycling.

In some other instances, such as the Timur Ruby, which was inscribed with the titles of four Mughal emperors as well as Nadir Shah and Ahmad Shah, the historic cut of the stones was preserved as were, in the case of the emerald girdle, the complete setting and Indian form of the ornament. This supports the view that employment in such an overtly political context of important royal gems was a case of meaningful re-use, and that this was done with some awareness of their political and—sometimes—of their historical and aesthetic value, despite the insensitivity of some of the alterations, especially the treatment of the Koh-i-Noor. The emerald girdle, which had been made for Sher Singh (d. 1843) out of stones used by his father Ranjit Singh (d. 1839) to caparison his favourite horses (Bury 1991: 113; Roberts 2010: 313), was greatly admired by the Queen, who lamented, however, that the emeralds were all cut flat (Bury 1991: 113).

Nonetheless, even when not worn, the items were kept as treasures and for their aesthetic value. The Indian enamelled armlet which had contained the Koh-i-Noor was also retained and set with rock crystal substitutes for the three diamonds (Roberts 2010: 312–13). It is noteworthy here that Garrard's necklace design for the Timur Ruby was of 'Oriental inspiration', so that despite its unmistakably European appearance, there was accordingly some attempt to reflect the Indian provenance of the spinels. Prince Albert not only designed an 'Indian-pattern Tiara' (Gere & Culme 1993: 156–7) but also, recognising its symbolic importance, purchased the crown of the last Mughal Emperor, Bahadur Shah II (Roberts 2010: 311). Royal pageantry and its associated symbols became important to the British Raj: David Cannadine has argued in *Ornamentalism* (Cannadine 2001) that these were used to retain loyalty, including that of the Indian rulers known as 'Native Princes'. Queen Victoria herself later insisted on high-ranking Indian visitors to her court wearing Indian dress and ornaments.

## CHANGING RE-USE: DESIGN REFORMERS, ARTISTS AND JEWELLERS

The 1851 Great Exhibition of the Works of Industry of All Nations, held in London, was seen by over six million visitors and represented the first major opportunity for the British public to view Indian jewellery. Popular accounts evinced excitement over its richness and splendour and *The Illustrated Exhibitor* saw "the crowning point" of the display of objects from India as the "gorgeous display" of jewels and jewellery: "a blaze of brilliants and a glow of gems"—diamonds and rubies in their rich gold settings, belts of emeralds, necklaces of pearls, fine silver filigree and bridal trappings "absolutely loaded with large and lustrous jewels" (*The Illustrated Exhibitor* 1851: 328).

However, a wider range of pieces was also on display, including those that, without valuable gemstones, showed fine qualities of artistry (see Plate 5.3). This is the point at which Indian jewellery not only began to become accessible to the general public in Britain, but also—by some at least—appreciated in its own right, rather than for the value of its stones, although the effects of both elements took some decades to work through. Here, we may find the beginnings of a more complex form of re-use than the appropriation of the most spectacular gemstones and the recycling of captured materials. This development came through the use of Indian pieces by design reformers as art objects for the education of the British public and eventually, by a wider public, in fashion. Indian jewellery, along with other art forms such as textiles and metalwork, was admired by the influential design reformers whose ideas were an important force behind the Great Exhibition. They saw the decorative arts of India as achieving a harmony and a balance between ornamentation and form and suitability of decoration to the purpose of the object which many British products had lost. Accordingly, six pieces of Indian jewellery were among the examples of decorative arts acquired for the new collections of what would become the South Kensington Museum (now Victoria and Albert Museum). Its purpose was to improve the quality of British design and public taste by selecting and exhibiting examples of good design from around the world. Indian jewellery played its part in the process of analysis by which this was to be achieved, as influential commentators, such as Richard Redgrave, attempted to establish scientific principles for good design (Redgrave 1852: 49–50, 72, 75–76, 88; 1857).

The catalogue of the South Kensington collection, published in 1853, comments on why the pieces were thought to exemplify this quality: an anklet from Kangra was admired for the nicely contrasted colours, the playful arrangement of forms and the judicious position of the pendant drops, alternating with the lines of ornament within the bands so that no direct line ran out of the subject (Department of Practical Art 1853: 252). The attempt to extract as much information as possible from the design characteristics of the Indian pieces can be seen in the catalogue record of another Kangra anklet (see Plate 5.4) where a diagram is used to support the analysis.

Of the six pieces selected for purchase, four were enamelled and came from the northern half of India, reflecting a clear preference among leading British design reformers such as Matthew Digby Wyatt (1851–1853: plate XI) and other eminent commentators such as the mineralogist Professor N. S. Maskelyne (1868) (see Plate 5.5). Although enamel, especially that of Jaipur, and the treatment of colour in Indian jewellery were consistently praised by British critics over the next few decades, not all the pieces were purely traditional. The royal blue preponderant in two enamelled bracelets from Dholpur in Rajasthan was popular in Victorian England but less typical of traditional Indian enamelling on gold, in which red, white and green were most favoured. A necklace from Calcutta was in the probably European-inspired cut-mole technique with faceted gold surfaces. The only acquisition from the south was work a bold and attractive gold neck ornament from Kerala, although this was, somewhat surprisingly, unfavourably compared to a Burmese gold necklace owing to the use of radiating rather than alternating lines and repetition of forms.

The Indian jewellery shown in the 1851 Exhibition included both traditional pieces and types that were now being made for the British market. Prominent among the categories was silver filigree from Cuttack which, as the Exhibition catalogue stated, was "only worn by Europeans" (Great Exhibition, 1851: 919).

Writers on the 1851 Exhibition and successive exhibitions continued to admire Indian jewellery and to see it as a resource for improving public taste. Charles Lock Eastlake in his influential *Hints on Household Taste*, first published in 1867, illustrated examples on loan to the South Kensington Museum and, describing them in typically admiring terms, endeavoured to use these and others to encourage the buying public to furnish their homes and persons with more aesthetically pleasing objects (Eastlake, 1872: 273–77). Indian jewellery—including the examples shown by Eastlake—had also been shown in the next great London exhibition of 1862, providing a further opportunity for the public to view it (Watson 1862: 258–70).

Reports continued to focus on the harmony of colour perceived in Indian jewellery, but some also admired the ornaments made with considerable beauty, harmony and splendour despite the use of relatively inexpensive materials (Maskelyne 1868: 612; Society for the Encouragement of Arts, Manufactures and Commerce 1872: 28–29; Science and Art Department 1872: 15–16). This was a popular theme among commentators, especially from the 1870s and 1880s, as the Aesthetic Movement developed, criticising heavy British commercial jewellery with its emphasis on diamonds and moving towards the use of more informal clothing and beads.[2] It is likely that the reaction of critics to Indian jewellery was a contributory factor to this development of taste and re-evaluation of European jewellery.

*\* \* \* \**

On her marriage to the Prince of Wales in 1863, Princess Alexandra was given a "Suite of Indian personal ornaments" by the Queen (Russell 1864: plate 22) (see Plate 5.6). Alexandra had an influence on fashion and this gift "established gem-set and enamelled Indian jewellery as a fashionable as well as an aesthetic commodity" (Bury 1991: 513; Gere and Munn 1989: 214). Although an association of Indian jewellery with the royal family in general and Alexandra in particular helped to make it more popular among the public, it was still often regarded as mere 'costume jewellery' (Field 1987: 96).

Some of the qualities that appealed to the design reformers may have encouraged the interest of certain artists in the Pre-Raphaelites' circle in Indian jewellery by the early 1860s. In part, no doubt, motivated by the desire to find ornaments that seemed suitably exotic for the subjects he was painting, Dante Gabriel Rossetti depicted Indian jewellery among the eclectic ornaments shown in the distinctive "large single-figure subjects" he painted from 1861 (Gere 1972: 145). The central female figure in *The Bride* or *The Beloved* (1865–66) wears a south Indian gold bracelet, subsequently owned by William Morris's daughter May (Bury 1976), while in Rossetti's painting *Rosa Triplex* (1874), the figure on the right (facing) wears an Indian necklace of the seven-string type. Other examples in his paintings came from China, Peru and North Africa.

---

[2] The criticism of the emphasis on commercial value and weight of precious metal at the expense of artistry and workmanship is also made by George Birdwood, Curator of the India Museum in London until its demise in 1879 and subsequently Referee for the India collections at the South Kensington Museum and an influential writer on India's crafts (Birdwood 1878: 64).

Rossetti bought the artefacts seen in his paintings from curiosity shops in Leicester Square and Hammersmith; clearly, such pieces were widely available in London at this time (Pedrick 1904: 29, 43). He also borrowed jewellery from the collection of another artist, George Price Boyce (Gere & Munn 1989: 109). The largest part of the jewellery listed in the catalogue of Rossetti's effects, made on his death in 1882, was described as Indian, although identifications were not always accurate (Wharton, Martin & Co. 1882).

The re-use of jewellery from India and elsewhere as exotic props, thus, not only reflected a new interest in it but would help prepare the ground for its later fashionableness, for its appearance in Rossetti's paintings encouraged a new perception of it among the Aesthetes—themselves later influential on fashion—as something that could actually be worn (Gere 1972: 99, 139). Rossetti's interest could thus be seen as the beginning of the re-use of Indian jewellery by a wider British public, led by artists and influenced by the work of design reformers, as props for paintings, as collectibles and ultimately as fashion accessories. Now, clearly, the interest was not merely in gemstones but in ornaments themselves, and often in non-courtly jewellery.

Other artists and designers who painted or drew Indian jewellery included William Burges in 1870, whose work was clearly inspired by interest in its forms (Gere 1972: 237), and Edward Poynter in 1881 and 1887, who used an adapted version of a Gujarati necklace for paintings of Helen of Troy, finding it suitably grand and exotic, unlike the actual jewellery excavated at Troy by Schliemann (Gere & Munn 1989: 82–83). Margaret Burne-Jones, daughter of the Pre-Raphaelite Edward Burne-Jones, who often bought jewellery, also owned at least three pieces of Indian jewellery, set with turquoises (Gere & Munn 1989: 151; Lochnan, Schoenherr & Silver 1993: 218–20, 224–25).

Artists were very influential in the Aesthetic Movement, whose members detested the typical, machine-made, mass-produced mid-Victorian jewellery and admired Indian jewellery's handmade character. The best-known shop catering to their taste, and that of numerous well-known artists, was Liberty and Co. (Gere 1972: 242; Gere & Munn 1989: 71), established in 1875, which stocked traditional, handmade Indian jewellery (Gere 1972: 144). Liberty's first catalogue, of 1881, includes silver bangles, Lucknow beads and a *rudraksha mala* rosary. The popularity of this sort of material by this time contrasts markedly with the exclusive emphasis of the first half of the century on courtly and valuable jewellery. It also differs from responses to the 1851 exhibition where, although more quotidian jewellery was present, interest was predominantly in the more expensive types.

\* \* \* \*

The 1872 Annual International Exhibition showed a vast display of Indian jewellery of many kinds. At the parallel Loan Exhibition of Ancient and Modern

Jewellery and Personal Ornaments at the South Kensington Museum, the lenders included British royalty, George Price Boyce, and Sir Matthew Digby Wyatt, whose jewellery collection included a large number of Indian pieces. By 1872, Indian jewellery was clearly not only admired but also collected in Britain, if only by an elite circle at this stage. The nature of the objects displayed from the collections of this influential and relatively well-informed group is interesting, for although they clearly included pieces of traditional work, there were quite a number of pieces that would have been made for the European market. These included *kuftkari* (which as jewellery was only made for Europeans) in the collection of R. H. Soden Smith—Keeper of the National Art Library and author of the catalogue's introduction—as well as several pieces of filigree, and other items of 'Modern Indian' work and crosses and brooches in Digby Wyatt's collection (Science and Art Department 1872).

The design reformers' intention that Indian jewellery should be used as a source of design inspiration does seem to have come about to some extent. By the late 1860s, interest had developed in Britain in an eclectic range of sources for jewellery. Although the greatest interests were in the antique and in Japanese work, the vogue included work from other regions such as Egypt and India. Robert Phillips of Cockspur Street, London, made a necklace whose plaques are modelled on the enamelling on a Mughal thumb-ring (Stronge, Smith & Harle 1988: 44, 101). The necklace is reversible, with the colours of the pendants on one side copying those on the inner side of the thumb-ring, while the red seen on the other side is a characteristic colour of Indian enamelling. The thumb-ring was in the collection of Colonel Charles Seton Guthrie, which had been exhibited in London in 1862. The Phillips necklace was exhibited at the Paris Universal Exhibition of 1867—where Guthrie's collection was also shown again—along with a locket by Phillips which was clearly inspired by a Mughal mirror-back in Guthrie's collection (Barnard 2008: 102–03).[3] Phillips (1810–81) drew on a very wide range of sources for his designs, including much from the ancient world as well as the examples from India such as "bonbon boxes of Louis XVI shapes, grafted on an Indian pattern in which much of the Indian feeling for colour is maintained" (Becker & Munn 1983; Haweis 1878: 104–05).

The firm of Watherston and Brogden in about 1860, as well as Robert Phillips in the 1860s and early 1870s, used Indian *theva* work plaques in some of their jewellery (Barnard 2008: 104; Janson 1971: figure 44, catalogue number 80). Made in Pratapgarh, Ratlam and Indore and often called 'Pertabgarh work' or similar, *theva* work used finely cut-out designs in gold chased with surface details overlaid on glass, held in silver-gilt mounts (see Plate 5.7). A necklace and matching brooch made by Robert Phillips between about 1860 and 1868 and bearing his

---

[3] Phillips also made feet of gold, enamelled and set with precious and semiprecious stones for two Mughal rock crystal bowls. See Becker & Munn (1983).

'RP' mark exemplifies this well (Becker & Munn 1983: 51). The pendants and clasp cover of the necklace and the brooch are composed of Indian-made silver-gilt cells containing gold and glass *theva* work units in the form of small plaques, which have been enclosed by Phillips in Britain with gold backs and sides, the latter decorated with applied twisted wires. The pendants have been attached to leaf motifs with a rather classical feel and strung on the necklace. Apart from the plaque covering the clasp of the necklace, worn at the back, which has the shape of a slightly elongated octagon, the *theva* work units are in the shape of four-leafed clovers. Unlike the octagon, a common shape in Indian jewellery, this motif is by no means traditional in India and these must have been made to order for Phillips. Curiously, however, although they were clearly designed as a set, the selection of subjects depicted on the plaques seems slightly arbitrary, with two rather similar depictions of parrots (one actually set on its side) flanked by one of larger birds on one side and a scene with mammals on the other, while on the clasp is a lion-hunt. The brooch carries a depiction of flowers, executed slightly more roughly than the others, though otherwise of very similar type. There is nothing unusual about this range of subjects in *theva* work and the slightly odd grouping may suggest that despite presumably commissioning the units, Phillips did not intervene too closely with the scenes to be shown on them.

A tablet of *theva* work from Sir Robert Hamilton's collection was shown by Eastlake in "Hints for Household Taste" and it is possible that this was among the tablets and other *theva* work objects from the same collection shown in the 1862 exhibition. Given Phillips' work with the Guthrie collection, shown at the same exhibition, these could have started his interest in the technique, although *theva* work had also been shown in the London 1851 and Paris 1855 exhibitions (Great Exhibition 1851: 919; Watson 1862: 265). He later exhibited "plaques slabs for bracelets" of *theva* work in the 1872 exhibition (London International Exhibition 1872: 167).[4] The units could be incorporated in boxes (such as a *qalamdan* or pen box presented to Queen Victoria by Maharaja Dalpat Singh of Pratapgarh in 1864), plates and other items as well as in jewellery. Indian designs and actual components of jewellery were thus being re-used by British jewellers both to satisfy and lead a developing new taste.

Relationships between the 'industrial arts' commentators and the leading designers were often close: Digby Wyatt describes examining two Keralan necklaces shown in the 1872 exhibition with Alessandro Castellani (Barnard

---

[4] It is known in the London International Exhibition 1872 catalogue as "Indore work". The 1862 Exhibition catalogue describing Sir R. N. Hamilton's pieces states that "the manufacture is peculiar to Indore", despite calling it 'Pertaubghur' work (Watson, 1862: 265). This is presumably because Indore was one of the three places it was made in and is the nearest big city to Ratlam, and one of the nearest to Pratapgarh, and perhaps also because Hamilton, whose collection must have done much to raise awareness in Britain of the technique, was stationed at Indore, 1844–59, where he was British Resident for Central India.

2008: 97–99, 104).[5] The Castellani firm had pioneered the vogue for 'archaeological' jewellery inspired by mainly Roman and Etruscan prototypes and influenced Phillips and many other jewellers (Becker & Munn: 1983).

Carlo Giuliano, who had worked for both Castellani and Phillips, made a necklace in the 1880s inspired by the Gujarati type shown in Poynter's paintings of Helen of Troy (Gere & Munn 1989: 82–83), although Giuliano's lacks the row of small finials topping the plaques in both the original necklace type and the paintings. In the late nineteenth century and up to about 1912, he and his son Arthur, continuing after Carlo's death in 1895, made several necklaces and other pieces of jewellery with Indian design influences (Gere 1975: 53; Gere & Munn 1989: 72–73, 75, 86–87; Munn 1984: 145–46; O'Day 1974: 58; Untracht 1997: 394).

European jewellery-makers were often happy to blend sources from different regions: Alexis Falize of Paris, for example, made a locket in about 1867 enamelled with flowers in an Indian-influenced style (Bury 1991: 478–80), but the design is quite divergent from traditional Indian enamelling.[6] Many of the Falize designs were in a Japanese taste and the asymmetry of the motifs on the exterior and the style of enamelling on the interior suggest influences from Japan, China and perhaps even Egypt. The overriding concern would of course have been what the public would buy, and it is quite likely that many British people would only distinguish quite vaguely between pieces from India and those from other parts of Asia. However, compared to the very definite and relatively specific interest in Japan, it is if anything surprising that British interest in Indian jewellery, given the imperial link, was not greater than it actually was. Nonetheless, a considerable volume came into circulation. Although some English manufacturers sold copies of popular Indian styles such as *swami* work, more subtle influences from Indian jewellery appeared in, for example, the shape of certain motifs (*The Queen* 1880: 534).

## FASHION: THE NEW POPULARITY OF INDIAN JEWELLERY IN BRITAIN

By the 1880s, the British public had had many opportunities to see Indian jewellery (see Plate 5.8).[7] Following the 1851 and 1862 exhibitions, the two exhibitions of 1872 in London had shown an enormous array and variety of pieces.[8]

---

[5] This is recorded in the Art Referees' Reports of the South Kensington Museum, 6 September 1872 (unpublished).

[6] The locket is V&A Museum number 1045–1871.

[7] These opportunities would have included, for those able to travel to Paris, the Paris Universal Exhibitions of 1878 and 1889.

[8] The Annual International Exhibition, 1872, and The Loan Exhibition of Ancient and Modern Jewellery and Personal Ornaments at the South Kensington Museum.

Indian jewellery would have been in general circulation after these four exhibitions. Interest among the British public in India increased after Queen Victoria was proclaimed Empress of India in 1876; and this included jewellery, which now became fashionable among a much wider public than hitherto (Gere 1972: 186). The Prince of Wales visited India in 1875–76 and the gifts he received there, which included some jewellery, were shown in a hugely popular touring exhibition and formed the principal component of the Indian display at the Paris Universal Exhibition of 1878.[9] This would have greatly stimulated the interest in India. Newly arranged Indian galleries at the South Kensington Museum opened in 1880 and the collection of jewellery and other artefacts was considerably increased by Caspar Purdon Clarke's purchasing tour in India, the objects officially acquisitioned in 1883. Purdon Clarke, who had designed the Indian pavilion in Paris 1878 and had also been responsible for the arrangement of the new South Kensington Museum displays, also designed Indian-style interiors for the Colonial and Indian Exhibition of 1886. He collected much of the Indian jewellery and other crafts displayed in this Exhibition, which further stimulated interest in India. This material was again on show in the Glasgow International Exhibition of 1888. More commercial ventures also increased public awareness of Indian crafts: London's two 'Indian villages' held in 1885–86 incorporated Indian-style architecture with streets and shops where Indian craftsmen demonstrated their skills, including, at the Albert Palace in Battersea, goldsmiths and silversmiths (Gere 2005; *The Queen* 1886a: 3; 1886b: 6).

By now Indian jewellery had become popular as a fashion item among a wide public rather than a collector's curiosity or design reformer's teaching tool. Doubtless, the work of artists and critics had done much to lay the groundwork for this and the development of the Aesthetic Movement and its tastes, so sympathetic to certain types of Indian jewellery, led and supported the new groundswell of interest in India. *The Queen* fashion magazine demonstrates the amount of Indian jewellery in circulation through its notices for purchase and exchange.[10] The magazine reported in 1884 that "Indian jewellery is much worn at present" (*The Queen* 1884: 673). Some of its fashionableness would of course have been at a very superficial and fairly ephemeral level, but, nonetheless, a genuine appreciation among artists and aesthetes formed the backbone of it.

This interest was matched by the availability of Indian jewellery from numerous sources. London outlets included Liberty's, the most influential and

---

[9] This included *theva* work from Ratlam. See Birdwood (1898: 12, 14). The jewellery collection among the gifts was "not extensive, but excellent" (*The Queen* 1876: 3).

[10] I am extremely grateful to Jane Perry who kindly made her research notes on this magazine available to me.

famous (*The Queen* 1886c: 95; 1883a: 57), but others who would have been very well known in their day were Procter & Co. (*The Queen* 1883b: 307) and Walter Thornhill. Some displayed their wares at international exhibitions. *Swami* work, high-relief designs, typically showing Indian deities, could be supplied by mail order by P. Orr and Sons of Madras. Even non-specialist dealers such as Silber and Fleming, who supplied an astonishing variety of household and industrial goods, sold Indian jewellery including a bangle of related type to that painted by Rossetti in *The Bride* (Barnard 2008: 106–07; Silber and Fleming Ltd [1881]: 18) (see Plate 5.9). A lot of jewellery would also have been in circulation having been sold off after the major exhibitions, and Britons resident in India would also have brought back a certain amount.

## THE RE-USE OF EUROPEAN JEWELLERY STYLES IN INDIA

What sort of jewellery was the British public acquiring? To answer this question, it is necessary to consider first the other side of the exchange, the re-use of European jewellery motifs and techniques in India. By the mid-nineteenth century, a wide range of different responses to European jewellery had been adopted in India. Some of these were relatively ephemeral, responding to a short-lived demand, while others had a more lasting influence. One of the key driving forces behind this new phenomenon was the loss of patronage for traditional jewellery as Indian rulers and their courts were marginalised by the spread of British power in the eighteenth and early nineteenth centuries. At the same time, a new market for jewellery emerged in the form of the increasing numbers of British people living in India, especially, from the first half of the nineteenth century, greatly increased numbers of women. Jewellery of an almost entirely European type came to be produced, using European gem-setting methods such as the open claw setting (Stronge, Smith & Harle 1988: 102) (see Plate 5.10). Ornaments of European form, such as the brooch, using European motifs, such as the dragonfly, were made, though often with aspects of distinctively Indian treatment. In the case of the dragonfly brooch, this is discernable through the size of the motifs and three-ball feature on the wings, a common feature of Indian jewellery (Stronge, Smith & Harle 1988: 104, illustration no. 118). Made presumably primarily for British residents in India; there is no special reason to think that copies of European-type ornaments would have been in particular demand in Britain, especially as an inevitable time lag in the transmission of ideas meant that styles were often still being produced in India after they had passed their peak of fashionableness in Europe. This is true too of a south Indian gold neck chain with its clasp in the form of a hand, symbolising love and friendship and characteristic of the European Romantic revival but made around 1853–54 at the very end of its popularity (Barnard 2008: 80–83).[11]

* * * *

The influence of European fashions had a bearing on jewellery worn by Indians, and nineteenth-century Indian commentators remark on the way Bengali men were wearing jewellery much less than hitherto (Tagore 1881: 1040–41; Mukharji 1888: 117). Sourindro Mohun Tagore wrote in 1881 that although the bangles once worn by women of rank had changed little, the bejewelled ornaments such as earrings, necklaces, armlets and bangles, once worn extensively by noblemen and wealthy gentlemen were no longer in fashion in Bengal, and now were being worn only as part of a bridegroom's wedding finery. The turban ornament presented to the titled nobility was still worn at state ceremonies and finger rings remained in use, but jewelled watch-chains and studs had become more fashionable than previously. Thus, as well as abandoning much traditional jewellery except for ceremonial use, Indians gradually adopted some Western jewellery forms, such as lockets. There is an example of the latter in the V&A's collection, probably made in England in the late-nineteenth century, which was commissioned by the industrialist J. N. Tata and contains photographs believed to be of his mother and sister. Similarly, the royal courts that did survive eventually turned to increasingly Westernised forms of jewellery, culminating eventually in the famous Art Deco resetting of the Patiala family jewels by Cartier between 1925 and 1928, the most spectacular of a number of enterprises involving Maharajas and European jewellers (Jaffer 2009: 211–18).[12] European motifs, styles and techniques were thus re-used both by Indian jewellers forced to seek new markets and by Indian consumers wishing to explore new fashions, although the apparently integrative nature of the latter should not conceal the force of the colonial expansion that lay in part behind it. A wide range of adaptations occurred, and the success of each type varied greatly, especially in their longevity. Some types of hybrid jewellery now used were adopted by Indian consumers and became part of mainstream production, while others remained primarily an export art. Some of the latter soon faded away, while others remained popular.

Some European techniques, applied to Indian forms, were absorbed and had a long-term influence. Traditionally, in India, gem settings that were closed at the back were used, such as the *kundan* method where the gem is enclosed and held in place at the front by very pure gold welded into shape at room temperature

---

[11] Ornaments with this motif certainly continued to be made in jet a couple of decades later. I am extremely grateful to Richard Edgcumbe, Judy Rudoe and Charlotte Gere for their comments and advice.

[12] Jaffer records that the pattern had begun as early as 1870, when Raja Rajaram of Kolhapur bought jewellery from Hunt and Roskell's on a visit to London (Jaffer 2009: 211–18).

to secure the gemstone around its edge. As the stone was not exposed to light at the back, reflective foil was set behind the stone to utilise the light entering from the front. European open claw settings, which secured the stone in place with small metal claws at the front but were open at the back, thus allowing the light to shine through the gem, gradually became more prevalent in ornaments worn by Indians. Indeed, one technique called *pachchikam* partially imitated the appearance of a claw setting, with claw-like raised elements surrounding the gem, but retained the closed back and Indian setting technique.

A technique prevalent in Calcutta by the 1850s used faceted gold surfaces to imitate the form used in precious stones and make the ornament sparkle. This was used in ornaments for Indian consumption as well as pieces made presumably for Europeans. It is probable that this derives from cut-steel work, which was developed in England in the seventeenth century and later became popular elsewhere in Europe (Stronge, Smith & Harle 1988: 64–65; Phillips 2000: 64). The technique was applied to traditional types of ornament and some of the objects are of a type only worn by Indians (such as a *kanphata*, in the V&A's collection, a large ornament covering the ear, clipping on to its outer curve, but also partly supported by a chain hooked into the hair) although there are often subtle elements of European influence in their decoration, presumably reflecting the large numbers of British people in the East India Company's capital city. This appears to represent a relatively integrative form of re-use, as local jewellery seems to benefit from the introduction of a new technique.

Traditional Indian techniques were often employed in ornaments made for the European market. Such ornaments typically reveal this characteristic by their form (such as brooches), although some examples show much more subtle transformation from traditional Indian ornaments to European purposes. Among the types of work popular for this was *babul* work (also known as *kikar* or *khardar* work), used in the Punjab and Rajasthan (Jain-Neubauer 2001: 78–79; Ganguly 2007: 115–16, 214–15), in which tiny gold or silver cones are soldered on to the surface of a hollow dome or tear-drop shape out of which the ornament is formed (Farmer 1996).[13] This technique, used for earrings called *gokhru*, came to be used in European ornaments in Delhi in around the 1840s (Kipling 1888: 26) (see Plate 5.11 top).

In such ornaments, the *babul* work could be combined with European techniques such as *cannetille* work, where curled gold wires are covered with trails of tiny gold granules, also visible in the dragonfly brooch (Stronge, Smith & Harle 1988: 104, 138). In one *babul* work brooch, a strongly Indian feel is retained by using a crescent-shape, often seen in north Indian jewellery, for the main ornament and deploying the three fused spheres used in traditional *gokhru*

---

[13] Ms Farmer carried out a microscopic examination of *babul* work pieces in the V&A and experimented in replicating the technique, revealing how it was done.

earrings as a pendant. In such ornaments, it is the Indian techniques and motifs themselves that are being re-used by the jewellers to produce a new type of ornament.

Miniature portraits of Sikh and Mughal rulers, painted on ivory in Delhi, were popular with Europeans in India in the mid-nineteenth century along with depictions of famous buildings in Delhi and Agra (Archer 1992: 215–27). Like *theva* work plaques, these could be set into caskets, but the portraits were often used in jewellery and are here combined with the *babul* technique (Kipling 1888: 26; Untracht 1997: 379–80) (see Plate 5.11 bottom).

*Theva* work, known in Britain as 'Pertabgarh work', is believed to have originated in Pratapgarh in Rajasthan in the late eighteenth or early nineteenth century and thus arguably developed in the context of the burgeoning Western market (Jain-Neubauer 1986; Mukharji 1888: 143; Untracht 1997: 300–03; Stronge, Smith & Harle 1988: 105–07; Watt 1903: 26). Rather than re-using a traditional Indian technique, it could be suggested that it was developed for European and Indian-type objects concurrently, for although a large number of the articles made are clearly for European use, others are of a somewhat more traditional Indian form (Stronge, Smith & Harle 1988: 105). The technique has been called 'quasi-enamelling' and superficially resembles enamelling but it fuses gold onto a sheet of glass rather than fusing vitreous paste onto metal. A delicate open-work design is cut out of a thin sheet of gold and overlaid onto coloured glass base (Untracht 1997: 300–03).[14] This is held in a silver-gilt frame, so that the resulting plaques can be used in a wide range of different types of object.[15] Following its success in the nineteenth century, *theva* work is still sold today and remains in production, albeit in part as a result of government-sponsored craft revival initiatives.

In *swami* work, high-relief depictions of Hindu deities in gold and silver were applied to European-type ornaments, deracinated from their religious meaning, and sold to customers around the world, as well as to Westerners in India (Orr and Sons 1877) (see Plate 5.12 right). Although this was almost certainly derived from *repoussé*-work images of gods in traditional south Indian jewellery, it is thought that the designs were often based on the illustrations in Edward Moor's *Hindu Pantheon* of 1810 (Untracht 1995). The need to consult a British book for accurate iconography would be consistent with European-led production, and indeed the principal maker of *swami* work was P. Orr and Sons

---

[14] The first part of the process was seen by the author in Pratapgarh in 2001. I am grateful to Jyotindra Jain for help in arranging this.

[15] Examples in the V&A's collection include earrings, a necklace, bracelets, brooches and a casket.

of Madras, who, by 1902, employed over 600 artisans in the largest factory of its kind in India (Watt 1903: 490). In this instance, it could be argued that the re-use of Indian jewellery techniques and motifs is being done here primarily by European businessmen rather than Indian jewellers. This Western method of organising production was unusual, however, especially outside the south of India, and small, independent family concerns, though quite often tied to a moneylender and dealer, continued to predominate in most parts of India (Kipling 1888: 26). Orr's work was prominent among the gifts received by the Prince of Wales from his tour of India in 1875–76, exhibited widely on their return, and *swami* work became very popular in England as well as in other countries such as Australia and America. However, a bracelet in the V&A's collection exhibited in the Paris Universal Exhibition of 1855 shows that the style was quite mature by the 1850s.

One of the most thoroughly Europeanised types of jewellery was the silver filigree made in Cuttack and other centres including Dhaka and Travancore, Karimnagar and elsewhere in the south (see Plate 5.12 left). Filigree caskets and other articles, including a pectoral cross and a rosary, were being produced for Portuguese commissions in the sixteenth and seventeenth centuries in Goa and elsewhere, and chests, toilet sets and rosewater sprinklers continued to be exported to Europe in the eighteenth century (Menshikova & Pijzel-Dommisse 2006: 21–23, 42, 46, 58–93; Silva 1996: 17–29, 190–91, 211–22). Jewellery of silver filigree in an unmistakably Western idiom was being produced entirely for sale to Europeans in Cuttack by 1851. Characteristically European-inspired motifs, such as roses, butterflies, hearts and crosses, were common and the objects made included brooches, bracelets, hairpins, cufflinks, bouquet-holders and card cases. As such, this jewellery has few integrative characteristics.

An interesting form of re-use is seen in the case of *kuftkari*, steel decorated with overlaid gold wires (see Plate 5.13). This was a traditional technique used in arms and armour in the Punjab and Rajasthan but not in jewellery (Hendley 1892: 6–7; Hendley 1906–1909: 51–53; Watt 1903: 44–45). However, by 1862, it had come to be used in jewellery made for Europeans and took very clearly European forms, such as the belt plaques, brooches and cross pendants made at Sialkot in the Punjab (Hendley 1906–1909: 48, 51).[16] These were often in a Victorian Gothic idiom, but with the surface decoration using Indian-style plant motifs. The new use of the *kuftkari* technique is almost certainly a result of force. It probably

---

[16] Gujrat, near to Sialkot, was another major centre of *kuftkari* and probably produced similar ornaments.

owes its inception to the annexation of the Sikh kingdom in the Punjab in 1849 when dispersed armourers had to seek new uses for their skills (Hendley 1892: 6). But the ban on the production of weapons imposed by the British after the war of 1856–57 is another possible cause and certainly a stimulus to the re-use of the technique (*The Queen* 1877: 285). Never in demand among Indian consumers, this type of jewellery was already on the decline by 1902.

Aspects of both European jewellery and Indian jewellery thus came to be re-used by Indian jewellery-makers during the nineteenth century as a result of British expansion in the subcontinent. The range of these transformations is considerable, from copies of European jewellery types made for mainly British customers to much more subtle adaptations which preserve distinctively Indian techniques and retain an obviously Indian character. The circumstances which brought them about also vary considerably, from the disruption of traditional production brought about by conquest to the adoption by elite groups of certain European fashions. However, even the latter trend was greatly encouraged by British presence and political power in the subcontinent. Despite the events which brought about this re-use, the skill of jewellers in adapting to the new circumstances is impressive, although several commentators expressed grave concerns about the effects of the demands of Anglo-Indian society on the artistic quality of Indian jewellery (Birdwood 1878: 49, 66; Maskelyne 1868: 612–13; Science and Art Department 1872: 16).

Some of this re-use was carried out by producers rather than Indian consumers. Of the various types of hybrid jewellery, some—such as *kuftkari* or Cuttack filigree—would have been bought almost exclusively by Europeans. Among the transformed styles described, during the nineteenth century only cut-work and, gradually, traditional ornaments using claw settings would have been purchased by a mainly Indian clientele, although they would have continued to buy the Indian forms of jewellery made with, for example, *theva* or *babul* work. It could therefore be argued that the re-use of European jewellery by Indian consumers was initially limited, but, nonetheless, it had a pervasive influence on Indian jewellery over a long period of time, and the increasing fashionableness of certain European types of jewellery among the wealthy had a powerful influence.

## INDIAN JEWELLERY IN BRITAIN: THE QUESTION OF CIRCULARITY

To what extent was the Indian jewellery fashionable in Britain by the late 1870s simply the sort made for the European market? In the first place, it is worth noting that many members of the public would probably not have been able to distinguish between traditional Indian jewellery and hybrid, Europeanised material, most of which would still have seemed distinctively Indian and quite different from European productions. Even among design reformers and connoisseurs, although concerns were sometimes expressed about hybrid jewellery, these types played an important role. As noted, Robert Soden Smith lent *kuftkari* work to the South Kensington Museum's 1872 *Loan Exhibition of Ancient and Modern Jewellery and Personal Ornaments*, and Maskelyne's report on the 1867 Paris exhibition extolled the virtues of filigree, although he also saw it as static art from (Maskelyne 1868: 610–11).[17] Eastlake's book included an example of *theva* work. Among the public, filigree was in wide circulation (*The Queen* 1870: 124a).[18] *Theva* work (*The Queen* 1880: 534) and *swami* work, advertised in 1876 as "the novelty of the season", were clearly popular (*The Queen* 1876: 68).An article in *The Queen*'s in 1884 reporting on the popularity of Indian jewellery also recorded "hat ornaments of tiger's claw", a novel use of a material used in traditional Indian amulets, and European-inspired objects such as brooches and hairpins. Indian ornaments were sometimes used in rather bizarre ways as they were adapted to the alien conditions of British costume and culture. In a very curious example of re-use, silver bangles were in 1884 being used as parasol handles or even knotted into the hair (*The Queen* 1884: 673).

More traditional Indian jewellery of a more traditional type was also in some demand from the public. The 1884 report refers to Jaipur enamelwork, and Delhi and Agra jewelled pendants. Indian bangles, the name derived from the Hindi *bangri*, though by now they had also become a stock European product, were "worn in numbers" in 1883 and Indian silver ornaments were also very popular (*The Queen* 1883: 307).[19] The latter is likely to refer partly to the sort of bazaar jewellery that could be purchased from Liberty's. Traditional jewellery types were often adapted for the European demand and this is clearly true of Jaipur enamel. This was highly regarded in Britain and one-third of the production was sold to Europeans. This was sometimes in the form of European articles such as "lockets, flat, English shape", card cases, and match boxes, although Indian articles like dragon-head bangles were also bought by Britons (Hendley 1883: 38–39).

Of the various types of jewellery the most popular included *swami* work, filigree, *theva* work, Jaipur enamel and silver articles. The first two of these, and

---

[17] Maskelyne was himself one of those concerned about the effects of Anglo-Indian demand on Indian jewellery, especially if Indian jewellers were bid to "copy the viler [...] forms of European bijouterie" (Maskelyne 1868: 612–13).

[18] There are also numerous references in other volumes of *The Queen*.

[19] Bangles may have gained popularity in Britain partly due to the French use of bangles inspired by North African jewellery, but British contact with India must have contributed significantly to their popularity in Britain, as the use of a Hindi-derived word for them suggests.

a sizeable part of the production of the second two, were made to be sold to Europeans. The type of Indian jewellery used in Britain was thus often, though not always, of a type already modified for this market, but still, in most cases, retaining Indian characteristics, which do appear in the late 1870s and 1880s to be partly what made it fashionable. Although a Jaipur enamelled sleeve-link or hairpin was not physically re-used, it is a clear case of Indian techniques and decorative style being re-used in a new British context.

Re-use of Indian jewellery among the Victorian public clearly took place, both through the use of actual ornaments in the new fashions and in the collections of connoisseurs. However, this re-use was part of a complex process in which some European themes had been adopted in Indian jewellery and the hybrid articles were then exported to Britain or sold to Britons in India. In addition to this, design reformers, arguably with some success, used Indian jewellery as one of the many weapons in their battle to improve the standards of British taste and design. In their turn, certain designers were influenced directly by Indian jewellery, and others (more subtly) by the general virtues of good design, which had inspired design reformers, concerns which found some echoes in the ideals of the Aesthetes and, ultimately, in the Arts and Crafts Movement.

## CONCLUSION

The nineteenth century saw the British use of stones removed from Indian ornaments, including those taken by force in times of war, which were then reset and sometimes re-cut, with relatively little interest in wearing the ornaments themselves, followed by a gradual awakening of interest in Indian jewellery in its own right. Despite the appreciation of Indian jewellery among design reformers which had begun in 1851, the extent to which this percolated through to the general public, even during its new-found popularity in the late 1870s and 1880s, clearly had its limitations and should be seen in the context of a general interest in jewellery of eclectic origins. Furthermore, a very significant proportion of the Indian jewellery worn in Victorian Britain was of a hybrid type, for re-use was carried out both in India and in Britain. This hybrid jewellery had arisen as some European and Asian jewellery styles were integrated in nineteenth-century India, albeit with a background of force in the creation of the historical conditions that brought this integration about. European styles, motifs and techniques were re-used and new ones developed in this new context. Meanwhile, further integration took place in Britain as designers responded to influences from India and consumers began to wear Indian and Indian-inspired jewellery. The circularity of the process, in which the Victorians re-used Indian ornaments and ornament types, some of which had already re-used European themes, is remarkable and indicates the complexity which an apparently simple instance of re-use may actually involve.

## PHOTO CREDIT

The photographs for plates 5.1, 5.2, 5.3, 5.4, 5.5, 5.6, 5.8, 5.9, 5.10, 5.11, 5.12 and 5.13 have been reproduced courtery of the V & A Images/Victoria and Albert Museum, London. The photograph for plate 5.7 has been reproduced courtery of the Fitzwilliam Museum, Cambridge.

## BIBLIOGRAPHY

Archer, Mildred, 1992, *Company Paintings: Indian Paintings of the British Period*. Victoria and Albert Museum, London and Mapin Publishing, Ahmedabad.

Balfour, Ian, 1987, *Famous Diamonds*. William Collins Sons & Co. Ltd., London.

Barnard, Nick, 2008, *Indian Jewellery: The V&A Collection*. V&A Publishing, London.

Becker, Vivienne & Geoffrey Munn, 1983 (October), "Robert Phillips, Underestimated Victorian Jeweller". *Antique Collector*, pp. 50–55.

Birdwood, Sir George, 1878, *Handbook to the British Indian Section*. Paris Universal Exhibition of 1878, Offices of the Royal Commission, London and Paris.

———, 1898, *Catalogue of the Collection of Indian Arms and Objects of Art Presented by the Princes and Nobles of India to H.R.H. the Prince of Wales on the Occasion of his Visit to India in 1875–1876*. Now in the Indian Room at Marlborough House, London.

Bury, Shirley, 1976 (February), "Rossetti and his Jewellery". *The Burlington Magazine*. Vol. 118, no. 875, pp. 94–102.

———, 1991, *Jewellery 1789–1910: The International Era*, 2 vols. Antique Collectors' Club, Woodbridge.

Cannadine, David, 2001, *Ornamentalism: How the British Saw Their Empire*. Oxford University Press, Oxford.

Collins, Wilkie, 2007, *The Moonstone*. Oneworld Classics, Richmond.

Davis, Richard, 1997, *Lives of Indian Images*. Princeton University Press, Princeton.

Department of Practical Art, 1853, *First Report of the Department of Practical Art*. George E. Eyre and William Spottiswoode, London.

Eastlake, Sir Charles Lock, 1872, *Hints on Household Taste in Furniture, Upholstery and Other Details*. Longmans, Green, and Co., London.

Farmer, Vivienne, 1996, "Work of Thorns: A Study of the Indian Technique of Babul, Khardar or 'Work of Thorns'". *Jewellery Studies*. Vol. 7, pp. 13–36.

Field, Leslie, 1987, *The Queen's Jewels: The Personal Collection of Elizabeth II*. Weidenfeld and Nicolson, London.

Ganguly, Waltraud, 2007, *Earrings: Ornamental Identity and Beauty in India*. B. R. Pub. Corp., Delhi.

Gere, Charlotte, 1972, *Victorian Jewellery Design*. Kimber, London.

————, 1975, *European & American Jewellery 1830–1914*. Heinemann, London.

————, 2005, "Dr Christopher Dresser: A Commercial Designer in the Victorian Art World". *Decorative Arts Society Journal*. Vol. 29, (Special edition *Decorative Arts Society 1850 to the Present*), pp. 8–22.

Gere, Charlotte & John Culme (with William Summers), 1993, *Garrard: The Crown Jewellers for 150 Years, 1843–1993*. Quartet, London.

Gere, Charlotte & Geoffrey Munn, 1989, *Artists' Jewellery: Pre-Raphaelite to Arts and Crafts*. Antique Collectors' Club, Woodbridge.

Great Exhibition, 1851, *Great Exhibition of the Works of Industry of All Nations, 1851*, Official Descriptive and Illustrated Catalogue, Vol. 2. Spicer Brothers, Wholesale Stationers; W. Clowes and Sons, Printers; Contractors to the Royal Commission, London.

Haweis, Mary, 1878, *The Art of Beauty*. Chatto & Windus, London.

Hendley, Thomas Holbein, 1883, *Memorials of the Jeypore Exhibition*, Vol. 1. London.

————, 1892, *Damascening on Steel or Iron, as Practised in India*. W. Griggs & Sons, Ltd, London.

————, 1906–09, "Indian Jewellery". *Journal of Indian Art and Industry*. Vol. 12, pp. 95–107.

*The Illustrated Exhibitor*, 1851 (4 October), "India and Indian Contributions to the Industrial Bazaar". *The Illustrated Exhibitor*. London, pp. 317–28.

*Illustrated London News*, 1852 (for the week ending Saurday, 24 July 1852), "Re-cutting the Koh-i-Noor Diamond". *Illustrated London News*. Vol. 21, no. 570, pp. 53–54.

Jackson, Anna & Amin Jaffer (eds), 2009, *Maharaja: The Splendour of India's Royal Courts*. V&A Publishing, London.

Jaffer, Amin, 2009, "Indian Princes and the West". In: Anna Jackson & Amin Jaffer (eds), *Maharaja: The Splendour of India's Royal Courts*. V&A Publishing, London, pp. 194–226.

Jain-Neubauer, Jutta, 1986 (December), "Gold Filigree on Glass". *The India Magazine of her People and Culture*, Vol. 7, no. 1, Bombay, pp. 57–61.

————, 2001, *Chandrika: Silver Ornaments of India*. Timeless Books, Manchester and Shisha, New Delhi.

Janson, Dora, 1971, *From Slave to Siren: The Victorian Woman and Her Jewelry, from Neoclassic to Art Nouveau*. The Duke University Museum, Durham, N. C.

*Journal of Indian Art*, 1889, "British Indian Section, Paris Universal Exhibition, 1889". *Journal of Indian Art*, Vol. 3, no. 28, October 1889, pp. 19–22 and plates.

Kipling, John Lockwood, 1888, "Industries of the Punjab". *Journal of Indian Art and Industry*. Vol. 2, no. 20, pp. 25–33.

Lochnan, Katharine, Douglas Schoenherr & Carole Silver, 1993, *The Earthly Paradise: Arts and Crafts by William Morris and His Circle from Canadian Collections*. Key Porter Books, Toronto.

London International Exhibition, 1872, *Indian Manufactures in Side Courts*. Indian Court, International Exhibition 1872, London.

Maskelyne, N. Story, 1868, "Report on Jewellery and Precious Stones. (Class 36.)". In: Great Britain. Royal Commission for the Paris Exhibition 1867, *Reports on the Paris*

*Universal Exhibition, 1867.* Printed by George E. Eyre and William Spottiswoode for Her Majesty's Stationery Office, London, pp. 610–14.

Menshikova, Maria, & Jet Pijzel-Dommisse, 2006, *Silver Wonders from the East: Filigree of the Tsars.* Lund Humphries, Aldershot and Burlington.

Moienuddin, Mohammad, 2000, *Sunset at Seringapatam: After the Death of Tipu Sultan.* Orient Longman, Hyderabad.

Mukharji, T. N., 1888, *Art-Manufactures of India.* The Superintendent of Government Printing, Calcutta, India.

Munn, Geoffrey, 1984, *Castellani and Giuliano: Revivalist Jewellers of the Nineteenth Century.* Trefoil Books, London.

O'Day, Deirdre, 1974, *Victorian Jewellery.* Letts, London.

Orr, P. and Sons, 1877, *P. Orr and Sons, Manufacturing Jewellers, Gold and Silversmiths, to His Royal Highness the Prince of Wales, by special appointment.* (Trade catalogue) Madras.

Pedrick, Gale (ed.), 1904, *Recollections of Dante Gabriel Rossetti and His Circle (Cheyne Walk Life) by the Late Henry Treffry Dunn.* E. Mathews, London.

Phillips, Clare, 2000, *Jewels and Jewellery.* V&A Publications, London.

*The Queen, The Lady's Newspaper and Court Chronicle,* 1870, "'The Exchange' – 'Ornaments'". *The Queen.* Vol. 47, 19 February 1870, pp. 124[a]–124[b].

———, 1876, "Indian 'Swami' Jewellery—The Novelty of the Season". *The Queen.* Vol. 60. S.O. Beeton, London, 22 July 1876, p. 68.

———, 1877, "The Inlaid Work of India". *The Queen.* vol. 62, S.O. Beeton, London, 27 October 1877, pp. 285–86.

———, 1880, *The Queen,* vol. 67, S.O. Beeton, London, p. 534.

———, 1883a, "London Fashions". *The Queen.* Vol. 73, S.O. Beeton, London, 20 January 1883, p. 57.

———, 1883b, "London Fashions". *The Queen.* Vol. 73, S.O. Beeton, London, 7 April 1883, pp. 306–07.

———, 1884, "Dress and Fashion. Fashions of the day". *The Queen.* Vol. 75, S.O. Beeton, London, 14 June 1884, p. 673.

———, 1886a, "India in London". *The Queen.* Vol. 79, S.O. Beeton, London, 2 January 1886, p. 3.

———, 1886b, "The Indian Village at the Albert Palace". *The Queen.* Vol. 79, S.O. Beeton, London, 2 January 1886, p. 6.

———, 1886c, "Specimens of Eastern and Modern jewellery from the collection of Messrs Liberty and Co". *The Queen.* Vol. 79, S.O. Beeton, London, 23 January 1886, pp. 95–96.

Redgrave, Richard, 1852, "Report on Design: Prepared as a Supplement to the Report of the Jury of Class XXX, of the Exhibition of 1851". William Clowes and Sons, London.

———, 1857, *Paris Universal Exhibition.* Report on the Present State of Design as applied to Manufactures. George E. Eyre and William Spottiswoode, London.

Roberts, Hugh, 2010, "State Jewellery". In: Jonathan Marsden (ed.), *Victoria & Albert: Art & Love.* Royal Collection Enterprises Ltd., London, pp. 309–16.

Russell, William Howard, Sir, 1864, *A Memorial of the Marriage of H. R. H. Albert Edward Prince of Wales and H. R. H. Alexandra Princess of Denmark*. Day & Son, London.

Science and Art Department, South Kensington Museum, 1872, *Catalogue of the Loan Exhibition of Ancient and Modern Jewellery and Personal Ornaments*, MDCCCLXXII. John Strangeways, London.

Silber and Fleming Ltd, *Latest Novelties in Jewellery, Watches, Card Cases, Optical Goods etc.* J. S. Virtue & Co., London.

Silva, Nuno Vassallo (ed.), 1996, *The Heritage of Rauluchantim*. Museu de São Roque, Lisboa.

Society for the Encouragement of Arts, Manufactures and Commerce, 1872, "Reports on the London International Exhibition of 1872". Bell and Daldy, London.

Stronge, S., 1996, "The Myth of the Timur Ruby". *Jewellery Studies*. Vol. 7, pp. 5–12.

———, (ed.), 1999, *Arts of the Sikh Kingdoms*. V&A Publications, London.

———, 2009, *Tipu's Tigers*. V&A Publishing, London.

Stronge, S., N. Smith & J. C. Harle, 1988, *A Golden Treasury: Jewellery from the Indian Subcontinent*. V&A Museum, London, in association with Mapin Publishing, Ahmedabad.

Tagore, S. M., 1881, *Mani Mala or a Treatise on Gems*, Vol. 2. I. C. Bose & Co., Calcutta.

Untracht, O., 1995, "Swami Jewellery: Cross-Cultural Ornaments". In: S. Stronge (ed.), *The Jewels of India*. Marg Publications, Bombay, pp.117–32.

———, 1997, *Traditional Jewelry of India*. Thames and Hudson, London and Harry N. Abrams, New York.

Waghorne, J., 2009, "The Power of Public Splendour". In: A. Jackson and A. Jaffer (eds), *Maharaja: The Splendour of India's Royal Courts*. V&A Publishing, London, pp. 76–104.

Watson, J. Forbes, 1862, *The International Exhibition of 1862*, A Classified and Descriptive Catalogue of the Indian Department. Printed for Her Majesty's Commissioners, London.

Watt, G., 1903, *Indian Art at Delhi, 1903*, Being the Official Catalogue of the Delhi Exhibition, 1902–03. Superintendent of Government Printing, Calcutta, India.

Wharton, Martin & Co., Auctioneers, 1882, 16, Cheyne Walk, Chelsea. *The Valuable Contents of the Residence of Dante G. Rossetti (Deceased), to be sold by Auction*. (Sale catalogue) London.

Wyatt, M. Digby, 1851–53, *The Industrial Arts of the Nineteenth Century: A Series of Illustrations of the Choicest Specimens Produced by Every Nation at the Great Exhibition of the Works of Industry, 1851*. Day and Son, London.

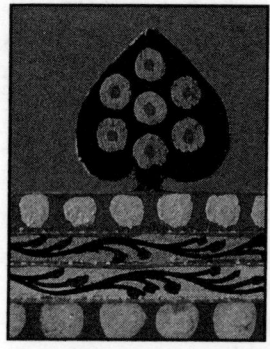

*Chapter 6*

# RE-USE IN THE YAKSHAGANA THEATRE OF COASTAL KARNATAKA

**BY KATRIN BINDER**

## INTRODUCTION

This chapter will explore aspects of re-use in the yakshagana dance drama performed in the coastal districts of Karnataka. A brief introduction to the art form below will provide an impression of Yakshagana's artistic complexity which integrates text, music, dance, improvised speech, stylised makeup and costumes. During its history as well as today, Yakshagana has been embedded in several sociocultural and religious contexts which often overlap. These inherent and contextual circumstances make Yakshagana a site of complex instances of re-use.

From a theoretical viewpoint, re-use in Yakshagana could be categorised broadly into textual and performative. In this chapter, I focus on textual examples of re-use in Yakshagana. I identify re-use of content as well as form in old and modern Yakshagana texts. Yakshagana texts were historically based on the epics and *Purana*s, with the poets drawing on the *bhakti* literature of the Kannada Dasas as well. Today, writers re-use storylines from diverse sources including local oral epics and popular films. In a particularly revealing case, I will show how the Yakshagana form of textual composition has been re-used itself. Performative examples of re-use in Yakshagana include its relationship with the religious storytelling genre Harikatha Kalakshepam or, more recently, ample borrowings from Indian cinema in its singing styles and dance movement repertoire. Re-use of Yakshagana can also be documented in the performative domain, with modern Kannada dramatists drawing on Yakshagana staging techniques in developing a contemporary indigenous theatre idiom.

This chapter will illustrate how re-use of form and content in Yakshagana texts is about the integration of material and techniques. In my examples, re-use surfaces as either a kind of 'copy-paste' method or as a blueprint for the creative adaptation of material. While the historical motivations for re-use are multilayered and hard to pin down, it can be shown that re-use is employed by Yakshagana writers and performers today to ensure the art's popularity and survival. To varying degrees, re-use in Yakshagana thus serves as a moderate means of emancipation and an antidote against existential anxieties.

## THE YAKSHAGANA THEATRE OF COASTAL KARNATAKA

Yakshagana (literally song or music of the *yaksha*s) is the name of several similar genres of performing arts across present-day Karnataka, Andhra Pradesh and Tamil Nadu. This chapter will focus on the dance-drama popular in coastal Karnataka. It is locally known as *bayalata* (play in the open air or open field) or simply referred to as *ata* (play). As is the case with many Indian performing arts, Yakshagana's origins and history remain largely undocumented. One theory is that Yakshagana originated as a system of music which existed prior to the formation of the Carnatic and Hindustani music styles (Karanth 1997: 82). Manuscript evidence suggests that Yakshagana as a style of literary composition in the Kannada language was firmly established by the early seventeenth century (Binder 2008: 323; Karanth 1997: 217ff). It is likely that Yakshagana as a performance genre developed around the same time (Binder 2008: 339). Kannada Yakshagana shares similarities in performance structure, costume, make-up, content and contextual situatedness with other theatrical forms across south India as well as some north Indian forms. Like these, it probably evolved from narrative story-telling genres (Binder 2008: 339).

Today, there are two sub-styles prevalent in coastal Karnataka. The southern style (*tenku-tittu*) (see Plate 6.1) is at home in Dakshina Kannada district and the northern areas of Kasaragod district in Kerala. The northern style (*badagu-tittu*) belongs to Udupi and parts of Uttara Kannada districts (see Plate 6.2). The two styles differ in music, dance style, costume and make-up, but use the same texts and share an identical performance format. Approximately fifteen professional troupes are active in each style at present. Between 2003 and 2005, I documented twenty-three troupes giving 'vow' performances (*harake-ata*). Customarily, people commission a performance in fulfilment of a vow (*harake*) connected with progeny or wealth. During the same period, seven troupes were organised along 'commercial' lines. This means that they perform inside tents (thus they are called 'tent troupes') and charge admission. Regardless of these differences, all troupes are attached to a temple in the region, most of them to a temple of a goddess. The relationship with the 'home temple' ranges from nominal attachment in the case of most commercial troupes to being directly managed and run by the board of temple trustees as are some *harake* troupes (Binder 2008: 254ff).

A typical performance lasts an entire night. The professional troupes perform almost every single night during the season from November to April. This season corresponds to the dry months of the year. Until the late nineteenth century, the plots presented on stage were exclusively based on the epics and *Puranas*. Since then, the scope has widened rapidly and boundlessly to incorporate local legends, historical events and figures, plots drawn from novels and popular Kannada movies. The 'play-texts' (*prasanga*s) normally consist of songs and poems. In performance, these are sung by the *bhagavata* or singer. He controls the rhythm of the performance with the cymbals (*tala*), and he is further accompanied by the *maddale* and *cende* drums and a harmonium to provide the drone (see Plate 6.3). The 'actors' dance to his singing, then 'improvise' their spoken lines. Content and style of these speeches is controlled by orally transmitted conventions. Yakshagana retains its own musical system. The dance is fast and vigorous, characterised by intricate footwork, jumps and twirls (see Plate 6.4). The use of hand gestures and codified facial expressions is limited in Yakshagana. Battles form the climax of most performances. Costume and make-up are colourful and elaborate with characteristic headdresses and ornaments suggestive of armour.

Historically an all-male affair, Yakshagana's vibrant amateur scene today comprises women and children. In the past, most performers would have been engaged in agricultural activities or other jobs during the off season, and even today the boundaries between the professional and amateur scene are fluid. In recent decades, the local Hindu religious establishment has taken an interest in Yakshagana, and the educated elite have discovered it as a platform to show off their eloquence. While there is some uncertainty as to the social background of artists in the past, there is no indication for one particular caste having been assigned with the performance of Yakshagana in a rights-cum-obligation system, which structured village life in pre-colonial times, including its ritual and performing arts (Bruin 1999: 62, 143ff). Sponsors of *harake-ata*s, historically from the wealthy landowning communities, nowadays come from a broader spectrum of the society and the audiences are equally socially diverse.

## TEXTUAL INSTANCES OF RE-USE IN YAKSHAGANA: 'OLD' *PRASANGAS*

A Yakshagana 'play-text' is called *prasanga*, which, in this context, means 'subject', 'topic' or 'event' (Kittel 1894: 1047) and is commonly translated as 'episode' (for example, Bapat 1998: 29). Unlike European or Sanskrit dramatic texts, they do not contain the lines to be spoken by the characters. They only contain songs and verses and very few prose passages. The combination of songs set in *raga* and *tala* with verses in certain Kannada metres in a single poetic work is characteristic of *prasanga*s. In the *prasanga*s themselves, this is referred to as the 'Yakshagana style'. In performance, the *bhagavata* will select certain verses from the *prasanga* text. During his singing, the actor-dancers enact the contents of the verses through dance and then elaborate on them in 'improvised' dialogues.

In exploring the depth of re-use in Yakshagana, I will begin by describing examples from the 'old' Yakshagana *prasanga*s. Normally, those texts written before the late nineteenth century are called 'old' (*hale*) *prasanga*s, while those written afterwards are the so-called new (*hosa*) *prasanga*s. In general, 'old' Yakshagana texts re-use stories, motifs and themes from the Sanskrit epics and *Purana*s. This is not unique to Yakshagana, as many theatrical performing arts in India draw heavily on this body of literature. The repertoire of re-used episodes is also strikingly similar across many genres. As far as I am aware, the popularity of episodes taken from the *Ashvamedha-parvan* of the *Mahabharata* is unique to Kannada Yakshagana. The reason for this popularity is that one of the most famous Kannada epics, the *Jaimini Bharata*, treats precisely this part of the great Sanskrit work. As I will show, Yakshagana poets have extensively re-used this and other Kannada epic poetry and its subject matter, prosody and language. Although there are speculations that Yakshagana began as a theatre of the *Ramayana* (Joshi 1994: 140), it is not limited to the performance of episodes from either the *Ramayana* or the *Mahabharata* but the repertoire also includes numerous *prasanga*s based on some of the major *Purana*s. Unlike some other forms of Yakshagana, especially those associated with the Thanjavur court in Andhra Pradesh (Rao 2004: 529), there is no evidence that the coastal styles have ventured into courtly theatre and associated subject matter. It is significant to note that the distinction between 'old' and 'new' *prasanga*s have a temporal dimension as well as implying a shift of content. Today, an 'old' *prasanga* may be written fairly recently but be based on the 'old' epics and *Purana*s, whereas a 'new' *prasanga* denotes one with a fictitious, historical or other plot. Given the fact that the overwhelming majority of troupes are affiliated to a temple of Devi, it is interesting that the plays and their performance in the past were mostly expressive of Vaishnava *bhakti*. Currently, only two professional troupes are attached to Vishnu temples. The reasons for this are not known, but as I will show, in recent years, the legends attached to the troupes' home temples as well as those of major pilgrimage centres have gained popularity with sponsors of vow performances.

The case of the adaptation of Sanskritic material for the Yakshagana stage is a particularly good example to explore how re-use in a performing art can be complex and involve several layers of material, technique and time. The main aspect of complexity in this case is due to the fact that the material is not taken directly from the Sanskrit 'originals'. Some authors of *prasanga*s may have had knowledge of Sanskrit, but one can easily show that they drew more immediately on the regional, Kannada-language versions of the *Mahabharata*, *Ramayana* and the major *Purana*s. The Kannada writer Shivarama Karanth, who pioneered research into Yakshagana, remarked: "Almost all the early *prasanga*s drew their material from various Kannada versions of our ancient epics and mythologies [*Purana*s]. These versions were well known at the time" (Karanth 1997: 56). In the context of the present chapter, it should be remembered that these 'translations' or 'adaptations' are in fact re-using Sanskrit sources. They are remarkably faithful to the 'original' while reworking the material in a new language and often with a particular motivation or agenda in mind. For example, the patron of the author appears as one of the main heroes or the text is used to illustrate the saving grace of the author's chosen deity. As sources for early *prasanga* texts, the *Karnata Bharata Kathamanjari* (also known as the *Gadugina Bharata*), the *Jaimini Bharata*, the *Kaushika* Ramayana and the *Torave Ramayana* as well as a *Bhagavata* are the most important works (Karanth 1997: 56). Probably written in the fifteenth and early sixteenth century, the texts precede the earliest *prasanga*s only marginally. These works are still held in high esteem by scholars of Kannada literature and enjoy considerable popularity to this day. In particular, the *Karnata Bharata Kathamanjari* and the *Jaimini Bharata* have a performance tradition of their own. They are commonly recited musically or sung, sometimes in semi-theatrical style with interspersed ad hoc commentaries (this is called *gamaka*, but can also take the form of a Harikatha performance). The popularisation of the material in the vernacular was thus already effectively achieved through these epic poems so that their further adaptation in the Yakshagana style (and, from a certain point onwards, for the Yakshagana stage) must have been motivated by different objectives.

Before speculating on these points, however, I will illustrate how the Yakshagana poets used a kind of 'copy–paste' form of re-use in reworking the Kannada sources. Close comparison reveals that they took metaphors, phrases and verses from these texts. Karanth already noted: "Authors of Yakshagana plays have often bodily lifted many stanzas from them [the source texts] and used them in their plays" (Karanth 1997: 70). In the following example, a verse from the *prasanga Abhimanyu Kalaga* can be traced back to the *Kannada Bharata*. Here, Kumara Vyasa writes:

> shivana beeDida sharava tege gaaN / Diivava bigi ninnishTadaivava / tavakadali nii beeDikombudu paramasadgatiy / avarivara havaNalla guru muni / davagaDisidare niluvanaavanu / bavarakeeLeeLendu jaridaru duutararjunana. (7, 4, 25/7, 5, 30)[1]

The *prasanga* reads:

> shivanoL beeDida sharava / nii tege gaaNDii / vava mige kuladaivava / tavakadi beeDiko avarivarantalla / avagaDisalu guruvingidir yaaruNTu. (21, 2)

Or compare the following verses between the *Kannada Bharata* and *Abhimanyu Kalaga*:

> terahugoDu phaDa phaDa jayadratha / herategedu saarenuta huuNiga / nurubidare maaraantu bhiimana kaDuha nilisidanu / maredu kaLeyabhimanyuvanu mai / mareyadennali kaadu maatina birubinali phalavillenuta kengoola toDacidanu. (7, 5, 64/7, 6, 69)

which becomes:

> terahugoDu phaDa phaDa jayadratha / horategedu nillendu / huuNiga / rurubidaDe maaraantu nindanu / harana varadi // terahugoDenindinali naDe naDe / maredu kaLeyabhimanyuvanu shashi / dharana kaaruNyaavalookana / viruvudenage //. (78, 3–4)

Within the scope of this chapter, it is not possible to go into detail but these two examples bear out the striking similarities between the *prasanga* and the epic. In my more comprehensive comparison it becomes clear that, in many cases, the dissimilarities are occasioned by the change of metre. Thus, apart from the literal overlaps, one can find that the author of the *prasanga* has substituted synonyms or used a different phrase to fit his metre.

---

[1] To make the textual examples more easily understood and the comparison clearer, I have adopted a compromised transliteration, which denotes long vowels through double vowels and cerebral consonants through capital letters (except cerebral 's', which is given as 'sh' and not distinguished). This transliteration is confined to textual examples in the present chapter. The verse numbering refers to Kuvempu & Ayyangar (2000) and Prasanna (2001) for the *Karnata Bharata*, and Fischer (2004) for *Abhimanyu Kalaga*.

Tracing metaphors, puns and some striking phrases from *Abhimanyu Kalaga*, I was able to confirm that many are directly taken from Kumara Vyasa (Fischer 2004: 79–80). What struck me most, however, was that a considerable number of metaphors have their roots in the Sanskrit *Mahabharata*. For instance, Abhimanyu's defeat by the Kaurava warriors is compared to that of a lion cub against elephants. While the phrase in the *prasanga* "*halavu gajavondaagi simhana mariyannu / kolisadantaaytu*" (95) directly invokes the *Karnata Bharata*'s "*halavu gajagaLu simha shishuvanu / gelida pariyantaaytu*" (7, 6, 65/7, 7, 68), the comparison also recalls the diction of the Sanskrit. A comparison between the youthful hero Abhimanyu and the adventures of Shiva's son Guha (the god of war, also known as Karttikeya) was found both in the *prasanga* and in the Sanskrit *Mahabharata*, while absent from the Kannada version (Fischer 2004: 80).

Not only content and vocabulary, but also compositional forms are re-used by the Yakshagana poets. Significantly, the same works that are the main referents for re-use in content also provide the sources for Yakshagana poetic forms. The most obvious formal difference between the epics and the *prasanga*s is that the epics are kept in a single metre throughout while the *prasanga*s are written in a combination of poems in a variety of metres alongside songs. The metres that are used in both the epics and the *prasanga*s belong to those Kannada metres counted in morae, the most popular being a group of six metres called *shatpadi*s with six metrical feet each. Occasionally, Sanskrit metres are used, predominantly in invocational stanzas which are either written in Sanskrit or exhibit highly Sanskritised vocabulary. The compositional format of Yakshagana songs is closely modelled on the songs of the Dasas (Dasa-*pada*). The Dasas were itinerant saint-singers in the late fifteenth and sixteenth century whose poetry flourished during the last decades of the Vijayanagara empire (collapsed 1565). In both, the songs of the Dasas and Yakshagana songs, the particular combination of *raga* and *tala* define the compositional form. The most important metres of the Dasa songs, the *ragale*s, have also been used in Yakshagana songs.

In the songs of Yakshagana *prasanga*s, the *raga–tala* combination is metrically more specific than the underlying metre (most often one of the morae-counting metres such as *shatpadi*s, *ragale*s or similar) and also determines the performance of the song. For example, a common compositional form is songs written in *bhamini-shatpadi* and *trivude-tala* (Bharadvaja 1998: 88). *Bhamini-shatpadi*'s six lines are defined as follows: In accordance with the general rules for all *shatpadi*s, the first three lines and the second three lines show an identical pattern. Additionally, the first two lines in each unit have the same number of morae, substructured in the same way. The final line of each unit always has half an extra line and ends in a long mora (the final mora counts long by definition, even if it is technically short). Thus, the pattern of morae for *bhamini* is:

3+4, 3+4
3+4, 3+4
3+4, 3+4, 3+4 + 2
3+4, 3+4
3+4, 3+4
3+4, 3+4, 3+4 + 2
(Kittel 1875: 122)

Within this pattern, certain combinations of long and short morae are es-
chewed, namely short–long in the three-morae sub-units, as well as short–long
and short–long–short in the groups of four morae. An example for a verse in
*bhamini* metre is the following verse from the *prasanga Shri Krishna Sandhana* attributed to Devidasa:

*hariya kaTTuvanivara kaaryava[-]*
*naritu gangaajaatanusurida*
*haraharaa maadhavana bigiva samarthanivanahude*
*maraNavanu bayasidiralaadasha*
*shirana soodararakaTa niiven-*
*dirade dhRtaraaSTrange tiLuhalu endanava marugi //* (Devidasa 2000)

The basic pattern clearly reveals why *bhamini-shatpadi* goes well with songs set
in *trivude tala*: This *tala* is counted as a seven- or fourteen-beat rhythm, hence fits
the number of morae of the poetic metre.

My aim in going into considerable detail here is to illustrate the way a 'basic'
metre intended for a recitative style of performance is re-used and adapted to
meet the requirements of musical rendering. It will emerge that the Yakshagana
poets creatively re-used the metrical patterns of earlier and contemporary works
and thus in all likelihood contributed to the variety of compositional forms in
Kannada literature. In the following example, I show how the metre coalesces
with the *tala* but also how the exigencies of the *tala* appear to override certain
aspects of the metre. The song is from *Abhimanyu Kalaga* again, and is set in
*raga-saurashtra*. This *raga–tala* combination is found frequently in this and other
*prasanga*s, always exhibiting the same pattern of differences compared with the
'basic' *bhamini* shown above. The main particularity of *trivude-bhamini* lies in the
third (and sixth) lines, which only have six morae and completely lack the final
long mora. To make my case as clear as possible, I have given the beat (*laya*)
count in the top line, followed by the mnemonics (*dastu*), before the lines of the
song. The emphasised beats are on count one, four and six:

As the stretching of words over the beats of the *tala* makes it difficult to make
out the lines properly, I give them here: "*ksheemavee samasaptakare nima / gaa ma-
haapaataaLalookada / siimeyoLu tava naariyaru pari / Naamisihare.*" The first thing to
note would be that the *shatpadi* metre is reorganised in the written text (morae

| 1 | 2 | 3 | 4 | 5 | 6 | 7 |
|---|---|---|---|---|---|---|
| ta | diku | taka | diku | taka | diku | taka |
| kshe- | e- | ma- | ve- | e | sa- | ma- |
| sa- | ap | ta | ka | re- | e | |
| | ni- | ma | ga- | a- | a- | ma- |
| ha- | a- | pa- | ta- | a- | la- | a- |
| lo- | o- | ka- | da- | a- | a- | a |
| si- | i- | me- | yo- | lu | ta- | va |
| na- | a- | ri- | ya- | ru- | u | pari |
| na- | a- | mi- | si- | ha- | re[2] | |

count: 14/14/14/6). So what we have here is actually the first three lines, with the extra 'half' in the third line receiving a separate unit. When we look at the distribution of the text over the *tala*, we notice that the three lines or four units are performed over eight repetitions of the defining mnemonics, or two full *tala* cycles (*avarta*).

The distribution of emphasised (*ghata*) and unemphasised beats in the *tala* enhances the inherent melodic qualities of the poetry. In the third line, the documented performance style chooses to leave a pause on the first, strong beat, beginning with the word only on the second, unemphasised beat. This is typical for this school of singing and creates an effective tension between textual rhythm and musical rhythm. In the last line, the final beat has a pause which functions as a pivot point between the cycles of the *tala* and the finishing *muktaya* sequence which would follow in the performance of this song. This is a purely rhythmic sequence, which is realised only through music and dance and leads into the performance of the next lines of text. It may surprise that the morae number of *bhamini* seemed to correspond perfectly with the number of beats of *trivude-tala*, while the example above revealed the choice of a different number of morae for the *trivude-saurashtra* type of songs. The underlying pattern is still *bhamini* because of the sub-organisation of the metrical feet, which is still basically 3+4 (Wendt 2006: 65). All *trivude-saurashtra* songs follow the same pattern; while, for example, songs in *trivude-tala*, *bhairavi-raga* also have a consistent, but different pattern—eight lines of 3+4/3+4 structure followed by

---

[2] This example cannot provide an 'authoritative' version of the song as performed in *badagu-tittu* Yakshagana. It approximates as far as possible the performance conventions for this song as taught to me by the late *bhagavata* Gorpadi Vitthal Pateel, a representative of an important style of northern style Yakshagana *bhagavatike*, or singing, of the twentieth century (see also Binder 2008: 64–65).

an 'irregular' refrain. Here, it should be made clear that none of the other *shat-padi*s have the 3+4/3+4 structure (Kittel 1875: 115ff). Thus, we can conclude that popular poetic patterns and techniques were adopted in Yakshagana songs but, at the same time, they were modified to meet performative needs and associated aesthetic considerations. It has been suggested that the *prasanga* poets also contributed to the variety of Kannada literary forms (Shetty 2005: ix). In re-using the metres creatively, as in the context of songs, the writers of Yakshagana *prasanga*s had models in the songs of the Dasas. However, the way they re-used literary forms from other literary contexts, creating new patterns and intertwining poems with songs in a single work, eventually led to the establishment of the Yakshagana style as an independent literary genre. Interestingly, the early Yakshagana poets do not seem to have rejected any metrical and compositional forms current in their time. Today, as we will see, the 'old' metrical forms are kept alive by contemporary poets.

As I have shown, the Yakshagana poets used a 'copy–paste' method when drawing on Kannada epics and *Purana*s to write *prasanga*s. This applies especially to the verbal level of textual re-use, as the authors sometimes copied quite literally. At the same time, the compositional format of the *prasanga*s required them to rework the material creatively. The compositional forms and metres in this sense provided a kind of 'blueprint' matrix for re-use. While the metric patterns themselves were re-used by copying them for other works, they provided a new framework for the textual content. Thus, the authors effectively reworked the material on several levels.

The largely formal examples above thus illustrate how textual material and technique undergo processes of conversion as well as integration into a different literary structure. On the level of textual content, it can be observed that instances of re-use are equally characterised by both these processes through what I call 'familiarisation'.[3] The episodes are brought 'closer to home' by the introduction of local place names, et cetera, and made more accessible by dwelling on emotional scenes that focus on themes such as marriage, death, relationships or duty (*dharma*). Performatively, 'familiarisation' is very often effected by characters such as women and jesters who are not the main characters or 'heroes' in the episodes. Their roles and appearances are less circumscribed by the written *prasanga* texts, thus providing ample scope for elaboration and interpolation. 'Familiarisation' techniques are an important part of the orally transmitted performance conventions (*nade* or *dari*) of 'old' *prasanga*s. For example, in *Abhimanyu Kalaga*, the parting scene between the young hero and his mother Subhadra is conventionally amplified by being played out at length

---

[3] On this issue, see Binder (2008: 172, 178).

and with heightened emotional expressiveness. Although most 'new' *prasangas* lack the detailed performance conventions that govern the staging of 'old' *prasangas*, I was able to identify a variety of instances of 'familiarisation' in my analysis of three contemporary performances. There were references to popular TV serials and oblique satire of politicians, but there were also long scenes with a 'traditional' feel, which was occasioned by their reliance on stock motives, dialogues and other techniques. Many of these scenes revolved around marriage issues. While I did not find that the female characters were portrayed as shy and submissive women of the Sita-ideal, the approach to marriage in all the performances reflected conservative Hindu values and cultural norms (for example, arranged marriage).

## MOTIVATIONS FOR EMPLOYING RE-USE STRATEGIES AND THEIR AGENTS

By the time Yakshagana emerged as a literary genre around the second half of the sixteenth century, some episodes from the epics and *Puranas* had apparently become 'canonical' as they not only appear as staged versions in many performing arts but also in several retellings for the Yakshagana stage. Some episodes seem to have been selected because of the popularity of their treatment in earlier Kannada works, for example those based on the *Jaimini Bharata* (that is, the *Ashvamedha-parvan* of the *Mahabharata*). Having discussed some of the technical details of re-use in Yakshagana *prasangas*, it remains to be asked why and by whom this strategy was employed.

Historically, I would cautiously argue for the surge of *bhakti* movements to have provided the impetus for the re-use of already widely circulated texts in a new literary genre and in a new performative style. However, I am wary of portraying Yakshagana exclusively as a religious propaganda tool. Its devotional facets emerge as equally important as its striking entertainment aspects. Today, as the religious establishment of Svamis and conservative politicians are starting to appreciate Yakshagana, they have a tendency to see in Yakshagana a once purely devotional theatre that has declined into worldly entertainment, and they clamour for the restoration of its 'traditional' form. But the situation was and is more complex. As I will show, even the preference for new, overtly religious themes such as temple myths have as much of a religious component as being expressive of cultural forces of identity.

The agents of re-use in the context of Yakshagana texts were—and are—the poets. When we look at the time of when the Yakshagana genre emerged, we see that there is a proliferation of literary forms—new versions of the Sanskrit epics and *Puranas* as well as the songs of the Dasas to mention but two. The Vijayanagara court stands as a focal point that provided an environment conducive to learning and the arts, while the subsequent regionalisation of power in south India strengthened local cultural centres, regional literatures and art forms. Significantly for the Yakshagana dance drama, the *dvaita* philosophy of Madhvacarya with its associated Vaishnava *bhakti* movement had its roots in the same coastal region of Karnataka where Yakshagana originated.

Most of the poets lived and worked here and in what is now the Kasaragod district in northern Kerala. This area remains, even today, the heartland of Kannada Yakshagana. There appears to have been some kind of overlap between the Dasas and early Yakshagana poets. Today, the tradition of the Dasas is upheld by the performers of Harikatha and there are several famous cases of Yakshagana performers who also belong to today's Dasas. While some historical Yakshagana poets are known by name, there is usually little that can be said about the dates and circumstances of their lives. Some *prasanga*s offer hints as to the favourite deities of the poet and thus to the area they probably came from in the invocational prayers. Hagiographic stories about some of the more prolific and esteemed poets abound (Fischer 2004: 61). Tentatively I would speculate that there may have been strong elements of personal *bhakti* or similarly motivated patron's wishes that prompted the individual poets to craft *prasanga*s from the epic storylines.

The association of Yakshagana with *bhakti* movements, especially with Vaishnava *bhakti*, today is confined to the content of most of the 'old' *prasanga*s. I have noted above that nowadays, most troupes are attached to Devi temples. And the devotional link to the troupes' 'home temples' seems to be strengthening. In *harake-ata*s, the deities are customarily offered Yakshagana performances. But it is particularly regionally important goddesses which are known as a 'Yakshaganapriya'—a deity with a special love for Yakshagana. For example, the Durgaparameshvari at Kateel is designated in this way (Binder 2008: 228). She is worshipped in a temple in Dakshina Kannada district that has five Yakshagana troupes attached to it, and where recently a permanent structure accommodating stages for four of them has been built. In Kumble in Kasaragod, Yakshagana artists in costumes dance facing the deity on its procession around the sanctum at major temple festivals (Gatty 2009a). In this case, it seems unknown whether this was a historical practice or has been introduced in recent years due to the rising importance ascribed to Yakshagana in the fabric of local cultural traditions.

It is often argued that the Yakshagana theatre was one of those genres that 'educated' the illiterate rural audiences in the narratives and values of Sanskritic Hinduism. Making the epic scriptures accessible to people in their own languages to a certain degree will have challenged brahminical domination.

This, however, does not mean that Yakshagana should be understood to have been a form of anti-brahminical resistance. While providing—quite literally—a stage for more or less oblique criticism, norms of Sanskritic Hinduism are reinforced rather than challenged through the content of most *prasanga* texts and their actualisation in performance. Besides, by the time Yakshagana emerged as a literary style and a performing art, the episodes and their religious and sociocultural messages were already widely known and accessible in Kannada. The earliest Kannada versions of the *Ramayana* and *Mahabharata* date from the tenth century, but they seem to have been completely superseded in popularity by the later versions that directly inspired Yakshagana *prasanga*s.

The issue is, however, made more complicated by the fact that for a large part of the population in 'Yakshagana land', Tulu, not Kannada, is the first language. In spite of sharing the same territory, Yakshagana did not belong to the distinctive Tulu culture with its own narratives and performative rituals. In the historical situation where Yakshagana would have been performed primarily at the request of wealthy landlords with their farm labourers providing the bulk of the audience, the theatre does indeed come across as a form that communicated Sanskritic Hinduism to people rooted in a different religious and cultural tradition. Below, I will show how the situation today has changed so radically as to include a Tulu Yakshagana as well. It has been argued that Tulu Yakshagana more openly challenges religious-brahminical and cultural-Sanskritic norms through the choice of language, subject matter and performance style.

## RE-USE IN 'NEW' OR CONTEMPORARY *PRASANGAS*

In the textual instances of re-use, I have shown that one can identify changes in the material on several levels, that is, over several textual layers (and historical periods) as well as changes in content and form. Some of the probably most consequential changes arise from contextual factors: intentions, audiences, historical and/or sociopolitical circumstances. The force of these contextual factors becomes especially obvious in the contemporary forms of re-use, which I will discuss in the following paragraphs.

To put contemporary instances of re-use in a contextual perspective, it seems necessary to provide here a summary of the theatre's situation today. Its present popularity is astonishing. It is unlikely that there have been as many professional and amateur troupes ever before in its history and it has become one of the most important visual icons of regional culture, to some extent, even serving as 'the' performing art form of the entire state of Karnataka. Yakshagana today also enjoys a considerable media coverage, which adds to its presence in the cultural life of the area and beyond. However, the theatre's situation and that of its proponents remains precarious. It is true that a large number of troupes are engaged every single night during the six-month season. Some of the *harake* troupes are now booked for up to ten years in advance and some temples maintain four troupes or more. Yet the scene is strikingly unstable in that troupes meander between a commercial and a *harake* orientation, between a fully professional status and different degrees of less stringent organisation down to amateur troupes with very few performances a year. Old troupes are being revived while newly founded ventures fold after only a few seasons. While especially the commercial troupes are increasingly exploring off season opportunities in the cities, venturing well outside Yakshagana territory to Bangalore, Mumbai and Delhi, a small number of troupes has started to experiment with new performance formats. Sponsors for *harake-ata*s do not appear to be lacking but audience turn-out at such performances seems to be low, especially as the night progresses. One *harake* troupe has therefore recently considered shortening their performances (Gatty 2009b). Other troupes profess to be particularly dedicated to performance quality and a 'traditional' performance style. These troupes present 'show-case' performances of two to four hour duration at social, cultural and religious events, often during the daytime or in the early evening. This seems to suit the increasingly urbanised, middle-class audiences.

Some artists today enjoy star-status and a considerable income. However, the majority of artists can just about survive on what they earn for their nighttime travails; most troupes only pay their artists for the six-month season, and as the contracts are renegotiated every year, they enjoy neither job security nor usually any social benefits such as pensions. Only through the interventions of a small organisation dedicated to artists' welfare called Yakshagana Kalaranga, performers now have access to affordable health insurance and life insurance schemes. Judging by troupe numbers and publicity, the late twentieth and early twenty-first century may seem like Yakshagana's 'golden age', but performance quality including the quality and content of the numerous new *prasanga*s is another aspect that remains hotly debated. The 'super hit' *prasanga*s of the commercial troupes may draw huge audiences, but rarely survive beyond one or two seasons. The state of Yakshagana is not least an issue of passionate opinions among coastal Kannadigas and Tuluvas living outside their native region, be it in another part of India or abroad. Their vocal participation in debates, for example in numerous online forums, on all issues concerning Yakshagana underpins the theatre's status of an icon for regional identity.

In the context of my exploration of re-use in Yakshagana, this broader situation has several implications. As I will show below, the theatre's state has a profound effect on which texts, themes and motives are re-used in Yakshagana *prasanga*s today. It even influences the messages conveyed and impacts on the motives for re-use in contemporary Yakshagana writing. It will become clear that the strongest motives that emerge surround Yakshagana's survival as well as issues of identity hinted at above.

\* \* \* \*

How and why, then, has the Yakshagana repertoire expanded boundlessly over recent decades? In spite of contextual and motivational changes, the processes of re-use as such remain similar. One of the most important repertoire changes within Kannada Yakshagana is the increasing popularity of explicitly local narratives as *harake-ata*s. The *sthala-purana*s and *sthala-mahatme*s of the temples with troupes (Mandarti, Maranakatte, Kateel, Dharmasthala, etc.) and those of regional centres of pilgrimage (Kollur, Shabarimala, Tirupati) have been reworked as *prasanga*s. While I cannot, at present, offer a detailed comparison between the original texts and their Yakshagana versions, it is important to understand the implications of this phenomenon of re-use. On a textual level, these episodes, like so many of the 'new' works, depart from the historically confined themes and texts. More crucially, these episodes and their success are an expression of Yakshagana's power in defining and underlining cultural significance and prestige. In the context of the present setup of the Yakshagana scene, it does not surprise that more *prasanga*s based on *sthala-purana*s are performed by *harake* troupes than by commercial troupes, and that in most cases, the troupe performs the story relating to their 'home temple'. Similarly, new versions of the *Devi Mahatmya* (*Devi Mahatme* in Kannada) are extremely popular choices for *harake-bayalata* performances, which reflect the affiliation of most troupes to temples of goddesses. The prevalence of these two types of episodes on the *harake* Yakshagana stage indicates a shift towards a more explicit link between performance and troupe deities. Rather than regarding the performance of any *prasanga* as an act of devotion, a more overt expression of loyalty to the deity seems to be favoured by many patrons. A few *prasanga*s of the *sthala-purana* type have become famous for more 'performative' reasons—their poetry and songs, their characters and associated novel costumes—and are now performed by several troupes.[4]

On the commercial stage, popular cinema films are frequently adapted for the Yakshagana stage. Their performances often draw immense crowds. Other instances of the re-use of new literary material include Shakespeare and Sanskrit dramas, historical as well as biographical stories and stories from other religious traditions. With the exception of historical plots, the impact of these more 'ambitious' new *prasanga*s on the Yakshagana scene is negligible.

---

[4] For more information on the popularity of these themes, see Binder (2008: 277ff).

The integration of new plots seems primarily motivated by a perceived need to cater to the tastes of potential audiences. Especially commercial troupes very often have one contemporary author who is bound by contract to churn out at least one new *prasanga* per season. Because the troupes thus invest rather heavily in their repertoire, the season's *prasanga*s are advertised prominently in the regional newspapers and by other means of publicity. One may speculate that audience expectations have changed through the influence of cinema and television to favour new repertoire. Interestingly, especially the adaptation of previously successful movie plots for the Yakshagana stage reflects an 'old' pattern: the stories performed in Yakshagana will be already known to many of the spectators; in fact, having enjoyed a particular movie, they are drawn to see the Yakshagana version. In all, this strategy can be seen to contribute to the survival and unbroken popularity of particular troupes with at least a section of the audience, but it consequently also contributes to the survival of Yakshagana in general. It should be remembered that the cinema, and today, home television, is Yakshagana's stiffest competition for audiences. Taking over movie plots (probably disregarding copyrights) is one of the ways in which Yakshagana rises to the challenge.

## TULU YAKSHAGANA

Since the 1950s, Tulu Yakshagana has gained ground. The performance of Tulu *prasanga*s is confined to the southern style. In the 1980s, Tulu had almost replaced Kannada as the stage language of *tenku-tittu* Yakshagana, a trend that seems to have recently reversed (Binder 2008: 288ff). While early Tulu *prasanga*s were translations of Kannada *prasanga*s, over time, the lore of Sanskritic Hinduism has mostly given way to fictional stories and staged versions of *paddana*s, oral epics connected with local deities (*buta*s or *daiva*s). While the rituals of these deities are enjoying an unprecedented vitality themselves, there are indications that the recitation of the *paddana*s no longer plays the prominent role in them as it previously did (Brückner 1995: 261). One could thus argue that the staged Yakshagana versions contribute to the preservation of these narratives. It has to be kept in mind, too, that the transmission and recitation of the *paddana*s was confined to particular communities or families, while the Yakshagana *prasanga*s are accessible to all. Here, too, I cannot, at present, comment on the textual relationship between the 'original' oral epics and their *prasanga* versions. The formal shift from the *paddana* style to the various metrical and musical forms of a *prasanga* must occasion dramatic changes. Many *paddana*s seem to be composed in a four beat rhythm (Brückner 1995: 178) and I can only speculate that there must be some problems involved in trying to accommodate the Tulu language in metres, which developed for the particularities of Kannada.

In the context of the theory of re-use, I find the appropriation of Tulu oral legends, besides that of contemporary movie plots discussed above, particularly significant. Tulu Yakshagana may be viewed as a strategy contributing to the search for and assertion of a regional cultural identity. While after Indian Independence, all of south India has been engaged in attempts to define its cultural distinctiveness from the north, such processes were spurred on by the reorganisation of south India which led to the foundation of Karnataka state along linguistic lines in 1956. The coastal areas of present-day Karnataka, however, have always been culturally somewhat separate (sharing more similarities with Northern Kerala), with Tulu adding a linguistic dimension to this distinction. Additionally, Tuluva culture had acquired a somewhat marginalised status. This was probably due to the lack of a script and the decisively non-Sanskritic rituals associated with a large body of its oral literature. The re-use of *paddana*s as Yakshagana *prasanga*s must also be regarded as part of the larger attempts at creating a written Tulu literature using the Kannada script (Upadhyaya 1996).

Overall, Tulu Yakshagana and the processes of re-use it involves are fine examples for the link between re-use and identity. While it clearly contains a component of challenging the dominant role of Kannada on a linguistic level, the choice of stories has been interpreted as being indicative of challenging brahminical domination (Bapat 1998: 238ff). To some degree this is reflected in the performances as well, as Tulu Yakshagana has dispensed with the performance rituals (Bapat 1998: 235). However, Tulu Yakshagana does not challenge the most basic messages of Yakshagana—the triumph of good over evil and the representation of a conservative, largely Hindu value system (Bapat 1998: 235). Even the clearly non-brahminical deities and rituals of the Tuluvas have been increasingly subject to an appropriation by the establishment of Sanskritic Hinduism, with Brahmin priests replacing the non-Brahmin specialists in rituals (Brückner 1995: 259–63), and the identification of the deities with major deities of the Hindu pantheon.

## POPULARISATION AND TRADITION

In response to the 'popularisation' of the commercial stage through the adaptation of movie plots and other 'fictional' (*kalpanika*) themes, the votive troupes present new versions of 'old' episodes. Thus, the re-use of epic material continues. Very often, the new versions combine several episodes or even strive to present the 'entire' *Mahabharata* or *Ramayana*. These developments can all be viewed as an effort to cater to changing audience tastes and demands. It is significant that similar developments in the treatment of puranic themes can be documented in the Kathakali dance drama. Here, too, the slow elaboration of confined episodes has partly given way to more comprehensive narratives such as *Sampurna Ramayana* (Jones 1983: 42; Zarrilli 1990: 351). It is generally thought that cinema and television have accustomed the audiences to a faster-paced mode of storytelling. In Yakshagana, however, this reasoning cannot explain the prominence of the spoken word sometimes observed in contemporary performances at the expense of dance and music, which tend to move the action forward.

The 'old' epic and pauranic material as well as some of the broader religious themes, regardless of whether they appear in a historical *prasanga* or a contemporary work are especially valued because they can be attributed with the label 'tradition'. Where this labelling translates into steady or new audiences, sponsorship and other forms of financial involvement, it directly contributes to the genre's survival. As a 'traditional' art form, Yakshagana can be appreciated by the educated, increasingly urbanised middle classes with conservative leanings that feed on a vague nostalgia for an idealised past that was safe, good and 'Indian' (mostly meaning: Hindu) as opposed to perceived threats of westernisation today.[5] The complex way in which Yakshagana is valued today primarily works via the 'old' material. These stories and themes are seen as part of that idealised past and all that it implies. From this point of view, Yakshagana, as a performing art, actualises the 'traditional', and it is from this fact that it derives legitimisation and value. Furthermore, it is appropriated as a tool to keep 'tradition' alive.

In summary, the fight for survival (which at the moment is more a fierce fight over audiences and sponsors to maintain a decent living for troupe proprietors, managers and artists) takes two shapes: one is 'popularisation', the other puts its stakes on 'tradition'. However, my research has confirmed that even 'tradition' is popularised to a very large extent: 'old' episodes are reworked, often combined and condensed into fast-paced narratives and 'new' religious themes have become prominent. Furthermore, the dichotomy between 'popular' and 'traditional' cannot be upheld as all sides draw on the legitimising label of 'tradition'.

However, the new repertoire is one of the main factors of change, altering the content and appearance of this dance drama in many ways. The new plots contain new character types which necessitates the finding of new costumes, while some of the old, magnificent ones are modified or abandoned. They also have facilitated the introduction of new styles of singing and dancing, which both often show a marked influence of Indian cinema. While performance styles now draw heavily on other genres of popular culture, this leaves the compositional

---

[5] See Peterson & Soneji (2008: 4ff) and many of the other essays in their volume.

form of even the most recent *prasanga*s unaffected. In general, it can be said that contemporary instances of re-use in Yakshagana texts are largely confined to the re-use of material. It seems particularly significant that material is often taken from contexts that Yakshagana competes with for audiences, such as cinema, television and (to a lesser extent), modern Kannada fiction and drama.

## RE-USE OF THE YAKSHAGANA COMPOSITIONAL FORM BY A CHRISTIAN MISSIONARY[6]

Re-use on a textual level does not only occur in Yakshagana, but the format of Yakshagana *prasanga*s has been re-used too. In 1862 Ferdinand Kittel, who served as a missionary in the Basel Mission, a Swiss–German missionary society that had been proselytising in coastal Karnataka from 1834 onwards, composed *Kathamale*. This was a selection of forty-three stories based on the New Testament. While it can be shown to have been modelled on a work by the German pietist Christian Gottlob Barth called *Zwey mal zweyundfünfzig biblische Geschichten für Schulen und Familien* (Two times fifty-two Bible stories for schools and families)—a selection of Bible stories hugely popular in nineteenth-century pietist circles and with missionaries, translated into a number of languages—Kittel, in effect, re-used the source in a similar way that Yakshagana poets re-used episodes from the epics. The missionaries' correspondence and reports consistently refer to Kittel's work being composed in 'Hindu metre' (Binder 2006: 232–33, 238). The similarities with Yakshagana *prasanga*s lie almost exclusively in the compositional form and, to a subtler degree, in the somewhat simple yet evocative vocabulary. Kittel's work differs from most Yakshagana *prasanga*s in that he chose not to use the full variety of metrical forms used by Yakshagana poets. All poems before chapter twenty-eight are either written in *bhamini* or *vardhika shatpadi*. After this chapter, some poems are in 'song' format. It is not documented why Kittel introduced 'songs' only in the later part of his work. Additionally, 'songs' in a Yakshagana *prasanga* can take various combinations of *raga* and *tala*. In contrast, Kittel only writes songs in raga *purvi* and *matte-tala*. This somewhat diminishes the similarities of the format of Kittel's text with Yakshagana *prasanga*s. However, while *raga-purvi* does not belong to the repertoire of *raga*s of classical Carnatic music, it is common in Yakshagana music, and the combination of *raga-purvi* and *matte-tala* is well-represented in *prasanga*s. It has been argued that Kittel was influenced by

---

[6] For a detailed discussion of Kittel's *Kathamale*, see Binder (2006).

Krishna Parijata, a performing art belonging to the Yakshaganas of northern interior Karnataka (Cabral 2006: 261). In-depth research in the mission's archives on the literary and linguistic activities of Kittel and his predecessors, however, have convinced me that while Kittel may have witnessed Krishna Parijata performances during the time he spent in north Karnataka, it is highly unlikely that this form influenced his writing of *Kathamale*; first, Kittel was working in Mangalore, right in the heartland of coastal Yakshagana, at the time, and most likely produced *Kathamale* with the help of a local '*munshi*' who would have been intimately familiar with Yakshagana *prasanga*s (Binder 2006: 250); second, archival documents reveal that Kittel's most eminent predecessors in the field of Kannada language and literature, Herrmann Mögling and Gottlieb Weigle, collected and studied Yakshagana *prasanga*s and regarded this poetry to be fit for instructing younger colleagues in the language. Mögling published a *Ramayana prasanga*, *Ravana Digvijaya* as part of his *Bibliotheca Carnataca* in 1852, and there were plans to include more *prasanga*s in this series (Binder 2007: 82ff). No such evidence exists for the texts used in Krishna Parijata. Unfortunately, there is no report by Kittel himself on the details of his writing. Poignantly, to date I have not come across any reference in the archives pertaining to the performance of Yakshagana or any other dramatic performance. It seems impossible that the missionaries never witnessed Yakshagana as they regularly travelled extensively through coastal Karnataka and especially attended major temple festivals to preach to the masses gathered on such an occasion. However, the missionaries probably shared with the colonial authorities a strong anti-theatrical bias. Although they regularly reported on indigenous customs and religious practices, the spectacle of a Yakshagana performance on the one hand may simply have been 'too much' for the missionaries, while on the other hand, they may not have grasped the full sociocultural and religious implications of the theatre thus overlooking its potential to communicate their own message.

Kittel's motivation to produce such a work in precisely this format must be seen in a need for new religious tracts among the missionaries in Karnataka at the time. Furthermore, the growing of a Christian community gave rise to calls for an indigenous Christian literature (Binder 2006: 237). Kittel himself firmly believed familiar literary forms would be more effective in communicating Christian beliefs to the Indian population.[7] In a later report, he generalised this to conclude emphatically: "Verse will eben der Hindu" ("The Hindu wants but verse").[8] This was an important part of his personal missionary strategy of becoming 'an Indian to the Indians', which was highly controversial in his missionary society and consequently forced him to realise it chiefly through linguistic and literary works.[9]

---

[7] Further details on this issue can be found in Wendt (2006: 65).

[8] The report is titled "Einige Notizen über Volksthümlichkeit". See Wendt (2006: 70ff; 2001).

[9] For several papers on this subject, see Wendt (2006).

Kittel published the first comprehensive Kannada–English dictionary (1894), and edited several important Kannada works such as Nagavarma's *Chandombudhi* (Ocean of Prosody 1875), culminating in his *Grammar of the Kannada Language* (1903) based on Keshava's indigenous grammar *Shabdamanidarpana*.

In many ways, the missionary's motives recall those of the earlier Yakshagana poets who were retelling Sanskritic material in locally spoken languages. In both cases, the communication of religious material is the key factor. This similarity of motivations between the Hindu Yakshagana poets from the sixteenth century onwards and the nineteenth-century Christian missionary leads to some interesting similarities in the way they have changed their respective materials when re-using it. In Kittel's case, his strategies to make Barth's text suitable for Indian audiences include not only the choice of format discussed above. The title *Kathamale* links his text to collections of Kannada stories such as a *Kathamanjari* (Binder 2006: 237). He even included an invocation ("shri yehovaya namah") and an introductory prayer (*vandanavakya*) directly modelled on the Hindu literary tradition. It appears that Kittel tried to concentrate on the central stations of Christ's life and the most essential stories of his teaching, avoiding episodes that he may have considered potentially ambivalent and disturbing for his Indian audience (Binder 2006: 246). To some extent, he also used 'familiarisation' strategies, although he did not make an attempt to overtly 'Indianise' the stories. While his most obvious way to 'familiarise' the material is the choice of compositional format, he also achieves it through his choice of idiomatic vocabulary and terminology (Binder 2006: 246ff).

In much the same way, Yakshagana poets drew on the mediaeval Kannada versions of the epics and *Purana*s to create their works, Kittel also re-used earlier, more literal translations of Barth's bible stories. However, while the Kannada epics were already in metrical form, Kittel's reference texts were in prose. Additionally, the sources which the Yakshagana writers re-used were already highly idiomatic and stylistic masterpieces. The earlier Kannada versions of the bible stories were less than idiomatic, echoing contemporary European 'biblical language' rather than esteemed Kannada literary works.

Although Kittel's arguments for the formation of a successful indigenous Christian literature betray insight and intimate knowledge, *Kathamale* can hardly be called a successful contribution to that end. Primarily, his fellow missionaries and the homeboard were not convinced that Kittel was on the right track. Many of his visions and works during this early time of his missionary career were seen to be going too far in the direction of 'going native'. Thus, *Kathamale* was never reprinted. No similar attempts were made by the missionaries to provide the seeds for an accessible Christian literature in Kannada.

## CONCLUSIONS

Across the descriptive and analytical examples of re-use in Yakshagana texts presented above, it has become clear that the processes involved are complex, multileveled and working in at least two directions. To summarise, I would like to address the key questions uniting the contributions in this volume, and again emphasise some of my interpretations.

In terms of what has been re-used, Yakshagana *prasanga*s historically drew on major Sanskritic epics and *Purana*s, their immediate sources being the later mediaeval Kannada versions of these texts. The poets not only re-used content, but also metrical and compositional forms from these and related texts. It is much less easy to determine what material was rejected both in terms of form and content. In contemporary *prasanga*s, the form largely remains unchanged, while virtually all imaginable sources are now re-used.

The poets were and are the main agents of re-use—prompted by patrons' wishes and audience preferences. In early *prasanga* writing, a link between the Yakshagana poets and the itinerant Vaishnava Dasas suggests itself. In the late nineteenth and early twentieth century, learned Brahmins have been identified as authors (Karanth 1997: 160ff).

Examining the motivations for re-use in the context of Yakshagana, there are remarkable similarities between the 'old' and 'new' *prasanga*s and in Kittel's *Kathamale*. They all illustrate a common strategy, which I have called 'familiarisation'. Within the present framework, 'familiarisation' emerges as a prime motive for engaging in re-use. At the same time, it shows most clearly how the poets creatively re-use(d) their sources.

One of the most important aspects of textual re-use in Yakshagana is, in my opinion, the historical continuity. Even the earliest Yakshagana poets were not the first to adapt the epics and even the reworking of particular episodes for dramatic representation did not occur in isolation as a number of parallel genres using similar texts developed around the same time. And if we compare the expansion of the Yakshagana repertoire today, we find similar processes occurring in these genres as well. From a theoretical viewpoint, the congruence of episodes across genres has consequences in that it may help to illuminate which material is re-used and why. Similar circumstances around the formation of these genres and their present situation will have played a key role in the choice of material. It has been suggested that the literary and performative genres I refer to were fostered by the arts patronage of the Vijayanagara Empire while gaining ground in the subsequent times of political fragmentation and unrest. Overall, however, these factors have not been sufficiently noted and analysed. I feel that such an analysis would benefit from drawing on the concept of re-use and, in turn, reveal important implications for the theory of re-use.

The historical continuity of re-use in Yakshagana *prasanga* writing is also an indication of the success of this strategy. The genre as a literary form has survived for more than four centuries now. Individual episodes, too, have had a long life. Today, many of the 'old' *prasanga*s have vanished from the professional stage; most 'new' *prasanga*s have a short stage life and are never printed, while others quickly become 'modern classics'. Historically, Yakshagana was one of the genres that familiarised people effectively with the stories and messages of the epics and *Purana*s. Today, it is more difficult to assess the message communicated through the stories performed but it cannot be denied that the new repertoire contributes to the theatre's survival. Largely through ongoing processes of re-use, Yakshagana seems to be finding a new identity between an auspicious occasion of thanksgiving to the gods, a playground for the assertion of social and cultural prestige and a commercial venture on the one hand. On the other hand, some of the changes are so profound that one has to ask where Yakshagana stops and a new genre emerges. In all, Yakshagana successfully employs re-use to evade its potential sidelining into an endangered species of entertainment, overshadowed by cinema and home TV. It thus actively transforms its role as a potential victim into an assertion of its popularity—using cinema scripts as well as using TV broadcasts of performances for its own ends.

It appears difficult to establish the differences between re-use and other strategies such as intertextuality. I believe that what we can learn from an example such as Yakshagana is that re-use may not only involve several levels in time, but also cut across different genres as well as working in at least two directions. Re-use as theory explicitly takes cognizance of motivations and contexts. In the study of Yakshagana, the approach could now be applied to other areas as well, beginning perhaps with performative examples. As some of the above has suggested (for example, Tulu Yakshagana, relationship with cinema), textual instances often coincide with or occasion performative instances of re-use. Within the approach, this continuity would be accommodated rather than ignored, which shows its integrative potential.

## PHOTO CREDIT

The Photograph for Plates 6.1, 6.3 and 6.4 are courtesy of Narayan A. Gatty. The Photograph for Plage 6.2 is courtesy of P. V. Jayan.

# BIBLIOGRAPHY

Bapat, Gururao, 1998, *Semiotics of Yakshagana*. Regional Resources Centre for Folk Performing Arts, Udupi.

Bharadvaja, Kabbinale Vasanta, 1998, *Yakshagana Chandassu. Ondu Adhyayana* [in Kannada]. Regional Resources Centre for Folk Performing Arts, Udupi.

Binder, Katrin, 2006, "A Garland of Stories: Kathamale". In: R. Wendt (ed.), *An Indian to the Indians? On the Initial Failure and the Posthumous Success of the Missionary Ferdinand Kittel (1832–1903)*. Harrassowitz, Wiesbaden, pp. 231–55.

Binder, Katrin, 2007, "The 'Ravana Digvijaya' in the Bibliotheca Carnataca". In: A. Frenz & S. Frenz (eds), *Zukunft im Gedenken—Future in Remembrance*. Books on Demand, Norderstedt, pp. 82–85.

———, 2008, "Yaksagana Rangabhumi: The World of the Yaksagana Stage". Dr. phil. dissertation [unpublished], Tübingen.

Brückner, Heidrun, 1995, *Fürstliche Feste: Texte und Rituale der Tulu-Volksreligion an der Westküste Südindiens*. Harrassowitz, Wiesbaden.

Bruin, Hanne M. de, 1999, *Kattaikkuttu: The Flexibility of a South Indian Theatre Tradition*. Egbert Forsten, Groningen.

Cabral, Hannibal, 2006, "Missionaries and Carnatic Music". In: R. Wendt (ed.), *An Indian to the Indians? On the Initial Failure and the Posthumous Success of the Missionary Ferdinand Kittel (1832–1903)*, Harrassowitz, Wiesbaden, pp. 255–65.

[Devidaṣa], 2000 [1978], *Srikrsna Sandhana* [in Kannada], Edited by M. S. Sunkapura. Kannada Adhayana Pitha, Karnataka Vishvavid[y]akaya, Dharwad.

Fischer, Katrin, 2004, *Yaksagana: Eine südindische Theatertradition. Mit Übersetzung und Text von 'Abhimanyu Kalaga*. Harrassowitz, Wiesbaden.

Jones, Betty True, 1983, "Kathakali Dance-Drama: An Historical Perspective". In: B. C. Wade (ed.), *Performing Arts in India*. University Press of America, Lanham, pp. 14–45.

Gatty, Narayan, 2009a, "Gods' Love for Yakshagana". Available online at http://rangasthala.blogspot.com/2009/02/gods-love-for-yakshagana.html (accessed on 26 September 2009).

———, 2009b, "Professional Troupes May Face Shortage of Artistes Soon". Available online at http://rangasthala.blogspot.com/2008_09_01_archive.html (accessed on 26 September 2009).

Joshi, M. Prabhakara, 1994, *Yaksagana padakosa* [in Kannada]. Regional Resources Centre for Folk Performing Arts, Udupi.

Karanth, K. Shivarama, 1997, *Yaksagana*. Abhinav Publications, New Delhi.

Kittel, Ferdinand, 1875, *Nagavarmana Kannada Chandassu. Nagavarma's Canarese Prosody*. Basel Mission Book and Tract Depository, Mangalore.

———, 1894, *Kannada English Dictionary*. Basel Mission Book & Tract Depository, Mangalore.

———, 1903, *A Grammar of the Kannada Language*. Basel Mission Book & Tract Depository, Mangalore.

Kuvempu & Masti Venkatesa Ayyangar (eds), 2000, *Kumaravyasa Mahakaviya Karnata Bharata Kathamanjari* [in Kannada]. Karnataka Sarkara Kannada Pustaka Pradhikara, Bangalore.

Peterson, Indira Viswanathan & Davesh Soneji (eds), 2008, *Performing Pasts: Reinventing the Arts in Modern South India*. Oxford University Press, New Delhi.

Prasanna, A. V. (ed.), 2001, *Kannada Bharata* [in Kannada]. Kannada University, Hampi.

Rao, Purna Chandra, 2004, "Yakshaganam". In: A. Lal (ed.), *The Oxford Companion to Indian Theatre*. Oxford University Press, Oxford, pp. 527–29.

Shetty, N. Narayana, 2005, *Yaksagana Chandombudhi* [in Kannada]. Yaksakala Pradhmapana Prakashana, Elatturu and Kinnigoli.

Upadhyaya, U. P., 1996, "Renaissance in Tulu Literature". In: U. P. Upadhyaya (ed.), *Coastal Karnataka: Studies in Folkloristic and Linguistic Traditions of Dakshina Kannada Region of the Western Coast of India*. Govindha Pai Research Centre, Udupi, pp. 1–12.

Wendt, Reinhard, 2006, "Between Cultures: Ferdinand Kittel's Missionary Ways in India Ranging from Strategies of Cultural Accom[m]odation to Scientific Research, Illustrated by Selected Documents". In: R. Wendt (ed.), *An Indian to the Indians? On the Initial Failure and the Posthumous Success of the Missionary Ferdinand Kittel (1832–1903)*. Harrassowitz, Wiesbaden, pp. 9–111.

————, 2001, "'Verse will eben der Hindu.' Ferdinand Kittels missionarische und philologische Arbeit zwischen Basler Konzepten und einheimischer Kultur". *Zeitschrift für Mission*. 27/1, pp. 27–45.

Zarrilli, Phillip B., 1990, "Kathakali". In: F. P. Richmond, D. L. Swann & Ph. B. Zarrilli (eds), *Indian Theatre: Traditions of Performance*. University of Hawaii Press, Honolulu, pp. 315–59.

*Chapter 7*

# INDIAN PAINTING AT THE BEGINNING OF THE TWENTIETH CENTURY

## MODERNISM AND RE-USE OF ANCIENT PICTORIAL TRADITIONS

### BY TIZIANA LORENZETTI

Between the nineteenth and the twentieth centuries—the age that saw the beginning of global communications—Indian painting, as had partly happened with architecture (Lorenzetti forthcoming), took in some of the trends of modern Western painting. Grounds for the development of lasting reciprocal influences, whether cultural or artistic, had already been laid at the beginning of the eighteenth century, by when the East India Company had consolidated its trade links on Indian soil, thus opening the way for the future British Raj. It was thus that Western painters—facilitated by an enforced coexistence—found inspiration in the exotic Indian landscapes (de Almeida & Gilpin 2005: 35–99; Guha-Thakurta 2003: 109–28; Tuli 1997: 184–87) while in India, preference for the Western-style oil portrait began to grow (Archer 1979; Archer 1997; Bayley

1990) to be followed later, by the diffusion of certain techniques such as lithography and incision on metallic plates (aquatints). We may cite, for instance, Ravi Varma (b. 1848) who introduced lithography in India, making it possible to go for a serial artistic production, articulated in various formats and sizes (Castelli et al. 2005: 18–39; Dolcini 1985: 105–15). These reciprocal influences are well known.

Eventually, at the beginning of the twentieth century, with the explosion of the Art Noveau Movement, India welcomed and elaborated elements suggested by the avant-garde of European Modernism (from Expressionism to Surrealism and Abstractionism to Cubism) which contributed to the birth of new artistic tendencies in the history of Indian painting (Mago 2001: 79–95; Mitter 2001: 189–219; Mitter 2008: 15–27; Tuli 1997: 183–240).

When the doors of British universities opened to Indian students at about the end of the nineteenth century, it certainly facilitated the diffusion of artistic innovations that were taking place in Europe, so much so that gifted painters such as Paritosh Sen (b. 1918) or Amrita Sher Gil (b. 1912) set up shop in the cosmopolitan Paris of the 1920s to study at the École de Beaux Arts,[1] while others such as J. Choudhary (b. 1939), J. A. Sabavala (b. 1922) or S. Das (b. 1939), to cite only a few, produced works inspired by Cézanne, Matisse, Munch, Seurat, Picasso and even Kandinsky (Mago 2001: 79–80). In this context, an exemplary work would be *Colour and Sound* by S. B. Palsikar (b. 1917) (Tuli 1997: 161–63), inspired by the celebrated painting *In Blue* and *Sky-blue* of the Russian master, where lines, geometries and fantastic figures seem to dance on an azure backdrop, suspended in the equilibrium of a timeless levitation.

It must, however, be said that many of the themes of modernist European paintings find a ready echo amongst Indian artists because, in my opinion, they are evocative of concepts and symbols already present in the Indian tradition. This is undoubtedly true with regard to Kandinsky since he drew some of his theories about art and the relationship between form, sound and colour directly from the Indian world.[2]

We know for a fact that early twentieth-century Germany was fascinated by the doctrines of the Theosophical Society,[3] spread mainly by Annie Besant and

---

[1] Amrita Sher Gil, in particular, notwithstanding her close contact with the Western artistic world (she was mostly influenced by Gauguin), in her mature works, turned to Indian heritage, already showing that the 'search for roots' that was to be typical of the post-Independence painters (Ramachandra Rao 1953: 36; Chopra 2004: 22–27; Dalmia 2006 59–75).

[2] To the relationship between colour, form and sound, Kandinsky dedicated significant proportions of his books, including the celebrated *The Spiritual in Art* (1989) published in the original in 1912.

[3] The Theosophical Society, whose philosophical–religious speculations were rooted in Indian thought (both Hindu and Buddhist), had been founded by Madame Blavatsky in New York in 1875. Sometime later the headquarters were moved to Madras, Tamil Nadu.

C. W. Leadbeater who republished in Munich (1908) the occult text *Thought-Forms*, first published in New York in 1896. Therein the authors described the relations between colour and energy (or rather vibrations) of the various bodies that were supposed to make-up a human being: the material one, the mental and the astral. The text was furbished with richly illustrated tables, inspired by the figurative universe of the *mandala*, where symbols get braided in a complexity of images, lines and colours that have no decorative or aesthetic value but are fixed by precise and inviolable rules. Rudolf Steiner, Secretary General to the European section of the Theosophical Society, set these theories down systematically, which in turn were thoroughly studied by Kandinsky and reproduced in his notes (Di Stefano 1993: 22). We may thus understand how it came to be that many Indian painters, perhaps even unwittingly, found in the works of the great Russian a source of inspiration.

The European expressionist tendencies attracted many Indian painters (Mago 2001: 80–82) precisely because, as we have hypothesised, some of its conceptions and intuitions, above all the existential ones, were not alien to Indian thought. Even Van Gogh, one of the mightiest roots of Expressionism, identified art in general—and painting, in particular—with the unity and the totality of existence, where reality is a continuous communication between subject and object (Argan 2001: 4). It is from this dialogue that the continuity and circularity of intrinsically creative movement issues, determining the formation of phenomenon as well as of thought. This is the 'vital impulse' which Bergson speaks of and which powerfully recalls the dynamic process of expansion from unity to multiplicity, the progressive dialogue between subject and object, which is a common heritage of most Indian philosophical schools (Tucci 1981: 121–25).

In this regard, let us cite a painter like Sayed Haider Raza (b. 1922) who devoted himself to those themes of European Abstractionism that were most consonant with the Indian sensibility. This is exemplified by certain recurring motifs in his works, such as the spiral or the expanding central point—see for instance *The Black Sun*, created in 1953 (Sen 2003: 134)—which are extraordinarily reminiscent of certain Indian cosmic symbols (for example, the *bindu*, the primordial point), or the visualisations of energy represented with great effect in the symbol of the *yantra*, the sacred diagram of an evocative character. This hypothesis seems to find confirmation in Raza's own artistic production, whose mature period reinterprets the dominant themes of his work in the light of the Indian tradition, which was, from the beginning, originally close to his inspiration. Hence, the vertiginously expanding central point, around which congeals and brims up that space which is at once nature and consciousness, is called *Black Sun* and, later, *Surya* (1986) (Tuli 1997: 159) and *Jalabindu* (1990) (Mitter 2001: 212).

This period of Indian painting which, despite being in accord with the sensibilities of the country, had gathered unto itself many themes, models and techniques of European Modernism, which enabled it to venture through a new phase soon enough. Indeed, already during the so-called nationalistic interlude, and especially after Independence, many Indian artists, in delicate equilibrium between global modernity and national identity (Mitter 2001: 189), reclaimed their artistic identity. In this regard Neville Tuli writes: "The search for '*Indianness*' is one focus; the oscillation between a traditional artistic heritage and the changing art norms of Western modernism being its main pendulum" (Tuli 1997: 183).

## THE SCHOOLS OF BOMBAY AND SHANTINIKETAN BETWEEN NEW LANGUAGES AND WESTERN INFLUENCES: SOME REMARKS

In the complex cultural and artistic panorama of the first decades of the twentieth century, two main centres of art may be mentioned: the Shantiniketan School of Arts founded in Bengal by Rabindranath Tagore (Guha-Thakurta 1992: 26, 2003: 120–22) and the Sir Jamshetjee Jeejeebhoy School of Art, established in Bombay in 1857.

Both schools proposed to engender a modern Indian painting that reflected the changing spirit of the new era, but, at the same time, retaining a desire to create a meaningful artistic dialogue between the past and the present of the country. Indeed, tradition and modernity were not postulated as necessary adversaries, but as mutually complementary phenomena. But the productions of the two schools, were quite different.

The Bombay school gave up those tendencies which had characterised its activities at the beginning—which had largely been related to the canons of Victorian British academies (Mago 2001: 46–48)—and generally promoted new orientations linked, especially in contents, to the ancient autochthonous traditions. For instance, senior students were encouraged to make copies of the frescoes at Ajanta and of other Indian masterpieces (Chaitanya 1994: 135–44; Mago 2001: 22–23). Of course, in many cases, the artists did not undertake pure and simple imitations, but effected fresh and genuine creations by assimilating elements from the past. But even in the multiplicities of its patterns and inspirations, the J. J. School of Bombay showed a general tendency to reinterpret themes and motifs of the Indian tradition (rather, of the Indian traditions) in the light of new Western influences (Mago 2001: 48). We may cite the example of Krishna Hebbar (b. 1912) who, at the age of twenty-five, started to teach at the School. Having gone beyond academicism and mannerism, he went on to blend different sources of inspiration (Jakimowicz-Karle 1988: 14). First of all, he gleaned what was great in Indian antiquities, incorporating in his own works motifs inherited from the past, both folk and classical, rendering them relevant to his day with a touch of 'social realism' (Jakimowicz-Karle 1988: 15). Besides, stimulated by a visit to Vijayanagar, he began to embrace art motifs and mythological scenes from the old sculpted panels of that ancient capital, combined with abstract grounds, as in *Govardhan* (Jakimowicz-Karle 1988: 19) or with impressionistic and postimpressionistic textures. As a matter of fact, Western influences were widely diffused, being even well considered by an independent group of young artists from Bombay, the so-called Progressive Artists' Group who, beyond the idea of an art involved in nationalistic politics or something like a 'colourless revival' of the past (Ramacandra Rao 1953: 56–63; Chaitanya Sambrani 2003: 21–27), intended to realise a new conceptual freedom in the use of colour and a 'vigorous synthesis' (Mago 2001: 69) of various schools of painting.[4] We can thus see how Western influences came, in a certain sense, to be deemed by the Progressive Artists' Group as being functional to their artistic conceptions. Cubism, in particular, attracted one of the most renowned members of the Group, Maqbool Fida Husain (b. 1915). In fact, within the undoubted originality of languages and patterns and despite the manifold sources of his inspiration,[5] Husain has depicted figures and episodes from Indian mythology that rear up in a continuous space wrapping and running through them, consonant with cubist formulations (Alkazi 1978: 34; Sen 2003: 130–31).

The Bengal school, on the contrary, created such a vocabulary of images so as to break with the pre-established schemes, taking its just distances from all Western influences—which Tagore himself considered 'rather restrictive'(Mago 2001: 59)—and giving life to multiple and unforeseeable results (Khanna & Kurtha 1998: 8–23; Mago 2001: 59–78).

In my opinion, it was not by chance that Bengal saw the birth of a new pictorial trend, marked by more typical Indian characteristics. Indeed, the majority of Eastern India—having been only marginally touched by the invasions of foreign peoples who in different ways and at different times, had run over the land—had kept the many autochthonous traditions more alive than elsewhere. Bengal, in particular, had been smitten only much later, at the end of the seventeenth century, by the violence of the Mughal emperor Aurangzeb and it was only towards the seventeenth century that the British had begun to make their commercial inroads, right from the territory around present-day Kolkata. In both cases, the Bengalis had put up an obstinate resistance at all levels to any

---

[4] In this regard, see the introductory note, written by Francis Newton Souza, to the first exhibition of the Group, held in Bombay in July 1949 (Mago 2001: 68–69).

[5] We may cite here, for instance, the Basohli miniatures and Gupta influences (Tuli 1997: 309).

attempt at deep-seated assimilation, creating—until India's Independence—a sort of 'hard nut to crack' that best defended their 'Indianness'. It would suffice to think of the cultural movement that led to the elaboration of the nationalist ideology and whose focal point was the self-same Kolkata, then known as Calcutta. This cultural stirring took place also in the visual arts, especially as regards the popular arts,[6] which have always been flourishing in the region and, in some cases, represented the continuity of very ancient autochthonous traditions.

It was precisely folk art and its rural cradle—the traditional microcosm that, to this day, notwithstanding the inevitable transformations, tenaciously opposes the runaway globalisation of Indian metropolises—that would be one of the main sources of inspiration for the painters of Shantiniketan (Mago 1986: 5–19). The extraordinary and variegated popular production was actually presumed to be able to best provide the primary root for a modern style, non-European in perspective. On one hand, the lack of an official academic culture seemed to guarantee an efficient opposition both to the influences of modernism and to those Indian paintings that had been bound too long to 'classical' traditions being, thus, hardly suited to express the ferments of a new era. On the other hand, the painters of Shantiniketan absorbed the great interest raised by popular art. Such a phenomenon might have had to do with the advent of Western avant-gardes, which had smashed the traditional aesthetic canons, making the fruition of folk art more immediate—in particular, that of painting which had always produced forms that were abstract, stylised and, in a certain sense, 'visionary'.

From the standpoint of an evolving national ethos, Guha-Thakurta sees the purpose of the Indian art movement in Shantiniketan as being:

> … directly engaged with the natural environment and physical realities of form (with everyday images of humans, animals, trees or landscapes), even in seeking out the visual ingredients for mythic and classical themes. Riding on this trend, it also now openly appropriated the 'popular' in the reformulation of its 'Indian' and 'modern' idioms. This was to be seen in the thematic involvement with rural life and culture, in the stylistic borrowings from folk art traditions like the *pattacitra*[7] and also in the new institutionalised concern with handicrafts…. The 'nation' was now located in the living traditions of village India. (Guha-Thakurta 1995: 29)

It thus came to pass that many Indian painters allowed themselves to be seduced not only by the landscapes and atmospheres of the rural world, but also

---

[6] We have used the term popular or folk art referring to the local or regional styles of various autochthonous groups.

[7] *Pattacitra* are paintings on cloth (generally cotton) treated with natural glue.

by its stimulating artistic production. The cardinal example is Jamini Roy (b. 1887) who, drawing upon the boundless reservoir of popular creativity—from the *pattacitra* of Bengal and Bihar to Kalighat paintings (Ghosh 1982: 119–23; Mookerjee 1939: 16–19)—, elaborated a new 'Bengali folk' style, stylised in its traits but pulsating with life (Archer 1987: 26). In his paintings, chromatic audacity and ample brushstrokes, probably derived from Kalighat painting (Appasamy 1987: 5–6), are often accompanied by angular lines, as in the *Boatmen* (Appasamy 1987: 8) which, all the same, yield to the softness of curves in the representation of female bodies.

Similarly, K. Sreenivasalu (b. 1932) reinterprets, with a brilliance of colours and a forceful and fluent line, the figures of popular art echoing those of the Lepakshi murals of Andhra Pradesh (see Plate 7.1). A good example is his *Plucking Flowers*, conserved in the Government Museum of Chennai (see Plate 7.2).

Finally, Binode Behari Mukherjee (b. 1904) and Manjit Bawa (b. 1941) represent the rural world with an extraordinary power of characterisation. Manjit Bawa, in particular, also takes inspiration from ancient folk ballads and popular sagas; his figurative narration, of languid rhythms and open spaciousness, introduces a use of colours not naturalistic but almost 'visionary', which concur to create, as in the well-known *Pink Field and Flute* (see Plate 7.3), the setting for a popular fable.

Obviously, the attainment of a modern Indian painting marked by new languages and patterns was not exclusive to the centres of Bombay and Shantiniketan; indeed, many other minor schools were to give voice to new vistas of research and many were the individual 'innovators' who, even though they did not belong to any academy or group, did respond to the diverse solicitations with original creations (Mago 2001: 143–94).

In this vast panorama—which deserves further study, especially from the perspective of an evolving national ethos, as much as it is very closely connected to the cultural and social history of India of the twentieth century—another phenomenon is to be remembered: less known but most interesting, it also contributed to the creation of a pictorial identity for the youthful India which, in step with her artistic production, was revealing an extraordinary unity in multiplicity. It had to do with the diffusion of ancient traditions and pictorial techniques, generally confined to a coterie of the elite, which were re-used and often re-elaborated by modern painters and opportunely divulged. Amongst these, two are worthy of special attention: the first one, better known—although it has not yet been the object of deeper examination—is the 'Thanjavur painting', born in the mid-eighteenth century and revived in the 1980s so much so that it is today found across most of southern India. The second one, far less known, is the so-called Brahmari painting, which, having risen in West Bengal at some indeterminate period, had again flowered between the nineteenth and the twentieth centuries in the artistic and cultural ferment that accompanied the Independence movement.

## RE-USE OF THE BRAHMARI PAINTING TRADITION

Towards the end of the nineteenth century, western Bengal found itself in the heart of an extraordinary cultural phenomenon, which as we have seen, represented one of the strongest roots of the Indian Independence movement. In this complex panorama, wherein flourished new orientations of art and thought, a group of Bengali artists, the well-known Acharya Chattopadhyaya (b. 1898) amongst them, re-used and divulged an ancient local technique, the so-called Brahmari painting which, perhaps because it was restricted to a coterie of artists, has not been an object of in-depth study until now.

This kind of painting, having risen at some indeterminate period, was brought back into vogue during the twentieth century and enriched with extraordinary chromatic harmony. In fact, according to one of the foremost contemporary exponents of this art, Buddhadeb Chattopadhyaya (1930–2002),[8] son of Acharya Chattopadhyaya, Brahmari paintings were originally made with the use of only four or five basic colours obtained from plants or mineral sources. Nowadays, pigments are very many and typically synthetic; often tempera is used. The great variety of colours contribute to the making of an extraordinary chromatic harmony that, without interruption of expressive continuity, favours the passage from one tint to another, whereby each sustains and accentuates the others in an unending crescendo. Thus came into being luminous and expansive areas whose confines are not a limit but a relaunch: indeed the lines, which in the ancient Brahmari paintings were contours, are now arabesques, assuring the circulation of the colour-lymph to the entire pictorial tissue.

But, even if the pigments have changed over time, the employed technique has remained the same. This is certainly a very particular case that has no clearly recognisable counterpart either in popular painting—which too was flourishing at the same period and place, such as the above mentioned Kalighat painting—or in classical circles, whose artistic production has always been based on technical texts (*citrasutra*).[9] However, in some of its traits, Brahmari painting may be associated with both traditions: with the popular or folk, in its abstract and

---

[8] Interview by the author with the artist Buddhadeb Chattopadhyaya, Uttarpara (Kolkata), January 1998.

[9] The *Citralakshana* of Nagnajit and sections of the *Vishnudharmottara Purana* are amongst the ancient sources, though neither is datable with certainty. Anyway, both do not date from before the Gupta period (fourth to fifth centuries CE) (Bhattacharya 1974: 4–10; Dave Mukherji 2001: 3–20).

imaginary forms, as with the classical, in the importance it gives to lineaments (*Vishnudharmottara Purana* III. 41.10–15), as well as to meditation.[10]

As a matter of fact, interior practice is inseparable from the Brahmari panting which, by virtue of this union, also becomes a means towards interior evolution. The already mentioned Buddhadeb Chattopadhyaya thus defined Brahmari painting:

> This process of art is a spiritual practice that utilises artistic expression in painting, music and dance. It is an inner operation of the rhythmical life energy, *prana*, inherent in every human being; the purpose of this process is to reveal the inner forms which lie in the deeper levels of the non-conscious mind, in order to attain spiritual self-knowledge.[11]

In practice, the creation of a Brahmari painting proceeds in several consequential stages, which follows a process of interior evolution: in the initial phase, meditation unleashes deep energies to 'guide' the artist's hand to trace a continuous line which wavers in a play of curves and designs according to a rhythm dictated by the interior intuition itself (see Plate 7.4).

As already pointed out, linkage between meditation and the artistic realisation—although rather different from what characterises the Brahmari painting—is certainly not alien to the Indian world: indeed, it is well known that the traditional image of every Hindu divinity (whether sculpted or painted) is made according to precise canons, defined *ab origine* by meditative visions. In other words, the Indian artistic tradition has always maintained a definite correspondence between the vision achieved through meditative intuition of spiritual masters and the form, colour and aspects of the various divinities reproduced by craftsmen. Therefore, every sacred image (*pratima*) is the precise copy of a psychological and religious phenomenon, and it stands in a relation to it which is one of absolute and conscious fidelity (Das Gupta 1940: 23; Zimmer 1984: 3–64, 123–80; Kramrisch 1961: 13–42).

Now, let us go back to the realisation of the Brahmari painting. After tracing the basic grid, vibrant with creative internal energy, the artist's conscious mind activates itself in discerning the triangular forms, which are coloured black. In the Brahmari painting, black is the colour of the unknown primordial energy, the energy that potentially contains all colours, all forms and all the possibilities that go on to take shape in the infinite variety of manifestation.

Starting with this new basic design, fusing the creativity of the unconscious intuition with that of the conscious mind, the artist then lets the original lines

---

[10] See, for instance, the edited and translated version of the *citrasutra* of the *Vishnudharmottara Purana* by Dave Mukherji (2001).

[11] Interview by the author, Uttarpara, January 1998.

evolve—in accord with their rhythm—into the creation of images that are comprehensible and yet fluid and allusive (see Plate 7.5). It entails the ordaining of a vocabulary of signs composed according to a syntax based not only on rational and logical constructs but, especially, on interior rhythms (*tala*) animated by the harmony and the pulsations of music.

Thus, from the structural grid diverse forms emerge, generally characterised by a curvilinear feature, which unravels through space with an outstanding plastic effect, suggested by the slightly undulated levels of the background lines. This is a singular figurative movement, which remarkably recalls the conception of the 'kinetic' form characteristic of certain European avant-gardes (Argan 2001: 54–87). These dynamic figures that have been always taken from Hindu mythology as well as from the natural world, propagate themselves in an elusive space, one that is dreaming and atemporal, one that has abrogated the levels of depth, to the point of becoming an integral portion of the very figures.

Finally, it is colour that completes the work: indeed, the painting is not complete until every colour achieves accord with the other tonalities to the best of its chromatic possibilities. Thus, the spatial rhythm acquires the extension and the depth suggested by this chromatic relationship (see Plates 7.6 and 7.7).

## CONCLUSION

To sum up, contemporary Brahmari painting can be conceived not only as an extraordinary revival of a traditional art, still awaiting its just recognition, but also as a vessel for inner visions, conveyed into comprehensible forms that come in the wake of procedures which might, in a certain sense, be said to take after the most ancient canons of the Hindu lore.

Adding on to this is the fact that in any case such painting undisputedly came across as 'modern', whether due to the peculiar figurative movement or the creation of a continuous space; we can thus see why it got re-used and divulged by nineteenth- and twentieth-century Bengali artists. It could be the epitome of a painting that looked modernist but was, at the same time, quintessentially Indian.

## ACKNOWLEDGEMENTS

My sincere thanks are due first of all to Prof. Julia A. B. Hegewald, formerly of the University of Manchester and now of the University of Bonn and to

Prof. Subrata K. Mitra, University of Heidelberg, for inviting me to present my contribution for the volume of essays entitled *Re-use: The Art and Politics of Integration and Anxiety*; to the Lalit Kala Akademi of New Delhi, for providing me with interesting bibliographical references, and last but not least to the artist Buddhadeb Chattopadhyaya, who passed away in Kolkata in May 2002.

## PHOTO CREDIT

All photographs reproduced in this chapter are by Tiziana Lorenzetti.

## BIBLIOGRAPHY

Alkazi, Ebrahim, 1978, *M. F. Husain: The Modern Artist of Tradition*. Art Heritage Publication, New Delhi.

Alkazi, Ebrahim, D. Elliot & V. Musgrave (eds), 1982, *India: Myth and Reality—Aspects of Modern Indian Art*. Museum of Modern Art, Oxford.

Appasamy, Jaya, 1980, *Thanjavur Paintings of the Maratha Period*. Abhinav Publications, New Delhi.

———, (ed.), 1987 [1973], *Jamini Roy*. Lalit Kala Akademi, New Delhi.

Archer, Mildred, 1977, *Indian Popular Painting in the India Office Library*. Her Majesty's Stationery Office, London.

———, 1979, *India and British Portraiture 1770–1825*. Sotheby Parke Bernet, London and New York.

———, 1997, *Company Painting: Indian Paintings of the British Period*. Antique Collector's Club, London.

Archer, William G., 1987, *The Art of Jamini Roy, 1887–1972*. A Centenary Volume. Birth Centenary Celebration Committee, Calcutta.

Argan, Giuseppe C., 2001 [1968], *L'Arte moderna, l'Ottocento e il Novecento*. Sansoni, Firenze.

Besant, Annie, 1896, *Thought Forms*. The Theosophical Press, New York.

Bhattacharya, Ashok K., 1974, *Citralakshana: A Treatise on Indian Painting*. Sarasvat Library, Calcutta.

Bayley, C. A. (ed.), 1990, *The Raj: India and British, 1600–1947*. National Portrait Gallery, London.

Bhavnani, Enakshi, 1974, *Folk and Tribal Designs of India*. Taraporevala, Bombay.

Brown, Percy, 1982, *Indian Painting*. Cosmo Publication, New Delhi.

Castelli, Enrico & Giovanni Aprile, 2005, *Divine Lithography*. Il Tamburo Parlante, New Delhi.

Chaitanya, Krishna, 1994, *A History of Indian Painting: The Modern Period*. Abhinav Publications, New Delhi.

Chaitanya Sambrani, 2003, "The Progressive Artists Group". In: Gayatri Sinha (ed.), *Indian Art: An Overview*. Rupa & Co., Delhi, pp. 121–27.

Chopra, S., 2004, "Past, Present and Future: Sher Gil and Beyond". *Indian Horizons*. Vol. 51, pp. 22–27.

Coomaraswamy, Ananda K., 1934, "The Technique and Theory of Indian Painting". *Technical Studies*. Vol. 3, no. 2, pp. 59–69.

Dalmia, Yashodhara, 2006, *Amrita Sher-Gil: A Life*. Penguin, New Delhi.

Das Gupta, S. N., 1940, *L'intimo aspetto dell'antica arte indiana*. IsMEO, Roma.

Dave Mukherji, Parul, 2001, *The Citrasutra of the Visnudharmottara Purana: Critically Edited and translated by P. Dave Mukherji*. Indira Gandhi National Centre for the Arts, New Delhi; Motilal Banarsidas, New Delhi.

de Almeida, Hermione & G. H. Gilpin, 2005, *Indian Renaissance: British Romantic Art and the Prospect of India*. Ashgate, London.

Di Stefano, Eva, 1993, *Kandinskij*. Giunti, Firenze.

Dolcini, Donatella, 1985, "'Raja' Ravi Varma: Senso dell'Indianità ed Eterno Feminino nella Pittura Indiana di Tardo Ottocento". *Annali di Ca' Foscari*. Vol. 24, no. 3, pp. 105–15.

Ghosh, D. P., 1982, *Mediaeval Indian Painting: Eastern School, 13th Century A.D. to Modern Times Including Folk Art*. Sundeepprakashan, Delhi.

Guha-Thakurta, Tapati, 1992, *The Making of a New 'Indian' Art: Artists, Aesthetics and Nationalism in Bengal c. 1850–1920*. Cambridge University Press, Cambridge.

———, 1995 (June), "Visualising the Nation: The Iconography of a 'National Art' in Modern India". *Journal of Arts and Ideas*. Nos 27–28, pp. 7–39.

———, 2003, "The Period of Colonialism and Nationalism, c. 1757–1947". In: F. M. Asher (ed.), *Art of India: Prehistory to the Present*. Encyclopaedia Britannica, Hong Kong, pp. 130–41.

Gupta, C. B., 2005, *Thanjavur Painting, Materials, Technique and Conservation*. National Museum, New Delhi.

Gupta, Shivani, 2004, "Harish Rathi: Painting the Cultural Heritage of India". *Indian Horizons*. Vol. 51, pp. 4–9.

Kulke, Hermann & Dietmar Rothermund, 1991, *Storia dell'India*. Garzanti, Milano [Originally published as: *A History of India*, 1990, Routledge, London].

Jackimowicz-Karle, Marta, 1988 (July–September), "K. Hebbar, Feeling for the Life-throb". *Kala Darshan, The Complete Magazine on Indian Arts and Culture*. Vol. 1, no. 3, pp. 13–22.

Karashima, Noboru, 1985, "Nayaka Rule in North and South Arcot Districts in South India during the Sixteenth Century". *Acta Asiatica*. Vol. 48, pp. 1–26.

———, 2002, *A Concordance of Nayakas: The Vijayanagar Inscriptions in South India*. Oxford University Press, New Delhi.

Khanna, Balaraj & A. Kurtha, 1998, *Art of Modern India*. Thames and Hudson, London.

Kramrisch, Stella, 1961, *Indian Sculpture in the Philadelphia Museum of Art*. University of Pennsylvania Press, Philadelphia.

Kandinsky, Wassili, 1989, *Lo Spirituale nell'Arte*. SE, Milano [Originally published as: *Über das Geistige in der Kunst: Insbesondere in der Malerei*, 1912. R. Piper & Co. Verlag, Munich].

Lorenzetti, Tiziana, forthcoming, "Interazione di forme fra l'Occidente moderno e l'India: da Lutyens a Correa". In: Pierfrancesco Fedi (ed.), *Atti del Convegno in ricordo di Maria Teresa Lucidi*. University of Rome 'La Sapienza', Rome.

Mago, Pran Nath, 1986, "Search for Roots: Exploration of Folk Arts for Identity". In: Pran Nath Mago (ed.), *In Search for Roots*. Lalit Kala Akademy, New Delhi, pp. 5–19.

——, 2001, *Contemporary Art in India: A Perspective*. National Book Trust, New Delhi.

Misra, Umesh Chandra, 1989, *Tribal Paintings and Sculptures*. B. R. Publishing Corporation, New Delhi.

Mitter, Partha, 1994, *Art and Nationalism in Colonial India 1850–1922*. Cambridge University Press, Cambridge.

——, 2001, *Indian Art*. Oxford University Press, Oxford.

——, 2008, *The Triumph of Modernism: India's Artists and the Avant-garde, 1922–1947*. Paperback, London.

Mookerjee, Ajit, 1939, *Folk Art of Bengal*. University of Calcutta, Calcutta.

Ramachandra Rao, P. R., 1953, *Modern Indian Painting*. Akshara, Hyderabad.

Randhawa, Mohinder Singh, 1981, *Indian Miniature Painting*. Roli Books International, New Delhi.

Rawson, Philip S., 1961, *Indian Painting*. Universe Books, Paris.

Sardesai, Abhay, 1998 (October–December), "The Abiding Power of Icons". *Art India: The Contemporary Art Magazine*. Vol. 3, no. 4, pp. 38–39.

Sen, Geeti, 1997, *Bindu: Space and Time in Raza's Vision*. Media TransAsia, New Delhi.

——, 2003, "Contemporary Art of India". In: F. M. Asher (ed.), *Art of India: Prehistory to the Present*. Encyclopaedia Britannica, Hong Kong, pp. 130–42.

Siva Kumar, R., 1997, *Shantiniketan: The Making of a Contextual Modernism*. National Gallery of Modern Art, New Delhi.

——, 2008, *Paintings of Abanindranath Tagore*. Pratikshan, Kolkata.

Sivaramamurti, Calambur, 1994 [1968], *South Indian Paintings*. Publications Division, New Delhi.

——, 1996 [1970], *Indian Painting*. National Book Trust India, New Delhi.

Tucci, Giuseppe, 1981 [1957], *Storia della filosofia indiana*. Laterza, Roma.

Tuli, Neville, 1997, *The Flamed-Mosaic, Indian Contemporary Painting*. Heart, Chidambaram and Ahmedabad.

Zimmer, Heinrich, 1984, *Artistic Form and Yoga in the Sacred Images of India*. Princeton University Press, Princeton [Originally published as: *Kunstform und Yoga im indischen Kultbild*, 1926. Verlags-Anstalt, Heidelberg].

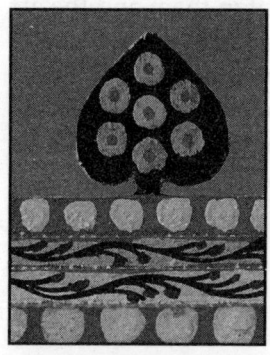

*Chapter 8*

# POLITICS OF ART AND THE ART OF POLITICS

## RE-USE OF 'TRIBAL' ARTS AND ARTEFACTS IN MODERN ORISSA

### BY PRASANNA K. NAYAK

## INTRODUCTION

Tribal works of art are basically priestly and/or shamanistic creations, an important men's affair, a manifestation of kingly pride and inspiration and therefore they receive sanction and certification from an authority above. Variations in art forms in tribal Orissa were due to intervention of local kings in the past. Hybridisation and decontexualisation of art forms today are due to the intervention of the Central/State governments. In the past, tribal cultures flourished under the patronage of kings, and the legitimacy of the king was dependent on an acknowledgement of tribal cultural beliefs and practices. Currently, in India, the central Government as well as the state Governments have not only pursued a positive discrimination policy for them but also have been supportive of preservation of their cultures and cultural artefacts. Be it tribal cultures in general or particular works of tribal art, politics is implicit in them and the art of politics in India today is based on ethnocultural divides, and, in the wake of globalisation, India is playing its cultural card in order to appropriate politico-economic dividends. Post-modern taste of people is displayed in the private sphere: to adore and acquire works of tribal art to decorate their drawing or living rooms. Everybody loves anything tribal and hence the re-use of tribal arts and artefacts.

## CONTEXT

Orissa is home to sixty-two tribes. They are officially listed as Scheduled Tribes, or *jana-jati*s. In the past, different tribal groups inhabiting the feudatory states, 'jungle kingdoms'[1] of Orissa enjoyed autonomy and had developed distinct sociocultural and political structures of their own. The kings of these states derived their legitimacy from the support of the tribes. Not surprisingly, therefore, a majority of these tribes claim royal ancestry and kingly connections. The cultural styles, arts and artefacts of individual tribes were appreciated and appropriated by the feudal lords for purposes of sustainable governance.[2]

Today, in democratic India, the government has adopted a policy of preservation of tribal cultures in their varied forms even while implementing a policy of development of tribes and tribal areas. Although translating development policy into practice has run into rough weather over the years (Nayak 2010), governments at the national and state levels have continued to use and re-use 'tribal' arts and artefacts for political purposes. Tribal cultural outfits, arts and artefacts in their varied forms are displayed in programmes sponsored by the government and political parties during the celebration of Independence Day, the Republic Day or during election campaigns.

In recent years, a more than usual interest has been evinced by government, non-government agencies as well as private persons in setting up of institutions and centres of tribal art and artefacts, in putting up exhibitions of tribal arts and artefacts under several themes and sub-themes, and also in organisation of tribal dance and drama. Government of India sponsors setting up of urban *hat*s

---

[1] Burkhard Schnepel uses the term 'jungle kingdoms' in his study of little kings of south Orissa (Schnepel 2002).

[2] In the early 1970s, the author had the opportunity of observing special interactions of two of the south Orissan tribes: the Gadaba and the Dongria Kondh, with their respective kings, the Maharaja of Jeypore and the Thatraja of Bissam, Cuttack. The tribal chiefs made special offerings of gifts of forest produce, *bheti*, to the kings and in return the kings presented them *pagarhi*s, turbans, which were specially designed; white *pagarhi*s with red borders to the Naiks, Gadaba chiefs, and red *pagarhi*s to the Mondals, Dongia Kondh chiefs.

(markets) in towns and cities of India for promotion of regional handicrafts, pre-eminently tribal arts and crafts.[3] Thus, recounting past cultural traditions and re-using them in one form or another serves the ends of political parties in India and imposes versions and images of the past on tribals cut-off from their roots.[4]

Drawing examples from the Orissan experience, the chapter intends to bring to light some of the less talked about aspects of the politics of art and the art of politics espoused by the little kings of the feudatory states in Orissa and the mutations these have undergone under a modern democratic dispensation. It seeks to demonstrate how these cut across regional distinctions and boundaries. In the globalisation process, global marketing of tribal arts and artefacts have enabled many government and private agencies and organisations to popularise and propagate tribal cultural products. They even hire artists and artisans for commercial production of their wares (see Plate 8.9). These agents of promotion of tribal art and artefacts, in the process of competing with one another, affect the interests of tribal artists and artisans adversely. As a result, the purpose of the tribal development programmes and strategies gets defeated. In the end, using the weaker sections to gain political leverage leaves these sections even more vulnerable.

## PROPOSITIONS

Hindus believe that Lord Brahma created the universe but Visvakarma, the Divine Architect, designed the universe in its multiple manifestations. Analogically, tribals or people of simple societies, most possibly in the distant past must have been the architects of all human cultures in their possible variations and later ramifications everywhere. The ideal design founded on a harmony between nature and culture is found almost intact in most of the tribal societies of Orissa today. The more 'primitive', the more pristine is the design. In the

---

[3] Especially beginning with the Fifth Five-Year Plan, the Government of India has sponsored setting up of Museums of Tribal Art and Artefacts in the premises of Tribal Research Institutes (Report of Woking Group 2002). In recent years, 'Urban *Hats*' and 'Craft Villages' have been set-up in many cities to promote and propagate tribal arts and crafts. Many NGOs also receive government grants to promote tribal art and craft. Every year, on the Independence Day and/or the Republic Day, the central as well as the state governments sponsor the organisations of week-long programmes of tribal dance and drama, and the tribals participate in it adorning themselves with traditional costumes.

[4] Youths drawn from tribal villages are being sponsored by the government to undertake training courses in art in art schools and colleges to become professionals in tribal art. During 2000–04, the author, while working as Director of the Tribal Research Institute, Bhubaneswar, was involved in many such government-sponsored programmes, and who had a thorough understanding of 'politics of art and the art of politics' in Orissa.

Indian context, the so-called tribes, more particularly the 'primitive tribes' and in many instances, the tribal-like caste groups, have kept to the standards of the early design and continue to follow the design in their day-to-day practices and strive to keep up the same spirit. Modern times, modern technology and influence of modern ideas have not fully eroded the foundational base of the simple and pristine cultures. The Hindus are like that. They change but maintain continuity in change. Culture grows in their case through a process of accretion. They value the past as much as they plunge into the future. The past enlivens in them, always with them. The globalisation spree in India has not been able to engulf the traditional cultures. Rather, they have appeared and reappeared in several designs and degrees and have grown and developed stronger and are also being used as instruments of power and politics in the country and as media of maximisation of politico-economic clout abroad. Thus traditional cultural practices are promoted to be on sale in the global market.

\* \* \* \*

Decontextualisation of art and artefacts narrows the definition of art. The art of living is also an art. Tribal arts of living are singularly remarkable and distinctive. If a piece of painting on the wall of a tribal dwelling could be viewed by us as a work of art—which the tribals see as their ritual scribing, their pantheon, a visual expression of their cultural identity—then there are many more tribal cultural artefacts which can be safely considered as works of art.

Tribal cultures as 'complex wholes', in every respect are artful in nature. In their lifestyle, one sees an art of living. In their food and drinking habits (see Plate 8.4), dress pattern (see Plates 8.5, 8.10), hair style, settlement structure, house pattern (see Plate 8.11), modes and means of earning a living, in raising crops in the swiddens, in their etiquettes, dealings and greeting behaviour, in their movement and gait, sitting habits and manners, dancing and singing, decorum in assemblies while taking decisions, propitiation of gods and spirits, and so on, one observes and encounters unique and unitary designs that are aesthetically artistic. Everything that you see in a tribal culture is as if it is a piece of art. And, in modern parlance, the work of art and painting that one notices on the walls of their dwellings, designs of their wood carvings, erection of memory stones and installation of stones under the trees (see Plate 8.3), propitiation of stones symbolising deities are unique to an individual tribe as if the entire culture in the context of a particular tribe is an art itself, a visual presentation, a cultural display, and every single tribal individual is a fully-grown artist himself.

\* \* \* \*

Be it tribal cultures in general or particular works of tribal art, politics is implicit in them and the art of politics in India today is based on ethnocultural divides, and in the wake of globalisation, India is playing its cultural card in order to appropriate politico-economic dividends. In *Chanakya Nitisloka*, one of the compilations of the famous Indian Sanskrit scholar Chanakya, in the second to third century BCE, one verse reads, in the form of a truism: "asma'pi yati devatvan mahadbhih supratisthitah" (even a stone can become god if it is installed by a great personality). Tribal works of art are basically priestly and/or shamanistic creations, a big men's affair, a manifestation of kingly pride and inspiration, and therefore they receive sanction and certification from an authority above. In the past, tribal cultures flourished under the patronage of kings and the legitimacy of the king was dependent on an acknowledgement of tribal cultural beliefs and practices. Indigenous tribal cultures are adaptive strategies of tribal groups and therefore involve decision-making at higher political levels within and without.[5] Currently, in India, the central government as well as state governments have not only pursued a positive discrimination policy for them but also have been supportive of the preservation of their cultures and cultural artefacts.

## JUNGLE KINGS AND TRIBAL ART AND CRAFT: QUALITY, PRECISION, STATUS AND PERSONALITY

In the historical past, 'little kings' or 'jungle kings' ruled over the hill and jungle tracts of Orissa (Schnepel 2002, 2005). These kings wooed the support of the local tribal chiefs and the latter in turn showed allegiance to the former. In many instances, the tribals were instrumental in the making of a king, and the king in turn had granted special privileges to the tribals (Schnepel 2004; Nayak 2007). Folk histories collected from south, north and western Orissa attest to this view (Das 1950, 1989; Chakravorti 2001). Some tribes trace their ritual bond of kinship ties with the kings. Although the kingdoms are no longer in existence and neither do the kings have any authority over the tribes, yet, ritual friendship and kinship between the present-day kings' families and the tribes people continues. Ritual exchange of gifts and symbolic interactions between the king's people and the tribes' people (Kulke 2010; Tripathy 2010) on the occasions of Dusselra and Rath Yatra today testifies the claims of most of the tribes' people that they are in their status positions kingly. On these occasions, the tribal representatives present themselves before the king in their traditional attire and impress upon the progenitors and present family members of the then kings about their cultural identity as a form of a unique visual art, which the former appreciate and acknowledge. They feel proud of their culture, which is no less

---

[5] On the basis of a four-decade long intimate encounter and experience with several tribes of Orissa, the author holds this view of tribal cultures as 'adaptive strategies'.

superior to any other culture around them and they value their dignity in life and living as comparable to the king's standard.

The Dongria Kondh, one of the so-called primitive tribes of south Orissa inhabiting the Niamgiri hills would never work as a labourer anywhere. They say that they are *raja-loka*, especially the descendants of the Niamraja. The Bhuiyan in north Orissa treat the king of Keojhar as their sister's son and therefore at the coronation ceremony the ritual practice follows that the would-be king is seated on the lap of the Bhuiyan Katei, the Bhuiyan priest. In western Orissa, the Binjhals used to claim royal ancestry. The fact of the matter is that the tribes' people in many ways than one claim their association with their local kings and express their kingly identity and cultural status. On these ceremonial occasions in the past, the kings would, in due recognition of their artistic cultural excellence, reward and honour the tribal chiefs by tying head gears of different colours and textures suiting to their level of artistic displays of their cultures.

Thus, the individual tribal communities with all their distinctiveness were well served by the kings and the kings never did anything to violate the cultural principles and practices espoused by the tribes' people. The kings used to facilitate the growth of diverse cultural lifestyles in their own kingdoms and helped promote arts and crafts. In the process, they promoted a culture of ingenuity and traditional technological excellence. The tribal chiefs on specific festival occasions would invite the kings to participate with them and be with the tribal congregations. By this the tribals used to get all patronage of the kings, which in turn helped them in maintaining and preserving what they had. In the kings' palaces, the tribal deities were installed, propitiated and adored and tribal priests and shamans made ritual offerings in their own style, drawing ritual arts on the floor and the walls of the temples.

The many wall drawings and figurines that we see in many Hindu temples must have been of tribal origin, although found in certain modified forms today. The Jagannatha Temple and its traditions at Puri is a striking example. The art and figure images one sees in the Jagannatha Temple walls and the wood carving of the chariots of the trinity and their decoration are all clear indications of the use of tribal art forms and techniques (Nayak 2001a). It is well known that Jagannatha is a tribal deity, and most of the temple priests and ritual functionaries are of tribal origin. They are called *Daita*s. Similarly, in most of the Shiva temples of Bhubaneswar, the main ritual functionaries are Mali Mohapatras, who are of tribal origin. However, now all these functionaries claim Brahmanical status.[6]

* * * *

---

[6] In 1990s, the author personally observed temple rituals in Puri and Bhubaneswar and confidentially interviewed the priests serving in these temples and came to know about their tribal origins.

It may be said that all tribal arts are ritual arts. Most importantly, they served a complex ritual purpose, and a sense of aesthetics is suffused in them. Often the components of a piece of art are made up of signs and symbols, and each sign and symbol used therein have meanings (see Plates 8.1, 8.2). The artists are no ordinary persons; rather they are specialists with born qualities in them. They are all gifted individuals who can communicate with the symbolic representations creating lively situations. They draw the symbolic figures which come in the dreams of these artists. These art works of the ritual specialists are used as magic wands. In order to be functional, the quality and precision of the ritual arts will have to be maintained. Any dereliction of the order may bring disaster to the artist himself or herself or to his or her family or the entire community. Quality and precision are never sacrificed because of fear of the wrath of the deity and the artists are experts in ritual art.

The status and personality of the artist is reflected in these ritual arts. Thus ritual arts in a tribal community have their own identity and all the arts are graded according to the status of the artist who is basically a ritual functionary. For the tribals, the king is the supreme artist under whose tutelage they perform their arts. The tribals see in their arts the spirit and the power of the king as well as that of the spiritual beings of the spiritual world.

In the walls of Hindu temples, mutated versions of the tribal arts find their prominence and the devotees, before paying their obeisance to the presiding deity of the temple, go on greeting and paying obeisance to the walled-in figurine deities. Figures on the walls of temples and residential houses have their significance. People believe that deities in their multiple variations reside on the walls of houses and temples and therefore the Hindus have the habit of submitting themselves by paying obeisance to the walled-in deities by touching their heads to the walls before they set out of their homes daily or occasionally, and also before entering any temples. However, the quality and precision in the depiction and drawing of art works had supernatural sanction as well as kingly or sovereign sanction and, by abiding by the standards, each piece of art had its status and the artists used to possess a high status in the society and maintain an uncompromising personality.

## DEMOCRATIC GOVERNMENT AND TRIBAL ART AND CRAFT: QUANTITY, CAMOUFLAGE AND CORRUPTION

In the remote tribal villages, the democratically-elected modern leaders are seen as go-betweens, between the government and the local people, who bring change and development in the area. But in their day-to-day sociocultural affairs, the traditional village councils continue to be functional and the traditional functionaries rule the roost and somehow manage to save the dying institutions and institutional practices, and so also the traditional art works. Modern leaders pay casual attention to traditional art and craft, but under the stimuli of making money out of selling their wares, they become instrumental in sending their little-educated young men and women for getting formal training in institutions of art and craft, mostly sponsored by government and non-government agencies under the policy of preservation of traditional culture and economic development schemes, such as income generation (Nayak 2001b, 2010). Many of the trainees in art and craft do not qualify for making ritual arts but make arts which are of secular and aesthetic value in a modern sense of art. Thus, they produce large varieties of mutated forms of art in considerable quantity.

Many voluntary agencies participate, partly to help preserve traditional art and promote tribal artists as neo-professionals and, at the same time, make money out of this new opportunities created by the government. Some of these agencies hire these artists to produce art and craft on a large scale in their art and craft centres—like industries situated in towns and cities—and then make huge profits by trading and often exporting them outside the country at a good price. The irony is that the traditional artists hardly intend to transgress the customary rules of art-making and therefore do not prefer to engage themselves in mass production of these arts, which have fallen out of their culturally-founded ritually-ordained context. Thus, they languish. The art works are gradually losing their meaning; rather they are viewed as material productions meant to please the outsiders, not insiders. Every piece of art appears to be a camouflage.

\* \* \* \*

In recent years, it has become a fashion to print new year's greeting cards with tribal motifs, to present tribal arts and crafts as gifts to high profile friends, colleagues and persons on their birthdays, marriage anniversaries and on innumerable other occasions as per the Hindu calendar. By giving gifts of tribal art in some form or other to decorate the private residences or office rooms of political masters and officers of high rank and file, one can manipulate interpersonal relationships with an ulterior motive to fulfil many a personal interest. The gift giver and the gift taker both may not genuinely appreciate the piece of art given as gift but pretend that the tribal traditions in the shape of the art products is to be preserved and they thereby join the foreign visitors and tourists in publicly propagating these arts. A whole of lot corruption creeps into the public space in the name of tribal art.

During Independence Day or Republic Day, the federal states of the Indian union display their respective cultural identities and the tribal cultural wares and artefacts get publicly paraded, displayed and exhibited in competitive spirit in the national capital of Delhi as well as in their state capitals to demonstrate

India's unity in diversity. The tribal dance troupes in their colourful attire and body movements show their mirth and excellence in the public, especially before the powers that be. All these are officially sponsored by the state and national governments and the best outfits in each item of cultural show are adjudged and awarded. A whole lot of politics is involved in it. While the Rajas and Maharajas, as well as the feudal lords, in the feudal past, used to appreciate each and every cultural show and artistic style, and recognise each as independent, in the democratic government setup, competitions among the states are growing stronger each day in cannibalistic spree.

## VARIATIONS IN ART FORMS IN TRIBAL ORISSA

Two major cultural variations along linguistic lines, such as Dravidian-speaking and Munda-speaking (Austro-Asiatic) tribal groups are observed among the tribal groups of Orissa (Nayak 2003). In the settlement pattern—house type and village plan and orientation—a marked difference is noticed among the Dravidian and Munda tribes and so also in their art work. But irrespective of their culture–linguistic divisions, local, subregional and regional variations, and variations within variations are also found, which is due to the intervention of local kings in the past. The Oriya (Indo-Sanskritic) speaking Hinduised tribes follow the practices of either of the Dravidian or of the Munda style, often being influenced by the caste Hindu practices of art forms. Due to modern influences and direct intervention of the government programmes, today there has occurred a hybridisation and decontextualisation of tribal art forms which has further added to the variations in tribal art.

\* \* \* \*

At the time of elections to the state assembly or to the parliament, regional and national political parties in order to woo the tribal voters have evolved strategies to re-use the tribal attires putting them on their shoulders as aprons or tie them as headgears, symbolising the tribal chiefs, *sardars* or the jungle kings. The modern tribal political leaders, in order to show their unity with the tribal cultures and demonstrate their identity with the forest-dwelling habitat, use twigs of leaves and flowers[7] made of plastic and decorate their heads in the traditional style and address the tribal congregations, preferably in the tribal market places on the market days. Under the patronage of Viswa Hindu Parishad (VHP), an

---

[7] The chiefs (*sardars*) of Bhuiyan tribe make offerings (*bheti*) of headgears made out of twigs of leaves and flowers to the crown prince to wear on the occasion of his coronation ceremony (Nayak 2007).

organisation of the Bharatiya Janata Party (BJP), a Hindu nationalist political party, photos of Hindu epic gods and goddesses like Rama and Sita and Krishna and Radha and their siblings and spouses in their original, exotic looks are being worshipped in the Saora tribal villages of Chandragiri and Kondh tribal villages of Phulbani, and for that, the villagers take Sundays off and participate in community prayers and *bhajan*s to counter the effects of the spread of Christianity and tacitly propagate the ideals of indigenous and indigenised cultural styles and art outfits and convey the message how these are integral to the ideals of a Hindu land. The educated young tribal men and women in these tribal areas draw their art—traditional art designs in a modern form—and decorate the walls and floors of the Sunday prayer rooms, which appeal the autochthones the most.

## RE-USE OF TRIBAL ARTS AND ARTEFACTS IN THE NEW CAPITAL CITY OF ORISSA

Under the personal patronage of the present Chief Minister of Orissa, the city administration and municipal corporation engage in city beautification by drawing, sketching and engraving tribal motifs on the walls of public buildings and public places or any space available for public gaze. Both the sides of VIP roads of Bhubaneswar, the state capital of Orissa, are beginning to wear a tribal look, re-using tribal paintings and stone art; an expensive project launched by the municipal corporation (see Plates 8.6, 8.7, 8.8). Works of tribal art, in some form or other, are found decorating government officers' rooms, most conspicuously in the secretariat buildings. The latest trends are being promoted by museums (see Plate 8.10) in India, which promote display and depiction of tribal art and artefacts, setting up of tribal huts and their re-use. People in the capital city have developed a postmodern taste for display of tribal wares in the private sphere: to adore and acquire works of tribal art to decorate their drawing or living rooms. There is also increased media coverage of tribal art and artefacts and tribal lifestyles through special channels under Taranga. These days everybody loves anything tribal. In recent years, a growing number of academics in the humanities and social sciences have displayed a keen interest in tribal studies crossing traditional disciplinary boundaries.

## CONCLUSION

Individual tribes in Orissa continue to retain their cultural distinctiveness and display their cultural excellence as a complete form of art to the appreciation of the people wielding political power and for the entertainment of the public at large. Indeed, the unified art of life and living of the tribals flourished in the past under the patronage and support of the little kings in the feudatory estates of Orissa. Democratic governments in modern India use and re-use tribal cultural outfits with a motto of preserving tribal cultures in some form or other. Political parties use tribal motives and insignia to woo the tribal electorate and the art of identity politics is gaining new ground in Indian politics.

Under the patronage of government and private agencies, many artists today create new arts on tribal cultural and ecological themes and re-use the ritual drawings, motifs and designs of tribals across cultures as tribal arts. Demand for tribal arts and crafts has stimulated the growth and spread of private institutions for preservation and propagation of tribal art and artefacts of mutated forms totally thrown out of the tribal cultural contexts. Tribal arts now are in the hands of middlemen. Bona fide artists languish in the woods and the enterprising non-tribals have captured the market for tribal art and handicrafts. Tribal art has become a lucrative profession for the non-tribal students of art.

## PHOTO CREDIT

All photographs reproduced in this chapter are by Prasanna K. Nayak.

## BIBLIOGRAPHY

Chakravorti, Debasis, 2001, *Kendujhar Parichiti*. Sansar Press, Telenga Bazar, Cuttack.

Das, Bipin Bihari, 1950, *Bhanjabhumi Kendujhari*, Part I. Neelachala Printing Works, Badabil, Kendujhar.

———, 1989, *Bhanjabhumi Kendujhari*, Part II. Neelachala Prakashani, Badbil, Kendujhar.

Kulke, Hermann, 2010, "Feudatory States of Orissa: Centres out There". In: Hermann Kulke & Georg Berkemer (eds), *Centres Out There? Facets of Subregional Identities in Orissa*. Manohar, Delhi, pp. 49–80.

Nayak, P. K., 1989, *Blood, Women and Rerritory: An Analysis of Clan Feuds of Dongria Konds*. Reliance Publishing House, New Delhi.

———, 2001a, "Jagannath and the Adivasi: Reconsidering the Cult and its Traditions". In: Hermann Kulke & Burkhard Schnepel (eds), *Jagannath Revisited*. Manohar Publications, New Delhi.

———, 2001b, "Revisiting Tribes and Reconsidering Tribal Development". *Adivasi* (Journal of the Scheduled Castes and Scheduled Tribes Research and Training Institute [SCSTRTI]). Vol. 40, no. 1, pp. 1–11.

Nayak, P. K., 2003, "Social, Cultural and Linguistic Variations in Tribal Orissa". In: *Tribes of Orissa*. SCSTRTI, Bhubaneswar.

————, 2007, "Owning the King: Ethno-cultural Politics in Bhuiyan Pirha". *Man in Society*. Vol. XVII, Journal of the Department of Anthropology, Utkal University, Bhubaneswar, pp. 19–69.

————, 2010, "The Rise and Fall of Tribal Development in Orissa". *The News Letter*. No. 53, pp. 20–21. IIAS, Leiden.

Government of India, 2002, Report of Working Group for Empowering the Scheduled Tribes during the Xth V year Plan, 2002, Ministry of Tribal Affairs, Government of India, pp. 29–31.

Schnepel, B., 2002, *The Jungle Kings: Ethnological Aspects of Politics and Ritual in Orissa*. Manohar, New Delhi.

————, 2004, "History of the Model". In: G. Berkemer & M. Frenz (eds), *Sharing Sovereignty: The Little Kingdom in South Asia*. Klaus Schwarz Verlag, Berlin, pp. 11–20.

————, 2005, "Kings and Tribes in East India". In: D. Quigley (ed.), *The Character of Kingship*. Berghahn Publishers, Oxford, pp. 187–208.

Tripathy, G. C., 2010, "The Transformation of a Tribal State into a Centre of Regional Culture: The Case of the Bhanjas of Keonjhar". In: Hermann Kulke & Georg Berkemer (eds), *Centres out There? Facets of Subregional Identities in Orissa*. Manohar, Delhi, pp. 81–112.

*Chapter 9*

# ANOTHER FORM OF RE-USE?

## INSTITUTIONAL CONTINUITY AND 'INDIGENISATION' OF WESTMINSTER PARLIAMENTARIANISM AND WESTERN PARTY POLITICS IN POST-COLONIAL INDIA

**BY CLEMENS SPIESS**

## INTRODUCTION

The gradual evolvement of modern Indian party politics and parliamentarianism after Independence, arising out of the clash between the inherited canon of liberal institutions and ideas, indigenous political traditions as well as residues of the British Raj and Indian nationalism, neither reflected a process of unidirectional transformation of Indian politics (towards an ideal type of liberal party politics and parliamentarianism based on the Western experience) nor was it simply a case of hybridity representing a synthesis of opposites and the mutation of new forms of political action. What took place instead was a process of 'indigenisation', whereby parties and parliamentarianism acquired local roots and adapted to indigenous conditions while retaining their canonical form and featuring institutional continuity. Can this be considered as another form of re-use? A strategic upholding of the institutions and ideas—used and practised by the former colonial rulers—which were to be filled with or adapted to 'indigenous life'? A 're-use' necessary, because these very institutions and ideas were seen to be the appropriate institutional and ideational 'containers' of what was to become a new and legitimate political order?[1] This chapter traces the decision for institutional continuity, that is, the retention of a (modified) Westminster institutional structure and its concomitant manifestation of party politics, back to strategic deliberations about the need for a not too thorough departure from the institutional model of the former colonisers. It investigates the ways and means by which Western party politics and Westminster parliamentarianism were 'indigenised' in post-colonial India, how they were imbued with locally embedded values, identities, perceptions and networks in order to provide a 'usable', or 'tried and tested' framework for the exercise of governance in a post-colonial context. Ultimately and from a conceptual angle, it asks to what extent the indigenisation of Western party politics and Westminster parliamentarianism in post-colonial India can be considered as a successful case of re-use.

## THE EMPIRE IS DEAD, LONG LIVE WESTMINSTER: INDIA OPTS FOR INSTITUTIONAL CONTINUITY

Contrary to India's nationalist myths, enamoured of immemorial 'village republics', pre-colonial history little prepared it for modern democracy. Nor was democracy a gift of the departing British. Democracy was established after a profound historical rupture—the experience, at once humiliating and enabling, of colonialism, which made it impossible for Indians to regard their own past as a sufficient resource for facing the future and condemned them, in struggling against the subtle knots of the foreigner's Raj, to struggle also against themselves. But it also incited them to imagine new possibilities: of being a nation, of possessing their own state, and of doing so on their own terms in a world of other states. By gradually raising the edifice of a state whose sovereign powers stretched across

---

[1] For the sake of analytical clarity, a distinction is made here between the concepts of hybridity and indigenisation. Whereas the former denotes a process whereby something (institutionally) new evolves out of the amalgamation of imported institutions and local traditions, the latter refers to imported institutions retaining their canonical form but acquiring local roots. The distinction between indigenisation and re-use is more difficult to draw. Here, the main difference is between indigenisation as a more or less unintentional process and re-use as the result of strategic, purposeful action. Re-use could thus be conceived of as the trigger that sets the process of indigenisation into motion.

the vast Indian landscape, the British made politics the unavoidable terrain on which Indians would have to learn to act. (Khilnani 1999: 17)

What Khilnani refers to in the section on 'democracy' in his widely acclaimed *The Idea of India*—the ambiguity of the colonial legacy in terms of its humiliating as well as enabling capacity regarding the search for a new political identity—can be used as a starting point for the analysis of the 're-use' and/or 'indigenisation' of Western party politics and Westminster parliamentarianism in post-colonial India. As a post-colonial state keen to embark upon a democratic project, but burdened with the formidable tasks of nation-building and meeting the development challenge, India could neither rely on any kind of pre-colonial traditions of political or social organisation—these were simply not suitable for the management of a territory and society as vast and diverse as India and given the nationalist elites' aspirations for social equality and universal citizenship—nor could it fully emulate the British model of parliamentary democracy and its concomitant manifestation of party politics because the struggle "against the subtle knots of the foreigner's Raj" (Khilnani 1999: 17) had just ended and some sort of a departure from colonial symbols and definitions had to take place.

What took place instead was some sort of a 're-use' of the operational parts of the Westminster institutions and the model of party and electoral politics exemplified through the former colonisers' political modus operandi, which were thought of as the best way to 'economise' power and uphold governance and social order amidst the political vagaries brought about by Partition, the integration of the former princely states or an often violent struggle to end colonial rule. At the same time, quite understandably, but unlike Sri Lanka, the ceremonial trappings of the Westminster model and British culture, were largely abandoned (Kumarasingham 2008).[2]

It was, however, clear that this re-use of the Westminster model and British-style party politics, a facade which the nationalist elite had already become acquainted with, for some time before Independence, had to encompass broad adaptations in order to promise success in sustaining democracy and governance, or, in other words, the chosen institutional arrangement had to match the nationalist elites' aspirations (for the sake of simplicity, let's assume they

---

[2] The part of the nationalist Indian elite that was to embrace the institutional continuity that a retention of the Westminster parliamentary model could provide, was so convinced of the need for an efficient parliamentarism that a 're-use' of the model of the former colonisers had to offer, that they even rejected the British idea of replacing the non-Asian nomenclature of the model (such as Governor, Prime Minister, Republic) with more indigenous titles borrowed from Indian history. The latter was a suggestion by Clement Attlee to Nehru dating back to 20 March 1949, and cited in a letter from Nehru to Patel (26 March 1949), in which Nehru described Attlee's letter as a "naïve document" (Patel 1971: 5–8).

were guided by ideas of 'welfare' and 'freedom of citizens') and had to be filled with local life to work in local contexts. But the fact alone that the Westminster model was chosen by the founding fathers of the Indian Constitution as an appropriate 'institutional fit' amidst a plethora of alternative and very often more indigenous models of governance—and against the 'ideological flavour of the day', which was much more inclined towards socialist or communist notions of governance—bears witness of both, the strength of the British institutional imprint, also the strategic character of the decision for maintaining the institutional arrangement of the former colonisers.

This choice was in no way predetermined; there were several serious state alternatives available such as, for example, the Gandhian vision of a decentralised web of village republics enhancing a bottom–up perspective of state formation, a Hindu state advocated by those critical of the Congress's secular commitment and arousing fears of minority suppression, a presidential system patterned along the American example or even a highly centralised, quasi-authoritarian state along the lines of the vice-regal model[3] and India's historical legacies pointed to a variety of possible outcomes. The Constitutional Assembly Debates (CAD) are interspersed with discussions on the need for a more thorough departure from the British parliamentary tradition,[4] but eventually the re-use of a 'tried and tested' institutional formula was accepted, essentially because—once

---

[3] For a detailed and perceptive account of the framing of the Indian Constitution and of the various alternatives of state formation that were discussed, see Austin (1966). Austin, in what remains to date the most sophisticated interpretation of the CAD, comes to the conclusion that "[m]embers spoke of democracy, socialism and the responsibilities of legislatures but not of the necessity for an 'Indian' form of government" (Austin 1966: 33).

[4] For example, K. Hanumanthaiya argued with regard to the 'British' character of the Indian Constitution and the way it was drafted:

> It is, something like this: we wanted the music of *Veena or Sitar*, but here we have the music of an English band. That was because our constitution makers were educated that way. I do not blame them rather, I would blame those people, or those of us, who entrusted them with this kind of work. (CAD, vol. XI: 616)

One Ramnarayan Singh lamented somewhat polemically that:

> [...] if you look into this Constitution it would be difficult for you to find anything Indian. I would go so far as to say that those of our future generations who might be unfamiliar with the History of this Constitution, would say that it was framed not at Delhi but at London. At least the people will have this suspicion. Some of them would have the suspicion also whether the representatives of the people of India framed this Constitution or whether the British of the White House in London were pleased to frame it [....] I regret to say that our countrymen have not forsaken the ways of their former masters and that they are ingrained in their minds. I am of the opinion [....] that we would experience much more difficulty in bidding good-bye to the ways of the British than we experienced in bidding good-bye to the British themselves. (CAD, vol. XI: 639)

adapted to local context and for reasons elaborated below—it suited the pursuit of governance and management of social order much better than any alternative, more indigenous or traditional form of political organisation.

Usually, the explanation of institutional continuity of the Westminster model in India is grounded in the argument of the "attachment to the familiar" (Morris-Jones 1964). Of course, there is a grain of truth in this proposition as the following quote from the CAD reveals. K. M. Munshi, member of the constitutional Drafting Committee, grasped the logic behind the incorporation of the former oppressors' institutions of governance into India's constitutional framework by referring to some sort of institutional familiarity:

> We must not forget a very important fact that during the last hundred years, Indian public life has largely drawn upon the traditions of the British Constitutional law. Most of us [...] have looked up to the British model as the best. For the last thirty or forty years, some kind of responsibility has been introduced in the governance of this country. Our Constitutional traditions have become Parliamentary, and we have now all our provinces functioning more or less on the British model. As a matter of fact, today, the Dominion Government of India is functioning as a full-fledged parliamentary government [...] After this experience, why should we go back upon the traditions that have been built for over a hundred years and try a novel experiment framed 150 years ago [the US-style presidential system, C. S.] and found wanting even in America?
>
> (CAD, vol. VII: 984–85)

Again, however, the decision for institutional continuity or, for that matter, for a re-use or appropriation of the institutions and, therefore, also the symbols of "those who had lost power" by the former "subjects of aggression"[5] can also be conceived of as a more deliberate undertaking, a strategic device in order to resort to the rather instrumental character of a state apparatus influenced by British political culture for the pursuit of a more state-oriented and less

---

[5] Conceptual references to the definition of 're-use' in quotation marks refer to the working definitions given in the panel description of the panel "*Re-use*: The Art and Politics of Integration and Anxiety" at the 20th European Conference on Modern South Asian Studies in Manchester (8–11 July 2008) where 're-use' is defined as "the intercontextual transfer of knowledge, design and belief by subjects of aggression, initially for the purpose of survival but ultimately for the construction of a new identity and the transformation of victim-hood into agency" and as a "strategic incorporation of the past into the fold of modern institutions" and to Hegewald & Mitra (2008: 1–2) where 're-use' is defined as:

> ... the attempt by conquering groups to appropriate the sacred sites, buildings and images of those who have lost power and transform them in a manner in which they could serve as symbols of their power. States—as holders of the monopoly of legitimate violence—need such symbols to economise the use of power. Success in the former often contributes to success in the latter.

society-centred approach to governance (or, as some would argue, to facilitate the preservation of elite privileges; see, for example, Washbrook 2001; Frankel 1978 or—as the 'classic' reference—Bardhan 1984) and/or in order to construct a new identity with the help of the unifying bond represented by the 'universalist' institutional blueprint of the Westminster model and by using the institutions or symbols of power of the former colonisers.

In a sense, the choice for institutional continuity along familiar lines despite widespread misgivings at the time the institutional fabric of Independent India was beginning to take shape holds true for the idea of political parties and party competition as the essence of modern representative democracy as well. By now, it is well-known that Gandhi, shortly before his assassination, called for the dissolution of the Congress party, which he saw in 'decay and decline'[6] and prone to corruption, and his general belief in the divisiveness, power obsession and unsuitability of modern political parties in the Indian context was shared by many in the Constituent Assembly.[7] Nevertheless, modern party politics—largely along the lines envisaged by the Westminster model of parliamentary democracy—prevailed, and party and electoral politics became the essence of Indian democracy. The latter is not the least visible from the high degree of 'partyness' that characterises political competition in India as illustrated, for example, by the fact that the aggregate vote share of independents in Lok Sabha (lower House of Parliament) elections was going down from 15.9 per cent in 1952 to 6.3 per cent in 1996 and that, concomitantly, the percentage of candidates

---

[6] The story was told to me by Sadiq Ali, former general secretary of the Congress party in an interview conducted at Gandhi Memorial, New Delhi, on 18 December 2000.

[7] The following quote from a speech by Ramnarayan Singh in the Constituent Assembly illustrates—sometimes, rather prophetically—this feeling of discontent that accompanied the general acceptance of modern party politics as the cornerstone of Indian democracy:

> The parliamentary system of government or the party-system of government has been provided for in this Constitution. I would like to say that it does not suit India. Unfortunately there are already too many parties in our country. There have been parties on the basis of the caste-system for a long time. Now if you introduce a new party-system what will be the outcome? If under the party-system you grant franchise to everyone, the result will be that some scoundrels and capitalists will combine and manage to monopolise all the votes. I know that they would not lack associates. Democracy cannot function in such a way. The way affairs are managed in Western countries has something of democracy in it but there too there is no real democracy. I hold that the government based on party-system strikes at the very roots of democracy. Under that system only a few persons rule […] It is right that in democracy everyone should have a vote and it is also right that an issue should be decided by the vote of the majority. But it should not be necessary that every person should belong to some party or other for arriving at decisions. The party decisions or the directions of a leader should not influence voting. Everyone should be free to vote and should do so honestly. The decision arrived at in this way will be a democratic decision and the country will benefit by it. Otherwise a party leader will give directions and others will vote accordingly. The decision arrived at in this way will not be a democratic decision […]. (CAD, vol. XI: 641)

who forfeited their deposits was going up from 39.8 per cent in 1952 to 90.9 per cent in 1996.[8]

Beyond the choice of the Westminster model as institutional cornerstone of the nascent Indian democracy, what is, however, even more puzzling is the fact that from a formal perspective, the institutional outlines of Westminster-based parliamentarism and its concomitant party politics remained more or less unscathed until today. That the institutional model of the former colonisers survived (and triumphed in becoming the single-most important determinant of political decision-making) stands in stark contrast to most of the other constituents of the post-colonial world: in particular, the Westminster model looks back at a history of failure in the post-colonial world.[9] Similarly, and again, in contrast to many of India's post-colonial Asian co-democratisers, India, once the institutional foundations of its polity had been laid, never attempted to experiment with other, seemingly more indigenous models of governance such as, for example, Sukarno's 'guided democracy' in Indonesia, Ayub Khan's 'basic democracies' in Pakistan or Nepal's '*panchayat* system' of democracy. Nor did it embrace a more radical (socialist or communist) model of governance prominent at the time of Independence as did so many other post-colonial or developing countries—despite the 'socialist' rhetoric that prevailed in official political discourse and economic policy planning immediately after Independence. What other post-colonial society has a similar record in that regard?[10]

---

[8] A security deposit is a small amount of money which the candidate has to bring forth for his nomination and which is lost if he fails to win one-sixth of the total vote. As Brass (1969: 40, table 5) has argued following Weiner (1968: 41):

> [a] large number of forfeited deposits in a state [...] [are] likely to reflect 'the number of individuals, unable to judge their capacity to translate personal influence into electoral votes.' More broadly, the index is likely to reflect the extent to which the electoral process is or is not dominated by organised parties, which have stable bases of support.

[9] See, for example, Munslow (1983) with regards to the failure of the Westminster Model in Africa.
[10] There are of course numerous other post-colonial countries that started their independent life on the basis of the Westminster model or some variant of it, a fact that led scholars to conclude that "[n]o other nation's system of government—certainly not the United States's—has been copied so extensively in such a wide variety of societies and continents. The sun had set on the British Empire but not on Westminster-style government" (Wilson 1994: 189). But the statement ignores the fact that the Westminster features of many of these countries' polities have either long been abandoned, compromised or broken down soon after independence. In Asia, the other prominent cases that displayed institutional continuity such as Sri Lanka, Malaysia or Singapore either engineered a constitutional change to a presidential system, embraced strong consociational features to counterbalance the majoritarian underpinnings of the Westminster model or qualify more as a semi-authoritarian regime than a truly democratic one. Where the Westminster system survived relatively unscathed for a long time, it was either cultural familiarity with the British institutional blueprint that was responsible for institutional continuity (as in the case of the [white] settler dominions; for example, New Zealand), or, the survival of the Westminster system was largely dependent on very specific contextual conditions as, for example, in the case of Botswana (low level of

At this point, the role of indigenisation comes into play: adapting the functioning of Westminster parliamentarism and party politics to local context, that is, to the 'mechanics' of indigenous forms and traditions of social and political organisation, made the (re-)use of an imported institutional arrangement and an (almost) alien form of political competition possible in the first place. At the same time, separating the rhetoric of Indian public discourse from political practice made it possible to merge contradictory traditions (an imported parliamentary and party tradition with local traditions of social and political organisation). What Varma (2005: 52) wrote about India's democratic experiment is true of the indigenisation of Westminster parliamentarism and modern party politics as well:

> The democratic experiment did not collapse prematurely—as happened in most other former colonies—because of a unique process of adjustment: the opposed traditions [the gothic façade of Westminster and the red sandstone of Sansad Bhavan] quickly carved out a complementary playing field, where neither could prevail fully, but both could survive. The alien graft both grew on, and was stunted by, the sap of the old.

As a consequence of this process of parties and parliamentarianism acquiring local roots and being adapted to indigenous conditions while retaining their canonical form, articulating interests in idioms of the modern state and featuring institutional continuity, the institutions of the Westminster model and the idea of modern party politics could be used to uphold governance and maintain social order while, simultaneously, acquiring legitimacy and serving as the base for the creation of a new post-colonial identity. Eventually, Westminster parliamentarism or, for that matter, its 'Indian' manifestation and modern party and electoral politics not only survived, but became the embodiment of Indian democracy whose success can be witnessed time and time again during election time (and beyond)—most recently in the run-up to the elections of the fifteenth Lok Sabha.[11] Such an interpretation is also a *riposte* to the many

---

social complexity and one-party-dominance). In addition, most of those countries, where a Westminster-based model of governance prevailed, did not operate it as effectively and successfully as India. The 'failure' of the Westminster system in so many a post-colonial states in Asia and Africa led Wilson, who described the Westminster-style government as one of Britain's biggest 'export hit' to conclude only ten pages later that India, as the exception to the rule, is an 'interesting anomaly' (Wilson 1994: 199) to this history of failure.

[11] As another consequence, instead of seeing the discrepancy between political discourse and rhetoric and actual policy implementation or political practice that so many observers of India's political economy lament as a result of an institutional crisis, a corruption of modern democracy by traditional values, it has to be seen as a structural response to the challenge of wedding the opposed traditions mentioned by Varma, a response necessary because it allowed the amalgamation of modern institutions and local context by granting both enough room to manoeuvre—be it for the smooth functioning of government, the working of representative democracy, the exercise of governance or be it simply for the much cherished pursuit of power.

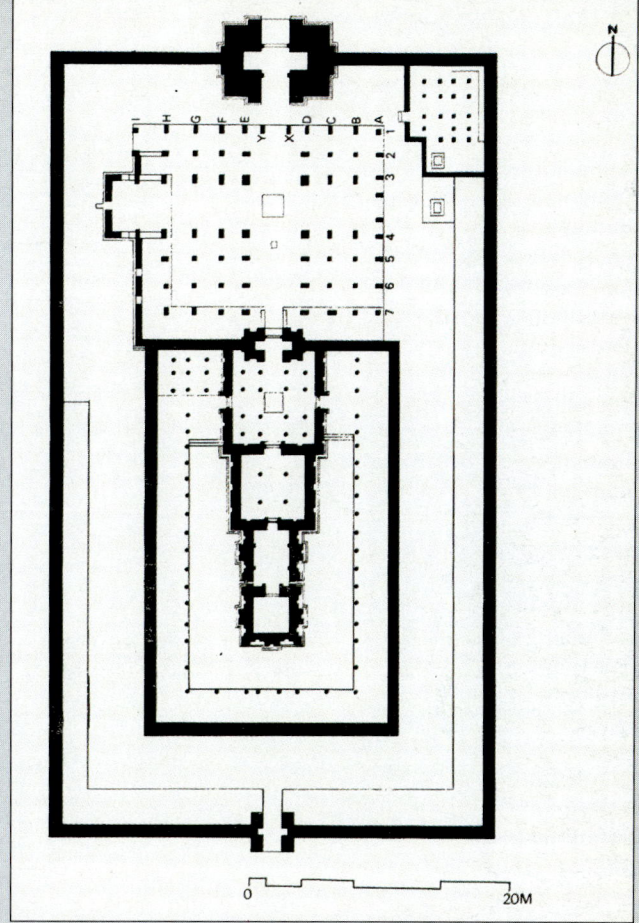

**Plate 4.7**
Kumbakonam, Ramasvami Temple, plan
(Courtesy Cambridge Kumbakonam Project).

**Plate 4.8**
Kumbakonam, Saranagapani Temple,
*gopura*, seventeenth century.

**Plate 4.9**
Kumbakonam, Kalahastishvara Temple, *mandapa* interior, eighteenth century.

**Plate 4.10**
Kumbakonam, outside Chakrapani Temple, chariot pavilion, eighteenth century.

**Plate 5.1**

Brooch: Gold, set with Golconda diamonds and turquoise, possibly from Tipu Sultan's turban; ram's head restricted warranty mark; Paris, 1819-38. (diam: 3.2 cm; given to the V&A by Miss M.A.A. Chambers; V&A IS.70–1963). © V&A Images/Victoria and Albert Museum, London.

**Plate 5.2**

The Duke of Wellington beginning the re-cutting of the Koh-i-Noor: With two representatives of Garrard of London, the Crown Jewellers, on the right and three of Coster of Amsterdam on the left. (*Illustrated London News*. Week ending Saturday 24 July 1852). © V&A Images/Victoria and Albert Museum, London.

RE-CUTTING THE KOH-I-NOOR DIAMOND.—(SEE NEXT PAGE.)

### M 14.—ANKLET, SILVER-GILT AND ENAMELED.

*Manufactured* at Kangra.
*Purchased* at £4 12s.

*Observations.*—The ornaments on this Anklet are well adapted to the different surfaces, the ornament on A tending in its main lines to develope length on the surface; while the direction of the ornaments on the surfaces B B, is the best that could be employed for leading the eye onwards

from the edge; the bands encircling the anklet on either side are prettily ornamented with lines calculated to aid the effect; whilst the ornament beyond leads the eye gradually into the portion of plain gold, the gold ornament consisting of two serpents' heads endeavouring to catch swans floating on water; had they been better executed, the whole would have been much improved.

**Plate 5.5**

Bracelet: Gold, enamelled and set with diamonds, Dholpur, Rajasthan, c. 1850 (w. of each of the three hinged sections: 5 x h: 2.4 cm); purchased by the V&A from the Great Exhibition of 1851, London; V&A 120-1820. © V&A Images/Victoria and Albert Museum London.

**Plate 5.6**

Bridal gift for Princess Alexandra, with "Suite of Indian personal ornaments." Sir W.H. Russell, "A Memorial of the Marriage of H.R.H. Albert Edward Prince of Wales and H.R.H. Alexandra Princess of Denmark," London, 1864. © V&A Images/Victoria and Albert Museum, London.

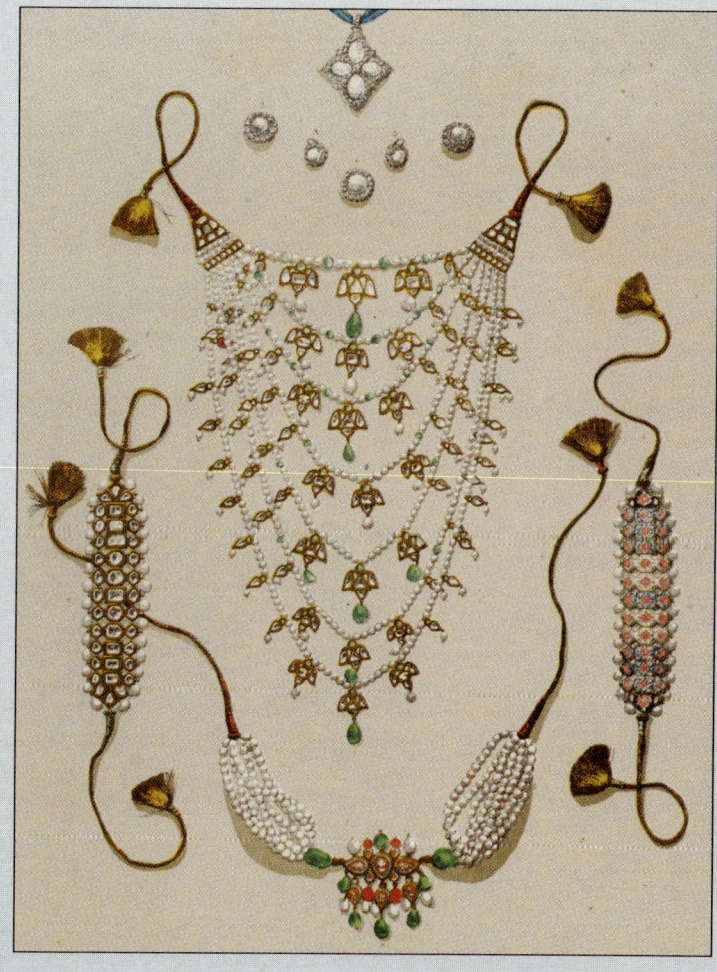

**Plate 5.7**

Necklace and brooch: Gold, with gold and glass plaques in silver-gilt and gold surrounds by Robert Phillips of Cockspur Street, London and unknown jewellers in India. The plaques: Pratapgarh, Ratlam or Indore. The necklace: London, c. 1860–68 (l. open 39.5 cm, w. of brooch 2 cm; given to the Fitzwilliam Museum by Mrs J. Hull Grundy, Fitzwilliam Museum M. 18-1983). © Fitzwilliam Museum, Cambridge.

**Plate 5.8**

The Indian Serai, Paris Universal Exhibition, 1889: Liberty & Co., Indian display including jewellery (*Journal of Indian Art*. October 1889, vol. III, no. 28, plate gg). © V&A Images/Victoria and Albert Museum, London.

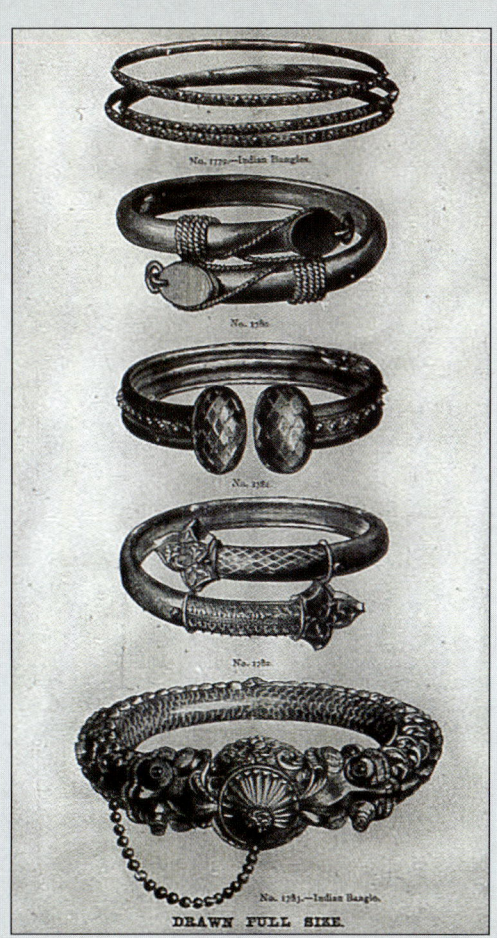

**Plate 5.9**

Details of a page from a Silber and Fleming Catalogue with "Latest Novelties in Sterling Silver Bracelets and Bangles", showing Indian Braceletes: Silber and Fleming Ltd, *Latest Novelties in Jewellery Watches, Card Cases, Optical Goods, etc.* London, [1881?]: 18, no 1779 and 1783.
© V&A Images/Victoria and Albert Museum, London.

**Plate 5.10**

Above: Dragonfly Brooch: Gold and gold filigree set with rubies and turquoise on the wings and pastes on the body, Madras, c. 1850 (4.9 x 7.2 cm; V&A 08661(IS)).
Left: Brooch: Gold set with six amethysts and one purple glass stone in open settings; Madras, c. 1850. (w: 3.2 cm); V&A 08637(IS)).
Right: Brooch: Gold set with a moonstone and amethysts in open settings, the pin missing, Madras, c. 1850 (2.5 x 3 cm; V&A 08637(IS)).
Below: Pendant (originally a brooch): Gold with an amethyst and red and green pastes, open-set, Madras, c. 1850 (3 x 2.8 cm; V&A 08639(IS)).
© V&A Images/Victoria and Albert Museum, London.

**Plate 5.11**

Above: Brooches: Gold, *babul* work, Delhi, India, c. 1853. Probably in the Paris Universal Exhibition of 1855.

Left: Crescent-shaped brooch (8.3 x 5.5 x 0.6 cm; V&A 03332(IS)).

Right: Greek cross-shaped brooch (7.8 x 5.5 x 0.9 cm; V&A 03334(IS)).

Below: Pair of earrings depicting Maharaja Ranjit Singh (r.1799-1839) (left) and Prince Akbar Khan (d. 1848) (right): Gold, *babul* work, with emerald simulants and miniature paintings on ivory. Delhi, India, second half of the nineteenth century (h: 3.1 x w: 2.2 cm; given to the V&A by Mrs Constance Morgan; V&A IM.26 & A-1924).

© V&A Images/Victoria and Albert Museum, London.

**Plate 5.12**

Right: Bracelet of five hinged plaques, showing incarnations of Vishnu: Silver, *swami* work, south India, c. 1853, probably in the Paris Universal Exhibition of 1855. (w: 19 x h: 4 cm; V&A 02676(IS)).

Left: Brooch with Floral Motif and Butterfly: Silver filigree, Travancore, c. 1853 (h: 10.2 cm; V&A 03371(IS)).

© V&A Images/Victoria and Albert Museum, London.

**Plate 5.13**

Ornaments in *kuftkari* work: Gold and steel Sialkot, Punjab, Pakistan, c. 1866, probably in the Paris Universal Exhibition of 1867

Above left: Buckle. (h: 5.1 x w: 5.1 x d: 0.9 cm; V&A 02709:1(IS)).

Above right: Brooch. (h: 5.8 x w (incl. pin): 5.6 x d (incl. pin): 1.3; V&A 02708(IS)

Below left: Brooch in the shape of belt (h: 3.7 x w (incl. pin): 4.6 x d: 2.3 cm; V&A 02711(IS)).

Below right: Pendant cross. (h: 8 x w: 5 x d: 0.3 cm; V&A 02706(IS)).

© V&A Images/Victoria and Albert Museum, London.

**Plate 6.1**

*Tenku-tittu*. A curtain entrance (*oddolaga*). Shri Manjunatheshwara Yakshagana troupe, Dharmasthala (Dakshina Kannada dist.). Photo courtesy: Narayan A. Gatty.

**Plate 6.2**

A scene between Jambavan and Krishna from the *prasanga* Jambavati Kalyana in the northern style. Photo courtesy: P. V. Jayan.

**Plate 6.3**

Female character (*strivesha*) dancing. Photo courtesy: Narayan A. Gatty.

**Plate 6.4**
The background musicians (southern style; standing in the traditional way).
Photo courtesy: Narayan A. Gatty.

**Plate 7.1**
Seventeenth century Mural from
Lepakshi, Andhra Pradesh.
(Pudukottai Museum, Tamil Nadu).

**Plate 7.2**

*Plucking Flowers* by K. Sreenivasalu. (Twentieth century, ca. 50 x 60 cm) (Government Museum of Chennai).

**Plate 7.3**

*Pink Field and Flute* by Manjit Bawa (Twentieth century, ca. 44.5 x 51.15 cm) (National Gallery of Modern Art, New Delhi).

**Plate 7.4**
Structural grid of a Brahmari painting
by Buddhadeb Chattopadhyaya, 1998.

**Plate 7.5**
Brahmari painting by Buddhadeb
Chattopadhyaya, photographed
in 1998.

**Plate 8.1**
Dongria Kondh wall paintings: Inner wall of Kudi, the shrine of the earth goddess.

**Plate 8.2**
Dongria Kondh wall paintings: Outer wall of Kudi, the shrine of the earth goddess.

**Plate 8.3**
Saora guardian deity represented by stones on the outskirts of village Sagoda.

**Plate 8.4**
Typical art of sitting and drinking, the Saora way.

accounts of post-colonial India "[...] which suggest that 'European modernity' has no place—or no roots—in Europe's Other, in '*Bharat*–India'" (Corbridge & Harriss 2000: 39). Most prominently in that regard is perhaps Inden (1990: 197), who identified the post-colonial Indian polity as a "nation-state that remains, ontologically and politically inaccessible to its own citizens. Its government continues to be just like its immediate British Indian ancestor, merely a neutral enforcer of unity on a morselised society, continually in danger of being pulled apart by 'centrifugal' forces." A statement which was proven wrong by empirical reality—given the endurance and liveliness of party politics and parliamentarism in India and the Indian political system's capacity to weld together the diverse strands of Indian society and a truly modern or Western idea of political representation and governance without being 'pulled apart'.

Similarly, despite the fact that political parties and party competition in India, as in the whole of South Asia, are, in essence, a product of the colonial encounter,[12] they have soon gained a (localised) life of their own without shedding their canonical form;[13] and even though Indian parties' and party competition's rationale is much more tilted towards the idea of the 'electoral/party machine' than to ideology and goal attainment (as the quintessential constituent of party politics according to the European party ideal), political institutionalisation through party rule helped to produce political order in times of rapid economic and social change.

This chapter further argues that the Westminster model of parliamentary democracy and its concomitant manifestation of party politics were deliberately chosen as the institutional fabric for the nascent Indian polity because they provided the (institutional) means to maintain governance and to economise power by vesting power in a strong executive centre, by making the state an all-pervasive instrument of governance (prior to the interest of any of its constituent members) and, at the same time, by offering the opportunity to engage in the power game and the equations of power as well as providing enough room to manoeuvre for local traditions of political management and accommodation

---

[12] European modernity has roots in India. Mitra & Enskat (2004: 3) rightly state that:

> [b]ereft of the nationalist gloss applied now to the history of anti-colonial struggle and the romantic aura of heroic sacrifice that accompanies it, the South Asian party tradition was born out of the incremental devolution of power by colonial rulers in order to create a buffer between themselves and the sullen peasantry.

[13] In that sense, the indigenisation of party politics and Westminster parliamentarism in India neither reflected a process of unidirectional transformation of Indian politics (towards an ideal type of liberal party politics and parliamentarianism based on the Western experience), nor was it simply a case of hybridity representing a synthesis of opposites and the mutation of new forms of political action. Instead, the institutional outlines remained intact but were interpreted and 'used' along locally relevant lines.

to be played out in the party political and electoral arena. In addition, institutional continuity prevailed, because it meant appropriating the (institutional) symbols of power of the former colonisers and thus proved that India could be a home to responsible government along the lines of its former 'masters'. Finally, it will be argued that the re-use of a modified Westminster institutional structure and its concomitant manifestation of party politics enabled post-colonial India to imagine a new nation state by turning them into the embodiment of Indian democracy (but that, in order for that to happen, a process of thorough indigenisation of the Westminster institutional fabric and modern party politics had to take place).

Though this contribution may be a little bit out of tune with the other articles in this volume, since it does not refer to "the attempt by conquering groups to appropriate the sacred sites, buildings and images of those who have lost power and transform them in a manner in which they could serve as symbols of their power," it nevertheless subscribes to the view that in the case of the indigenisation of Westminster parliamentarism and party politics in post-colonial India, a strategic re-use (inclusive of adaptation) of the institutions and ideas (of democracy) of the former colonisers took place because these very institutions and ideas were seen to be the appropriate institutional and ideational 'containers' of what was to become a new and legitimate political order. In other words, the kind of re-use the chapter deals with is not about a merely strategic incorporation of the past into the fold of modern institutions, but rather about a strategic 'upholding' of modern institutions—'imported' from the past wielders of power—to be filled with local/traditional life.

## NOT SIMPLY AN ATTACHMENT TO THE FAMILIAR: MAKING RE-USE OF THE COLONISERS' INSTITUTIONS OF GOVERNANCE

Despite the interpretative acrobatics, Lijphart undertook to turn India into an "impressive confirming case" (1996: 259) of his consociational theory[14] India always was (and remains) a relatively clear-cut case of Westminster parliamentarism, formally at least. Of the main elements of the Westminster model of

---

[14] Simplified, consociational democracy as delineated by Lijphart can roughly be conceived of as the counterpart to a majoritarian/winner-takes-all democracy essentialised in the Westminster model. Democracy's compatibility with a regional context of a deeply divided society, according to consociational theory, is conceded only under the condition of an institutionalised power-sharing arrangement comprising as its main characteristics: "(1) grand coalition governments that include representatives of all major linguistic and religious groups, (2) cultural autonomy for these groups, (3) proportionality in political representation and civil service appointments, and (4) a minority veto with regard to vital minority rights and autonomy" (Lijphart 1996: 258).

government and its surrounding operating culture, the bigger part is realised in India's institutional and constitutional setup.[15] There is a concentration of executive power with the prime minister and cabinet, which was—initially at least—fuelled by one-party and bare-majority cabinets; there is a fusion of the legislature and the executive (with ministers drawn from the parliament), there are separate roles for the head of state and head of government and there is cabinet responsibility to parliament. A largely asymmetric bicameralism prevails and a plurality or first-past-the-post system determines elections to the Lok Sabha and to the Vidhan Sabhas (State assemblies). And even some of the more glaring aberrations from the Westminster model such as India's federal set-up, the office of the president or a written constitution could—upon closer scrutiny and with some goodwill—be traced back to original Westminster principles.[16]

Parliamentary sovereignty as the most fundamental principle of the Westminster system, though formally confined by a written constitution, a Supreme Court, a second chamber representing the States' interests (Rajya Sabha) and the office of the president, in the Nehru era at least reigned supreme. Nehru himself made it very clear in the Constituent Assembly's debate on compensation

---

[15] It is rather difficult to find a clear scholarly consensus on what constitutes the essential elements of the Westminster model, precisely because the Westminster system is essentially a convention-based parliamentary system. For a more constitutional approach to the nature of the Westminster system, see Dicey (1908), Wheare (1960) or Jennings (1957), all of them arguing largely in the tradition of Bagehot's original formulations; for a more political approach, see Lijphart (1984) or Wilson (1994); for an approach focusing on the Westminster manifestations in Asia and the Pacific, See Rhodes & Weller (2005) or Kumarasingham (2008); for India, see Morris-Jones (1957).

[16] India's federal system, a clear deflection from the Westminster system's requirement for unitary and centralised government, features strong centralist tendencies such as the (in)famous President's rule, the constitutional right of the centre to invade the legislative and executive domain of the States, the uniformity of jurisdiction and administration, financial supremacy of the central government, appointment of the governor by the President and the right of the parliament to alter the territorial boundaries of the States; it has therefore been described as a mere "quasi federalism" (Wheare 1956: 28) or as a "federalism from above" (Rothermund 1995: 385). Likewise, the Indian President, though elected and formally endowed with extensive powers, is much more of a ceremonial figurehead than his namesakes in conventional presidential systems. As the Indian cabinet was informed by Krishnaswami Aiyar: "[...] there is no sort of comparison between the positions of a President under the American Constitution and that of the President under the Indian Constitution, who, in every way, is in the position of a constitutional monarch." (Note by Aiyar, 8 October 1951 in Prasad (1984–95: 291). His role as a potential institutional veto-player/point vis-à-vis the executive and parliament was anyway curtailed very early on in India's post-colonial history, especially after Nehru ended the first President's (Prasad) power to be an effective source of horizontal accountability on Indian prime ministers in the course of the Hindu-Code Bill controversy. And even the written constitution—though without doubt compromising India's Westminster underpinnings—can be seen as (merely) a requirement of the federal system did not stand in the way of a process of decision-making largely determined by interpretation and convention, and has relegated many substantial policy objectives to a catalogue of nonjusticiable Directive Principles.

for property (redistributed through land reforms) that "[n]o Supreme Court and no judiciary can stand in judgement over the sovereign will of Parliament representing the will of the entire community [...] ultimately the whole Constitution is a creature of Parliament" (CAD, vol. XI: 1195). That later on judicial activism gained much more prominence, to the extent that in 1973 the 'basic structure' doctrine declared amendments attacking certain fundamental parts of the constitution as unconstitutional, is a different matter and is related to the strengthening of the federal principle and a growing perception that parliamentary sovereignty could also be used to curtail judicial and constitutional leverage and to protect those in power, as became clear during the Emergency (1975–77). Nonetheless, some of the aberrations from Westminster, especially India's federal set-up, have to be considered as necessary adaptations to local context, a form of indigenisation needed to succeed in operating a kind of power-sharing arrangement within the institutional confines of a majoritarian Westminster democracy.

But beyond the technicalities of constitutional interpretation, what is of interest here, are two different questions: why did India opt for institutional continuity at all—not taking into account the obvious connotation with the attachment to the familiar? And, how did it make use of an institutional arrangement of parliamentary democracy that provided specific institutional incentives for executive strength and political and institutional flexibility, state-centrism and parliamentary sovereignty, government stability and room for a localised process of political mobilisation to gain momentum, but was a clear legacy of the former colonisers—given the fact that a strong anti-British sentiment prevailed at the time of Independence or an indifference towards those institutions from the West, at least among the masses. That such a sentiment (or indifference) prevailed is visible from the fact that "Indian historical culture, rather than British historical culture, was creatively used to justify Westminster institutions for India" (Kumarasingham 2008: 39). Benegal N. Rau, the Constitutional Adviser to the Constituent Assembly, who was commissioned to explore constitutional practices all over the world in order to bring home a 'constitutional toolbox' for the Constituent Assembly to ponder on, walked the extra mile to prove the rootedness of Westminster-style cabinet government in (pre-colonial) Indian political thought by referring to evidence of 'parliamentary traditions' and ancient equivalents of cabinet-style government as well as of other official procedures of (Westminster) parliamentarism such as 'motions', 'resolutions' and 'voting' derived from the *Sukraniti*, the *Mahabharata* or from writings dating back to the era of Emperor Asoka (Rau 1960: 315–19). The Nehru Report of 1928, in a sense the document on which the debate on India's constitutional future was based, was less categorical in rejecting British historical culture as the basis for choosing the principles of the future constitution of India, but made the point that this culture had taken on a new form, one of acculturation to the Indian way of thinking: "[...] what India wants and what Britain has undertaken to give her, is nothing else than Responsible Government [and] the assimilated tradition of England has become the basis of Indian thought" (All India Congress Committee [AICC] 1928: 6–7).

The reasons for the ready acceptance of the Westminster model are to be found in the extraordinary close institutional match it offered for the situation at hand. First, the Westminster model with its strong focus on prime ministerial and cabinet power endorsed by executive-legislative fusion, a minimum of institutionalised veto points and, usually, one-party and bare majority governments favours a strong centre and governmental stability. The same holds true for the winner-takes-all logic of the plurality electoral system, which is an integral part of any Westminster system. It also applies to the principle of parliamentary sovereignty, which enables the government to get through its desired policies without too much consideration of judicial oversight. That India opted for "the strongest and most centralised government achievable in a democracy—the British cabinet system" (Bernard 1992: 49) is, therefore, no wonder, given the need for a strong state and government able to preserve national and territorial integrity, to handle the turmoil produced by Partition and the integration of the princely states (as well as militant Hinduism and revolutionary communism), to manage the country's social diversity—while upholding governance—and to push through social reforms and planned economy (in the face of Indian society's rigid caste hierarchies and in the wake of the Bengal famine of 1943 and a serious food crisis at Independence).[17] At the same time, given a strong anticipation of Congress dominance in the evolving post Independence party political arena, the choice of the Westminster model with its most prominent corollary, the first-past-the-post electoral system, and its in-built feature of executive–legislative fusion meant making an already strong government (strong by institutional disposition) even more powerful by almost

---

[17] For example, the main argument in favour of a plurality system in the CAD was the need for governmental stability in a divided society. There was, however, considerable resistance to the decision from the socialists, communists and representatives of various religious communities. They suggested changing the prevailing electoral system to some form of proportional representation, which is conceived of to be more inclined to the provision of social and societal representativeness than to the provision of governmental stability. Hartmann (1971: 16) describes the reactions of Ambedkar (a vehement critic of the Congress) and Nehru:

[...] Dr. Ambedkar energetically opposed the proportional representation system. He stressed that for the minorities a properly functioning Government is necessary which cannot be achieved through the principle of proportional representation. Nehru added that he could not imagine a weaker Government than that which is elected on the basis of the system of proportional representation.

'naturally' delivering the desired majorities for the Congress—a rather convenient outlook for the party elite.

India's, or rather the nationalist elites' desire for a strong state even went beyond the mere upholding or 're-use' of the Westminster institutional model when it came to devising the new institutional framework, adopting an approach which brought the nascent polity yet closer to its colonial precursor.[18] As a statement of conscious adoption, the Government of India Act of 1935, by itself the outcome of the process of constitutional development before Independence dating back to the Indian Councils Act of 1861, the Morley-Minto Reforms (or Indian Councils Act) of 1909 and the Montagu-Chelmsford Reforms (or Government of India Act) of 1919, became the blueprint of the Indian Constitution; about 250 of the constitution's 395 articles were taken from the 1935 Act verbatim, or almost intact.[19] Among the 'strong state' features it encompassed the role and reserve powers of the Governor (in its 'national' manifestation as Governor General, later on to become a constitutional president, and as the respective Governors in the territorial subunits or Provinces), a legacy of British Paramountcy (the Crown's supremacy over the princely states engineered to facilitate British hold over India through 'indirect rule') stand out in their almost unconditional acceptance for adoption into Independent India's new constitution by the Constituent Assembly.[20] These vice-regal relics made their

---

[18] This desire for a strong state is a common phenomenon in the post-colonial world, even more so in case of divided societies. In South Asia, as Mitra (1990: 1) put it rather bluntly, "the national aspiration for a strong, unified state, ironically mimicking that of the colonial power, lay beneath the struggle for independence."

[19] Washbrook (2001: 83–84) critically brings out the ripples of the colonial past resonating in India's post-colonial trajectory when referring to the impact of the Government of India Act of 1935:

> There is perhaps no clearer indicator of this subtle post-colonial influence than the ultimate fate of the 1935 Government of India Act, originally designed to undermine the national integrating functions of the Congress, to submerge the voices of *demos* beneath those of executive authority and aristocratic privilege, and to keep India tied to the apron-strings of Westminster. The Act did not entirely die with the rule of the King-Emperor: when India wrote 'her own' constitution in 1950, she took more than 250 of its clauses straight out of the relevant Parliamentary publication.

[20] Brass (2000: 67–68) notes on the ready acceptance of this 'strong state' feature by the Constituent Assembly that "[t]his ideal of a strong Centre was itself so strong that members who criticised any of the emergency provisions of the Constitution felt obliged to preface their remarks with the defensive statement that they, too, shared the common goal". In order to prove that the nationalist elites' concern over the security of the Indian state even took precedence over fundamental rights, he goes on to quote the Assembly member Brajeshwar Prasad:

> I feel that if there is a conflict between the security of the State and the personal liberty of the individual I will choose the former and lay stress on the security of the State. For the first time in the chequered history of India we have got an independent State of our own; are we going to barter it away in the name of some newfangled notions which have been discredited in their own homelands?

way into the new polity's institutional framework in form of the (in)famous Articles 352 and 356 of the Indian Constitution, the emergency provisions, that is, the authority to suspend fundamental rights and declare a state of emergency and the so-called President's Rule under which the president assumes executive power over the State's administration and the State is ruled directly by the union executive through the State's governor. Due to Westminster convention, both presidential powers are actually the prime minister's. Article 352 has been applied only once under Indira Gandhi from 1975 to 1977, the notorious period of the Emergency. Emergency powers vested in the president under Article 356 have been tested very often and have given the central government considerable leverage over state politics. Designed to be used in times of crisis, this article has given Indian federalism a unitary face and gives the central government a powerful tool that has often been used in a partisan manner.[21]

India needed a strong centre for essentially two reasons: to prevent disorder and to promote social reform through a planned economy. And the strong centre was epitomised in the centralist features of the Westminster model and the traditions of the Raj, of which extensive use was made in the immediate post Independence period and beyond.[22] In addition, the executive dominance inherent in the Westminster system and the centralism of the vice-regal tradition also display a state-centric approach to governance that stands in contrast to the more accommodative and society-centred approach to governance that characterised the precolonial subcontinental empires. This state-centric approach to governance is to be found in post-colonial India's obsession with bureaucracy and the 'omnipresence' of the state (the all-pervasive occupation of organisational and

---

[21] The unitary character of Indian federalisms, which is also reflected in uniformity of jurisdiction and administration, financial supremacy of the central government, appointment of the governor by the president and the right of the national parliament to alter the (territorial) boundaries of the states, led some scholars to go as far as to describe Indian federalism as "Paramountcy Federation" (Rau 1960: 13) or to conclude that "Indian Government virtually re-created for itself the powers of paramountcy without its obligations" (Hodson 1996: 502). According to Weiner (1989: 81) "the viceregal model is thus just as much a part of the British tradition as the Westminster model".

[22] Examples of making (re-)use of the former colonisers' institutions of governance are too numerous and manifold to be dealt with here. They range from the military intervention in the princely state of Hyderabad to the imposition of President's rule on the State of Kerala, where the communists had been elected as the first and only non-Congress government in the period up to 1967, to the establishment and 'above politics'-elevation of the Planning Commission by virtue of executive authority. In essence, they followed a similar rationale, which was perceptively described by Rudolph & Rudolph (2008: 187) in terms of the contradictory principles of parliamentary sovereignty and judicial oversight: "Nehru and the Congress left were deeply concerned that the judiciary would create obstacles to the realisation of socialist objectives, while hard state advocates led by Patel were concerned that the courts would jeopardise the state's capacity to maintain law and order." There were of course other legacies from India's colonial past that were 're-used' in order to prevent disorder and to promote social reform through a planned economy, such as the Indian Civil Service (renamed as Indian Administrative Service).

representational 'space' by state agencies in the economic and political arena) and it also originates from the desire to prevent disorder and to promote social reform through a planned economy, but instead it has spawned rather different and less welcome results such as the notorious licence-permit Raj (the practice of state-issued licences and permits over business and its accompanying red tape) and a preponderance of excessive patronage politics.

The second reason why the nationalist elite was attracted by the Westminster model is related to the flexibility attached to Westminster parliamentarism that readily allows indigenous interpretations and modifications (in contrast to the more rigid American presidential system or any kind of even more rigid socialist state variant, as well as in contrast to the even more flexible but too permissive indigenous traditions and models of governance). Since the Westminster system is essentially a convention-based parliamentary system, with a minimum of formal and institutionalised veto points, there is plenty of room to manoeuvre for individual incumbents to direct and interpret their role and relationship with the rest of the political structure. Nehru as the first prime minister used this room to manoeuvre to define the constitutional space available to the constituents of government, especially with regard to the relations and horizontal accountability of the president, prime minister and cabinet.[23] He held India's first president, Rajendra Prasad, at bay when Prasad wanted to test the presidential powers bestowed upon him by the constitution during the Hindu Code Bill controversy, thus making presidential restraint and prime ministerial power the hallmark of executive governance in India.[24] At the same time, by turning the president into a more or less mere figurehead, thereby according to Westminster conventions,[25] the president could become a symbol

---

[23] Even though the Indian Constitution is one of the longest in the world and extremely rich in detail, the section dealing with the executive of the Indian Union is relatively short and lacking in clarity, deliberately left to convention and constitutional practice.

[24] The controversy was based on the attempt by Jawaharlal Nehru to standardise Hindu personal law and incorporate some practices such as monogamy, divorce and alimony which some orthodox Hindus took objection to. However, Nehru also took the horizontal accountability of the executive, inherent in the Westminster system and guaranteed by parliamentary oversight, seriously and made a point of discussing his policy decisions in parliament and submitting them to parliamentary scrutiny. That later the same flexibility provided by the Westminster system and the early establishment of prime ministerial superiority, was misused by Indira Gandhi, is a different matter.

[25] The Indian president therefore resembles the Governor General of the Raj or the constitutional monarch of Westminster much more than some would say it was originally envisaged by India's republican constitution. In this regard, Kumarasingham (2008: 72) rightly points out that "India may have been a Republic, but it was still an institutional Westminster *mutatis mutandis*." As an illustration of India's "faithfulness to Westminster norms", he quotes Sir Ivor Jennings' comment on visiting Sansad Bhavan: "[...] true the Queen and the Crown have disappeared, but the Governor-General and the Governors reappear as President, Governor and Rajpramuks. Quite often the draftsmen had difficulty in finding a phrase to replace 'Crown'" (Kumarasingham 2008: 66).

of integration while staying out of party political power games and largely remaining above politics.

Of course, by virtue of convention, executive accountability and checks and balances or, for that matter, a responsible government, are all also a part of the Westminster parliamentary tradition, but in the first two decades after Independence, these were compromised by Congress dominance, which, at the same time, granted enough latitude for the nationalist elite to adhere to such parliamentary norms as accountability, collegiality, regard of the principle of opposition, and so on. Contrasting the Indian case with the Sri Lankan experience of a more or less rigid adoption of the Westminster model inclusive of Bagehot's 'dignified parts' without any serious indigenous interpretations and modifications and against the background of a culturally much more homogenous society, Kumarasingham (2008: 13) comes to the conclusion that:

> [...] in India, the acculturation to Westminster cultural feature of collegiality was aided by the institutional background of a strong Congress party—and also by institutional and social complexities that made the Westminster cultural feature of flexibility seem very appropriate. Such flexibility rather than rule-bound rigidity seemed to the Indian political elite to be essential if the new country was to experience 'good government', especially in light of its post-independence federalism and of the sheer complexity and volatility of India's vast society—whose potential for communal violence had been displayed in the Partition massacres.[26]

Parliamentarism in independent India started life on the basis of a clear, one-sided party power configuration. The competitive 'infrastructure', which is the premise upon which the Westminster model holds the executive accountable, was confined to one dominant party. Consequently, there was no (urgent) need to evoke a culture of compromise or coalition and party discipline. On the contrary, to ensure a functional equivalent for a weak opposition, the internal pluralism or factionalism within the dominant party had to perform a sort of 'watchdog role', controlling the executive's decision-making power. In this regard, the interdependence of government and parliament, inherent in Westminster parliamentarism, offered an institutional incentive for factional leaders to adhere to political exchange deals and informal arrangements.[27]

---

[26] However, India, like Sri Lanka, was also falling back on some of the well-rehearsed parliamentary conventions of the British Westminster role model for rather pragmatic reasons. Until 1978, India retained the practice of standing orders (rules of procedures) as used in the House of Commons (the House of Commons was referred to in Article 105 of the constitution verbatim) in order to avoid "the difficult task of having to formulate their own parliamentary rules" (Kumarasingham 2008: 256).

[27] At a more systemic level, the Westminster system normally works best—some would contend only—with a two-party system. Again, India defied the odds by making the Westminster system compatible with, first, one-party-dominance, then multi-partyism.

The flexibility inherent in the Westminster parliamentary tradition not only allowed to establish the supremacy of prime ministerial power but also to push through instruments and policies, such as the Planning Commission or land reforms, devised to tackle the need for economic restructuring by circumventing the often paralysing effects of democratic consensus building.[28] In sum, given the institutional incentives the Westminster model and vice-regal institutional traditions had to offer at a time, when (institutional) uncertainty reigned supreme—when relevant party loyalties and identities had to be produced anew (or 'from scratch'), conflict and contestation had to be coordinated along unfamiliar institutional lines, mobilisation and participation had to be channelled for the first time and when the room to manoeuvre for political actors was naturally more flexible, the institutional rules of the (democratic) game were not that clear and the functions ascribed to the representational system differed from those in the established democracies of Western provenance—anything else than a re-use of the former colonisers' institutions of governance, was largely unthinkable.

In the words of Morris-Jones (1992: 220), one of the most astute observers of the early history of Indian parliamentarism, who tried to describe the 'paradoxical logic' of institutional continuity in post-colonial India:

> Since history abounds in paradox, it should not be unexpected that the post-imperial state is at once a reflection of and a reaction against the preceding imperial state. The founding fathers, who then normally became the first rulers, of new successor states sought both to bring down and re-build, both to replace and to reproduce. The past regime was anathema but at the same time a model worthy in some respects of preservation or imitation. The rulers certainly were to be changed but the rules of ruling might be carried over.

And the successes of this strategy were remarkable: "power relationships were sorted out constitutionally; the parliamentary system became entrenched, democracy not only survived Nehru's charisma, popular participation strengthened it ..." (Austin 1999: 36). The fact, however, that the institutional outlines of

---

[28] At the same time, however, the necessity of candidate-centred local mobilisation, in-built into the Westminster based single-member simple-plurality electoral system, meant making the Congress (as well as other parties) dependent on a strategy that entailed the need to let the party being 'corrupted' by local, sectional and regional elites (mainly those elites representing the traditional social order and being able to 'purchase votes' in exchange for material gains, that is, access to state resources) and by regional aspirations (which they tried to co-opt by means of a cooperative federalism). Ambitious policies and reform plans thus often got derailed. But the need for localised mobilisation also meant localising potential sources of conflict and melting down modern institutions and party politics with the "little loyalties of the 'little community'" (Morris-Jones 1978: 212).

Westminster-based parliamentarism and its concomitant party politics remained relatively unscathed until today, has to be accounted for by different reasons.

## BACK TO THE ROOTS: THE INDIGENISATION OF WESTMINSTER PARLIAMENTARISM AND PARTY POLITICS

The 'indigenisation' of the two most important democratic imports to India—parliamentarism and party politics—took place at two different levels: the macro-level of the institutional framework, or polity, and the micro-level of the actor-based political process or politics. At the macro-level, the context-driven need to actively shape and mutate the Westminster legacy found expression in three distinct features of the Indian polity, all catering to the requirement to reconcile Western-style parliamentarism with India's sociocultural hetero-geneity: federalism, group rights and the operation of a kind of power-sharing arrangement within the institutional confines of a majoritarian Westminster democracy. At the micro-level, closely related to the working of party politics, indigenisation took the shape of localised and regionalised machine politics, an aggregation of and adaptation to local conditions.

The federal principle in India—though reinforced by subsequent assertions of regional aspirations, which were accommodated through various reorgani-sations of the country's administrative fabric—is not the result of an agreement of powerful constituent units but rather a federalism by imposition. Federalism in India thus displays an initial agency or conscious modification of the inherit-ed Westminster legacy for the sake of accommodation of the country's cultural pluralism. Ambedkar, the pre-eminent figure among the drafters of the Indian Constitution, made this very clear by stating in rejection of characterising India as a 'federation of states' that:

> [...] though India was to be a federation, the federation was not the result of an agreement by the States to join in a federation, and that the federation not being the result of an agreement, no State has the right to secede from it. The Federation is a Union because it is indestructible. (CAD, vol. VII: 43)

It was a bold decision, largely against the Westminster tradition of a unitary system of government insofar as the federal principle requires a whole range of institutional features—a written constitution that specifies the division of pow-ers, a powerful judiciary to interpret the constitution, an upper house, a Head of State to deal with federal crises—that contradict parliamentary sovereignty and born of the desire to integrate the princely states and the trauma of Parti-tion. But this creative institutional response to the imposition of an imported model of government, flexibly combining parliamentary sovereignty and the federal principle, worked rather well and contributed enormously to sustaining representative democracy on 'foreign' (Indian) soil.[29] As Chakrabarty (2008: 88) has lucidly argued:

> For the Westminster model to strike roots in a diverse society, federalism seems to be the most appropriate political arrangement for two important reasons. On the one hand, federal principles ensure segmental autonomy by formally recognising the importance of the segments for the whole; they also, on the other, firmly establish the relative strength of the constituent units that can be undermined only at the peril of the federal state.

Parliamentary federalism in India thus represents a successfully indigenised system of government that—in addition—can be both, unitary and flexible, depending on the situation at hand.[30] As Dasgupta (2001: 49) notes, "[…] India's bold experiment of combining democratic responsiveness to cultural differences with a federal conciliation of regional community, identity, and autonomy claims and a nationally concerted promotion of regional capability, has tendered to ensure a novel mode of multicultural development." That the experiment got rewarded to the point that by now few would see any practicable alternative to the federal principle as a mechanism to reconcile effective governance with India's cultural pluralism—simultaneously quarantining conflict at the state level and accommodating the countless ethnic and regional identities prevalent in Indian society—is proof of the thorough acculturation to this (indigenous) adaptation of the original Westminster heritage. In a sense, Indian federalism bears yet another trace of institutional continuity and indigenisation, that of its linkage with pre-modern as well as colonial forms of governance on the subcontinent. In the words of Rudolph & Rudolph (1987: 66):

> The strategy propounded in the fourth century *Arthasastra*—that subordinate rulers shall be preserved and respected in their customs and territorial jurisdiction if they acknowledge, via respect and tribute, the superior authority of a ruler of rulers—governed the statecraft of subcontinental empires in Mughal and British times. After independence, India's federal system became its modern embodiment within the twentieth century subcontinental empire.

[29] It is not the place here to go into the role (merits and demerits) Indian federalism plays for the Indian democracy. The literature on the working (and success) of Indian federalism is enormous. See, for example, Dasgupta (2001) or Manor (2001).

[30] As mentioned before, Indian federalism displays strong unitary features such as President's Rule or uniform administration and jurisdiction, but is, at the same time, rather flexible, for example, when it comes to giving into regional demands by carving new states out of existing administrative units.

Regarding the second distinctive institutional feature of India's "novel mode of multicultural development", the (constitutional) incorporation of group rights into the policy process as another innovative form of adaptation and indigenisation of the Westminster framework (to make it comply with or strike roots in the country's diverse society), what was aimed at was also a gradual eradication of the blatant manifestations of socially sanctioned inequalities prevalent in Indian society. At the same time, however, the incorporation of group rights can also be understood as a tribute to the past, to more traditional and group-accommodative forms of governance and social order. Group rights or group-based privileges such as the reservations and quotas for minorities such as the Scheduled Castes and Scheduled Tribes, the granting of customary law to parts of the tribal population in India's Northeast, linguistic federalism, separate personal laws for Muslims and other religious communities, cultural autonomy in educational matters, consideration of the vernaculars through the three-language formula and selective distribution of development programmes constitute an aberration from the individualism and equality of rights-approach inherent in the Westminster model of governance. Though the AICC's (the party's general assembly) statement that "[o]ur aim should be to evolve a political system which will combine efficiency of administration with individual liberty [...]" (AICC 1954) clearly reflects the "liberal obligation to recognise the civil and political rights embodied in the Westminster model" (Rudolph & Rudolph 2008: 55), the "traditional obligation of the ruler to recognise and uphold the jurisdiction of prior social groups" (Rudolph & Rudolph 2008: 56) found expression in the bestowment of special rights upon some of these prior social groups.[31]

Finally, the third manifestation of indigenisation or adaptation of the Westminster framework at the macro-level, the operation of a kind of power-sharing arrangement within the institutional confines of a majoritarian Westminster democracy, was closely related to as well as critically dependent on the overwhelming dominance of the Congress in the party political arena of the two decades following Independence. The benign effect of the 'Congress system' (Kothari 1964) was essentially to establish, within the formal design of a majoritarian democracy, an informal arrangement of a consociational democracy (Lijphart 1996). Not a perfect one, but given India's institutional underpinnings as a majoritarian democracy (power concentration in the executive, one-party governments based on clear majorities, an electoral system undermining proportional representation, and so on), the fact that "[t]he combination of the Congress

---

[31] The more accommodative approach to governance that characterised the pre-colonial (and, in a sense, also colonial) subcontinental empires thus prevailed over the European tradition of state formation and the nation-state "whose strength rested on the extinction of regional cultures and identities" (Rudolph & Rudolph 2008: 54).

Party's inclusive nature and political dominance has generated [consociational] grand coalition cabinets with ministers belonging to all the main religious, linguistic, and religious groups" (Lijphart 1996: 260) is quite remarkable. As Nicholson (1975) and Pai Panandiker & Mehra (1996) have demonstrated, Congress cabinets were always largely representative of all sociocultural groups in society—if not sometimes to the extent that some minority groups were overrepresented. Although there had been no institutionally anchored agreement on power-sharing arrangements (as, for example, in Malaysia), the maintenance of a party's dominance with a composite character in a competitive environment, virtually necessitated this kind of accommodation (and consent) of all relevant societal groups. Grand coalition cabinets and the group rights mentioned above were necessary to uphold the dominant party's catch-all image, ensuring both, the societal anchoring of the Indian National Congress (INC) and a fair degree of power-sharing, necessary for the reconciliation of majority rule with the aspirations of social and cultural (minority) groups (Spiess 2009).

At the macro level then, the three distinct features of the Indian polity described above, all indicate a thoughtful (and working) adaptation or modification of the Westminster model to make it match indigenous conditions, thus contributing to its cultural acceptance and longevity. Again, contrasting the Indian case with the Sri Lankan experience of a more or less rigid adoption of the Westminster model without any serious indigenous interpretations and modifications, one can see how successful India was in indigenising her inherited Westminster legacy. India's inimitable form of federalism, the provision of group rights and an informal power-sharing arrangement unquestionably prevented the communal strife seen in Sri Lanka.

At the micro-level, indigenisation, fuelled by the need for localised mobilisation inherent in plurality electoral system usually attached to Westminster democracy largely meant that Indian parties, above all the Congress, while retaining their canonical form, adapted themselves to the local power structure, the traditional, informal hierarchies of power and authority, rather than following the party-voter linkage characteristic of Western democracies. As a consequence, instead of animating a liberal vision of party competition where parties aggregate the interests articulated by society and compete with each other by offering programmatic bundles to voters who rationally weigh up a given party's issue position with their programmatic preference or orientation, for the first two decades after Independence at least vote banks and machine politics reigned supreme. Mitra et al. (2004: 3) in their survey of *Political Parties in South Asia*—though still searching for a Western homologue rather than conceding to the regional context a unique adaptation of the Western blueprint to indigenous conditions—capture the essence of this difference between the Western and the South Asian party context, historically a result of a top–down rather than a bottom–up process of party and party system formation:

Bereft of the nationalist gloss applied now to the history of anti-colonial struggle and the romantic aura of heroic sacrifice that accompanies it, the South Asian party tradition was born out of the incremental devolution of power by colonial rulers in order to create a buffer between themselves and the sullen peasantry. The South Asian party was thus born essentially out of supplication, and therein lies their difference from the European masterscript. More helpful to the understanding of the South Asian party is the American image of the political machine and hard-bargaining men in smoke-filled rooms than coherent ideologies and disciplined party organisations that are more the hallmark of European political parties. (Mitra et al. 2004: 3)

Especially below the district level, where, traditionally, a strong proclivity to venerate power prevailed,[32] parties were operating essentially along neo-patrimonial lines. And modern party politics provided a fertile ground for the social traditions and structures of the past to be played out in a 'modern', party-based way. Westminster-style majoritarian democracy suited this cooptation of modern institutions of representative democracy rather well, because it puts emphasis on the rewards of the democratic process rather than on the democratic idea per se. Engagement in party politics promised, at the same time, upward mobility and, for the entrenched classes, a means to enhance status and to reinforce existing patterns of domination and hierarchy.[33]

In 1967, Weiner, in his path-breaking study of the Congress' early dominance in post-colonial India's nascent party-political arena, came to the following conclusion:

[...] Congress party leaders, in order to succeed politically, are concerned, first and foremost, with doing whatever is necessary to adapt the party to its environment. This proposition is deceptively simple, but it immediately calls attention to the difference between the Congress party and many other political parties in the developing world. Elsewhere, many governing parties are concerned with either mobilizing or controlling the population. In contrast, Congress is primarily concerned with recruiting members and winning support. It does not mobilize; it aggregates. It does not seek to innovate; it seeks to adapt. Though a few Congressmen dream

---

[32] This proclivity for veneration of status and power also results in a prevalence of charismatic leadership in Indian party politics, which manifests itself, for example, in the success of film stars-cum-politicians in Tamil Nadu from the late 1960s onwards and in Andhra Pradesh in the 1980s—long before famous actors also became famous politicians in the West.

[33] Varma (2005: 45) comments on this interplay of modern democracy and traditional society as follows:

In India, the working of democracy has effortlessly adapted to the undemocratic social structures of the past. Obviously, the two are mutually opposed; in other societies the contradiction would have asphyxiated the institution. In India the older tradition *co-opted* the younger institution. People flocked to polling booths but voted mostly according to caste affiliations. Numerical majorities prevailed, but candidates continued to represent segments of the established hierarchic structure.

of transforming the countryside, in practice most Congressmen are concerned simply with winning elections. In its effort to win, Congress adapts itself to the local power structures. It recruits from among those who have local power and influence. It trains its cadres to perform political roles similar to those performed in the traditional society before there was party politics. It manipulates factional, caste, and linguistic disputes, and uses its influence within administration to win and maintain electoral and financial support. It utilizes traditional methods of dispute settlement to maintain cohesion within the party. (Weiner 1967: 14–15)

From a different perspective, however, one could also argue with Varma that "the older tradition *co-opted* the younger institution[s]" (Varma 2005: 45), that traditional society was gradually creeping in modern party politics and that the kind of indigenisation Weiner describes was the only way for modern party politics to strike roots in Indian society. And of course, with the democratic machinery getting entrenched, something slowly changed: since numerical strength was now the *sine qua non* of the power game, traditional loyalty gradually gave way to loyalty with the one who is the strongest numerically, a change that is responsible for subsequent 'democratic upsurges' to be witnessed most prominently in the rise of the various parties drawing on the support of former untouchables and backward classes in the North of India. In the countryside, however, party and electoral politics, though very often speaking in the modern idiom of socioeconomic and political organisation, remains thoroughly 'indigenised' to date. Sharma (1999), going beyond the realm of mere party and electoral politics, draws a rather bleak picture of the interplay of modern, formal and traditional, informal structures as a result of his fieldwork in India's rural areas:

> In the village, block, and district (and even in some states), the formal and informal structures of rule and governance become woven into the same tapestry, a process that over time has further reduced central authority and eroded its efficacy in the countryside. Under these conditions, local notables and seasoned political brokers (some located ambivalently between state and society) have been able to extend their powers, actively pursuing the interests of their constituencies as well as their own individual imperatives [...]. Through stratagems of collaboration, patronage dispensation, building of supportive coalitions with clientele groups, and opportunistic manipulation of the formal apparatuses of the state (e.g. the courts, bureaucracy, police, various political and administrative structures), the local notables and power brokers have legitimised their power and authority and enhanced their rent-seeking capacities. (Sharma 1999: 53)

However, this article would contend that despite the social injustice and upholding of traditional power structures that the indigenisation of party and electoral politics or, for that matter, of modern institutions produced, it made the survival of (liberal) representative democracy altogether possible—to the point that that the re-use of a modified Westminster institutional structure and its concomitant manifestation of party politics enabled post-colonial India to imagine a new nation state by turning them into the embodiment of Indian democracy. What Sharma describes above and what many today see as a crisis of democracy in India is therefore the result of a rather genuine process; a process, which so far was quite successful in wedding modern, imported institutions to foreign (culturally different) Indian soil. As Bhargava notes:

> [...] the current crisis of liberal democracy is due in large part to its own success. The introduction of civil liberties gave voice to the mute, and the stage for action was set by the democratic process for those hitherto debarred from the public domain. They entered it with new modes of speech and action to which the initiators of liberal democracy were unaccustomed, and in numbers that greatly exceeded the tiny upper crust that led the national movement. It is no doubt true that those empowered by institutions of liberal democracy do not come from a cultural background with an obviously liberal or democratic character. However, it would be mistaken to conclude from this that this newly empowered class is wholly maladjusted to these institutions. Considerable evidence exists of its successful adaptation to these Western institutions (and of these institutions to these groups!). (Bhargava 2000: 27)

## BIBLIOGRAPHY

All India Congress Committee (AICC), 1928, "The Report of the All-Parties Conference", Part I. AICC, Allahabad.

———, 1954, "Resolutions on Economic Policy and Programme, 1924–1954". AICC, New Delhi.

Austin, Granville, 1966, *The Indian Constitution: Cornerstone of a Nation*. Clarendon Press, Oxford.

———, 1999, *Working a Democratic Constitution: The Indian Experience*. Oxford University Press, New Delhi.

Bardhan, Pranab, 1984, *The Political Economy of Development in India*. Basil Blackwell, Oxford.

Bernard, Jean-Alphonse, 1992, "The Presidential Idea in the Constitutions of South Asia". *Contemporary South Asia*. Vol. 1, no. 1, pp. 41–51.

Bhargava, Rajeev, 2000, "Democratic Vision of a New Republic". In: Francine Frankel, Zoya Hasan, Rajeev Bhargava & Balveer Arora (eds), *Transforming India: Social and Political Dynamics of Democracy*. Oxford University Press, Delhi, pp. 26–59.

Brass, Paul, 1969, "Political Participation, Institutionalization and Stability in India". *Government and Opposition*. Vol. 9, no. 1, pp. 23–53.

———, 2000, "The Strong State and the Fear of Disorder". In: Francine Frankel, Zoya Hasan, Rajeev Bhargava & Balveer Arora (eds), *Transforming India: Social and Political Dynamics of Democracy*. Oxford University Press, Delhi, pp. 60–88.

Chakrabarty, Bidyut, 2008, *Indian Politics and Society since Independence: Events, Processes and Ideology*. Routledge, London.

Government of India, 1949, "Constituent Assembly Debates (CAD), Vol. VII". Government of India, New Delhi.

———, 1949 "Constituent Assembly Debates (CAD), Vol. XI". Government of India, New Delhi.

Corbridge, Stuart & John Harriss, 2000, *Reinventing India: Liberalization, Hindu Nationalism and Popular Democracy*. Polity Press, Cambridge.

Dasgupta, Jyotirindra, 2001, "India's Federal Design and Multicultural National Construction". In: Atul Kohli (ed.), *The Success of India's Democracy*. Cambridge University Press, Cambridge, pp. 49–77.

Dicey, Albert Venn, 1885 [1908], *Introduction to the Study of the Law of the Constitution*, Macmillan, London.

Frankel, Francine, 1978, *India's Political Economy, 1947–1977*. Princeton University Press, Princeton.

Hartmann, Horst, 1971, *Political Parties in India*. Meenakshi Prakashan, Meerut.

Hegewald, Julia A. B. & Subrata Kumar Mitra, 2008, "Jagannatha Compared: The Politics of Appropriation, Re-use and Regional Traditions in India". *Heidelberg Papers in South Asian and Comparative Politics*. No. 36, January 2008, pp. 1–37. Available at http://hpsacp.uni-hd.de/ (accessed on: 21 July 2011).

Hodson, H. V., 1996, *The Great Divide: Britain—India—Pakistan*. Hutchinson, London.

Inden, Ronald, 1990, *Imagining India*. Basil Blackwell, Oxford.

Jennings, Sir Ivor, 1957, *Constitutional Laws of the Commonwealth*. Oxford University Press, London.

Khilnani, Sunil, 1999, *The Idea of India*. Farrar, Straus and Giroux, New York.

Kohli, Atul (ed.), 2001, *The Success of India's Democracy*. Cambridge University Press, Cambridge.

Kothari, Rajni, 1964, "The Congress 'System' in India". *Asian Survey*. Vol. 4, no. 12, pp. 1161–73.

Kumarasingham, Harshan, 2008, *Westminster Regained: The Applicability of the Westminster System for Executive Power in India, Ceylon and New Zealand after Independence*. Doctoral Thesis awarded by the School of History, Philosophy, Political Science and International Relations of the University of Wellington. Available at http://researcharchive.vuw.ac.nz/handle/10063/275 (acessed on: 21 July 2011).

Lijphart, Arend, 1984, *Democracies: Patterns of Majoritarian and Consensus Government in Twenty-One Countries*. Yale University Press, New Haven.

———, 1996, "The Puzzle of Indian Democracy: A Consociational Interpretation". *American Political Science Review*. Vol. 90, no. 2, pp. 258–68.

Manor, James, 2001, "Centre–State Relations". In: Atul Kohli (ed.), *The Success of India's Democracy*. Cambridge University Press, Cambridge, pp. 78–102.

Mitra, Subrata K., 1990, "Introduction". In: Subrata K. Mitra (ed.), *The Post-Colonial State in Asia: Dialectics of Politics and Culture*. Harvester Wheatsheaf, New York, pp. 1–19.

Mitra, Subrata K. & Mike Enskat, 2004, "Introduction". In: Subrata K. Mitra, Mike Enskat & Clemens Spiess (eds), *Political Parties in South Asia*. Praeger/Greenwood Publishing Group, Westport and London, pp. 1–30.

Mitra, Subrata K., Mike Enskat & Clemens Spiess (eds), 2004, *Political Parties in South Asia*. Praeger/Greenwood Publishing Group, Westport and London.

Morris-Jones, W. H., 1957, *Parliament in India*. Longmans, Green and Co., London.

————, 1964, "Parliament and Dominant Party: Indian Experience". *Parliamentary Affairs*. Vol. 17, no. 3, pp. 296–307.

————, 1978, *Politics Mainly Indian*. Orient Longman, New Delhi.

————, 1992, "Shaping the Post-Imperial State: Nehru's letters to Chief Ministers". In: Mark Twaddle (ed.), *Imperialism, the State and the Third World*. British Academic Press, London; pp. 220–42.

Munslow, Barry, 1983, "Why has the Westminster Model Failed in Africa". *Parliamentary Affairs*. Vol. 36, no. 1, pp. 218–28.

Nicholson, Norman K., 1975, "Integrative Strategies of a National Elite: Career Patterns in the Indian Council of Ministers". *Comparative Politics*. Vo. 7, no. 4, pp. 533–58.

Pai Panandiker, V. A. & Ajay Mehra, 1996, *The Indian Cabinet and Governance of India*. Konark, New Delhi.

Patel, Vallabhbhai, 1971, *Sardar Patel's Correspondence, 1945–50*. Navajivan Pub. House, Ahmedabad.

Prasad, Rajendra, 1984–95, *Dr. Rajendra Prasad: Correspondence and Select Documents*, Volumes I–XXI. Valmiki Choudhary (ed.), Allied Publishers, New Delhi, pp. 277–99.

Rau, B. N., 1960, *India's Constitution in the Making*. Orient Longmans, Madras.

Rhodes, R. A. W. & Patrick Weller, 2005, "Westminster Transplanted and Westminster Implanted: Exploring Political Change". In: Patapan Haig, John Wanna & Patrick Weller (eds), *Westminster Legacies: Democracy and Responsible Government in Asia and the Pacific*. University of New South Wales, Sydney, pp. 1–23.

Rothermund, Dietmar (ed.), 1995, *Indien—Kultur, Geschichte, Politik, Wirtschaft, Umwelt. Ein Handbuch*. Beck, München.

Rudolph Lloyd I. & Susanne Hoeber Rudolph, 1987, *In Pursuit of Lakshmi: The Political Economy of the Indian State*. University of Chicago Press, Chicago.

————, 2008, *Explaining Indian Democracy: A Fifty-Year Perspective, 1956–2006. Volume II. The Realm of Institutions. State Formation and Institutional Change*. Oxford University Press, New Delhi.

Santhanam, K., 1960, *Union-State Relations in India*. Asia Publishing House, London.

Sharma, Shalendra D., 1999, *Development and Democracy in India*. Lynne Rienner, Boulder and London.

Spiess, Clemens, 2009, *Democracy and Party Systems in Developing Countries: A Comparative Study of India and South Africa*. Routledge, London.

Varma, Pavan K., 2005, *Being Indian*. Penguin, Delhi.

Washbrook, David, 2001, "The Rhetoric of Democracy and Development in Late Colonial India". In: Niraja Gopal Jayal (ed.), *Democracy in India*. Oxford University Press, Delhi, pp. 82–96.

Weiner, Myron, 1967, *Party Building in a New Nation: The Indian National Congress*. The University of Chicago Press, Chicago.

———— (ed.), 1968, *State Politics in India*. Princeton University Press, Princeton.

————, 1989, *The Indian Paradox—Essays in Indian Politics*, Edited by Ashutosh Varshney. SAGE Publications, New Delhi.

Wheare, Sir Kenneth, 1956, *Federal Government*, 3rd edition. Oxford University Press, London.

————, 1960, *The Constitutional Structure of the Commonwealth*. Oxford University Press, London.

Wilson, Graham, 1994, "The Westminster Model in Comparative Perspective". In: Ian Budge & David McKay (eds), *Developing Democracy*. SAGE Publications, London, pp. 189–201.

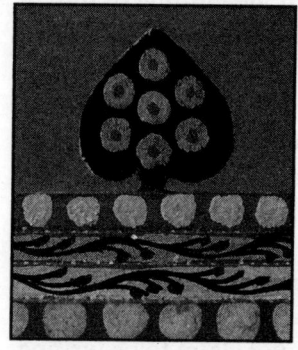

*Chapter 10*

# MYTH, IDEA, DREAM AND VISION

## NEHRU'S DISCOVERY OF INDIA

**BY JIVANTA SCHÖTTLI**

> She [India] is a myth and an idea, a dream and a vision, and yet very real and present and pervasive.

> (Nehru 2004: 627–28)

Jawaharlal Nehru is a towering figure in India's modern political history. As Shashi Tharoor, author of the recent book, *Nehru: The Invention of India*, explained in an interview to the Carnegie Council, "Nehru was a giant of his age, an iconic figure of twentieth-century nationalism who for sixteen years after Mahatma Gandhi's assassination also incarnated India as a country, as an idea, as a civilisation, and as a presence on the world stage."[1] As an individual, bearing such a historical responsibility, it becomes imperative for us to deconstruct Nehru's own idea of India and to determine how he reconciled India's elusiveness on the one hand, as implied in the quote above, with the very concrete reality of its resilience through centuries of time. To do that,

---

[1] See http:/Tharoor 2003/www.cceia.org/resources/transcripts/1075.html

this chapter conducts a close examination of Jawaharlal Nehru's book titled, *Discovery of India*. First published in 1946, it is Nehru's understanding of Indian history, his quest for the sources of India's cultural stability or, the 'spirit of India', as he himself puts it (Nehru 2004).

Nehru's coming to terms with his country's heritage draws upon mechanisms of understanding and rationalisation that were prevalent in Europe during the nineteenth and early twentieth centuries, namely, an approach that emerged under the influence of two important movements, that of romanticism and utilitarianism. The text therefore can be read as a window into the mind and person that was Nehru as well as an example of how the past is refracted through the lens of his present. Whether Nehru was consciously using a particular set of analytical tools to decipher the past is not sure. He does not claim to be writing according to the rigours of a historical study and, given that Nehru chose predominantly English-language sources on Indian history, shows that he was not really being confronted with a range of interpretive options. Nevertheless, there was a clear objective behind his efforts: the search for continuity with the past so as to lend coherence to his project of nation and state building. Hence, the *Discovery of India* was a very real attempt to re-use the past in order to bestow legitimacy on the future.

\* \* \* \*

The chapter begins with a short background to Nehru and the book and then applies the concept of a 'social imaginary', which has been used by Charles Taylor in his analysis of modernity to encompass three central aspects that underwent drastic change in the transition from pre-modern to modern: the economy, the public sphere, the emergence of a polity ruled by the people (Taylor 1999: 91–124). Modernity is crucial to understanding Nehru's dialogue with the past because his project of nation and state building was firmly entrenched within a vision of modernity. Mirroring the three pillars that Taylor identified, Nehru was a strong advocate of industrial and economic development as the bedrock to a modern, independent state, a public sphere that would be kept clear of private issues such as religion, language, community, a democratic political system that would ensure representation and a constitution that would emphasise the fundamental rights of its citizens. Nehru's writing is loose and narrative, and the 'social imaginary' helps to contextualise Nehru intellectually because it is, in the end, up to the analyst to 'interpret' the statements that are presented or, to draw out the theoretical assumptions and ideas that are being implicitly invoked by the author. The aim of this section is to demonstrate Nehru's particular cast of Indian history in terms of a 'social imaginary' or, in other words, to delve into Nehru's imagined notions of how the Indian state took shape through history and his depiction of its various avatars.

\* \* \* \*

The state is a central theme because Nehru sought to deny the importance of other sources of collective identity, such as the role of culture and religion, which he tended to regard as being divisive rather than unifying forces. Instead, he applied a utilitarian outlook, one which held that institutions, once designed properly, would bring about the necessary changes both in material conditions as well as in people's way of thinking and behaviour. The mould of Nehru's state is European, or more precisely British, and in fact, ironically, represented great continuity with some of the dominant colonial practices and priorities. The chapter ends by positing that Nehru acted as a central agent in the transfer of an essentially Western 'social imaginary' into the Indian context. What is, however, of particular interest, is how weak Nehru's own institutional legacy has actually been—something which emerges if one looks closely at policies that he was personally involved in the making of (Schöttli 2012). Instead, the Indian state that established itself through the 1950s can be seen to have represented a gradual appropriation of Nehru. Hence, by the time of his death in 1964, he could be hailed as founding father of the nation despite the fact that his policies and vision of a modern, secular, self-sufficient India represented a veneer, barely concealing a reality, which had remained largely unchanged.

## A BACKGROUND

Born in 1889 into a wealthy, Kashmiri Brahmin family settled in Allahabad, in the northern state of Uttar Pradesh, Jawaharlal had a childhood that was exposed to both, great religiosity on his mother, Swarup Rani's part as well as the highly Westernised habits and views of his father, Motilal Nehru.[2] From 1901 to 1904, Jawaharlal was educated at home by a European tutor and was then sent, at the age of sixteen, to Harrow and from there to Trinity College, Cambridge, where he graduated with a Lower Second in the Natural Sciences Tripos in 1910. In accordance with the wishes of his father, Motilal Nehru, a highly successful barrister and political figure in his own right, Jawaharlal went on to read law at Gray's Inn, London, the same place where before him, Mohandas Karamchand Gandhi and Muhammad Ali Jinnah, among others, had studied. It is during this time that Jawaharlal encountered the movement of Fabian Socialism,[3] popular at the time in Britain.

---

[2] For example, in 1899, Motilal made his first trip to England and was officially excommunicated by his caste members when he refused to perform a purification ceremony upon his return.

[3] A British socialist movement, with its origins in the nineteenth century, whose central idea was that Socialism could be advanced through gradual reform, and not through revolution. At the core of the society were Sidney and Beatrice Webb, authors of various studies on industrial Britain and the Soviet Union. See for example, Webb & Webb (1936).

Jawaharlal returned to India in August 1912 and began to work for his father's law practice in Allahabad. Politics, at this point in time in India, was relatively quiet with leaders of the Swadeshi movement[4] in jail. The outbreak of World War I in 1914 stirred the political environment and prompted anti-British movements to take shape. The Defence of India Act, passed in March 1915 empowered the government to suppress civil liberties and imprison anyone deemed to be a threat to British interests. Rallying together, the Moderates and Extremists reunited in 1915 and initiated the Home Rule Movement, which, in addition to demanding self-government, argued that the British war effort was to be supported not opposed in exchange for concessions later on. The Muslim League[5] also accepted the argument and in December 1916 the Indian National Congress and Muslim League reached an agreement, known as the Lucknow Pact in which the Congress accepted separate electorates,[6] and the League accepted under-representation for Muslims in Muslim-majority areas in return for over-representation in Muslim-minority areas.

\* \* \* \*

Responding to the events around him, Jawaharlal's views began to take a clearer shape, in particular as he engaged directly in politics, for example, through Annie Besant's Home Rule League.[7] Meeting Mohandas Karamchand Gandhi for the first time in the winter of 1916 at the Lucknow Congress of the INC, Jawaharlal was unable to relate to his style and rhetoric of politics, which he found to be an unfamiliar blend of grass-root activism, asceticism, religion and philosophy. However, in 1919 when the Rowlatt Act was passed, extending wartime repressive legislation into peacetime, it was Gandhi who galvanised the Indian response through his first nation-wide campaign in an all-India *satyagraha*[8] to resist the Act through non-violent civil disobedience. This entailed courting arrest, returning of titles bestowed by the Raj, boycotts of schools and colleges, withdrawal of lawyers from courts, campaigns against the use of foreign cloth. Another major event in 1919 which marked the beginning of Jawaharlal's direct involvement in active politics was the Jallianwala Bagh massacre, which soon eclipsed the Rowlatt Act. On 13 April, opening fire on a peaceful gathering of

---

[4] *Swadeshi* translates as 'Self-Sufficiency'. Mahatma Gandhi had developed a strategy of boycotting British products and reviving local production methods and products.

[5] Founded in 1907 to safeguard the rights of Muslims, the Muslim League eventually became the political group agitating for a separate Pakistan.

[6] Separate electorates here referred to provisions which would create constituencies where only Muslim candidates could stand and only Musliams were eligible to vote.

[7] Launched in 1916 by an English reformer, Annie Besant's Home Rule League was modelled on the Irish experience and was one of the first successful attempts to create an all-India mass protest movement. The INC till this point was largely an elite organisation without the grass-root political networks which Gandhi was later to create.

[8] Coined by Gandhi, *satyagraha* can be translated as 'truth force'.

people, General Dyer's battalion killed hundreds of people, official estimates put the number of dead at 379 though it was widely agreed that the actual figure was much higher. The Congress began to organise relief work in the Punjab and set up its own enquiry committee in which Jawaharlal was involved and which brought him into close contact with Gandhi.

The 1920s seem to have marked a turning point in Nehru's political career for he also began to gain first-hand knowledge about working conditions in factories and the state of the peasantry. In 1920, Jawaharlal participated in the Congress' Allahabad district conference and was elected vice-president of the district committee, his first official position. This was also the year when Jawaharlal 'discovered' the peasants in his first rural campaigns within the Kisan (farmers) Movement. Carrying Gandhi's message of non-violence to the *kisan*s in the Uttar Pradesh countryside, it was precisely these principles of *satyagraha*, entailing self-restraint which was to clash with Jawaharlal's own inclinations towards socialism and its ideals of radical and revolutionary change. However, for both the Nehrus, this seems to have been a period of transition and greater involvement in active resistance against the government and on 6 December 1921, both father and son were arrested and sentenced to six months in jail each.

Briefly released, Jawaharlal was re-arrested on a new charge and this commenced his first long spell of imprisonment that lasted till 31 January 1923. Upon his release, he agreed to become chairman of the Allahabad (UP) Municipal Board where Jawaharlal gained experience in administrative work. Disillusioned with the abrupt ending of Non-Cooperation and Gandhi having withdrawn himself to reflect and reconsider the methods of the struggle, Nehru sought other sources of inspiration. The aftermath of the Russian Revolution was felt in India during the mid and late 1920s with the growth of left-wing parties, workers' and peasants' parties, an increase in trade unionism, worker's agitations and strikes. In this context, Nehru's intellectual moorings began to lean more towards the Left.

Nehru was back in jail on 26 December 1931 to begin his longest term that lasted until 30 August 1933. As has been noted by many of his biographers, this was a time that he put well to use, reading and writing widely. A book of essays and letters to his daughter, Indira Gandhi, written during this time was published as *Glimpses of World History* in 1934.[9] To quell the growing vagueness surrounding his thoughts and political inclinations, Nehru published *Whither India*

---

[9] Zachariah (2004: 70) lists some of the books Nehru read during this first long phase of imprisonment: Shakespeare, a number of books on China, a book on eugenics, Oswald Spengler's *Decline of the West*, Emil Ludwig's historical biographies, Ruskin and Carlyle, Bukharin's *Historical Materialism*, Kropotkin's *The Great French Revolution*, Trotsky's *My Life*, Bernard Shaw, Radhakrishnan's *Hindu View of Life*, a great deal of history, French and British literature, Nietzsche's *Beyond Good and Evil*, R. H. Tawney's *Religion and the Rise of Capitalism*.

in October 1933 in a pamphlet form which sought to answer questions about what was to come after Independence and the implementation of socialism into policies. Arrested again in February 1934 for having denounced imperialism and tried for sedition, Nehru was sentenced to two years imprisonment during which he wrote his autobiography (published in 1936 with the same title).

\* \* \* \*

Elected as President of the 1936 Congress, Jawaharlal's statements implied a turn towards socialism, alarming businessmen and Congress members on the Right of the ideological spectrum and adding to the strains that were emerging in response to a central dilemma about the nature of Indian nationalism. Was the Indian nationalist movement to be defined as a loose, broad, all-inclusive, secular movement but one that essentially failed to develop an ideological core? 'Right-wing' tendencies within and without the Congress tended to be Hindu, upper-caste property owners, the dominance of whom was likely to alienate the 'Depressed Classes', minorities, and particularly Muslims. On the other hand, the Muslim League at the time was also inclined more towards maintaining the *zamindar* (land owner)-based social order, pushing Muslims in favour of radical social change closer to the Leftist within the Congress. At the same time, conservative, prominent businessmen, such as G. D. Birla and political figures like Vallabhbhai Patel and Bhulabhai Desai also identified themselves as 'Gandhians'.

\* \* \* \*

Till the mid-1930s, the philosophy of the Congress-led movement had been to provide an institutional umbrella, incorporating all hues of political outlook. The crisis over Subhash Chandra Bose's re-election as Congress president in 1939 brought tensions to the fore, allowing Nehru to emerge as a consensus candidate. By this time, Nehru had begun to appear as one of the few possible unifiers within the Congress movement. In November 1937, an anonymous article appeared in the Calcutta-based *Modern Review*, titled "The Rashtrapati" (President) that warned that there was a tendency to see Nehru as a kind of saviour and that the man might be in danger of seeing himself as a latter-day Napoleon or Caesar. It turned out later that Nehru himself was the author and while the intentions behind publishing such a piece are debated, the point is that he was increasingly in the limelight. From 1937, following the first provincial elections in which the Congress won easily in six of the eleven provinces and dominated two more, Jawaharlal took it upon himself to become the "conscience of the ministries" (Zachariah 2004: 90), reprimanding premiers of various provinces on their policies and statements, as well as lecturing Congress on the need to keep an eye on the main goal of Independence. Afraid of losing the collective momentum, as the day-to-day running of provincial administrations distracted Congress members, and observing the growing fractionalisation within Congress, the 'Mass Contact Programme' was launched in 1937 with Jawaharlal Nehru as one of its main leaders. Aimed at bringing Congress into close contact with those who were not yet Congress supporters, Muslim mass contact was deemed a priority.

Drawn into 'high' politics more directly, Nehru's views on the role of religion in politics and the potential for communal violence took on a harder line. For instance, writing to Stafford Cripps, at the time an upcoming figure in Labour politics to whom he had been introduced to by his friend, Krishna Menon, in London, Nehru was intent on demonstrating the strong influence that Congress had on the Muslims, claiming that:

> I come into greater touch with the Muslim masses than most of the members of the Muslim League. I know more about their hunger and poverty and misery than those who talk in terms of percentages and seats in the councils and places in the state services. (Wolpert 1996: 223)

Issuing such an open challenge which was released in the form of a statement to the press, Nehru's actions had the effect of spurning the Muslim League to launch a far more successful 'mass contact' campaign of its own as well as setting the leader of the Muslim League, Muhammad Ali Jinnah, onto a war path. Other examples can be given of occasions when Nehru's publicly advertised principles did not serve the cause of gaining support for the Congress and are an early indication of his discomfort with, and inability to manage religion as a force in politics. Approaching the problem of communal politics in highly dichotomous terms, Nehru more often than not depicted the Congress as "an advanced organisation" pitted against "a politically reactionary organisation like the League" (quoted in Zachariah, 2004: 93–94). This ruled out the possibility of Congress sharing power with any minorities in the provincial ministries, a scenario which could have helped to dispel accusations that Congress provincial rule, particularly in the heavily Muslim-populated state of Uttar Pradesh, was discriminatory and repressive against Muslims.

For most of World War II, Nehru was behind bars, jailed from November 1940 to December 1941 and again, from August 1942 to June 1945. Using this time to write, for instance, *Discovery of India*, while he was a prisoner at Ahmadnagar Fort jail, Nehru was able to take advantage of his confinement. He could draw upon his fellow class-A prisoners who were articulate and important figures in their own right, and who were afforded the luxury of being able to order books and newspapers while interned. As a result, *Discovery of India* is an impressive and accessible account of India from the time of the epics until 1944. Expansive and sweeping, the book asks itself a core question, posed both at the level of individual and of country, of whether it is possible "to have a union of poise and inner and outer progress, of the wisdom of the old with the science and the vigour of the new?" (Nehru 2004: 34). This dilemma pursued Nehru throughout his political career for, as the parliamentary debates reveal, he was constantly confronted by forces that he considered to be retrograde.[10]

\* \* \* \*

Nevertheless, it is noteworthy that one of the first images evoked in *Discovery of India* is that of Nehru immersing his wife Kamala's ashes in the Ganges in accordance with Hindu ritual. Despite the battles that Nehru was to fight with religion in general and Hinduism in particular, through the pages of his books and as political leader, even he could not shirk the final rites that marked the passing of a life. As Nehru implies in the text, it is ultimately the rituals of death that link the individual to the vastness and anonymity of the past. This need to feel connected through time, across space as well as reaching to the masses is something that resonates throughout the book, and appears to be a central concern if not a self-conscious source of insecurity.

\* \* \* \*

Though the word 'identity' does not appear in the text, Nehru can only be alluding to it when he writes about something that has bound the innumerable successions of human beings, "India is a geographical and economic entity, a cultural unity amidst diversity, a bundle of contradictions held together by strong and invisible threads" (Nehru 2004: 627). Herein lies an intriguing tension in Nehru's conceptualisation of the state and nation. On the one hand, he denies the compulsions of identity and yet, at the same time, recognises the need for something greater than the self as the individual's reference point. *Discovery of India* is his attempt to identify the lineage of India's stateness and to cast this as a source for the country's resilience and unity.

## THE SOCIAL IMAGINARY

In his article titled "Modern Social Imaginaries", Charles Taylor (2002) seeks to address the rise and spread of modernity by highlighting two central elements of Western modernity: the 'moral order' and 'the social imaginary'. The moral order is a clear set of ideas about how one should act and why the social world is arranged in the way it is, while the social imaginary is defined as the ways in which people imagine their social existence which "is often not expressed in theoretical terms [but rather] it is carried in images, stories and legends" (Taylor 2002: 106) but which give people a sense of a shared collectivity. Europe's moral order originates in the late Middle Ages, and finds, according to Charles Taylor,

---

[10] See, for instance, Mitra's analysis of the cow debate in Mitra (1991: 755–77).

its mature expression in the political philosophy of Locke and Grotius whose natural law theory posits that individuals have innate rights and obligations towards one another. Politics, as it emerges in its new 'modern' form, is no longer working towards a specific ordering of the world but rather towards serving the individual's search for happiness or, in other words, a non-political end. This new principle of a general equality among individuals, Taylor argues, transformed the social imaginary or the lived practices through which people engaged each other and through which a self-understanding of their collective life emerged.

Tracing the 'long march' through which the modern social order emerged, Taylor demonstrates the gradual transformation of three central forms of the social imaginary: the economy, the public sphere and popular sovereignty. The economy is the first of the social imaginaries to be transformed as it moves from being a management of existing resources into a mesh of interlocking activities serving a mutual social benefit. Similarly, in the public sphere, a new forum emerges where people can form a unit of mutual interests outside the state. The final form of the modern social imaginary, according to Taylor's scheme is popular sovereignty which lays yet another basis upon which people conceived of themselves as constituting a group.

\* \* \* \*

Although Taylor has little to say about the non-Western experience of modernity, the two concepts of moral order and the social imaginary are useful tools with which to compare Nehru's understanding of India's state traditions and processes of collective-identity formation. They are useful because they serve to illustrate the extent to which Nehru was a carrier of Western ideas of modernity and liberal politics.

## THE 'INDIAN' SOCIAL IMAGINARY

Central to the Indian 'moral order' is the caste system and hence it is important to examine Nehru's analysis of it. Linking the caste system to the economy, Nehru in fact seemed to imply that it was the caste system which hindered the emergence of a new social imaginary in line with the emerging productive forces of the economy. Instead:

> The caste system was a barrier to such a change. For all its virtues and the stability it had given to Indian society, it carried within it the seeds of destruction ... So long as that structure afforded avenues for growth and expansion, it was progressive; when it reached the limits of expansion open to it, it became stationary, unprogressive, and later, inevitably regressive. (Nehru 2004: 240–41)

The caste system was considered by Nehru to be one of three central compo-nents of the Indian social structure along with the joint-family system and the autonomous village community. It is important to keep in mind that rather than drawing upon these as foundations for strength, Nehru presented a narrative through which he demonstrated the inevitable decline of these institutions, their lingering presence and negative effects, and the importance of policy as a mechanism through which to ensure their removal.

Recognising some of the caste system's strengths, Nehru conceded that it provided for a certain amount of resilience and flexibility to the ancient Indian polity, creating a sense of solidarity and ensuring that "no minority need submit to a majority, for it could always form a separate autonomous group, the only test being: is it a distinctive group large enough to function as such?" (Nehru 2004: 271). Furthermore, despite the tendency to regard Indian society as structured according to groups rather than individuals, Nehru did point out that "there has always been an individualistic tendency in India ... Partly that individualism was the result of the religious doctrine which laid emphasis on the individual" (Nehru 2004: 271). Nehru went as far as to write that in ancient India, "the democratic way was not only well-known but was a common method of functioning in social life, in local government, trade-guilds, religious assemblies etc. Caste, with all its evils, kept up the democratic habit in each group" (Nehru 2004: 275). The old Indian social structure is therefore presented as a source of resilience, integration and innovation.

* * * *

Turning however, to processes of change and adaptation, India's ancient moral order, in Nehru's opinion, failed to respond, first to the intellectual challenges of the ninth and tenth centuries, and later to the military challenges that began in earnest with the eleventh century invasions from the north-west. Instead of giving rise to a new social imaginary, the ancient social structure gradually petrified as it turned inwards, rejecting challenges rather than incorporating or accommodating them. Despite the subsequent centuries that witnessed examples of strong rulership, visionary leaders and compassionate generals, India entered into a phase of terminal decline, culminating in colonial rule under Britain. This phase was unlike anything before, given that the British maintained throughout, their centre of command outside India or, as Nehru put it, in a sub-title, "India Becomes for the First Time a Political and Economic Appendage of Another Country" (Nehru 2004: 328).

* * * *

The colonial phase is a crucial part in *Discovery of India* and in fact occupies more than half of the book. This period is the most important for it is used by

Nehru to demonstrate his thesis, to position himself and to cast his vision of an independent India.

## THE STATE IN NEHRU'S DISCOVERY OF INDIA

It is useful to note that Nehru held India's cultural and social decay accountable for the failure to develop a state capable of withstanding the onslaught of the British who represented a superior form of political and military organisation. Even the Mughal Emperor Akbar, whom Nehru casts as an admirable figure and as one who not only succeeded in enhancing the brilliance of the Mughal court but also in fusing Hindu and Muslim aesthetics in art and architecture and creating a sense of oneness but who ultimately failed to lay the foundations for social change. Shackled by the caste system, the old Indian social structure confined success and opportunities to the upper classes, degraded a mass of human beings and led to the puetrfaction of India's economy and life. Nehru is categorical in his analysis:

> In the context of society today, the caste system and much that goes with it are wholly incompatible, reactionary, restrictive, and barriers to progress. There can be no equality in status and opportunity within its framework, nor can there be political democracy and much less economic democracy. Between these two conceptions conflict is inherent and only one of them can survive. (Nehru 2004: 277)

Nehru advocates two central mechanisms necessary to break the mould of stagnation and paralysis. Both of these were to be state-led, top–down initiatives: social reform and planning. Through the Congress party, or rather under the influence of Mahatma Gandhi's leadership, two dramatic steps of transition were to be undertaken in one go: a reworking of the moral order and the creation of a new social imaginary. In the European narrative presented by Charles Taylor, the former had led to the latter, as norms and attitudes were gradually altered, moving from the way the economy was organised to the public sphere and finally giving rise to a new domain of popular sovereignty. In the case of India, Nehru believed that the new social imaginary necessary to kick-start the emergence of an independent, modern nation state, could be both instilled and installed, simultaneously.

The National Planning Committee is the theme of a substantial subsection in *Discovery of India* and must have been intended as a statement of objectives given that Nehru was in prison at the time and possessed no other means of communicating his ideas and aspirations to a wider audience. Planning was to serve various purposes at once. It was to address the very real problems of backwardness, poverty and unemployment, of national defence and economic regeneration and the urgent need for industrialisation. At the same time, it would also make "people come out of their narrow grooves of thought and action, to think of problems in relation to one another, and develop to some extent at least a wider co-operative outlook" (Nehru 2004: 436). More explicitly, Nehru prophesied that planning would:

> [...] lead towards establishing some of the fundamentals of the socialist structure [...] limiting the acquisitive factor in society, removing many of the barriers to growth, and thus leading to a rapidly expanding social structure [...] [it would serve] the benefit of the common man, raising his standards greatly, giving him opportunities of growth, and releasing an enormous amount of latent talent and capacity. (Nehru 2004: 441)

Planning, it would seem, was being offered to his readers and followers as the panacea for India's social ills, economic woes and political deficiencies, all at once.

Maintaining the unity of India was a central concern in *Discovery of India* both in terms of being a philosophical, historical puzzle as well as a practical challenge. The book's last chapter contains an important section on "India: Partition or Strong National State or Centre of Supra-national State?" (Nehru 2004: 583) in which Nehru discussed the possible scenarios and what he observed to be a general trend towards the multinational state or large federation such as the United States or the Soviet Union. It is interesting to note that here, in the final pages of a book which highlighted and occasionally hailed the invisible threads binding India and Indians together, Nehru dismisses "the tendency towards abstractions and vague ideals, which arouse emotional responses and are often good in their way, but which also lead to a woolliness of the mind and unreality" (Nehru 2004: 592). Instead, a brief attempt is made to describe the federal shape to come where defence, customs, trade, economic planning would provide that intermediate sphere of joint and separate functioning. This then was to be the answer of the modern age to the past and the 'old enchantment' of an India that was a myth, an idea, a dream and a vision.

## NEHRU'S VISION OF INDEPENDENT INDIA

Key developments in the political and intellectual climate of turn-of-the-century Britain were to play a crucial role in shaping the policies of both post-war Britain and Independent India. Amongst these, the influence of the Fabian society is an important prism for the observation of the change and continuity in ideas and practices from the age of Victorian utilitarianism to the post-war social democracy and welfare politics of the Labour party. Founded in 1883, the Fabian society attracted a number of intellectuals including among others, George Bernard Shaw, H. G. Wells, Annie Besant, Harold Laski, Beatrice and Sidney Webb. What is interesting is how closely Nehru's thoughts on the state, modernisation and development reflected the twin sources of ideas popular at the time in Britain—utilitarianism and fabianism.

As Governor-General of India in the mid-nineteenth century, Lord Dalhousie upon reviewing his years of administration, is supposed to have described the railways, electric telegraph and uniform postage, which he introduced to India, as the "three great engines of social improvement" (Quoted in Ghosh 1978: 97). Such a reading of legacy reflected the philosophy of utilitarianism, as articulated by Jeremy Bentham and James Mill. In his *History of British India*, Mill had questioned the values of Indian society and proposed reforms along Benthamite ideals. Despite being a Conservative, Dalhousie was therefore advocating that the key to progress in India was the introduction of Western science and knowledge. It is crucial to note that the utilitarian idea of progress was not only progress brought about through scientific innovation but also reform of the existing social order. Hence, Dalhousie saw it as his duty to tackle the problems of infanticide, female education and the treatment of Hindu widows. Unity of authority, uniformity of management and legal practices were essential principles within this vision of governance. Codification was to emerge as one central instrument to put these principles into practice. References by Dalhousie to "the good of the community", "the interests of the public" and "the welfare of mankind" were echoes of the central utilitarian, "Greatest-happiness precept" (Stokes 1959).

\* \* \* \*

His farewell address on 5 March 1856 in Calcutta is a good example of this:

> While we have a right to congratulate ourselves on what has already been done, while we may regard with complacency the introduction into the East of those great instruments of public benefit which Science has long since created in the West; while we may rejoice that measures have been already taken for opening new sources of public wealth, for ministering to the convenience of increasing the happiness, and for raising the mental and social condition of the endless millions, whom providence for its own wise ends has committed to our charge; I trust we still shall feel that all we have yet done must be regarded as no more than the first beginning of greater things that are to come. (Ghosh 1978: 108)

Nehru, in some ways represented continuity with this line of thinking. His speeches and writings often claimed the interests of mankind and of society as a whole, to be at stake. Even more striking was his propensity to believe in the wisdom and acumen of eminent individuals who could conceptualise and grasp the good of the community and take action from a neutral, benevolent position. His tendency to concentrate power and decision making in the hands of a few individuals, his persistent monitoring and correspondence with chief ministers throughout his term as prime minister, attest to this.

Fabianism, as a current of political thought, emerged in response, or rather in dialogue, with the dominant ideas and in reaction to the experiences of industrialisation during the Victorian Age. Believing in the possibility of gradual transition and reform, the Fabian society rejected notions of class struggle and revolutionary change advocated by Marx's followers. Instead, it was argued that evolutionary and constitutional methods, the use of persuasion and permeation would bring about a gradual process of socialisation.[11] Although Fabianism came to be embraced by the post-war Labour government, it was never a doctrinal set of principles. The main goal of its adherents was to tackle the great injustices wrought by the capitalist system and to spread the theory of evolutionary socialism. As a result, democracy was to play a central part in the Fabian outlook as it provided the opportunity to bring about change, peacefully and gradually.

\* \* \* \*

The position of Fabianism on the state did not reject the utilitarian notions of the 'greatest happiness for the greatest number' and the need for society to be reorganised from above but instead, sought to extend them. Sidney Webb, for instance, is a good example of how utilitarianism was enhanced through his faith in positivism. Hence, science and experts were to be essential sources of neutral, rational advice. Much of the activity of government then could be left to "the disinterested professional expert who invents, discovers, inspects, audits, costs, tests of measures" (Bevir 2002: 242) so as to pinpoint the facts about social life and its requirements. The knowledge, accumulated by the scientist, would enable them to administer effectively and to indicate priorities on policy matters. Elections, while not to be abolished, were to some extent in Webb's view a symbolic exercise through which popular consent for expertly designed policies could be raised. A belief in the inevitability of society to become ever more differentiated into functional units, held together through cooperation and coordination, meant the broad path of social development was set and the job of politicians and experts was to develop proposals that would ease the way along this route.

\* \* \* \*

A strong alternative to Webb's view was represented at the time by John Maynard Keynes who advocated fiscal and monetary measures to stimulate

---

[11] See, for instance, Shaw (1889).

the economy essentially by expanding demand and employment. Furthermore, unlike Webb, Keynes focused on the individual as opposed to the common good. Reacting to the depression and unemployment of interwar years, Webb criticised Keynes for advocating short-term solutions within the framework of a capitalist economy when what was needed was a long-term industrial reorganisation within a collectivist economy. Turning therefore to the Soviet Union, which he visited in 1932 and 1934, solutions such as 'planned production for community consumption' appeared to have rationalised the economy for the social good in a way that had abolished "mass unemployment, together with the devastating alteration of commercial booms and slumps" (Webb & Webb 1936, vol. 2: 602). In spite of the control exerted by the Communist Part, Webb regarded the Soviet political system as a 'multiform democracy' in which the individual can participate as a citizen, producer and consumer (Webb & Webb 1936, vol. 1: 427). Ignoring the ineluctable place of conflict in social life, Webb was committed to the ideal of there being an evolutionary movement towards a society where conflict would be largely absent since everyone would be working towards a common good upon which they agreed. Seeing the market as the epitome of immoral and irrational conflict, Webb did not want to recognise the extent to which the Soviet model too embodied violence and conflict. Nehru's thoughts and ideas about the role of the market and state and the nature of societal development carry a striking resemblance.

* * * *

In many ways Nehru was a great believer in the importability of institutions and ideas. His writings are littered with references to lessons that could be learned from the advances and achievements of others. However, what is in fact surprising is how little he *discovers* that is indigenous upon which to build his vision of independent India. Compared to his contemporaries including Gandhi, Tagore, Bose, Prasad, Savarkar, Nehru's writing is curiously lacking in hybridity. The book speaks in one voice and does not generate the impression of an author torn between multiple identities. When Nehru wants to be elegant, he cites Yeats.[12] When he refers to an ideal contemporary society, he invokes the Soviet Union. Furthermore, when, in *Discovery of India*, he finally describes the kind of India he would like to inculcate, his depiction is rather vague and rambling, referring as he does to:

> [...] the wisdom of the ancients, the buoyant energy and love of life and nature of our forefathers, their spirit of curiosity and mental adventure, the daring of their thought, their splendid achievements in literature, art and culture, their love

---

[12] See *Discovery of India* (2004: 9) for a citation of Yeats' poem, "An Irish Airman Foresees His Death".

of truth and beauty and freedom, the basic values that they set up, their understanding of life's mysterious ways, their toleration of other ways than theirs, their capacity to absorb other peoples and their cultural accomplishments, to synthesise them and develop a varied and mixed culture. (Nehru 2004: 567)

No doubt Nehru himself was a hybrid, "a queer mixture of the East and West, out of place everywhere, at home nowhere" (Nehru 1953: 596), as he put it in his *An Autobiography*, first published in 1936, but the social imaginary which he embodied did not carry a strongly indigenous imprint. Instead, as he crossed the length and breadth of the country campaigning for elections, it is as though he was trying to convince himself of what linked him to the crowds he encountered as well as what it was that drew them to him. The past may represent an idealised essence providing both an implicit and conscious source of pride and unity, but *Discovery of India* ends by highlighting the need for a rupture with the past. All aspects of the present were ready for change, in his final opinion, and it is useful to sum up by paraphrasing the 'social imaginary', which he sought to replace the existing superstructure with. First and foremost, it was necessary for India "to lessen her religiosity and turn to science" (Nehru 2004: 579) in order to unlock the shackles that had stunted the spirit and productivity of the people. Caste, as a social organisation, was to have no place as "the concept of abstract rights is (to give) place to that of functions" (Nehru 2004: 580) and a system of 'democratic collectivism' would address India's economic woes of colonial exploitation and stagnation. Thus, the three central forms of the social imaginary as articulated by Charles Taylor above, that of the economy, the public sphere and popular sovereignty were firmly entrenched in Nehru's outlook of India's modern future.

## CONCLUSION: ENDURING NEHRU

If one briefly considers the three realms mentioned above of the economy, the public sphere and popular sovereignty, it is intriguing to note how little Nehru sought in the end to appropriate from the past. With regards secularism, which corresponds somewhat with his notion of the public sphere, Nehru advocated a strict exclusion of religion from political life, a radical break with past traditions of traditional Hindu rulership where religion was seen as a way of life regulating not just the personal but also political, public life. Likewise, Nehru's national goals of industrialisation, socialism and nonalignment represented ideas that were essentially alien to the Indian experience of polity and social order. For instance, the *Arthasahastra* Kautilya instructed that foreign policy ought to be entirely based on expediency and could include the use of both alignment and nonalignment, depending on the situation. While Nehru may have, on occasion, conceded that nonalignment simply meant the pursuit of national interest, the ambiguity that was left surrounding India's foreign policy was in itself meant to be an instrument, a tool for self-defence or self-aggrandisement. Furthermore, even into the 1950s, Nehru's own ideals had in fact received little public endorsement. As Bhikhu Parekh notes in his article, "Nehru and the National Philosophy of India" (1991: 35–48), some of the goals contained in Nehru's national programme were embodied in the Constitution of India passed by the elected Constituent Assembly, others had formed part of the Congress party's programme promulgated during elections. However, the constituent assembly was elected on a very limited franchise and more than half the electorate never voted for Congress in any of the elections held under his leadership (Parekh 1991: 45).

Nevertheless, buttressed by a strategic consolidation of power, Nehru's ideals eventually gained predominance, emerging out of the power mongering of the early 1950s. Furthermore, despite the drastic changes in foreign policy engineered by his daughter, Indira Gandhi, the attempt to bring religion under the purview of the state by his grandson, Rajiv Gandhi, and the efforts of a Congressman, Manmohan Singh, to dismantle the licence-permit Raj, one of the enduring vestiges of the planned economy, Nehru retains a potent symbolic value. Revived and rediscovered at election time or at international gatherings, Nehru's legacy is underscored in Congress election manifestos and statesmen's speeches. These are nevertheless adapted to suit the times as can be seen, for instance, in the 2009 Congress election manifesto which reads:

> The Indian National Congress is fully aware that the world economy faces the worst crisis in 50 years. This crisis has been caused by a failure of financial markets in the USA and in other developed countries. However, the Indian economy has shown considerable resilience under the most adverse international circumstances. This is the outcome of the policies of successive Congress governments. This is the direct result of a vibrant public sector that is the legacy of Jawaharlal Nehru, government ownership of banks that is the legacy of Indira Gandhi, and a strong private sector that matured and flowered during the tenure of Rajiv Gandhi and thereafter. (The Manifesto of the Indian National Congress 2009)

While the 'vibrant public sector' may not quite reflect reality and most of the core elements of Nehru's vision have not been fulfilled, he continues to be used as a legitimating device and symbol of higher ideals. This stretching of Nehru to fit expectations and challenges of the day may not be endlessly feasible and as India's democracy asserts its own distinctive character, it may become necessary to reassess some of the self-understandings that underpin India's institutions of modernity.

# BIBLIOGRAPHY

## Secondary Sources

Bevir, M., 2002 (June), "Sidney Webb: Utilitarianism, Positivism and Social Democracy". *The Journal of Modern History*. Vol. 74 , no. 2, pp. 217–52.

Ghosh, S. C., 1978, "The Utilitarianism of Dalhousie and the Material Improvement of India". *Modern Asian Studies*. Vol. 21, no. 1, pp. 97–110.

Mill, James, 1840, *The History of British India*, 4th edition/with notes and continuation by Horace Hayman Wilson. J. Madden, London.

Mitra, Subrata K., 1991 (October), "Desecularising the State: Religion and Politics in India after Independence". *Comparative Studies in Society and History*. Vol. 33, no. 4, pp. 755–77.

Nehru, Jawaharlal, 1933, "Whither India". In: *1973 Selected Works of Jawaharlal Nehru*. S. Gopal (General editor). Orient Longman, New Delhi, pp. 1–31.

———, 1953, *An Autobiography*. The Bodley Head, London.

———, 1984, *Glimpses of World History*. Oxford University Press, New Delhi.

———, 2004, *Discovery of India*. Penguin Books, London.

Parekh, B., 1991 (5–12 January), "Nehru and the National Philosophy of India". *Economic and Political Weekly*. Vol. 26, no. 1/2, pp. 35–48.

Schöttli, J., 2012, *Vision and Strategy in Indian Politics: Jawaharlal Nehru's Policy Choices and the Designing of Political Institutions*. Routledge, London.

Shaw, G. B., 1889, *Fabian Essays in Socialism*. Scott, London.

Stokes, Eric, 1959, "The Doctrine and Its Setting". *The English Utilitarians and India*. Clarendon Press, Oxford, pp. 1–47.

Taylor, Charles, 1999, "Modern Social Imaginaries". *Public Culture*. Vol. 14, no. 1, pp. 91–124.

———, 2002, "Modern Social Imaginaries". *Public Culture*. Vol 14, no. 1, pp. 91–124.

Tharoor, Shashi, 2003, *Nehru: The Invention of India*. Penguin, New Delhi.

Webb, Sidney & Beatrice Webb, 1936, *Soviet Communism: A New Civilization?*, 2 Vols. Scribner, New York.

Wolpert, Stanley A., 1996, *Nehru: A Tryst with Destiny*. Oxford University Press, Oxford.

Zachariah, Benjamin, 2004, *Nehru*. Routledge, London.

## Internet Sources

http://www.cceia.org/resources/transcripts/1075.html (accessed on: 15 April 2009).

Manifesto of the Indian National Congress (2009). Available at http://www.indian-elections.com/pdf/manifesto09-cong.pdf (accessed on: 30 June 2010).

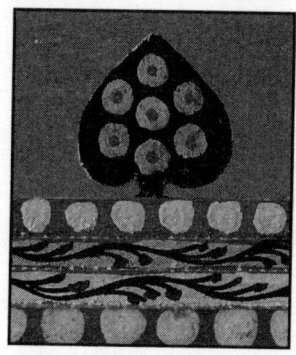

*Chapter 11*

# USE AND RE-USE OF 'PAKISTAN' IN THE INDIAN MUSLIM PRESS (1932–47)*

**BY THIERRY DICOSTANZO**

## INTRODUCTION

Provided the use of proper keywords, a brief look at the internet these days will make one surprised to discover that the dream of a more united South Asia concerned mainly the very official circles of the South Asian Association for Regional Cooperation (SAARC). More stupendous is the impression that the old idea of Indian Muslim separatism, called the idea of 'Pakistan' in the 1940s, is surprisingly not dead even sixty years after the creation of a homeland

* This essay is based on my PhD dissertation which has just been published in Germany [L'idée séparatiste dans la presse anglo-musulmane du Bengale: le cas du Star of India, 1937–1947, *Anglo-amerikanische Studien*, 42 (2011): 291 pp]. A shorter version of this essay was also published in French [Essai de définition du concept de Pakistan dans la presse anglomusulmane selon le modèle de dominion et selon le modèle irlandais, 1932–1947, *Cultures of the Commonwealth: Essays and Studies*, 17, Winter (2010–11)]. I am grateful to Subrata Mitra and Julia Hegewald for their support in wanting the result of this study to be published in English for the first time ever.

for Indian Muslims. Sites advocating the re-use of former sub-concepts like 'Muslimistan' and 'Islamistan', dating from the old pre-Partition ideas of Pakistan, abound next to sites having coined new but similar-in-meaning concepts like 'Mughalstan', 'Urdustan' or even 'Mohajiristan'.

In the north-eastern region of the subcontinent, old and new also coexist: the old 'Bangistan' and the new 'Bengalistan' both advocate a kind of regional ethnic or ethnic-religious nationalism that is sixty years old, in a way.[1] This 're-use' of the old concept is no 'abuse' at all of the word 'Pakistan' and its historical sub-meanings. In the 1930s and 1940s, such sub-uses were already apparent in the Indian press. This incredible renewal and modernisation of these much bandied-around terms requires one to return to the period in question.

This chapter attempts to tackle one particular aspect of the immense issue of the 1947 Partition, that of the birth of Indian Muslim nationalism[2] in journalism. A form of unitary Indian Muslim nationalism existed among Indian Muslims before 1947 as especially apparent in the Bengal Muslim press.[3] After the concept of 'Pakistan' appeared in Muslim dailies, it was used and re-used to such

---

[1] Some of the sites quoted here are only given as examples of the huge amount of 'hate' or militant material found on the net:

For Urdustan, look at the MQM's video: http://www.youtube.com/watch?v=ResU1IbXyj8, http://www.youtube.com/user/Urdustan

For Mughalstan or Mughalistan, look at Hindu Nationalists' sites advocating for the canto-nalisation of Muslim-majority districts in India: http://www.hindujagruti.org/activities/cam-paigns/national/india-map-controversy/mughalstan.php, http://www.bengalgenocide.com/mughalistan.php

For Islamistan, look at the minimal but enlightening definition found on Wikipedia: http://en.wikipedia.org/wiki/Islamistan

For Bangistan: http://rupeenews.com/tag/greater-bright-bangladesh

For Bangalistan: http://www.worldproutassembly.org/archives/bangalistan/

[2] On Indian Muslim nationalism, Torri provides a comprehensive and clear summary, unfortu-nately only available in Italian (Torri 1996).

[3] If we apply Rashid Khalidi's findings from *Palestinian Identity: The Construction of Modern National Consciousness* (1997), on Palestinian nationalism to the Indian context, we will find and agree with the following: Holders of the new idea of Pakistan reject both the idea of an exclusive and eternal Hindu India—which is so dear to Hindu nationalism—and the idea of an exclusive and eternal Islamic Pakistan or Bangladesh—which is so dear to Islamic militants and Jihadists. There exists a rightful and legitimate Indian Muslim nationalism, as its emergence is a direct consequence of the Indian Muslims' rejection by Hindu nationalists from the Indian national-ist scene. The Indian context can be seen as similar to that of post-World War II Palestine: end of Empire and British colonialism, intense activity of exclusivist movements on both sides. Khalidi's study numbers five main themes that we can also apply to the South Asian context. First, the emergence of national identities of India, Pakistan and Bangladesh; then, the role of foreign powers in the shaping of those identities; after that, the role of education in the build-ing of political identity; certainly, the shaping of great historical accounts on South Asia as a region must also be a perspective—there is a serious lack of an historiographical project on Indian Muslims despite the existence of Iggers' and Mukherjee's master study on India and the world (Iggers & Mukherjee 2008: 38, 97, 227–37, 284) that deal with Indian historiography or Islamic countries, not with the situation of Indian Muslims. Finally, the most important for us is the impact of the press in the shaping of new community awareness.

considerable and different significations that one may say that it was occasionally in contradiction with the original idea of Pakistan.

We will start from the early 1930s, when the last constitution of colonial India was put into place, to reach the aftermath of Partition in August 1947, a period of time that corresponds, more or less, to the span of life of a daily paper called *Star of India*. The main thread of this chapter is, the idea of Pakistan as this concept appears in the editorials of the *Star of India*, an Indian Muslim daily paper from Calcutta. Our objective will also be to determine at what precise moment the daily adopted the use of the word 'Pakistan', and what it meant by it.

To understand the issue fully, we will seek to know who were the agents of this new form of Indian anti-colonial nationalism—the Indian Muslim idea of Pakistan—in the press and what motivated them. First, we are simply seeking to analyse the geographical, social and ideological origin and identity of the *Star of India* journalists dealing with the important question of the idea of Pakistan. We will focus our attention towards the Bengal Muslim journalists in particular. Second, we will try to know at what precise moment and in which manner the famous and first-ever Muslim daily in English from Calcutta decided to put pressure on Muslim opinion in eastern India for it to support a form of Indian nationalism that was different from mainstream nationalism. Third, we will consider what was re-used from Indian nationalism in the idea of Pakistan and what was rejected. After that, the idea of Pakistan as a branch of unitary Indian nationalism having failed, we will consider the causes of its failure. The *Star of India*'s propagation of the idea of Pakistan being rather successful, we will try to understand why it was so, the main reason probably being the multifaceted shape of the concept, the possibility for the paper to re-use its vague catchphrase for as long as negotiations on the future of India were open. We will finally look at the present and the fact that 'Pakistan' has, in the end, produced less integration and more anxiety concerning the future of Muslims in South Asia.

We will show that the *Star of India* was in constant evolution when using the concept of Pakistan. The paper offered its columns to numerous sensibilities of the anti-colonial movement in India and was in favour of a united India able to guarantee special community rights for the Muslims rather than a full territorial separation between the two main religious groups. Let us insist on the fact that most of the paper's collaborators rejected both the centralist ideal and the extreme solution of territorial separation. In fact, the journalists were far from being unaware of the dire consequences that the idea of a separate territory for Pakistan would have meant for all Indians. Few supported a strict divide of India into two inward-looking, antagonistic and suspicious independent states. Yet, Partition and violence is what happened in 1947.

If we consider the Bengal Muslims writing in the *Star of India*, it is clear that they opposed radical Partition, not so much of India but of their own province. In 1947, they were still debating three possible scenarios for Bengal. We can shortly present them here. We have one group supporting the idea that the province should be declaring its independence unilaterally, in order to be neither a part of India nor a part of Pakistan. Another category insisted that Bengal should simply benefit from a strong dose of freedom from the Indian Central Union. Finally, a last group estimated that north-east India was to be the rightful property of Pakistan.

We can clearly see that none of the groups that controlled the *Star of India* was satisfied at the time of Partition. Therefore, we found them a generation later in East Pakistan, as militants for stronger autonomy and opposing the very same who favoured the ill-orchestrated 1947 Partition of India and Bengal. In this article, we are thus trying to explain the origin of the fracture within the pro-Pakistan Bengal Muslim groups too.

This chapter is originally based on my PhD work presented in 2005 at Rennes University, France. Transcripts of articles published in the *Star of India* available on forty-one microfilms are mainly originating from the Library of Congress. These microfilms are copied from the issues of the daily printed between 17 August 1932 and 30 June 1948. The only microfilm copied from the British Library includes a period going from 3 January to 10 August 1949, the period going from 31 May to 12 July of that year being missing. The study of the daily paper called *Star of India* was undertaken from microfilms copied by these two libraries, none of which could boast a full collection.

The scope of this chapter is modest and the lack of diversity in the sources we were able to exploit could provoke controversy. For instance, it would have been interesting to compare the *Star of India* to other newspapers published in Calcutta and other big cities in India, but collecting the proper material demanded special financial means unavailable to us. However, the study of the *Star of India* makes it possible for one to become rather well acquainted with the world of the Indian press in late colonial times, in particular the study of the idea of Pakistan in public opinion and its surprising semantic use and re-use.

Our constant endeavour in this analysis was to have sufficient distance, in particular when giving views on the various forms of the idea of Pakistan in the Indian Muslim community. Nationalist hagiographies often hamper a proper reading on the issue. The study will then try to show how absurd all types of territorial fragmenting along religious lines can be. In the 1940s' Indian case, we are unhesitatingly asserting that Partition was a catastrophe and the real cause for the most exclusive Indian Muslim brand of nationalism are those that pushed for a hurried and low-cost decolonisation of India.

## THE STORY OF 'PAKISTAN' IN THE *STAR OF INDIA*

Together with Lahore and Delhi, Calcutta was one of the three main centres of Indian Muslim journalism. In the context of the 1930s—the Indian press as a whole was undergoing massive commercialisation—the *Star of India* wished to provide advice and respond to the needs of a well-to-do readership at a time when Indian society was going through social, economic and political upheaval. The daily offered the possibility for Muslims to experience a new and proud sense of community through the vision of a common language, history and culture in its columns. It also expressed that new community pride in a code tolerated by either the regime or the anti-colonial movement.

The *Star of India* was created on 17 August 1932 in Calcutta, the future epi-centre of Partition. Between the years 1932 and 1947, the time when the Anglo-Muslim newspaper existed, the Indians decided that their religions separated them and that it was better to divide India along communal lines. Calcutta was deeply wounded by the 1947 Partition and the *Star of India* left for Karachi in August 1949.

Our material often offered quite varied and contradictory analyses on the causes of the break-up between Hindus and Muslims, but it also allowed for a clear grasping of the special context that preceded the set-up of two antagonistic States in 1947 South Asia. More than sixty years after, the *Star of India* can still bring one to understand what continues to oppose—often violently—the different political families of a State created from the secession of East Pakistan in 1971. Indeed, Bangladesh still refers to ideological conceptions of the nation that were already visible in the newspaper columns (DiCostanzo 2003).

Just like the *Star of India*, the first modern dailies in India and Bengal were born in the interwar period and had a circulation of hundreds of thousands.[4] The readership for the dailies written in English was very influential in Indian society even if quite insignificant in numbers and readership. The *Star of India* was indeed the daily paper of the elite of one of the most consequent communities in colonial India, the Indian Muslim community.

Immediately after World War I, Indian papers were defending a rather moderate point of view concerning community rights, at a time when anti-colonial feelings were common in the Indian press. The press was in favour of elaborating some sort of official recognition for the various minorities of India or was on the side of granting some form of autonomous powers for the Indian

---

[4] On the history of the colonial Indian press, see Israel (1994); on the Congress press, see Moitra (1969) and Natarajan (1962); on the Bengal or Indian Muslim press, see Nurul Islam (1973) and Talbot (1988).

Imperial Provinces. After 1926, an extreme form of hatred, communalism, clearly increased among some journalists. Those editors openly rejected the official federal communitarist policy offering particular political representation to the Muslims.

When the *Star of India* was created in 1932, the daily was in no way in favour of a strict separation between Hindus and Muslims. It supported a moderate anti-colonial line and wished to offer a different product from the district, Congress or pro-regime press. Of course, editorial opinion in the *Star of India* changed concerning community rights issues, or autonomy and separatism. Between 1932 and 1936, first editor-in-chief, Horace George Franks, supported some kind of political communitarianism within the limits of Calcutta only. Between 1936 and 1939, Lawrence Patrick Atkinson developed some kind of more province-oriented communitarianism until the publishing of an aggressive editorial that caused his resignation.

Atkinson had endangered the paper's mission of propagating the idea of a territorial Pakistan that the *Star of India* took up after the so-called historic Muslim League Resolution of Lahore. Between 1942 and 1945, it was no less than the towering figure of Indian journalism, Pothan Joseph (1892–1972), who submitted the paper to the orders of the Central League, even if only for a short time.[5] Usman Ahmad Ansari was his successor and showed himself more open to various opinions held within the Indian Muslim community concerning the risks emanating from the much-debated idea of a territorial Pakistan, if it were applied too strictly to the particularly complex context of the administrative province of Bengal.

After 1947, the *Star of India* stopped being Indian and became Pakistani. Of course, the idea of Pakistan that it supported was the very cause of its disappearance; however, it soon became alive again in Karachi under the similar name of *The Star*. That newspaper still exists: it is the evening edition of a famous daily, originally founded by Muhammad Ali Jinnah (1876–1948), *Dawn*. Today, the *Dawn* and *The Star* both belong to one of the most prestigious press group publishing in English in modern-day Pakistan, the Dawn Group and Publications which is part of the Haroon family economic empire.

The paper belonged to an upper-middle class group of wealthy Muslims living in Calcutta or in its economic hinterland.[6] The group was in favour of a certain selective economic protectionism, but was also open to outside influences—especially British and American, not so much Islamic. The government had first appointed experts, but professionals were also recruited from other communities, before Muslims provided quality supervision to the

---

[5] On Pothan Joseph, see George (1992) and Joseph (1979).
[6] On Calcutta Muslims, see McPherson (1974).

first modern Muslim newspaper ever published east of Lucknow. Above all, the paper had in store the launching of a soft approach and version of community modernisation and therefore dealt with numerous aspects of Muslim history, language and culture rather than politics. It was true that the *Star of India* was mainly preoccupied with local news and did not debate so much on complex political issues.

Right away, the name *Star of India* (also the name of colonial India's official flag) showed the moderate political stance of that modest anti-colonial paper: ideologically right-wing and in favour of a Dominion status for India—something denied since 1926 by the regime. As many other papers of its time, the *Star of India* was community-oriented. However, its pro-Muslim community stance was particular in the sense that it perceived itself as the only voice for the Muslim community in the eastern region. Politically, it regarded the Muslims as a whole as the only community who deserved official recognition as a minority at the federal-central level. Besides, the paper maintained that the colonial regime should grant territorial protection (sometimes called Pakistan) to the Indian Muslim community unless the most powerful Indian nationalist movement, the Congress, recognised the demand for a federal protection of that minority.

The chronology of the different forms of the debate on the Pakistan idea and use of this concept must be examined in the paper's columns. It will therefore be possible to understand what precise form of the idea of Pakistan the paper was inclined to believe. On the idea of Pakistan in either the editorial column or the interior politics column, three main periods can be isolated. In the years 1939 and 1940, the *Star of India* published about a quarter of all articles found to be relevant to the theme of the idea of Pakistan. Between 1941 and 1944, another quarter bore on the issue. However, most of the articles dealing with the issue were to be found in the 1945–47 period.

For the first time in 1933, the *Star of India* mentioned Chaudhury Rahmat Ali (1895–1951) and his Pakistan project in its columns—the original idea of poet Iqbal's project is surprisingly not mentioned till the 1940s. It is most interesting to note that at the time of the first-ever quote of the word 'Pakistan' in its columns, the paper viciously attacked the idea as being extreme although said to gain more and more importance in the north-west regions of the Indian British Empire. Between the date of the 1936 elections and the declaration of war, the paper very much preferred the clearer and less ambiguous expression of 'Indian Muslim State' to that of 'Pakistan'. The *Star of India* considered the possibility of some sort of a large autonomous province that would be part of a federally administered India. It rebuked the use of the term 'Pakistan', which had a kind of student-like, immature, irresponsible, fancy and unrealistic idealism—again probably an indirect reference to Rahmat Ali's group of student supporters, but this remained unclear.

It was only at the end of 1939 that the *Star of India* fully adopted the word-use of 'Pakistan' as a synonym of 'Indian Muslim Nation'. At that time, the paper partially and temporarily rejected the federal idea for India for the idea of an Indian confederation. At the same time, the use of 'Pakistan' infiltrated the everyday language of the paper and was not any longer the trademark of a handful of extremists. The Resolution voted at its Lahore session of March 1940 by the All-India Muslim League provided a new meaning and use for the word 'Pakistan', quite different from Rahmat Ali's version: all of India's Muslim-majority provinces (and not just the Muslim West) were to form several entities gathered into a Muslim Confederated State affiliated to a united India.[7] Princely States where Muslims were in a majority—like Kashmir—were to decide whether they would freely join the Indian Muslim Confederation in a near future. It must be insisted upon that even after 1940, the *Star of India* endlessly repeated it was attached to Indian unity, considering the option of total independence as nothing but a most extreme possibility.

At that time in the *Star of India*'s history, the editors decided to open its columns to members of the Indian National Congress who did not oppose the Confederation idea. The main point the paper defended was that two Indias could constitute two united dominions within the British Empire in India. Indeed, some of the *Star of India* collaborators underlined how interesting the creation of a Pakistani state would be for India as the Muslim dominion would be a sort of buffer state between the Muslim world, China and the Soviet Union, consequently reducing the size of India's future defence budget.

Between 1940 and 1942, the concept of Pakistan became problematic. How solid was British India as it had to deal with the advance of the Japanese in Burma? India being also at the forefront of the anti-colonial battle in the world, any official recognition of territorial limits for a would-be Pakistan on Indian territory could have had as a consequence the Ulsterisation of India. *The Star* defended itself against such solution and remained attached to an at-one-go independence of India, for Ulsterisation would have meant maintaining the Western lands of India, called 'Pakistan' under even tighter colonial domination. Many journalists therefore refused the make-up of a separate Indian Muslim State in India in *The Star*.

However, geographic Muslim predominance in the East and West logically made it possible for a national territory to be cut out there for the majority of the community. With Indian Muslim separatism being based on religion, not on ethnicity or language, the *Star of India* had a premonition that, at the end of the day, the very diversity of Indian Muslim society could threaten the mythical project

---

[7] For a vivid account of the debates concerning the Lahore session of 1940, see Ahmad (1975).

of an Indian Muslim nation. Even if the paper, along the official 1941 census, attempted to support that a Muslim language (Urdu) and an Indian Muslim ethnic group (that was not necessarily Islamic) had always existed, its stand on the fact that Muslims made up a homogeneous group remained unconvincing. In the *Star of India*'s columns at the time, it was quite clear that the proposed Indian Muslim nation state could become just as heterogeneous as the country it was breaking off from and could itself fall prey to internal separatist tendencies quite rapidly. Some of the Bengal journalists unknowingly and unwillingly anticipated what would happen a generation after Partition: the secession of East Pakistan.

Between the end of war and the time of Independence, the paper used the word 'Pakistan' more and more often. It used it in its titles first during the year 1945 and then both in its titles and contents during the following year. The break-up with the idea of the two-dominion idea dated from the middle of 1946 when the paper then opted for the idea of a completely independent State for Indian Muslims. If Pakistan were reduced to the meanest share—that is, a territory constituted of Muslim-majority districts alone—the separatist project entailed creating a nonviable State along with the brutal break-up of old and solid economic links, especially in Bengal and Punjab, in spite of the numerous assertions of Aligarh economists in the *Star of India*.

What has just been drawn here is a broad outline of the paper's discourse concerning the idea Pakistan between 1933 and 1947. In spite of an initial rejection of a term akin to extremism and provincialism, the *Star of India* adopted the word 'Pakistan' in order to give it a special bi-national form and finally a fully independent flavour.

However, we must clearly understand that the will to separate was fragile between 1938 and 1947: it is what we can make out through the study of the *Star of India*. For Muslim public opinion, objective elements were lacking for it to determine exactly what the Indian Muslim nation would be and any subjective awareness of forming a nation proper is far from obvious for all. *The Star* could not prevent numerous journalists from expressing serious doubts on the issue of Pakistan. Around 1947, some Muslim Socialists even voiced their main priority in the right-wing paper: the reducing of social inequalities was superior to the creating of a Muslim State that could continue to fall prey to the traditional collaborators of the colonial regime, that is, religious clerics, rich business people, *zamindars* and the top military brass.

There were numerous signs suggesting that the idea of Pakistan remained in the realm of extremely fringe political fantasists within the community. The idea of Pakistan, at best, could have been the consequence of frustrated regionalist feelings. It can be argued that supporting this idea was just the ultimate resort some Muslim quarters had, when confronting a very stubborn Indian National Congress that would not bend to moderate communitarianist and particularistic demands. Indeed, most of the articles defending a separatist view were simply content with an attack on the Congress' refusal to grant basic Indian Muslim demands for more political autonomy or full minority rights. Hence, the raised bid of using the vague catchphrase of 'Pakistan, Pakistan'.

Until the very eve of Partition and full Independence, there were several possible compromises between League Separatists and Congress Centralists. We will examine one main example of that type of dialogue in the *Star of India*, that of Abul Hashim. Together, the League and the Congress were seeking to officiously recognise the distinct character of the Indian Muslim minority and even trying to adapt a kind of particular status within the future unitary state normally emerging with the time of Independence. Those different parties explored the potential of federal and bi-national solutions which could offer a form of autonomy to the Muslim minority. Between 1939 and 1946, there were many long articles illustrating that principle in the *Star of India*.

One can only regret that such agreement could not be reached immediately after the war in a context of communal violence and fragilised central authority. Many Muslims in colonial India were worried about the uncertain consequences of their own separatist demands. Their will to cut the British Empire in India into two, bore the risk of an armed conflict with the British expeditionary corps, the non-Muslim regiments of the local army and the ultra-Hindu militias. Even though the *Star of India*, out of bravado, claimed the Muslims were ready for a civil war, it remained vague on possible alliances with other Muslim countries and on the opinion of military officers who never wrote in the paper. The Communal conflict starting in Calcutta with Hindu Nationalist militias was certainly less intense than a full-blown civil war. However, this conflict put an end to the dialogue started between peace activists, in spite of ultimate and isolated convulsions.

Interestingly, many Muslim journalists in the *Star of India* deplored that British colonial rule—unlike Mughal rule—and had not been willing to hit at particularist tendencies in India. Of course, the regime had drastically altered the social, cultural and territorial frontiers that had existed at its advent. However, many believed in India that particularists had won over universalists in 1947. This chapter attempts to show, albeit reluctantly and begrudgingly, the use of the concept of a fully independent Pakistan after being in favour of the full territorial integrity of India.

## 'Pakistan' as the Rejection of the British Model for India

In 1939 and 1940, the *Star of India* considered that the direct causes for progress of the idea of Pakistan within Indian Muslim opinion was the Congress's strict support for majority rule and the total inexistence of a genuine Indian nationalism, whose goal would be the reunion of all anti-colonial political parties. The Calcutta Muslim daily was not against a strong dose of central rule; it even started defending a version of the centralist idea offering special guarantees to religious minorities of India.

Originally, the editorial board pleaded for the granting of a third of all seats to Muslims at the central executive and the federal legislative assembly as well as the instauration of US-inspired institutions for India. The British—as most Indian Muslim commentators writing in the *Star of India*—wished India had had a less centralised political system. Year 1942 was the utter and definite end of federalism in the paper and the first editor to bury the idea formally was Pothan Joseph, of a Christian Southern background. After 1942, the board regularly supported the concept of confederation. The idea of creating two fully independent states relaying the Imperial regime only came at the last minute.

Debating steadfastly about India's unity and federal communitarianism nevertheless remained alive and well till 1946. More than the idea of a territorially-recognised Pakistan, it was that version of the idea of Pakistan—the recognition of an all-India religious minority—that the *Star of India* thought should have been installed since 1939. The paper's position perhaps showed that, for a long time, Indian Muslim opinion in Calcutta viewed with disfavour the idea of a radical territorially-based Pakistan.

We saw that the paper wished for a centralised communitarian federalist system (a kind of federalism bunched up with 'affirmative action' measures as we would say today) and was waiting for an agreement to be signed at the federal level up until the Lahore Resolution. Many articles published at the time were trying to demonstrate how dysfunctional large existing state federations could be. The paper's evoking the situation of American Blacks could obviously be seen as a sign that Indian Muslim opinion looked towards the outside for models and support—in this case, the English-speaking world. Though the idea of a united central India survived the war, it could not live through the 16 August so-called, Great Calcutta Killing.

The Muslims' federal communitarianism was different from Gandhi's unitary nationalism which was repeatedly attacked in the paper's columns, especially between 1937 and 1944. For a long time the paper viewed the failure of that federal idea as being due to the opposition of one man only, Gandhi; it must be noted that a leader like Nehru was hardly directly criticised and that the *Star of India* sometimes called for the construction of a genuine Indian nationalism later described by Nehru. The paper rejected the Gandhian project of an inherent Hindu identity for Indian Muslims and all other minorities. In the context of World War II, the paper played on the reader's sensitivity to the ambiguous position of the Congress towards Japanese advance. What seemed to make the paper more radical in its views was also the increasing influence of extremist

Hindu Nationalist philosophy within the Congress, especially between 1940 and 1942. The *Star of India* therefore rejected all forms of nationalism that could be inspired by Hindu Nationalist ideology. Further, the military successes of Nazi Germany, which certainly did not encourage trust of Hitler-inspired theories of radical Hindu groups on the possible future of Muslims in India, did not help either. Hence, the temptation to create a Muslim Ulster or a separate Pakistan in India inspired some Muslims in case ethnic cleansing, persecution or extermination was to be orchestrated by extremists collaborating with the Nazi or Japanese authorities.

## 'Pakistan' as Part of the Two-Dominion Idea

It was no wonder that, in the *Star of India*, the idea of an Indian confederation appeared within the six months preceding the Muslim League's 1940 Lahore Resolution. Some commentators supported the creation of two Muslim zones (one in the north-west and one in the north-east) and two Hindu zones (one in the north and one in the south). Others at the same time favoured the creation of one-only Muslim and Hindu zone. Of course, the debate generally bore on the definition of the borders of these future confederated cultural-religious zones. Should the two Indian States be contented with districts where a religious majority existed? Alternatively, should they remain bounded to existing administrative provinces? The last case would have meant the remodelling of provincial borders to fit language, ethnicity, religion and culture. There were also numerous supporters of the organising of population exchange between the two or four Indian zones, although other opinions refused the scenario and simply asked for an equal share of power at the central level or a cantonal system based on the Swiss model.

Consequently, it was no surprise to discover that it took one year exactly after the Lahore Resolution, for Jinnah to use the word 'Pakistan' when giving a speech in Aligarh University. On 12 March 1941, on page 3 of the *Star of India*, Jinnah was quoted defining Pakistan as being anti-communal and the proper tool to reduce conflict between Hindus and Muslims in India. The article is called "Muslims Can Accept Nothing but 'Pakistan'", and promised Pakistan would be an economically viable Muslim territory carved out from about twenty ethnic–religious Indian provinces:

> What is Pakistan? It is, in a word, the creation of separate ethnic or cultural states within suitable territorial boundaries, so as to avoid communal and cultural frictions. It contemplates two central governments [...].

'Pakistan' for Jinnah had no revolutionary connotation in 1941 and the Muslim leader did not require full sovereignty for his Pakistan, which remained united to India (Jinnah 1976). Not everyone in the Muslim camp shared the Qaid's view though. Students in Bengal saw it slightly differently, surely. Calcutta was to be the capital of the future Eastern Indian Muslim State.

Anyhow, in 1942, the principle of an Indian confederation seemed suddenly favoured by the regime in dire search of Indian allies, so the League was ready to open negotiations with the Congress. Jinnah rejoiced at what Richard Stafford Cripps (1882–1952) had to offer. Two years later in Bombay, Gandhi, the Congress Right, and Jinnah were, then, quite ready to find a successful compromise between hardcore Congress centralists and radical Muslim separatists of the Rahmat Ali kind. How unfortunate for the colonial authorities not to have launched a daring administrative reform in order to modify the limits of India's provinces as numerous political groups were demanding. That administrative reorganisation might have opened the way to a compromise between the two Indian sides. In any case, be it on the issue of provincial frontiers or the choice of a future national idiom for India, the *Star of India* opened up the debate without providing a readymade solution; it therefore fulfilled its role as a press and information organ rather well within the institutional setup and 'Pakistan' still remained ill-defined.

In 1946, the *Star of India* gave full support to the Cabinet Mission even if the Mission's awkward behaviour buried the bi-national solution forever. From mid-1946 onwards, the paper therefore forgot about the confederated solution for India.

## Independent and Separate 'Pakistan'

At the start of the war, the *Star of India* had also opened up its columns to the kind of Muslims that supported the idea of a totally independent Muslim territory carved out for Islamic believers only. This kind of closed nationalism could be seen as the natural Muslim reaction to the growing success of extreme Hindu nationalist theses. However, the rise of Muslim extremism, much visible in the press, seemed only a tactic to counterbalance Hindu Nationalists within the Congress. Discarding Hindu groups would allow for an immediate and historic agreement between League and Congress, the paper claimed. It was ironic that this version of Pakistan idea presented then in the *Star of India* was originally a creation of Lala Lajpat Rai (1865–1928), a Hindu nationalist.[8]

The paper also asserted that there was already a separatist precedent in the colonised world and even in the Indian Empire. After all, India would not

---

[8] Lala Lajpat Rai belonged to the Arya Samaj, a reformist Hindu religious movement that wished Hinduism would become the official religion of an independent India.

be in such upheaval as the country was experiencing religious intolerance. In 1940, the Bengal Regionalist Left lead by Congress-expelled Subhash Chandra Bose wished that British and Congress recognised both the Pakistani and the Bengali identities, the only solution to solve the communal impasse all over India.

During the war, the Muslim League supported a strong anti-Fascist line and, therefore, put any radical and exclusive territorial idea of Pakistan aside. After 1945, opinions trying to demonstrate that Hindus and Muslims were to be separated forever were more present in the paper. In spite of the *Star of India*'s strong defence of either federalism or the bi-national concepts, we might have forgotten that in the paper were also present the views of radical separatists, who not only favoured territorial break-up but also a cultural and religious war in India.

## 'PAKISTAN' AND THE MUSLIM STUDENTS

At the start of the 1930s, the 'idea of Pakistan' as such was a project perceived as suspicious and synonymous of 'Greater Afghanistan', more simply, a plot to give the fiercely independent and never-colonised Pashto Kingdom, a cheap and convenient access to the sea. That Pakistan project was then emanating from a small group of Punjabi intellectuals, among whom was Rahmat Ali. The Regionalists originating from the Provinces concerned by such idea—the North-West Frontier Province (NWFP) Pashtos, the Indian Baluchis, the Northern Bombay Province Sindis and the Muslim Punjabis—ferociously denounced and derided the project at the time.

Muslims from the Western Provinces of India being a numerical minority among Indian Muslims, that original 'Pakistan scheme' also found little echo in Indian Muslim opinion in general. Up until April 1939, the *Star of India* and other Muslim papers like the *Khyber Mail* accused the defenders of the scheme of being manipulated by both Congress and Hindu Nationalists—the creators of the concept in 1925—in order to divide the Muslim effort for unity.

The Pakistan idea supporters later became more popular among pro-League Muslim student groups who connected more with poet Iqbal's imprecise project than with Rahmat Ali's Jihadist views. However, up to 1946, the mainstream Muslim League and the *Star of India* itself felt very ill at ease using the word 'Pakistan'; for them, the word had a radical, fanatic and anti-Shi'a Muslim Establishment connotation. The height of absurdity was that, in the end, the All-India Muslim League created a country called 'Pakistan' only a few months after shuffling the term's use. So, what happened for the party to change its opinion on the use of the much-disparaged word?

## First Uses of the Word 'Pakistan'

The first time the *Star of India* mentioned the word 'Pakistan' was at the time of the Round Table negotiations held in London. The 'Pakistan' or 'Pak-stan' project was said to have been inspired by an official declaration made by poet Iqbal when holding the Muslim League leadership in 1930. Iqbal had wanted the division of British India into a Hindu, a Muslim, a Princely and a Burmese Buddhist part.

The Punjabi students presenting the scheme themselves envisaged things slightly differently. They wanted the five administrative units making up north-western India, all Muslim-majority units, to be regrouped into a single state called 'Pakistan'. That state would obtain a dominion status and would belong to the Commonwealth. That 'Pakistan' was to be a buffer State between Afghanistan and India, and an ally of both Britain and Hindu India. Certainly, Bengal, also a Muslim-majority province of British India, remained a problem unaddressed, but the *Star of India* journalist reporting on the Round Tables on 14 April 1933, on page 4, in "Federation of Muslim States? Scheme Which May Eventually Evolve", envisaged the unrealistic constitution of such a state only to take shape in a very remote and improbable future:

> The present century might not see the establishment of Pakistan [...] at the moment; however, Muslims can no more than view it with academic interest.

A few months later, the *Star of India* reproduced an article from some unreferenced Irish newspaper, which bore on a Dublin university student called Rahmat Ali. Ali was then presented as the leader of Western Indian Muslim student groups who were present at the Round Tables and who pleaded for the creation of an independent Muslim State in the Western region. The article dated 28 November 1935, claimed on page 5 in "New Muslim Nation, Plans of a Dublin Graduate" that Rahmat Ali was simply an Urdu language militant, claiming that his language was being threatened by colonial rule, just like Irish Gaelic had been before 1921:

> [...] he clings to Urdu as his native tongue with greater patriotic tenacity than any of our people in the 'Gaeltacht'.

Otherwise, another sign of the lack of popularity of the concept in the press was that four years were necessary for the word 'Pakistan' to be mentioned again in the paper's columns. The Bihar Muslim Students Federation was the first to revive the use of the word by pointing out that Muslims, who had once governed India, deserved their own state as foreseen by Iqbal. This state was to be called

'Pakistan' and the Bihari students considered the creation of that state as the only solution to the 'Indian problem'.

We now know that, on the right of the Muslim political exchequer, some Muslims flirted with the idea that the future Indian Muslim nation, whatever its name, would have to become exclusively Islamic. The most moderate among militants of the faith thought that Islam's recovery had to be done through total submission to religious values. For them, the idea of Pakistan was very ill-defined and boundaries for the projected country were vague. At best, if Pakistan proper came to existence, it would be the result of the rampant exterminating threat coming from Hindu Nationalist extremists, nothing else, since Pakistan could be everywhere in India.

These moderate militants of the faith enjoyed significant support from the wealthy Shi'a *zamindar* of Mahmudabad, who represented them in the highest instances of the Muslim League and occasionally wrote in the *Star of India*. Very much like Gandhi, as far as Hinduism was concerned, Mahmudabad fought modernity and Westernisation. He preached the return to the glorious Mughal past and to rural-based religious values. Indian Muslim territory was strictly the abode offered by Muslim-majority provinces. Mahmudabad wanted a non-violent and socially and politically conquering Islam. For him, the creation of a separate Indian Muslim State called Pakistan was a first step towards a world conquest and the total reformation of Indian Islam.

As we know, it was the Lahore Resolution which made the use of the word 'Pakistan' more widespread or acceptable. Still, many *Star of India* journalists were reluctant to use the imprecise term. For instance, in the early 1940s, we have seen that 'Pakistan' kept a bad connotation when used as a synonym for an 'Indian Ulster', which could have remained under British rule. The paper found it more interesting to provide news on the 1941 census and the Cripps mission that gave recognition to whatever 'Pakistan' was to be. Indeed, the census took into account the self-proclaimed and subjective specificity of Indian Muslim national feeling.

At that moment, the paper claimed that the Muslim community had a real national identity within India and, for a long time, Indian Muslim nationalism in the *Star of India* was felt to be of a different kind compared to the originally more regionally-based Pakistani kind of nationalism. It also accepted articles from those who used biology to justify the existence of the Indian Muslim group—whose origins were supposed to be rooted in Ancient Sind. It allowed other articles whose contents used pure religious identity to define nationality, together with those saying that anyone foreign to the Islamic religion was not to be a part of the new nation even if belonging geographically. However, up until the very eve of freedom, the use of the term 'Pakistan' was to be shunned by numerous key people in the anti-colonial movement writing in the paper.

## Rahmat Ali's 'Pakistan'

Only weeks before World War II was declared, a *Star of India* London correspondent came up to explain Rahmat Ali's views more precisely. Ali was reported to have claimed that there existed a solution to the communal hatred and conflict if Hindus and Muslims were to consider being nationals of different countries. The Muslim nationals would be attributed the North-West and the North-East of India—to be called Pak-stan while, for the first time ever in Ali's plans, the Indian North-East was mentioned as 'Bengsam', on page 1 of 1 June edition of the *Star of India*, in an article called "Hindus and Muslims Two Different Nations". The planned Indian Muslim states would both be independent and belong to the Commonwealth. Post-1935 British Burma was to be the model for such a scheme.

For Ali, the mere fact that India had never been united in its pre-colonial history could justify the demand for multiple Muslim states. India was very much like Europe under Napoleon and had been artificially forced to unite by the British. The name 'India' was a pure British fabrication ('India' was the name they gave to the united conquests) as they had conquered not just one 'India' but several 'Indias'. Moreover, the *Star of India* correspondent underlined the sacrifice made by Indian Muslims between 1914 and 1918, which, according to him, represented eighty per cent of all Indian loss, thus making legitimate any demand for separate Muslims States. However, this report was clearly an exception in the columns of the *Star of India*. The paper never did give much echo to this obscure Pakistan movement, only a preposterous number of paragraphs were to found hidden away amongst the huge quantity of articles dealing with politics and the future of India.

Generally, these type of articles went a little further when using the registry of fear, openly leaning towards conspiracy constructs, involving Christian powers being allied to the Indian Hindu political leadership in their will to control a world devoid of any large-scale Muslim power. India would thus be of real importance as it would remain at the centre and forefront of a war between religious civilisations.

The absolute rejection of the 'Indianity' of India's Muslims by Hindu militants had caused a rejection of anything Indian in Islam by Ali. His radicalism became obsessed with the idea of a return to the Arab origins of a purified, though mythical, Islamic faith. Also for him, a war with Shi'a Islam could not be avoided, for Shi'as, who did not seek to place the Muslim territories of India in the Middle-Eastern orbit, controlled the League. The Muslims who belonged to other areas than the west of India (let us point out that they were the majority of the Indian Muslim population) were, for Rahmat Ali, mere instruments in a permanent fight between eternal Pakistan and an ungodly Hindustan whose fate was to be submitted again to another era of Muslim rule. The future Pakistan had to become a proselytising and aggressive state.

On 11 April 1940, the most interesting article ever published by Ali in the *Star of India* was to be found on page 6. It is called "After 1302 Years, the Millat and the Menace of 'Indianism,' Choice between Asia and India, President Pakistan Movement". Here is one of the few times the *Star of India* reproduced the ideology of the initiator of the use of the term 'Pakistan', Rahmat Ali. Understandably, this was done at the time of the Lahore resolution. Ali asserted that the future Indian Muslim State, called Pakistan, would become a full-blown Middle-Eastern country which would break off all geographic and historical links with South Asia, to which it never naturally belonged. Pakistan, according to Rahmat Ali, would become a country turned towards the central Islamic world, in direct continuity with the Sind conquest declared by the ancient Arabs. Originally, Pakistan nationals were not from South Asia.

Also, Rahmat Ali desired a theocratic State inspired by Wahabi ideology. He wanted to lead a permanent offensive war against an irreligious India that had always denied the existence of the ethnic, geographic and cultural Pakistani nation. In order to achieve this goal, Ali recommended instrumentalising the Muslims of India who were to constitute a sort of fifth column already infiltrated within the enemy's camp. Rahmat Ali therefore rejected all federal and bi-national ideas. He wanted the immediate independence of the provinces of the north-west and pleaded for a radical rejection of all form of union or alliance with the remainder of India.

If the bi-national project had been possible in 1933, at the time of the first Pakistanist project, it was henceforth invalid once World War II had started, Rahmat Ali asserted. He rejected the bi-national concept so dear to British imperialism, to leaders of the Muslim League and Congress, and to officials and members of the Muslim Establishment. The word 'India' was, according to him, an artificial invention of the British. Even the concepts of Gandhian or British liberal inspiration considered India and the Indians as Hindus. Rahmat Ali therefore found ridiculous this impossibly schizophrenic double identity that was to be present in the very name of the 'All-India' Muslim League.

For Rahmat Ali, 'Pakistanians' were not 'Indians' for their religion was not Hinduism, as others living in southern Asia. In Pakistan, the official religion was to be Islam, and the nation was to adopt national symbols marking this adhesion, in particular a flag ornated with a moon crescent and a star. This state was to be theocratic and the *millat* (a term that designates the Elect) could well reject the non-Sunni leaders, such as Jinnah, numerous in the Muslim League. Besides, according to Ali, the old Muslim League would have to be replaced by the League of Muslim nations regrouping Pakistan, Bengal and Usmanistan (the name that Ali gave to the Princely State of Hyderabad in the south of India).

Finally, Pakistan was to be the enemy of imperialist Hindu India. Rahmat Ali denounced that imperialism by branding it 'Indianism'—indeed, even if granted autonomy, would not the Muslims inside India be threatened with elimination and extermination? The Muslims therefore had to create a state capable of enforcing their survival. It was necessary for them to oppose Indian expansionism by creating permanent hotspots of instability like Bengal, Kashmir and Usmanistan (strangely, we notice that it did not refer to the United Provinces) where the Muslim majority population was fighting for self-determination. Pakistan, the future enemy of India, could therefore bring assistance to Muslims residing in the provinces of Bengal and Hyderabad, in order to confront Hindu expansionism and to weaken the much-hated enemy.

As early as 1940, Rahmat Ali's speculative comments in the press were to prove partly ominous of the antagonism that would oppose the two independent nations in the decades to follow. More than sixty years later, the situation is still unstable with Bangladesh and Kashmir, and the existence of numerous Muslim presence in India is a cause of disagreement between the three countries. After the publication of this article, Ali was never allowed to express himself again in the *Star of India* since we think he had probably gone too far in voicing his opposition to the principal Indian Muslim leaders.

Around 1945, the fanatical Muslims publishing in the *Star of India* were sensitive to the conspiracy theory. They obeyed the injunctions of a closed Islam and wanted to launch a holy war and constitute a new Empire. For them, the recourse to an international Islamic offensive would allow the opening of an anti-religious frontline in India. *The Star* seemed to be less shocked by the ideas of these fanatics than by the Hindu Nationalists' similarly mad theories. Even the Indian Muslim Secularists who proposed an interesting Turkish-inspired project did not seem to notice the danger posed by the new brand of Islamism. In 1971, they would nevertheless be the target of these very same Islamists. Only *The Star* collaborator Atay denounced these theories while reminding the reader of the more modest and realistic objectives of Jinnah's nationalism. Despite that, in 1945, it seemed the *Star of India* supported a reinforcement of an electoral alliance between the League, the Orthodox, the non-violent Reformers (like Mahmudabad) and the radical Islamists.

## 'PAKISTAN' AND BENGAL

Especially after the 1940 session of the League in Lahore, the *Star of India* certainly wanted to convince the main provincial personalities of the necessary unity of the Indian Muslim camp at a time when autonomist leaders of Bengal were demanding the recognition of an almost independent Eastern Pakistan within a future Muslim State. It was Talebur Rahman who did it. However, much later, the 'Great Killing of Calcutta' seemed to weaken the concept of an Eastern Pakistan separated from the remainder of Muslim India. Muslims from the Hindu majority districts of Western Bengal, like Suhrawardy himself, then took over the defence of the idea of a Greater Hindu–Muslim Bengal.

One position that was particularly interesting at the time was that of Hashim, also a native of these Western Bengal districts. Hashim wanted an India-confederated Bengal, not a Western Pakistan-confederated Bengal, as India would be more akin to acknowledge the Bengali context. Akram Khan, a native of the Calcutta division himself, envisioned an Eastern Pakistan that included the left shore territories of the Hooghly. His and other Muslims' bitterness at the division of Calcutta is thus perceptible in the newspaper at the time of Partition. That bitterness would reappear some years later, at the time of the movement for the defence of the Bengali language.

A detailed account of the meaning of the Lahore Resolution was published in the *Star of India* on 8 April 1941, page 7, in "Eastern Pakistan or Greater Bengal, a Nationalist Point of View". The article written by Talebur Rahman reinforces the hypothesis that a debate actually took place between Regionalists and Centralists within the League. On the anniversary day of the Resolution, this supporter of a Greater Eastern Pakistan idea implicitly honoured the conceivers of the project, Fazlul Haq (1873–1962) and Suhrawardy, who had promised the advent of a new Muslim state in India, a tolerant and open Eastern Pakistan.

The Eastern Pakistan project foresaw the division of India not in two, but in three sovereign states: Pakistan in the North-West and India, plus another Pakistan in the North-East, constituted of the Assam and Bengal provinces. Only the creation of such a state could make it possible to avoid the decline of Eastern India. Rahman used several arguments to underline the very strong internal consistency and sense of identity of the north-eastern Indian area: geography, economy, demography, language and ethnicity.

The main religious tradition of the north-eastern province only appeared in the article title "Eastern Pakistan", in parallel with another geo-cultural concept called 'Greater Bengal'. According to Talebur, although Bengal was part of India's political and economic body, it would always be isolated from other Indian regions because of geography, history, culture and population.

For the author of the article, this more modern form of nationalism was inspired by a post–World War I ethno-linguistic ideal that gave birth to the new states in the Germanic, Balkanic, Slavic, Baltic and Scandinavian regions of Europe. The Bengalis rejected the unitary and geographic nationalism of British, French, Italian and South American origin of the Congress.

For Talebur Rahman, the religious identity of the population was another component of local nationalism and Bengal was very different from other Indian regions, as a sort of religious syncretism existed in this province. Indeed,

Rahman asserted that the Bengalis were not Indo-European and that only upper-class Bengal Hindus had a pure Indo-European origin. The remainder of the population had pre-Aryan ethnic origins and thus the Bengali ethnic group was, according to Rahman, an exception in north India.

From an economic and social point of view, the Hindus' activities were totally complementary to the Muslims in Bengal. The Hindus held administrative and financial power, while the Muslims possessed agricultural resources. Together, Hindus and Muslims made Bengal the highest contributor to the central Indian budget among the provinces of India. Talebur reminded the reader that the Bengalis were well represented at the top of the colonial elite, either in the central public service or in the liberal professions.

The Bengalis were fighting at the forefront of the anti-colonial nationalist movement, and were spreading unrest to the rest of the Indian subcontinent, thanks to their very developed interprovincial network. Last but not the least, from a historic standpoint, the Bengalis had been very advanced in their own nation-building enterprise—in India, their intellectuals played an equivalent role to what the French intellectuals' had played in Europe. The proliferation of superlatives was the brand of a provincial patriotism that we had not suspected until then.

Talebur continues on this mode, with a specially benevolent concern for Muslim input, asserting that the Bengalis had only been temporarily submitted to central power in history and had always obtained a legal and semi-independent status and that there had been an uninterrupted historical Bengali tradition of power in this country. Talebur also denounced colonial ideologies that pretended that Bengalis were effeminate and sterile, as a way to oppress a formerly conquering and soldiering nation by providing it with few jobs in the colonial army, adding that it could be a sort of vicious central authority design to put down Bengali pride efficiently. At the time of World War I, the regime had only exceptionally recruited Bengalis in the army, but the nation had nevertheless counted many military heroes throughout history. Those had fought against central mismanagement from the Sultans, Mughals and British or had even succeeded in subverting overseas territories, such as Ceylon. In an article dated 8 April 1941 (page 7) titled "Eastern Pakistan or Greater Bengal, a Nationalist Point of View", it said:

> The heroic deeds and acts of bravery done by the great Bengali warriors, Vijayasimha, Isa Khan, Pratapaditya, Ilyas Shahi, Mirmadan, Mohanlal, Sirajuddaulah, Mir Qasim and a host of others can be a pride to any nation in the world. Even in the last Great War, our brave boys magnificently fought in the various fields of battle.

In the *Star of India*, eulogist Talebur Rahman declared the Pakistan idea a form of Bengali nationalism. However, it was necessary to await the end of the war to see this project discussed publicly.

## Independent Greater Bengal

Discussing Bengali nationalism was what happened when, in an interview given to the *Associated Press of India* and published in the *Star of India* on 28 April 1947, on page 5, called "Plea for United Bengal, Partition Fraught with Unending Mischief", provincial Premier Husain Shahid Suhrawardy voiced his own unofficial interesting opinion knowing that the Muslim League and the Congress had not succeeded in any lasting political compromise to counter the mounting violence in 1947.

First, Suhrawardy wanted to remind the reader of the current context. From a geographic point of view, the Congress was trying to obtain Pakistan to limit its territory to Muslim majority districts only. The League desired a Greater Pakistan delineated by current Muslim majority provincial borders. For the Central League at the time, the two countries had to become religiously homogenous and had to proceed to exchanges of populations, something Suhrawardy opposed since the Noákhali massacres.

The Central League being in favour of a single independent Indian Muslim state pressed for the Partition of India while Suhrawardy underlined that Bengali identity remained a thorny problem for the League's project. The Suhrawardian project objected it concerned Bengal only and was to avoid any mention of the situation in Punjab or in other provinces. Suhrawardy was also merely trying to rally some of the Hindus opposed to the Partition of Bengal and was offering a compromise to the secularist elements among the Congress and to East Bengal Hindus whom he protected at the time of the Noakhali massacre.

He opposed mostly Western Bengal Hindu-majority district Hindu militants who wanted to obtain power on a reduced portion of the province, and who were supported by Hindu Nationalist parties campaigning for a referendum on local self-determination. He also protested against powerful press organs like the *Amrita Bazaar Patrika* (a Goliath newspaper, let us point out, compared to the Samson-like readership of the *Star of India*) that had published for free Hindu Nationalist petitions in its columns. Suhrawardy also rejected the opinion of Minister Muhammad Fazlur Rahman favouring an exclusive Muslim Bengali identity and territory linked to Western Pakistan.

Suhrawardy asserted that the newly established state in the north-east should recognise the real economic social and professional importance of the Hindus of Bengal, an importance not reflected in the demographic and political position of the minority community. The Greater Calcutta non-Bengali speaking population, be it Hindu or Muslim, was made up of immigrants from the interior who were also entitled to Bengali citizenship. Even if an official religion was necessary for the Muslim state in the north-east, he wished to build an open and tolerant kind of nationalism. Being opposed to an expulsion of the

Hindus of Bengal (in contrast to his minister M. F. Rahman), he reminded the reader that Bengal was isolated from the rest of the Muslim world, unlike the Muslim-world bordering Western Pakistan. A united and independent Bengal would progress rapidly and would be unlikely to generate any conflict. On the contrary, if Partition took place, the two Bengals would stagnate, decline and become enemies. If Bengal remained united and depended on a central government, it ran the risk of becoming the victim of a new famine, like in 1943.

Bengal, according to Suhrawardy, was the richest Indian region from an agricultural, industrial and commercial point of view. Its economic growth was one of the best in India. The province had therefore to redistribute its wealth to all its population. The nation state of the united Bengal had the ambition to be modern, open and powerful. Suhrawardy proposed to summon a sovereign constituent assembly in order to decide the future of Bengal. The assembly had to pronounce itself on the form its electoral college would have and declare either full independence or the joining of Pakistan, India or an Indian–Pakistani confederation. At the end of the day, the Bengal Muslim leader claimed that only in case the project of an ethnic and linguistic independent Bengal failed, a communal project could be envisioned, regrouping the Muslim-majority districts of Bengal and Assam.

## The Bengal–India Confederacy Idea

Shortly after Suhrawardy's article, an interesting and quite neglected actor in these fateful months, secretary of the Bengal League Abul Hashim, opted for an Eastern Pakistan–India confederate solution.

In an article dated 30 April 1947, page 2, called "United Bengal, Remedy for All Present Ills, Abul Hashim Exposes Hollowness of Partition Move", Hashim was not voicing the same views as his brother-in-law, Suhrawardy. Going a step further, Abul Hashim was offering a return to an intercommunal agreement in Bengal leading to the reestablishment of peace in the much-troubled province. He rejected political violence and advocated an open idea of Pakistan, advocating the choice of a confederacy uniting India and Eastern Pakistan. He called for the local ex-Congress Secularists to sign a new Bengal Pact, once initiated by his father, Abul Kasem in the early 1920s.

Hashim invited the students campaigning for the Muslim League to found an intercommunal alliance respecting the old tolerant traditions of Bengal. According to him, such an alliance would be in direct line with the actions of the historic personalities of the first Congress and the non-Gandhian figures of the 1920s. Abul Hashim strongly denounced adventurist and so-far marginalised communal leaders like Nazimuddin (1894–1964).

The Bengal League's secretary also rebuked Hindu Nationalist radicals', Marwaris' and Anglo-American business interests', as their hidden intention was to preserve their economic monopoly by encouraging the division of Bengal. For Hashim, the idea of dividing Bengal into two parts could only be the result of a 'divide and rule' neocolonial conspiracy. To prove this fact, Hashim sustained that the respective militias of the Mahasabha and Central League, the Rashtriya Swayamsevak Sangh and the National Muslim Guard, were both armed by Britain and the United States. Although Abul Hashim was in favour of an alliance with the Hindus in order to destroy the old Conservative guard of big Muslim interest from the East of the province, he was also a firm believer in the application of the spirit of Lahore, that is, the idea of an Indian Muslim Eastern Pakistan. Nevertheless, Hashim used the term of 'Pakistan' only twice in his article, preferring the one of 'united and independent Bengal'.

To the difference of Suhrawardy, he envisioned the creation of Indian confederate States, on an ethnic and religious basis. With Hashim, Lahore was not synonymous of an exclusive idea of Pakistan (a sort of Muslim irredentism), favouring centralism and the total religious homogenisation of two Indias. He found it unrealistic to divide Bengal and Punjab, and denounced the illusory aspect of declaring a single official ideology there. A separate Bengali Muslim State would, according to Abul Hashim, integrate the Hindus into full citizenship and admit the existence of a variety of sources in legal systems: both *sharia* and *shastra*. Hashim considered the break-up of Western Bengal as a demonstration of Indian imperialism, and therefore the start of a new colonial occupation.

Therefore, for Hashim, reducing Pakistan to the smallest share seemed dangerous for any peace plan, and Bengali Muslims had to fight to preserve the integrity of their homeland. Hashim supported a renewed bi-national solution and noticed that the creation of an eastern truncated Pakistan would not be the better strategy India could implement in order for her to reintegrate this territory into the Indian Union. Through this particular Pakistan project, Hashim showed he remained attached to the unity of India, and might have been coming closer to the ideas of Abul Kalam Azad (1888–1958) and other Congress Muslims.

*The Star* was opposed to all kind of provincial and ethnic sense of identity in its columns, where few articles appeared on this question. The newspaper refused the creation of a second autonomous Pakistan that would group together all the Bengali-speaking regions of East India and Burma. This project, supported by some prestigious intellectuals of Bengal Muslim origin (not necessarily all Bengali-speaking), seemed, for a moment, to be losing momentum after the Great Calcutta Killing. Being threatened by Hindu residents, the Regionalists appeared fuzzier on the project of a Greater Eastern Pakistan in the end.

Certain Muslims went for the creation of an independent and intercommunal Bengal, while others desired to return to the bi-national idea, becoming suddenly aware of the dead-end situation which they were being lead into. However, a last, more opportunistic group was certainly happy with a truncated Pakistan in the East, related to a truncated Pakistan in the West. The members of this group claimed they were faithful to Jinnah, and honestly thought that the administrative division of Calcutta would have remained Pakistani. It was necessary for them to have a little time to become disillusioned with the Partition deal. This accounted for the later malaise that the *Star of India* went through after Independence.

## CONCLUSION

In this study, we tried to understand the evolution of the editors of a major Indian Muslim newspaper concerning the use of the word 'Pakistan', during the period going from 1932 to 1947. In the *Star of India* daily, a pioneer Indian Muslim paper in Eastern India, 'Pakistan' had several, very different meanings. The main but intermittent moments when the word 'Pakistan' was used in the *Star of India* were the first three years of the war, then 1945 and 1947 only. For as long as the paper defended the idea of federal communitarianism, the use of the word 'Pakistan' was shunned and even rejected. The concept can be seen as being re-used—quite differently from its original conception—by the Muslim League with the advent of the confederacy idea or the idea of a national or religious homeland designed for the protection of Indian Muslims.

Fifteen principal editors defended the different conceptions of the word 'Pakistan', definitely a vague and fuzzy term. Hashim accepted the word only to illustrate the confederacy idea. Rahmat Ali used the word differently as a pan-Islamic jihadist concept. In the more restrictive and problematic territory of Bengal, Mahmudabad used the word 'Pakistan' very much like a synonym of the peaceful jihad. Suhrawardy favoured the use of 'Pakistan' as an ethnic Bengali nation.

In all cases, 'Pakistan' meant a rejection of the concept of unitary Indian nationalism so dear to Banerjea, between 1932 and 1940. We saw that the *Star of India* campaigned for community autonomy in a federal framework. More importantly, the anti-colonial Muslims of India rejected the strict centralist conception of mainstream Congress that was envisioned for any future independent state in India. Then, in a very cautious manner, the paper was seen to rally the territorial separatist camp in 1940. The Lahore Resolution, voted that year, allowed for the official use of the word 'Pakistan', but the use of the term was only temporary, timid and hesitant in the columns of the Muslim press in

English. 'Pakistan' certainly evoked the possibility of Indian Muslim separation but—no contradiction—also the possibility of a united Indian Independence.

'Pakistan' meant the possibility of a bi-national or confederate solution. London recognised the use of the word in 1942, and after that, strangely enough, the newspaper did nothing to defend the idea of a Muslim territorial independence any longer. When Gandhi accepted the validity of the idea of Pakistan in 1944, the newspaper still chose to advocate the case for the creation of a Greater Pakistan integrated with an Indian confederacy. This use of the word 'Pakistan', as synonymous of 'two commonwealths', lasted till the beginning of large-scale communal unrest and violence in August 1946. The final outcome, as we know, was a million deaths and millions of exiles (Hindus, Muslims and Sikhs). The newspaper therefore reluctantly went for a new idea of Pakistan, that of total separation and Partition on the basis of the existing provinces or Muslim-majority divisions.

It can be said that, from 1940 to 1947, the Indian Muslim editors of the *Star of India*'s use of the word 'Pakistan' oscillated for the making of various demands. If most of the published articles were in accordance with the central Muslim League orders, atypical ideas were also expressed in the columns of the *Star of India*. The native editors originating from the two main Muslim majority provinces, Punjab and Bengal, which had a long and proud tradition of autonomy, mostly developed some of the particular uses of the Pakistan concept. Commentators supporting a worldwide Islamic union or a closed Indian Muslim nationalist project elaborated other uses of the Pakistan concept. However, the *Star of India* wholeheartedly desired an agreement between the League and the Congress, an agreement that was never concluded.

Therefore, especially after August 1946, the elite of the Muslim-majority province of Bengal who wrote in the newspaper columns constantly supported the idea that India had to remain united—or the opinion that Bengal had to. Some of the extracts presented in our study give a different perspective on the wider and rarely imagined use of the word 'Pakistan', and show that, in contrast to the commonly held idea in Western opinion, Muslims from north-eastern India were hesitating as for the radical division of their country, despite the peak of communal violence starting in 1946. The Muslims of Burdwan, the Westernmost region of Bengal, who expressed themselves in the *Star of India* were fiercely opposed to the division of their province (even if not to the division of India) and wanted to declare the independence of Bengal or benefit from an autonomous statute within the Indian Union or Pakistan. The paper was open to famous politicians and Bengal journalists who did not always respect the orders emanating from the central League.

The newspaper was deeply disappointed at Partition. It only grudgingly defended what Jinnah had obtained and began supporting this part of the political elite that were to mobilise for the autonomy of Eastern Pakistan within

Pakistan. Long before 1947, various currents, that were at odds with the idea of separated and opposing Indian nations, confronted each other and found a way of expressing their feelings in the newspaper. They were joined very early by the extremely dissatisfied partisans of the embryo of a new idea of Pakistan, the ethnic autonomist 'Bangalis' (Bengalis Hindus and Muslims from Eastern Pakistan). Less than a generation later, this new group, already apparent in the newspaper, led this part of Pakistan to secede.

In 1949, the Delhi and Calcutta Muslim press migrated towards Karachi or Dacca. Suhrawardy and Abul Hashim joined the opposition, while Akram Khan had still not chosen his camp. He would do so three years after, when the provincial government declared Urdu an official language. Manhandled by Partition, the pre-1928 former Congress Muslims, such as Akram Khan or Hashim, who had been the masterminds of Bengal Muslim unity, finally became the architects of a new idea of Pakistan, ethnic Bengali East Pakistan or Bangladesh.

The secession of Eastern Bengal less than a generation later confirmed the tendency for multiethnic non-democratic states arising from Partition to be heading towards inevitable break-up. The separatist phenomenon is a no-exit. In our case, it puts a true problem (social), but offers a false solution (cultural) to the contradictions of colonial India and British imperial ideology.

Today, the Bangladeshi newspapers continue to be confronted to the harsh and thorny question of national identity that is presenting as either strictly Bengali Muslim, or geographic and accidental. If we consider the historic inheritance of Partition in the Eastern region of India, every camp (the religious nationalist one and the geographic and ethnic nationalist one) bears its own contradictions and generates deeply-anchored violence. Maybe this was the extreme consequence of the type of politics that encouraged small differences and strong, exclusive identity.

Then, would it be necessary to go back to a sort of political union in Southern Asia, a union that would try to erase sixty years of religious fanaticism, wars and fratricidal conflicts in this tormented region? Again, this perspective seems remote. To those who asserted that the birth of Pakistan was decided in 1940 in Lahore, we wanted to oppose the results of our research: the will for Pakistan was intermittent, at least in Bengal, and made many Muslims hesitant and uneasy, even on the eve of independence and Partition.

Islamists, who became much more important during the Cold War, had already drawn, in the pre-Partition Indian Muslim press, their project of a permanent holy war. However, the reading of articles written by other Muslim intellectuals makes it possible to understand that there exists no historical fate, and that peace was always possible in South Asia in 1947. Then, the life of millions of people would not have tipped into hatred and violence, now a difficult element to obliterate. Today, the entire world pays the consequences of this cheap, rushed and badly carried-out decolonisation.

# BIBLIOGRAPHY

## Primary Sources

Reel 1 to 42: shelf n° NP 1515, *The Library of Congress*, 101 Independence Avenue, SE, Washington, DC 20450-4570.

Reel number 2, issues from 01 January to 30 April 1933: 14 April 1933, p. 4, "Federation of Muslim States? Scheme Which May Eventually Evolve".

Reel number 10, issues from 01 September to 31 December 1935: 28 November 1935, p. 5, "New Muslim Nation, Plans of a Dublin Graduate".

Reel number 22, issues from 01 September to 31 December 1939: 11 April 1940, p. 6, "After 1302 Years, the Millat and the Menace of 'Indianism,' Choice between Asia and India, President Pakistan Movement".

Reel number 23, issues from 01 January to 30 April 1940: 12 March 1941, p. 3, "Muslims Can Accept Nothing but 'Pakistan'".

Reel number 26, issues from 01 January to 30 April 1941: 8 April 1941, p. 7, "Eastern Pakistan or Greater Bengal, a Nationalist Point of View".

Reel number 39, issues from 01 January to 30 June 1947: 28 April 1947, p. 5, "Plea for United Bengal, Partition Fraught with Unending Mischief".

Reel number 39, issues from 01 January to 30 June 1947: 30 April 1947, p. 2, "United Bengal, Remedy for All Present Ills, Abul Hashim Exposes Hollowness of Partition Move".

## Secondary Sources

Ahmad, Abul Mansur, 1975, *End of Betrayal and Restoration of Lahore Resolution*. Koshroz Kitab Mahal, Dacca.

DiCostanzo, Thierry, 2003, "Il Bangladesh, una democrazia in crisi". In: Elisa Guinchi, Corrado Molteni and Michelguglielmo (eds), *L'Asia prima e dopo l'11 settembre*. (Asia Major 2002, Centro studi per i popoli extraeuropei Cesare Bonacossa, Università di Pavia), Il Mulino, Pavia, pp. 127–42.

———, 2011, "L'idée séparatiste dans la presse angol-musulmane du Bengale: Le cas du Star of India, 1937–1947", *Anglo-amerikanische Studien*, 42: 291 pp.

George, T. J. S., 1992, *Pothan Joseph's India: A Biography*. Sanchar, Delhi.

Iggers, Georg G. & Supriya Mukherjee, 2008, *A Global History of Modern Historiography*. Pearson, Edinburgh.

Israel, Milton, 1994, *Communications and Power: Propaganda and the Press in the Indian Nationalist Struggle (1920–1947)*. Cambridge University Press, Cambridge.

Jinnah, Muhammad Ali, 1976, *The Quaid-e-Azam Papers 1941–42 Compiled by Rizwan Ahmad*. East and West Publishing Company, Karachi.

Joseph, Pothan, 1979, *Idylls Past and Present: An Editor's Wet Copy*. Orient Longman, Delhi.

Khalidi, Rashid, 1997, *Palestinian Identity: The Construction of Modern National Consciousness*. Columbia University Press, New York.

McPherson, Kenneth, 1974, *The Muslim Microcosm: Calcutta, 1918 to 1935*. Beiträge zur Südasienforschung, Südasien Institut, Universität Heidelberg, Band 8, Franz Steiner Verlag, Wiesbaden.

Moitra, Mohit, 1969, *A History of Indian Journalism*. National Book Agency, Calcutta.

Natarajan, Swaminath, 1962, *A History of the Press in India*. Asia Publishing House, Bombay.

Nurul Islam, Mustafa, 1973, *Bengali Muslim Public Opinion as Reflected in the Bengal Press (1901–1930)*. Bangla Academy, Dhaka.

Talbot, Ian, 1988, *Provincial Politics and the Pakistan Movement: The Growth of the Muslim League in Northwest and Northeast India (1937–47)*. Oxford University Press, Karachi and Oxford.

Torri, Michelguglielmo, 1996, "Nazionalismo indiano e nazionalismo musulmano in India nell'era coloniale". In: Mario Mannini (sous la direction de) (ed.), *Dietro la bandiera Emancipazioni coloniali, identità nazionali, nazionalismi nell'età contemporanea*. Pacini, Ospedaletto (Pisa), pp. 139–99.

## Internet Sources

http://www.youtube.com/watch?v=ResU1IbXyj8 (accessed on 7 November 2011).

http://www.youtube.com/user/Urdustan (accessed on 7 November 2011).

http://www.hindujagruti.org/activities/campaigns/national/india-map-controversy/mughalstan.php (accessed on 7 November 2011).

http://www.bengalgenocide.com/mughalistan.php (accessed on 7 November 2011).

http://en.wikipedia.org/wiki/Islamistan (accessed on 7 November 2011).

http://rupeenews.com/2008/06/23/4749/ (accessed on 7 November 2011).

http://www.worldproutassembly.org/archives/bangalistan/ (accessed on 7 November 2011).

*Chapter 12*

# BUDDHISM AND COLLECTIVE EMANCIPATION IN MODERN INDIA

## B. R. AMBEDKAR'S RE-USE OF THE BUDDHA'S *DHARMA* IN THE DALIT MOVEMENT

**BY EDWARD A. RODRIGUES**

### INTRODUCTION

On 14 October 1956, Dr B. R. Ambedkar together with nearly eight *lakh* scheduled castes, drawn predominantly from the Mahar caste, converted to Navoyana Buddhism. In a ceremony marked by simplicity and religiosity, Ambedkar and his followers renounced Hinduism to swear allegiance to a new spirituality that was neither the Buddha's *dharma*[1] of the ancient world nor the Buddhism practised in many parts of the modern world. The conversion ceremony itself scripted in a political idiom marked a watershed in the nearly century-long

---

[1] *Dharma* is Sanskrit for the Pali term *dhamma*, also often used in connection with Ambedkar's re-used form of Buddhism.

struggles of the Scheduled Castes. Within modern Indian society the Scheduled Castes or Dalits[2] comprise about 16.2 per cent of the total Indian population (Shah 2006: 36). Notwithstanding efforts by the Indian state to improve their material conditions, many of them continue to live in abject poverty and in severe and inhuman conditions.[3]

The re-use of cultural symbolism and practices from India's ancient past is not a new phenomenon and Ambedkar's own attempt to re-use the Buddha's *dharma* must be understood in this larger context of the social and religious reform movements, which had emerged in colonial India from the middle of the nineteenth century (Sumant 2004: 64). These reform movements, as has been argued by several writers (Panikkar 1998; Jones 1999; Sarkar 1986), represented an engagement of different social groupings with colonial modernity. Yet as Guha (1998) rightly observes, this overarching power structure of colonial modernity witnessed dual relations of dominance and subordination, between rulers and ruled and between upper castes and lower castes. These relations were the sites of deeply contested claims and assertions by the different caste groups in their dealings with the colonial rulers.

As a concept highlighting symbolic strategies and spheres of engagements, culture re-use necessarily evokes a political context. Cultural re-use brings into play the capacities and resources of those participating in re-use to establish both internal group compliance as well as external societal acceptance. Additionally, as we shall observe in this chapter, when components of culture re-use get invested with new assertions by its practitioners, it becomes intricately linked up with the identity politics of its practitioners. Cultural re-use in this latter sense aims to create new solidarities of resistance wherein the practice of resistance becomes the object of re-use in the contemporary present. The re-forming or reinventing of Hinduism in the nineteenth century as King (1999: 112–17) suggests was deeply involved with the politics of identity. The efforts to create a pan-Indian Hindu solidarity by Hindu nationalist leaders involved the re-scripting of several Hindu religious practices into practices of resistance against British imperialism. For the purpose of this chapter, I want to suggest that understanding the dynamics of cultural re-use involves a consideration of

---

[2] Dalits (a Sanskrit word denoting that beneath the feet) are perceived as ritually defiling and prohibited from participating in the rituals of the caste Hindus as well as entry into their temples. Outcast from traditional society, they are forced to live outside the villages and compelled to earn their livelihood by performing all the defiling and demeaning occupations within the village community. Several good works have documented the Dalit movement in India; see Omvedt (1994), Guru (1997) and Zelliot (1992).

[3] Exploitation and oppression of Scheduled Castes in India has been the focus of several government investigations like the annual reports of the Schedule Caste Commission (a Government of India publication). Similarly nongovernmental organisations like Human Rights Watch and Action Aid have also investigated the violations of Dalit rights as well as the persistence of discrimination. See Broken People (1999), Teltumbde (1997) and Shah (2006).

two different aspects of the phenomena. First, the role of subject agency in shaping the representations and practices of cultural re-use. Second, the processes of contestation or resistance involving those asserting cultural re-use. How cultural re-use eventually gets integrated into the life of the community that can tell us a great deal about its success of these latter processes.

In this chapter, I consider Ambedkar's re-use of the Buddha's *dharma* in two parts. In part one, I briefly look at the historical context in which the Buddha's *dharma* emerged in ancient India pointing to its key doctrinal features and how its followers went on to make it a major religion of the ancient Indian civilisation. Yet Buddhism in India came to an end by the sixth century CE and I consider some of the reasons attributed to this demise. I conclude this section by briefly considering the revival of the Buddha's *dharma* in the nineteenth century under the label of Buddhism and show how Orientalist interests in the religion combined with growing interest amongst lower castes, especially in South India which saw a minor revival of the religion. In the second part of this chapter I look at the specific way in which Ambedkar sought to re-use this ancient religion by infusing it with a modernist doctrine of collective emancipation. Finally in my conclusion I look at how Ambedkar's re-use of Buddhism came to be accepted by both his followers and detractors. I argue that notwithstanding Ambedkar's radical vision of Navoyana Buddhism, its impact on the Dalit Movement has not been of any revolutionary significance. On the contrary, even if individually, Dalits have a better self-perception and self-esteem of themselves as Buddhists, Buddhism has yet to have any large-scale impact on Indian society. Finally I may add here that given the important role of subject agency in shaping culture re-use, I have oriented this enquiry from the standpoint of how Ambedkar himself understood the past of Buddhism as well as how he sought to reshape this past in the contemporary present.

## THE RISE OF BUDDHISM IN ANCIENT INDIA

Even though he was neither a historian nor an Indologist, Ambedkar's keen interests in the study of India's ancient past was fuelled by his lifelong intellectual endeavour to demystify and critique the irrational truth claims of modern Hindu caste society.[4] In an unfinished volume, *Revolution and Counter Revolution*

---

[4] B. R. Ambedkar was both a lawyer and economist, yet, even in his early days in Columbia University, his 1916 anthropology seminar paper on "Castes in India: Their Mechanism, Genesis and Development" (Ambedkar 1989: 3–22) was evidence of his ability to critically interrogate as well as intervene in the ongoing debate on caste. In several other works, namely, *Annihilation of Castes* (1989: 23–98), *The Untouchables* (1990: 238–380), *Who were the Shudras* (1999: 11–235), *Revolution and Counter Revolution* (1987: 3–40), one encounters a range of historical insights on ancient Indian society. Importantly, his knowledge of both Sanskrit and Pali facilitated him in separating myth from fact in the study of ancient Indian society.

*in Ancient India*, Ambedkar had set out to document a detailed history of ancient Indian society. Yet as he observes at the very outset of this work, "Ancient
Indian history must be exhumed. Without its exhumation Ancient India will go
without history. Fortunately with the help of the Buddhist literature, Ancient
Indian History can be dug out of the debris which the Brahmin writers have
heaped upon in a fit of madness" (Ambedkar 1987: 152). It is with the help of
Buddhist literature that Ambedkar develops his understanding of Aryan society at the time of the Buddha. For Ambedkar, this pre-Buddhist Aryan society was one inflicted by great moral decadence and its Brahmin priesthood
were completely bereft of any religious spirituality (Ambedkar 1987). Whether
these observations are historically correct or not, what is important to us is that
Ambedkar saw the arrival of Buddhism as a revolutionary transformation of
ancient Indian society.[5]

Historically, Gautama Buddha, the founder of Buddhism in the sixth century BC, lived in a period when early Indian society was undergoing rapid and
turbulent changes characteristic of what historians refer to as the second urbanisation. Chakravarti (1987) observes that the period not only saw the flourishing of agrarian societies, it also marked the growth of town and cities and,
above all, marked the beginnings of State formation in India characterised by
the transition of clan based societies 'the *ganasangha*s' to the rise of kingship
and monarchies. Brahmanism proved incapable of successfully responding to
this second urbanisation. The *dharma* of Gautama Buddha, as Ambedkar (1987)
notes, contested the claims of brahminical ritualism with its irrational beliefs
and wasteful practices. More importantly, as Chakravarti (1987) notes, the Buddha's *dharma* came to enjoy political and social patronage from the emerging
new classes of landowning and trading groups, 'the *gahapatti*s', as well as the
labouring populations of the peasantry, namely, the Kammakaras and Dasas.
It becomes the religion of the empire under Ashoka. Under the Mauryan and
post-Mauryan dynasties of the Kushanas in the north-west and Satavahanas in
western India, Buddhism spread far and wide across the entire Asian continent
carried by monks who travelled far and wide proselytising whole populations
wherever they went (Bapat 1999). Additionally, Buddhist monasteries came up
along trade routes developing over time into power centres.[6] Archaeological
evidence in both central and peninsular India point to the coexistence of political capitals, market towns, production centres and Buddhist monasteries at
urban centres (Thapar 1966).

---

[5] It is important to note that all of Ambedkar's writings on Buddhism were carried out in the period
following his decision at the Yeola conference of 1935 that he would never die a Hindu.
[6] Buddhist monks sought patronage of the mercantile guilds and the royalty and, in turn, provided
not only for the security of the merchant and his caravan at staging points along the route and
investment facilities but also a flexible attitude to usury and money lending, thus attracting the
support of the mercantile and guild communities.

Yet this dynamic spread of Buddhism came to end by the early mediaeval period. Sectarian rivalry arising out of doctrinal differences, the decline of the *sangha*s, the loss of patronage from the mercantile communities following the collapse of the Roman Empire, the revival of the popular Hindu sectarian orders of Shaivism and Vaishnavism and their hostility to the *shramanic* tradition are important factors that account for this decline. Although surviving till the tenth century in pockets of eastern India, Buddhism was gradually absorbed in the Vaishnava pantheon. Ambedkar accounts for the decline by pointing to the ritualisation and the alienation of the *sangha* from the laity. The *bhikku*, he notes, had become a beggar of alms far removed from the laity whom they were supposed to serve. Yet, even if the tree appeared withered, he believed that the roots of Buddha's *dharma* were still very strong within Indian civilisation (Ambedkar 1987).

Buddhism witnessed a kind of revival in the mid-nineteenth century. Alexander Cunningham, John Marshall, James Prinsep (Ajanta and Ellora) and James Fergusson (monasteries of western India) discovered ancient Buddhist sites, Aurel Stein's attempt to retrieve Buddhist manuscripts along the silk route and Rhys Davids wrote on Buddhism and founded the Pali Text Society in 1882. Notwithstanding these Orientalist and archaeological concerns, as King (1997: 145) quite rightly puts it, the labelling of Buddhism like Hinduism as 'religions' was essentially an Orientalist invention of nineteenth century colonialism. European Orientalists, he argues, were quick to draw parallels between the reformism of Martin Luther and that of Gautama Buddha. Not surprisingly then, it is this reformist nature of Buddhism that made a deep impression on its admirers both in the East and the West.[7] In 1937, Dharmanand Kosambi founded the Buddhist Bahujana Vihara in Bombay's working class district. In 1940 he published a Marathi work on the life of the Buddha. In the reformist environment of the nineteenth century, such efforts were not out of place. Indian reformers like Rammohan Roy, Dayanand Saraswati, Vivekananda, Ramakrishna, and so on, relied heavily on India's ancient past in developing a religiosity for modern Indian society. Yet this re-emergence of Buddhism in the nineteenth century exhibited none of its earlier greatness as a doctrine, which once attracted such great followings from amongst the peoples of the subcontinent. Unlike the emergence of Hinduism, which was intricately linked up with the larger right-wing nationalist project of creating a Hindu nation, the re-emergence of Buddhism presented no such political aspiration. Not only were the followers

[7] Interest in Buddhism was shown by the Theosophical Society, from which several Europeans even converted to Buddhism. In 1891, Dharmapala, the Sri Lankan convert to Buddhism, formed the Maha Boddhi Society of India. Even before Ambedkar, he was advocating the view that because of Buddhism's proximity to democracy, it was ideally suited for the depressed classes of India (Kuber 2001).

of the Buddha *dharma* a miniscule proportion of the population, the *dharma* as a practice of lived spirituality had largely vanished from the everyday life of Indian society. It was Ambedkar's decision to re-use the Buddha's *dharma* for a modern society that saw a major revival of Buddhism in modern India.

## AMBEDKAR'S RE-USE OF THE BUDDHA'S *DHARMA*

It is fair to surmise that Ambedkar, given the range of his intellectual and political concerns, was familiar with some of these developments taking place within the revivalist phase of Buddhism.[8] Yet it is important to mention here that according to his biographer Keer (1995), Ambedkar's choice of Buddhism as a religion for the Dalits was the result of a long and rigorous study of several religions including Sikhism and Islam. Notwithstanding this rigour, it is equally important to note here that his quest for a religion was as much a search for redressing the asymmetrical power structure of the Hindu caste system. As Fitzgerald (2004) observes, religion and politics were deeply enmeshed in the quest for Dalit liberation. Not surprisingly, as we shall see, this political face of Navoyana Buddhism turned out to be its most enduring legacy.

The scripting of the Buddha *dharma* into a doctrine of Dalit emancipation was the culmination of a long drawn out struggle led by Ambedkar against the oppression of Dalits by the upper castes. Ambedkar was himself a product of this Dalit resistance to caste both during the colonial period as well as the post Independence period. He came from the Mahar caste, which provided the most assertive face of Dalit resistance in western India. Ambedkar was a modern political leader, who was profoundly influenced by modernist ideas. His biographers have identified him as a Republican, a Liberal and a Rationalist.[9]

The issue of a mass conversion to Buddhism in 1956 must, however, be explained from within the larger context of the Dalit struggle in the first half of the twentieth century. It is from within this larger context that I wish to draw attention to two important aspects of Dalit emancipation that affected Ambedkar deeply and to which he attempted a variety of strategies.

The first concerned the identity of the untouchables. It is a well-known fact that in the course of their political struggle for emancipation, Ambedkar sought to identify the untouchable castes by several names such as Bahiskrut, labouring

---

[8] In the unpublished preface to *Buddha and his Dhamma,* as provided by Eleanor Zelliot, he recounts a dispute he had with his father who insisted that he read the *Ramayana* when he instead preferred reading the life of the Buddha.

[9] There are very good works on the life of B. R. Ambedkar by Zelliot (1992), Keer (1995), Omvedt (2004), Kuber (2001), which all position him as India's foremost modernist thinker and political leader.

classes, Depressed Classes, Scheduled Castes, and so on. These identities, however, proved incapable of placing the group outside and beyond the stigma of untouchability. The inability of these identities to embrace a universal category which could include both Dalits and non-Dalits simply meant that caste Hindus would continue to see them as defiling and unclean. Ambedkar also rejected the term Harijan given by Gandhi seeing it as too paternalistic and like the others trapped within the particularism of caste. If Dalits should live with dignity ad self-respect, they clearly needed an identity that was completely removed from the stigma and historical memory of untouchability. Such an identity could only emerge if that what it signified included both Dalits and non-Dalits.

Related to this problem of identity was the second issue concerning the persistence of exclusion in the sphere of social relations encountered by the Dalits in their everyday life experience. Ambedkar saw this as neither an economic nor political problem. He was himself a victim of such exclusionary practices by caste Hindus. Notwithstanding the individual's identity or religion or ideology, exclusion was practised by everyone including the untouchable castes in modern Indian society. Exclusion lay at the very heart of the social fabric that holds together Hindu caste society. So deep rooted was the practice of caste exclusion, that no matter what they did and however meritorious they become, Dalits in particular continued to experience the worst forms of exclusions in their everyday world. Ambedkar was convinced that Dalits could only live in dignity and self-respect in a social world structured on inclusive norms and practices. I wish to suggest here that Ambedkar's re-use of Buddhism in the modern context must be seen as a response to both these issues.

Ambedkar's declaration at the Yeola conference in 1935 stating that even though he was born a Hindu, he would not die a Hindu, was the first time he publicly acknowledged his intention to renounce Hinduism. Yet it would be another two decades before such a decision would become a reality. Preceding the Yeola conference, Ambedkar had launched several struggles against caste oppression: setting up the Bahiskrut Sabha; the Mahad Satyagraha guaranteeing free access to water for Dalits from public places; unifying the untouchable castes under the Depressed Classes Federation; the struggle with Gandhi and the Congress over the issue of separate electorates; struggle with the Communists and the establishment of the Independent Labour Party; were events that not only made Dalit struggles visible all over India, additionally, they had succeeded in making their demands for the abolition of untouchability central to the political aspirations of the Indian National Congress.

In considering Ambedkar's mass conversion to Buddhism, it is important to assert that even though he led masses of Dalits into conversion to Navoyana Buddhism and despite the fact that his followers today give him the venerated status of a *bodhisattva*, he was himself not a religious leader. Ambedkar, till the very end, remained a political leader rooted in a worldly struggle of the Dalits against caste oppression. His appropriation of religion and what he meant by this term was an act deeply infused with political intent.

The immediate antecedent to the Yeola declaration by Ambedkar was the Dalit struggle over entry to the Kalaram Temple in Nashik, Maharashtra. As opposed to Gandhi's change of heart approach amongst the upper castes, Ambedkar was deeply disgusted and sickened by the rigidity of the caste Hindus.[10] Notwithstanding their claims to reforming Hinduism, or their insistence of India being one nation and one people, the temple entry movement had brought to the fore the deep-rooted divisions that persisted within caste society. Ambedkar was deeply disillusioned with the prospects of a future life for the Dalits within a caste Hindu society.

The search for a religion that would take forward the prospect of Dalit emancipation was not at all a simple matter. On the contrary, as Jaffrelot (2005), Keer (1995) and several others have observed, Ambedkar was approached by the leaders of many religions within India including Islam, Sikhism and Christianity. Equally there were even leaders from the Hindu Mahasabha who tried convincing him to follow in the footsteps of the Arya Samaj. Mahasabha leaders believed that this way Ambedkar's religious quest would remain within the fold of Hinduism in a civilisational sense (Keer 1995). Ambedkar sought to deal with this search for a religion from the perspective of both identity and exclusion which faced Dalits everywhere. Not surprisingly, concerns of social equality, the practice of caste, problems of adjustment and inclusion were all issues that accompanied the search for a new religion. In addition, Jaffrelot (2005) observes how Ambedkar was also interested in the electoral arithmetic that would result from Dalits adding their numbers to different religious communities within the democratic arena. Such an exercise would provide a deeper understanding of how the increased numbers within the religious group would affect political prospects of the Dalit population.

It is interesting to note that Ambedkar firmly believed in a larger civilisational conception of Indian society and culture of which Hindu society was just a part and he believed that Dalits were a part of this larger civilisational culture of India. Even if Dalits did convert to another religion, it was important to him that such an act does not widen the gap between them and the rest of the Indian society. To that extent, he excluded both Islam and Christianity on grounds that

---

[10] In conversation with Gaikwad and other Dalit activists involved in the Kalaram Temple agitation, he is known to have asked of them to call off the agitation, notwithstanding their insistence to carry on. Ambedkar made it known to them that irrespective of the outcome, his mind was made up that no matter what, caste Hindus would never give up their practice of ritual exclusion when it came to the Dalits (Keer 1995).

these religions were alien to Indian civilisation. Whether Ambedkar was correct or not in this observation, what is interesting is that his views coincided with those of the Hindu Mahasabha.

When exactly did Ambedkar decide that Buddhism would be the religion he would convert to is not very clear, what we do know is that, as Zelliot (1992) observes, from a very young age Ambedkar's encounter with K. A. Keluskar who gifted him the first book on Buddhism, to the period of the 1930s when he read extensively on Buddhism important, among these was *Essence of Buddhism* by Lakshimi Narasu (1993), to meeting and engaging eminent Buddhists and scholars like Anand Kausalyayan. Sangharakshita, his writings and speeches as well as his travels to Buddhist countries in Asia attending Buddhist conferences, and so on, had made it clear that Buddhism would be the eventual religion of conversion. Yet what was also clear is the fact that the eventual choice of Buddhism was motivated by several factors, though none of these were strictly of a religious nature. They were rather aspects that revealed his deeper concerns of how he viewed Buddhism both as an identity for the Dalits as well as in the possibility it offered for reconstructing a world of inclusive social relations for both Dalits and non-Dalits in modern India.

Ambedkar saw Buddhism as an intrinsic part of the Indian civilisation. Conversion to Buddhism would not separate or alienate the Dalits from the culture and civilisation of India. Unlike the other religions that he had surveyed, Buddhism was the only religion that was constructed on strong moral foundations and was the only religion that espoused a moral universe embedded in the value of equality. Buddhism did not have any holy book nor did it have any centralised authority which could undermine or threaten his own project of developing a *dharma* that would respond to the needs of the Dalit population. In such a society where the majority practiced Buddhism, the stigma associated with Dalits could disappear forever. He was convinced that Buddhism could be re-used to ensure its continuing relevance for modern times.

This re-use of Buddhism was essentially an intellectual engagement aimed at making Buddhism relevant for a modern society. A closer look at this exercise clearly shows that what Ambedkar was attempting in the form of Navoyana Buddhism involved a fusing of modern political ideas with the teachings of the Buddha as represented in his work *The Buddha and his Dhamma*. Though he never produced a text on Navoyana Buddhism, it is clear from his other writings on Buddhism, Hinduism as well as on Marxism, that he traced the lineage of many of the cherished values of modernity, liberty, equality, fraternity, socialism, rationality, and so on, to the teachings of the Buddha. For Ambedkar, not only did the Buddha espouse all these modern values, in an ancient period, more importantly, he had a far richer depth and understanding of these ideas in comparisons to the modern counterparts. If one face of this cultural re-use involved the connection of modern ideas with the ancient teachings of the Buddha, its other face involved a political practice of Buddhism deeply tied up with the creation of a new identity for the Dalits completely removed from the memory and stigma of untouchability. As Buddhists, Dalits and non-Dalits could give shape to an undifferentiated world of social interaction and social intercourse rooted in the morality and rationality of the modern world as represented in Buddha's teachings. Unlike other nationalist leaders who often espoused the idea of giving up modernity to return to ones traditions, Ambedkar's emphasis was just the reverse insisting that in their new identity as Buddhist, both Dalits and non-Dalits could successfully engage with the modern world.

Giving shape to this cultural re-use of Buddhism involved developing a critique of three very different sets of ideas. Each of these, Ambedkar believed, represented a major concern for establishing the legitimacy of Navoyana Buddhism. There was first the need to rationally demonstrate why Hinduism as a religion had to be rejected. Second, the need to show why the Communist doctrine of equality could not be a relevant ideology for modern Indian society. Finally, he had to demonstrate why existing practices of Buddhism the world over were unsatisfactory and hence the need for Navoyana Buddhism.

## THE CRITIQUE OF HINDUISM

Ambedkar's critique of Hinduism involved a long and critical interrogation of the *Manusmriti* and several other texts in his essay titled "Philosophy of Hinduism" (1987). It is in this essay that one gets an insight into his understanding of religion. Borrowing from European scholars of religion like Robertson, Smith and Max Mueller, his effort was aimed at developing a common framework through which any religion could be examined and evaluated for its relevance to modern society. He was convinced that not all religions were positive or relevant for a society at any given time. In distinguishing religion between its antique character rooted in utility and its modern nature rooted in justice, he set down what he believed was the core to not only evaluating other religions, additionally, it would emerge as the foundation for his reworking of Buddhism. Ambedkar observes, "I take [modern] Religion to mean the propounding of an ideal scheme of divine governance the aim and object of which is to make the social order in which men live a moral order" (Ambedkar 1987: 14). This emphasis on morality as explicating a normative domain of right and wrong became the yardstick in his evaluation of Hinduism: interrogating Hindu sacred texts on values of equality, liberty and fraternity. It were these modern values that served as his yardstick of evaluation of an ancient religion. Ambedkar made a forceful case to show that based on the doctrinal assertions of Hinduism, notwithstanding recent attempts at reforming it, the religion was deeply inegalitarian, completely devoid of a fraternal sense of community and outrageously unjust and dehumanising to the individual within the Hindu social order. In short, Ambedkar was at pains to show how Hinduism lacked a moral order as it consistently collapsed the moral and the social, rendering any consideration of moral principles irrelevant. Thus, the social structure of the Hindu social order functioned with the two contradictory principles, that of status protection (*chaturvarna*) and social exclusion (*jati*). Both these processes were, in turn, legitimised by the doctrines of *karma* and *dharma*. Ambedkar pointed out that the absence of a moral domain that justified right from wrong made Hinduism nothing but a set of prescriptions that one had to follow, notwithstanding the deep sense of injustice associated with their practice. Hinduism could never be the religion of modern Indian society as it proved incapable of giving shape to either a sense of community or, for that matter, unite the nation into a progressive solidarity. Instead, what Hinduism had succeeded in doing was keeping vast sections of the Indian population in ignorance and darkness, enforcing a structure of widespread caste inequalities and instilling a consciousness of hatred and antagonisms amongst the different communities. Buddhism, on the other hand, could serve as the moral and religious foundation for creating a new Indian solidarity, additionally with its emphasis on learning and compassion. It could be the civilisational framework on which to construct a new, vibrant and progressive social order.

## The Critique of Marxism

Ambedkar was deeply aware that of the major modern ideologies that dominated the world of his times. Marxism, with its egalitarian emphasis, proved to be a major force of economic political and social transformation. His engagement with the Communists in Bombay in the first half of the twentieth century revealed to him the limits of their emancipative agendas. At the level of practice, he observed that Communists came from the upper caste and were unable to transcend their caste identities. At a more theoretical level, Ambedkar was dissatisfied with Marx's response to the question of inequality.

His writings on Marxism as an egalitarian ideology in the modern world[11] clearly point to an engagement with Marxism by one who had already positioned himself as a Buddhist. Not surprisingly, his evaluation of Marx came by way of a comparison with the Buddha's *dharma*. Thus, even though he appeared to

---

[11] These two of writings are, namely, *Buddhism and Marxism* and *Buddha and Karl Marx*, to be found in Ambedkar (1987, vol. 3).

be in agreement with Marx's analysis of poverty and capitalist exploitation, he was in complete disagreement with how these should be resolved.

His antipathy to violence as a means of creating the egalitarian society was matched by his fervour for the Buddha's path of persuasion and compassion to achieve the same ends. He believed that Communism was antithetical to democracy and that all dictatorships including that of the proletariat could not create an egalitarian society, since all dictatorships undermine individual freedoms and liberties. On the contrary, he believed that Buddhism was a far more superior social philosophy since it was able to achieve equality within the *sangha* without the use of violence and advocating the highest norms of democratic practice. He further believed that Buddhism was superior to Marxism in that it emphasised a social world that was materialistic and yet founded on strong moral principles of equality and justice. Notwithstanding the validity of these comparisons, it is interesting to note how Ambedkar critiqued ancient Hinduism from the standpoint of the modern, and then goes on to critique Marxism from the standpoint of ancient Buddhism. On both counts, one cannot help but observe the workings of cultural re-use with an undoubtedly clear political intent.

## THE CRITIQUE OF EXISTING BUDDHISM

Ambedkar did not appear to be impressed with any of the existing Buddhist doctrines either in India or in other parts of Asia. In general, he was of the view that compared to the period of its origins, the Buddhism of the present period had become another antique religion losing completely the moral core that made it once stand out as a religion that shunned rituals, add superstitions and which enunciated a path of liberation through knowledge and compassion. He was highly critical of the existing *sangha* institution within modern Buddhism. The *bhikkus* were in fact transformed into beggars of alms and had completely lost the initial objectives for which the *sangha* was set up. Yet Ambedkar was convinced that Buddhism was the only religion for a modern society based on science and rationality (Ambedkar 1987). In the extensive literature of Buddhism, especially the translated works that he accessed, there existed a rich possibility of rendering the Buddha's *dharma* as a philosophy of emancipation in a modern world. Whether Ambedkar was correct in his historical assessment of Buddhism as an emancipative doctrine in the contemporary setting has been a disputed issue; after all, there was no historical evidence anywhere in the world where Buddhism had functioned as an emancipative doctrine for the oppressed. Everywhere in the modern world, wherever Buddhism flourished, it appeared to have state patronage and was by-and-large a very conservative status quo force, yet Ambedkar's position seems to subsume such a dispute. Citing Christianity as a religion which started out as a religion of the oppressed, he believed that the struggle for emancipation was intrinsic to modern religion (Ambedkar 1987).

## NAVOYANA BUDDHISM

In having established the immorality of Hinduism, the coercive nature of the Communist ideology and the passivity of modern day Buddhism, Ambedkar believed he had laid the foundations for the development of Navoyana Buddhism. Given his belief that Buddhism was at its core, the teachings of the Buddha, it is these teachings he turned to so as to read into them a modernist vision of morality, justice, equality, rationality and compassion. Ambedkar's strategy was neither to author a new bible for Buddhism, nor did he try to build on any existing school of Buddhism. Instead, *The Buddha and his Dhamma* (1992) is a selective compilation as he claims of Buddhist texts on the life of the Buddha. It is through this richly lyrical yet argumentative text that Ambedkar sought to direct the reader to the teachings of the Buddha. Through these writings on the life and teachings of the Buddha, the reader is made aware that the Buddha took *parivraja* (renunciation) to prevent violence breaking out between warring clans, that the gospel of the Buddha is not pessimism but a path to an enlightened consciousness, that the Buddha rejected the Hindu doctrine of *karma* and rebirth, that the *bhikku* was not a perfect being but rather a learned and compassionate being in the service of society. Whether these are the authentic translations from the Pali or not, or whether Ambedkar is using the person of the Buddha to present a new interpretation of Buddhism, what is important for understanding his re-use of Buddhism is his manner of presenting Buddhism as a project of Dalit emancipation. In the period after Independence, Ambedkar was undoubtedly the most important and revered leader of the Dalits in western India. For the Dalits who converted to Navoyana Buddhism, conversion was not about a quest for an authentic Buddhism. Rather, for Dalits it was a way out of untouchability and social exclusion. Ambedkar was himself convinced that Navoyana Buddhism was a vehicle of social transformation for both Dalits and non-Dalits given that untouchability and exclusion were problems of the Hindu social order and not of Dalit creation.

Ambedkar was very clear that the Buddha's *dharma* was a social engagement grounded in a morality aimed at transforming social relations in the everyday world. Since *dharma* was the pursuit of moral righteousness in the real world, it had to be social, involving human relationships of all kinds with other human beings. For Ambedkar, "The purpose of *Dhamma*, as a social teaching is to reconstruct the world" (Das 1979: 231). Moral righteousness was an expression of group sentiment. This quest for a moral righteousness in the everyday world of lived social relations, Ambedkar believed, was what distinguished Buddhism from all other religions. Seen in this way, the Buddha's *dharma* seeks to alleviate human suffering through moral intervention in the everyday world. More importantly Ambedkar sought to present this process of moral engagement as one of collective emancipation. It was an emancipation that was simultaneously both moral and political in its realisation. In modern societies, religion and morality coincide such that morality is the religion of modern man. For Ambedkar, the Buddha's *dharma* espoused a moral righteousness that emphasised the alleviation of human suffering through moral interventions against issues of injustice and inequality. For Ambedkar, the Buddha sought to overcome suffering in the world not by renouncing the world but by intervening in it to bring about change. As a political force, Navoyana Buddhism sought to achieve this moral righteousness through the pursuit of rational learning and the practice of compassion in everyday social relations.

The emphasis on developing a rational understanding of the world through the pursuit of scientific learning was a key objective of Navoyana Buddhism. In *The Buddha and His Dhamma*, Ambedkar showed how the Buddha successfully dispelled superstitions and irrational beliefs through a sustained, persuasive and rational interrogation of the issue under consideration. Ambedkar invested hugely in the education of Dalits. He sincerely believed that education and the pursuit of knowledge was central to the project of Dalit emancipation. Not surprisingly, Dalit converts to Navoyana Buddhism emphasise the policy of "educate, mobilise and agitate" as Ambedkar's message to them (Jaffrelot 2005; Zelliot 1992).

## CONCLUSION

The strategic shift in the way that Navoyana Buddhism emphasised the collective emancipation of the untouchable castes proved to be the crucial component of change in the re-use of ancient Buddhism. The radical interpretation of Navoyana Buddhism as a social doctrine of revolutionary significance was quite clearly an attempt to ensure that Buddhism would not only provide a new and universal identity to the Dalits, equally Navoyana Buddhism would serve as the moral and political foundations for Dalits and non-Dalits to participate in a just and inclusive social order.

More than half a century later, how does one understand Ambedkar's re-use of the Buddha *dharma*? How does one understand the nature of Dalit solidarities in the period after the conversion? And how did mainstream Hindu society come to terms with this re-use of Buddhism?

As argued earlier in this chapter, Navoyana Buddhism was, at one level, a response or strategy to address issues of identity and exclusion faced by the Dalit movement in India. The conversion ceremony in which the Mahar converts promised to give up all attachments to Hinduism was a poignant and powerful political assertion of the new identity and solidarity that the new converts were now a part of. The assertion of this Buddhist identity, both politically and culturally by Dalit converts, continues even to the present period.[12] Yet, as Beltz (2004) rightly observes, little has happened by way of the institutional development of Navoyana Buddhism either in western India or elsewhere in India. Perhaps Ambedkar's untimely passing away left a large part of realising Navoyana Buddhism to other less competent and committed, as he was to this task. Equally there is the real problem of whether Dalits could actually live up to the values of moral righteousness as represented within Navoyana Buddhism. To the extent that Navoyana Buddhism proved incapable of bringing about any radical transformation in the oppressive and exploitative material conditions of Dalits, its impact remained culturally tied up to the identity politics of a fragmented and divided Dalit movement. Other scholars like Fitzgerald (2004) have argued that even amongst the converts, many continued to practice both Hinduism and Navoyana Buddhism and working with different identities depending upon the demands of the situation.

What is most significant however is the fact that the mainstream Hindu society has accepted the converted Buddhists as part of Hindu society. Major events of the Buddhist calendar are now part of state patronage. Further, unlike Dalit converts to other religions, Dalit converts to Buddhism are entitled to state reservations in education and employment. As a community engaged in the re-use of Buddhism, there are no doubts that the Buddhist identity has significantly diluted the stigma of untouchability and many Buddhist converts have taken to education and made substantial progress in their personal lives. As a community, however, they continue to function as another caste group within the larger pantheon of castes, as Beltz (2004) observes, their different identities continue to exist and flourish, notwithstanding the radical claims of Navoyana Buddhism.

---

[12] Even to this day, the anniversary of the conversion ceremony is marked by Dalits all over the country as occasions when they continue to convert and, whenever they do, the conversion is always a collective event marked by their rejection of Hinduism.

# BIBLIOGRAPHY

Ambedkar, B. R., 1987, *Dr. Babasaheb Ambedkar: Writings and Speeches*, Unpublished Writings, Vol. 3, edited by Vasant Moon. Education Department, Government of Maharashtra, Mumbai.

———, 1989a, *Dr. Babasaheb Ambedkar: Writings and Speeches*, Vol.1, edited by Vasant Moon. Education Department, Government of Maharashtra, Mumbai.

———, 1989b, *Dr. Babasaheb Ambedkar: Writings and Speeches*, Vol. 5, edited by Vasant Moon. Education Department, Government of Maharashtra, Mumbai.

———, 1990, *Dr. Babasaheb Ambedkar: Writings and Speeches*, Vol. 7, edited by Vasant Moon. Education Department, Government of Maharashtra, Mumbai.

——— 1992, *Dr. Babasaheb Ambedkar: Writings and Speeches*, Vol. 11, *Buddha and his Dhamma*, edited by Vasant Moon. Education Department, Government of Maharashtra, Mumbai.

Bapat, P. N., 1999, *Two Thousand Five Hundred Years of Buddhism*. Government of India publication, New Delhi.

Beltz, J., 2004, "Contesting Caste, Hierarchy and Hinduism: Buddhist Discursive Practices in Maharashtra". In: S. Jondhale & J. Beltz (eds), *Reconstructing the World: B. R. Ambedkar and Buddhism in India*. Oxford University Press, New Delhi.

Chakravarti, U., 1987, *The Social Dimensions of Early Buddhism*. Oxford University Press, New Delhi.

Das, Bhagwan (ed), 1979, *Thus Spoke Ambedkar: Selected Speeches*, Vol 3. Ambedkar Sahitya Publications, Bangalore.

Fitzgerald, T., 1995, "Religious Studies as Cultural Studies: A Philosophical and Anthropological Critique of the Concept of Religion". *DISKUS*. Vol. 3, no.1, pp. 35–47.

———, 2004, "Analyzing Sects, Minorities and Social Movements in India, the Case of Ambedkar's Buddhism and Dalits". In: S. Jondhale & J. Beltz (eds), *Reconstructing the World: B. R. Ambedkar and Buddhism in India*. Oxford University Press, New Delhi, pp. 267–82.

Guha, R., 1998, *Dominance without Hegemony: History and Power in Colonial India*. Oxford University Press, New Delhi.

Guru, G., 1997, *Dalit Cultural Movement and Dialectics of Dalit Politics in Maharashtra*. Vikas Adhyayan Kendra, Mumbai.

Jaffrelot, C., 2005, *Dr. Ambedkar and Untouchability Analysing and Fighting Caste*. Oxford University Press, New Delhi.

Jones, K., 1999, *Socio-religious Reform Movements in British India*. Foundation Books, New Delhi.

Keer, D., 1995, *Dr. Ambedkar: Life and Mission*. Popular Prakashan Private Limited, Bombay.

King, R., 1999, *Orientalism and Religion: Post Colonial Theory, India and the 'Mystic East'*. Routledge, London.

Kuber, W. N., 2001, *B. R. Ambedkar*. Ministry of Information and Broadcasting, Government of India, New Delhi.

Narasu, P. Lakshimi, 1993, *The Essence of Buddhism*. Asian Educational Publishers, New Delhi.

Narula, S., 1999, "Broken People: Caste Violence against India's 'Untouchables'," Human Rights Watch, India.

Omvedt, G., 1994, *Dalits and the Democratic Revolution: Dr. Ambedkar and the Dalit Movement in Colonial India*. SAGE Publications, New Delhi.

————, 1996, *Dalit Visions: The Anti-caste Movement and the Construction of an Indian Identity*. Orient Longman Ltd., Hyderabad.

————, 2004, *Ambedkar: Towards an Enlightened India*. Penguin, New Delhi.

Panikkar, K. N., 1998, *Culture, Ideology, Hegemony: Intellectuals and Social Consciousness in Colonial India*. Tulika, New Delhi.

Sarkar, S., 1986, *Modern India: 1885–1947*. Macmillan India Limited, Madras.

Shah, G., 2006, *Untouchability in Rural India*. SAGE Publications, New Delhi.

Sumant, Y., 2004, "Situating Religion in B. R. Ambedkar's Political Discourse". In: S. Jondhale & J. Beltz (eds), *Reconstructing the World: B. R. Ambedkar and Buddhism in India*. Oxford University Press, New Delhi, pp. 63–78.

Teltumbde, A., 1997, *Impact of New Economic Reforms on Dalits in India*. Occasional Paper Series: 1, University of Pune, Pune.

Thapar, R., 1966, *The History of India*, Vol. I. Penguin, New Delhi.

————, 2000, *Cultural Pasts: Essays in Early Indian History*. Oxford University Press, New Delhi.

Zelliot, E., 1992, *From Untouchable to Dalit: Essays on the Ambedkar Movement*. Manohar, New Delhi.

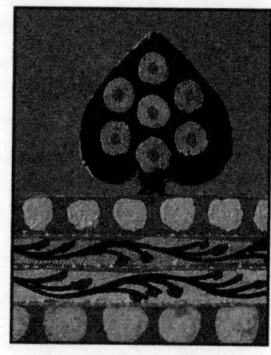

*Chapter 13*

# 'THE JAIN WAY OF LIFE'

## MODERN RE-USE AND REINTERPRETATION OF ANCIENT JAIN CONCEPTS

**BY SABINE SCHOLZ**

## INTRODUCTION

This chapter will focus on the re-use and reinterpretation of concepts within jainism, one of the oldest religious traditions which has its origin in the Indian subcontinent.

Although always a minority, Jains[1] have been wielding substantial influence in different fields for many centuries, and continue to do so even today. During

---

[1] 'Jain' or 'Jaina' is the term for those who follow the teachings of the Jainas, literally 'victor'. Jaina describes a human being, who has attained omniscience and teaches others the way to spiritual liberation. In the following, I will use the term Jain instead of Jaina, since the organisations mentioned and discussed in this chapter use it as a self-designation in their respective names and English publications. For a general introduction to history, doctrine, philosophy and religious practice of the Jains, see Dundas (2002) and Jaini (1979). For a concise encyclopaedia of Jain terms and eminent Jain organisations and persons, see Wiley (2006).

mediaeval times, Jain scholars contributed strongly to philosophy, Indian vernacular languages and literature, as well as to other intellectual fields. The Jains' absolute emphasis on vegetarianism, most probably, had its impact on the dissemination of a vegetarian lifestyle among non-Jains, especially in south India. Up to the present day, a large number of Jains are engaged in trade and their economic power supersedes that of most other Indian communities.

The Indian census of 2001 states the number of Jains in India as 4,225,053, around 0.2 per cent of the total population.[2] Today, most Jains live in the Indian states of Maharashtra, Rajasthan, Madhya Pradesh, Gujarat and Karnataka, though small communities of Jain traders can be found in all parts of India.

Unlike Buddhism, which decreased in its influence in its country of origin, while prospering elsewhere, Jainism has always been confined to the Indian subcontinent. Nevertheless, more recent times have witnessed the growth of a Jain diaspora. For this chapter, the Jain diaspora in Britain and North America and organisations founded there are of special importance since here we find the development of new interpretations which did not stay confined to the diaspora context, as will be shown in the course of this chapter.

## IMMIGRATION AND THE JAIN DIASPORA

For centuries, Jain merchants have been moving in small groups throughout India for business purposes. From the end of the nineteenth century, however, a large-scale migration of Jains, mostly from Gujarat and belonging to the Shvetambara image-worshipping tradition,[3] to East Africa started. Due to political unrest, many East African Jains started moving to Britain from 1968 onwards. Today, there are approximately 25,000–30,000 Jains residing in Britain,[4] most of them in the Greater London area, while a substantial number of Jains settled in Leicester. It has to be noted that, as anywhere else, the Jains in

---

[2] For the data of the Census of India 2001, see http://www.censusindia.gov.in/Census_Data_2001/ Census_Data_Online/Social_and_cultural/Religion.aspx.

[3] Jains are divided into several traditions or sects, the two main ones consisting of the Digambaras (sky-clad) and Shvetambaras (white-clad). Their names refer to the practice of clothing of their male ascetics, in case of Digambaras to their absolute nudity. Differences between both groups are mainly differences in practice. Among the Shvetambaras, further sectarian divisions led to the existence of reformist groups whose members do not practice image worship, while the traditional image-worshipping section still forms the majority of the Shvetambaras. For a general introduction to the different Jain sects, see Dundas (2002: 46–59, 246–71) Jaini (1979: 4–6, 38–41) and Wiley (2006: 14–15, 78–79, 203–04, 208, 214–17).

[4] Paul Dundas states the number of Jains residing in Britain and other parts of Europe in the year 2002 as 25,000–30,000 (Dundas 2002: 271). According to the webpage of the British newspaper *The Guardian*, in 2002, there were around 25,000 Jains living in Britain (http://www.guardian. co.uk/world/2002/oct/30/religion.uk16). Kristi L. Wiley in 2006 estimated the number of Jains in the whole of Europe, with the majority in Britain, as about 30,000.

Britain do not form a homogeneous group. While many families have migrated from East Africa, some have come directly from India. Jains are not only divided into several sects, but also belong to different castes, some of which are made up of Jains and Hindus. 'Caste identity' often proves to be stronger than a 'Jain identity'.[5]

With the liberalisation of the immigration laws, Jains in larger numbers began to settle in the United States as part of the so-called brain drain of highly educated professionals, arriving from South Asia after 1965.[6] A number of the Jain immigrants to the US and Canada did not come directly from India, but, as in case with immigrants to Great Britain, from East Africa, where they had been settled as businessmen or professionals. The given numbers of the North American Jain population differ between approximately 50,000 (Wiley 2006: 19) and more than 100,000, as stated by the Jain Associations in North America (JAINA, (http://www.jaina.org/about/, p. 1). Apart from the immigrant Jain communities in Britain and North America, smaller groups of Jains, mainly engaged in business and trade, can be found in East Asia, Australia and Western Europe.[7]

As has been noted before and has to be stressed again, the importance of caste as an identity marker, in many cases, supersedes the notion of a Jain identity. Regarding Jain immigrants, this becomes evident by the fact, that the first Jain temple in the East African diaspora was only built in 1926 at Nairobi, while before worship and rituals had been performed at home or at centres belonging to the specific castes (Dundas 2002: 272). Though the notion of a distinct 'Jain identity' and 'Jain community', as in case with other Indian religious traditions such as Hindus and Sikhs, has gained more popularity in the course of the twentieth century, in many cases, caste still plays a dominant role. In the European disapora, the first Jain *samaj* (association or organisation) was founded among Shvetambara Jains of the Srimali and Oswal castes. The initial cooperation, however, did not last long, and in subsequent times, most of the Oswal members broke away. In 1980, a partial reconciliation of both groups took place and in 1982, the Leicester Jain *samaj*, still dominated by the Srimali caste, became known as the Jain Samaj Europe (Banks 1992: 159–73; Dundas 2002: 272–73). From the 1980s up to the present day, several Jain organisations have been founded in Britain.[8] Some of them represent different castes or Jain sects, while some, such as the Institute of Jainology, founded in 1983 in London,

---

[5] A strong focus on caste affiliations, however, is not a diaspora phenomenon. Although the concept of caste is regarded rather as a social than a religious sanctioned institution within the Jain tradition, a strong caste consciousness nevertheless developed among Jains, which has been attacked by progressive Jain reformers from the end of the nineteenth century onwards.

[6] For the rise of immigration from South Asia to the US after 1965 and the 'brain drain', see: Williams (1998: 181–82).

[7] For more details on Jain immigration, see Banks (1991: 242–43; 1992: 125–59), Dundas (2002: 271–75), Kumar (1996: 94–103) and Wiley (2006: 19–20).

[8] For a list, see http://www.jainology.org/?q=en/resources/Jain-Organisations-In-the-UK.

aim at providing "a platform for interaction between different Jain communities and organizations, where all sectarian traditions jointly promote the faith and engage in discussion amongst themselves, encouraging Jain unity" (http://www.jainolgy.org/?q=aboutus, p. 1).

In North America, the first Jain centre was opened in New York in 1966. The 1970s witnessed the arrival of two Jain ascetics: Acharya Sushil Kumar and Shri Chitrabhanuji. Their visits have to be regarded as extraordinary events for the diaspora Jains, who, similar to other Indian immigrant groups, have been organised and led by professional laymen (Williams 1998: 183–84). Since their ascetic vows do not allow fully initiated Jain monks and nuns to travel by any mechanical conveyance, the two ascetics' visits of immigrant Jains in the diaspora only became possible due to their disregard of the ancient rules. Acharya Sushil Kumar contributed to the establishment of several Jain institutions, such as community and teaching centres at several places in North America, and a temple in Toronto, Canada (Kumar 1996: 174; Williams 1998: 184). After Acharya Sushil Kumar and Shri Chitrabhanuji, several ascetics have taken a more liberal approach towards the traditional ban on an ascetic's travel abroad and have visited the Jain diaspora. Within the Shvetambara sect of the Terapanthis, a new class of novice mendicants was established in 1981 whose members are permitted to travel by all kinds of transportation. This development can be seen as an aim to reach out to the Jain immigrant communities. Religious specialists, however, remain rare in the context of the Jain diaspora and, more or less, all leading and organisational tasks are taken care of by lay followers.

In 1981, the first Jain Convention was held at Los Angeles and at this occasion the federation of JAINA got initiated. The umbrella organisation, started with the blessings of Acharya Sushil Kumar and Shri Chitrabhanuji, was formally established in 1983 and is a federation of sixty-two North American Jain organisations (http://www.jaina.org/about/, p. 1).

Among the Jain organisations formed among immigrant Jains in Europe and North America, youth associations are of special importance for the topic of this chapter. The concept, to found an organisation for young second or third generation Jains, had first been articulated in Britain when a group of young Jain professionals in 1987 formed the 'Young Jains UK'. The association targets at the age group between eighteen and thirty-five. This group, however, includes not only second and third generation Jains, who aim at coming to terms with their family's religious tradition in the context of their British environment, but also include non-Jains, particularly young people who take a very sceptical approach to religion, among their main target group. The events, meetings and courses organised by the group centre around discussions instead of sermons, the use of English instead of high Gujarati and stress the aspects of individual self-realisation and the leading of an ethical way of life.

Starting from the UK, the Young Jains movement was also adopted among American Jains. In 1991 the 'Young Jains of America' were founded. In 1994, they held their first convention and in the following year their website was started. Like JAINA, the Young Jains of America also work as an umbrella organisation, bringing together several Jain youth organisations, targeting the age group between fourteen and twenty-nine. In 1998, another association focusing on young Jains, the 'Young Jain Professionals', held their first convention. The Young Jains of America and Young Jain Professionals have not been the only Jain youth associations established after the example of the Young Jains UK. In subsequent years, other immigrant Jains have founded the 'Young Jains Nairobi', the 'Young Jains Perth' and the 'Young Jains Singapore'. What had started in the diaspora among second and third generation young professionals finally came back to the 'homeland', India, in 2005 when the 'Young Jains of India' came into existence.

## THE YOUNG JAINS OF INDIA

The establishment of the Young Jains of India[9] was highly influenced by the Young Jains of America. Two active members of the latter organisation, one coming back to India after having spent ten years in Boston, were instrumental in its founding. In accordance with the concept of the earlier described Young Jains groups, the YJI targeted young Jains and professionals.

The following description of the YJI is based on the program booklet for their first convention, held at Indore in December 2005, personal observances and communication with some members conducted during a period of field research for my PhD thesis in 2006 and 2007 at Dharwad, Hubli and Varur (Karnataka) and on written communication with leading members via the internet. According to their self-description, the YJI are "[a]n organization dedicated to promote Jainism as a way of life, a practice, and an observance" (YJI Program Booklet 2005: 1). This concept becomes further illustrated in the words of a leading member:

> Our aim is to simplify Jainism without compromising on the basic principles and fundamentals so that the youngsters do not perceive religion as a complicated set of Do's and Don't to follow, rather they get guided towards self-realization with deeper understanding of Mind, body & Soul.
>
> We do not preach Jainism as a religion but as a way of life that can be adopted/followed by any individual regardless of caste/creed/religion.

---

[9] In the following, the short form YJI will be used.

> We believe that Jain Way of Life is based on very scientific and logical principles which help in improving the quality of one's life. So not only Jains but anyone can and should learn to understand and practice it.[10]

What is the 'Jain Way of Life' mentioned in this statement? The Jain Way of Life,[11] according to the YJI, consists of three concepts, which form 'core Jain principles' (YJI Program Booklet 2005: 13). These principles are: *ahimsa* (non-hurting, non-violence), *aparigraha* (non-possessiveness) and *anekantavada* (non-onesidedness). Before we start with a discussion of the YJI's modern interpretation of these 'three A's', it is crucial to have a look at the meaning of the concepts from the traditional Jain perspective.

## THE JAIN CONCEPTS OF AHIMSA, APARIGRAHA AND ANEKANTAVADA

As there is no single authoritative Jain scripture, comparable to the Bible in the Christian tradition, there is also no homogenous Jain community. Nevertheless, all Jain sects agree that the Jain tradition describes a system, taught by omniscient human beings, which leads to individual spiritual liberation through the destruction of negative *karma*. Among ethical practices for spiritual progress and liberation from the circle of death and rebirth, the most important is *ahimsa*. The principle of *ahimsa*, non-hurting of every life form, though also an essential value in other Indian traditions, is mostly elaborated within the Jain system. It is already found in the earliest rules for monks, which are based on the principle of *ahimsa*.[12] It is the first of the five vows an ascetic takes, though, in a less strict interpretation, it can also be taken by Jain householders. The remaining four vows, non-lying, non-stealing, sexual restraint and non-possession or non-possessiveness are commonly regarded as elaborations of the first vow, non-hurting by actions of the body, speech or mind (Dundas 2002: 160). In Jain practice, the principle of *ahimsa* led to a very elaborate set of rules for an ascetic's daily routine, especially regarding travelling and the bodily functions. To avoid any possible hurt to small life forms, ascetics are not allowed to travel during the four months' rainy season, when many small living beings are considered to come into existence. While within the Shvetambara sects of the Sthanakvasis and Terapanthis, ascetics wear a mouth-shield to avoid hurting life forms in the

---

[10] Personal (written) communication from a leading member of the Young Jains of India, June 2008.

[11] In the following, the short form JWOL will be used. This short form is frequently used by Jains on websites and in the YJI Indore Convention Booklet of 2005.

[12] See Dundas (2002: 158–59) and Wiley (2006: 22). For a more detailed discussion about the usage of *ahimsa* as an ethical principle in ancient Jain literature, see Dixit (1978).

air while speaking and breathing, Jain ascetics of all traditions carry a broom, made out of different materials, to gently wipe the floor before lying or sitting down in order not to harm any insects. In this regard, the two objects non-Jains often associate with Jain ascetics, mouth-shield and broom, then, can be considered outward symbols for the strict practice of *ahimsa*. Every aspect of an ascetic's life is regulated by rules which aim at *ahimsa* to the utmost possible extent. Regarding bodily functions, the acts of eating and drinking underlie much stricter rules than the avoidance of any kind of meat, eggs or honey. Water has to be filtered or boiled, before it is suitable for usage and some kind of vegetarian food, such as root vegetables or vegetables which are considered to contain a large number of seeds are to be avoided. Absolute vegetarianism is also compulsory for lay followers, and in lay practice, *ahimsa* becomes most visible in a strict vegetarian lifestyle.

The traditional interpretation of *ahimsa* as the highest ethical principle, whose practice is considered absolute crucial for any spiritual progress, however, differs from the (Christian) Western concept of non-violence not only in as far as all kind of life forms are included. For instance, it may seem strange for a Western observer that ancient and mediaeval Jain history includes a number of rulers, generals and soldiers among followers of the Jain tradition. The fact that a successful general, whose professional life involved warfare, at the same time, could be praised in Jain literature as a pious Jain, shows the complex nature of the Jain concept of *ahimsa*. Violence, then, according to the traditional Jain interpretation, has to be regarded in relation to an individual's intention and professional occupation. To kill in self-defence or, in case of a soldier, in fulfilling his duty, for instance, could be interpreted as an act which did not involve *himsa*, or violence.[13]

The second principle, *aparigraha*, which can be translated as 'non-possession' and 'non-possessiveness', is also part of an ascetic's and householder's vow. The stress on *aparigraha* as a core value for an ascetic can also already be found in earlier scriptures about monastic rules (Dixit 1978: 28–42). Regarding lay Jain rules of conduct, the vow of *aparigraha* consists in the voluntary limitation of the own possessions. To strengthen one's commitment to the concept of *aparigraha*, a lay follower may take further vows, for instance, to restrict the area of the own activities and travels or to put a limitation on the objects of food, clothes, and so on, to be used (Jaini 1979: 187). Though it is impossible for a householder to renounce all possessions, *aparigraha* for a lay follower means the cultivation of a feeling of non-attachment, restraint from greed and the limitation of one's possessions. Jain ascetics, on the other hand, are supposed to renounce all possessions. In case of male ascetics of the Digambara tradition, the vow of *aparigraha* also includes any kind of clothes. In this regard, the naked

---

[13] See Dundas (2002: 160–63). For a study of the image and symbol of the ideal warrior in Digambara Jainism, see Dundas (1991).

Digambara monk begging for food can be seen as an extreme example for both the principles of *ahimsa* and *aparigraha* (see Plate 13.1). Having renounced all kind of clothes and moving around in complete nudity, his only possessions are a water pot (*kamandalu*) and a brush made out of peacock feathers (*pinchi*). The water pot contains water which has been boiled by lay followers and may only be used by the ascetic to wash hands and feet and to clean himself after excretion. The brush, ideally made out of peacock feathers found in the forests (without causing any harm to the animal), is used to sweep the ground to avoid injury to small insects. Since the Digambara ascetic is not allowed to possess a begging bowl, the food, which has been prepared according to strict regulations, following the principle of *ahimsa*, is put directly into the ascetic's cupped hands. Should during the process of begging or being fed any violation of the rules occur, the monk or nun is supposed to rather go without food for a day than carry on eating (see Plate 13.2).

The third of the 'three A's', propagated as the JWOL, unlike the first two, is no part of the vows, but a metaphysical concept and philosophical method. The term *anekantavada* can be translated as the "theory of non-onesidedness", or the "theory of the many-sided nature of reality" (Matilal 1981: 1). Reality, accordingly, is manifold and cannot be described in an unconditional statement. The soul (*jiva*), for instance, can be said to be both permanent and impermanent, depending on the viewpoint. In this regard, the Jain tradition grants partial truth to other religious systems, which are either based on the theory of permanence or impermanence (Wiley 2006: 36). Jain philosophy, however, rejects any philosophical system, which claims to contain the absolute truth as *ekanta*, 'onesided'. As a philosophical method, also known as *syadvada*, which can be translated as the 'doctrine of qualified assertion', *anekantavada* was used by mediaeval Jain monks as a polemical weapon in religious disputes, by making it possible to defend the own doctrine, while pointing out that rival systems, like Hindu traditions and Buddhism, only contained the partial truth.[14]

## THE JWOL: TOWARDS A NEW JAIN IDENTITY

How, then, are the principles of *ahimsa, aparigraha* and *anekantavada* interpreted within the JWOL framework? The YJI Indore convention program booklet from 2005 gives the following explanation:

> The world today is in a dire need of the Jain principles of Non-Violence (Ahimsa), Non-Possessiveness (Aparigraha) and Non-Onesidedness (Anekantvaad). When

---

[14] For the Jain doctrine of *anekantavada*, see Cort (2000: 325–27), Dundas (2002: 229–33), Jaini (1979: 89–97), Matilal (1981) and Wiley (2006: 36).

we read the newspaper or turn on the television, we hear of hatred and anger along with on-going wars and acts of terrorism. The spirit of ahimsa is urgently needed. Today, there is ever-increasing greed for money, power, fame and other materialistic objects. The principle of aparigraha offers a solution to overcome the greed and live a life of contentment. Fundamentalism and differing views divide us to the point of violence. The principle of anekantvaad also referred as multiplicity of views, makes us realize that the reality may be perceived differently from different points of views. (YJI Program Booklet 2005: 2)

Within this modern interpretation of Jainism and the creation of a JWOL, the focus on *ahimsa* as such seems to be nothing new and therefore does not come as an unexpected surprise. But the re-use of *ahimsa* as one important pillar of a modern JWOL represents a shift of focus from *ahimsa* as a means for individual spiritual progress to *ahimsa* as a solution for the modern world's problems. This stress, however, does not originate with the YJI and the JWOL, for we already find it from the beginning of the twentieth century onwards in the first English apologetic writings of a small Western educated intellectual Jain elite. Here, Jainism, and especially its central doctrine of *ahimsa*, is represented as the sole 'remedy' for the troubled world. This, for instance, is illustrated in the following statement, published in 1921 in the English language organ of progressive lay Jains, *The Jaina Gazette*:

> Every body in all the four corners of the globe is groaning against all the miseries, political, social, economic and of all kinds. Many remedies are prescribed and tried. But only one can cure, and that always comes from Jainism. [...] India is to be led. M. Gandhi rises to lead it in a most difficult stage; he charms all hostility into silence, or inactivity. What makes him so harmless and so exempt from the hostility of all? His non-violence or *ahimsa*, which is the first step and a *sine qua non* of the life, thought, speech and action of all rational beings according to Jainism. Let the world read its riddle and misery in the light of the mere A.B.C. of Jainism in an unprejudiced attitude of sympathy and faith; and it will at once find the cleanest, clearest solution to its riddle and cure for its misery. (Jaini 1921: 304)

This modern interpretation of *ahimsa*, however, is not unique to Jains. As Jain apologetic writers have stressed the Jain influence on Gandhi's politics of non-violent resistance[15] and tried to propagate *ahimsa* as an instrument for world peace, advocates of the so called 'Neo-Hinduism' have also been engaged in propagating the principle of *ahimsa* as India's most valuable 'spiritual gift' to the world. Nevertheless, the modern representation of Jainism is often based on the claim that the Jain tradition, from ancient times up to the present day,

---

[15] Among Jains, the influence of a Gujarati Jain layman, who became known as a mystic under the honorific name of Shrimad Rajacandra (1867–1901), on Mohandas Gandhi has been stressed. See, for instance Mehta (1929: 200). For a short account of Shrimad Rajacandra and his impact on Gandhi, see Dundas (2002: 262–65), Wiley (2006: 176–77).

has been the purest representative of the ideal of *ahimsa*. This assumption, for instance, finds its expression in the English account of Jainism by a present day Digambara monk, Upadhyaya Munishree Kamakumar Nandi, who writes in a chapter about *ahimsa*: "The fact as to how zealously the slogan of disarmament is shouted today in the UNO by experimenting the unparall[el]ed weapon of non-violence is the gift of Jainism alone" (Upadhyaya Munishree Kamakumar Nandi, n.d.: 56). In the modern context, vegetarianism becomes more than a necessary practice for followers of *ahimsa*. Furthermore, vegetarianism is propagated as part of a healthy lifestyle, which, for modern Jain apologetics, proves the compatibility between Jainism and science.[16]

When we look at the second pillar of the JWOL, the concept of *aparigraha*, as with *ahimsa*, we also witness the focus shifted from the original stress on individual spiritual progress. In the modern interpretation, *aparigraha* as 'non-possessiveness' becomes an important instrument for a responsible approach to the environment and the saving of natural resources. In this regard, *aparigraha* is considered a substantial means to create a fairer world. While, according to the traditional interpretation, the attachment to worldly belongings is regarded as a hindrance for spiritual progress, here it is seen as an obstacle to universal justice and peace. In the context of the individual, *aparigraha* in its modern interpretation does not only focus on the otherworldly, which means the way to individual spiritual liberation. The voluntary limitation of the own possessions is furthermore seen as a way to attain peace of mind by living a life of contentment in a materialistic world.

The most interesting reinterpretation and re-use concerns the third of the 'three A's', namely, the concept of *anekantavada*. This modern interpretation has also already been promulgated in academic and popular accounts of Jainism from the beginning of the twentieth century onwards. Here, *anekantavada* gets interpreted as 'intellectual *ahimsa*'. The term 'intellectual *ahimsa*' was coined by the Indian scholar A. B. Dhruva, who first used it in 1933 (Cort 2000: 327).[17] In this context, *anekantavada* is regarded as tolerance towards other opinions. John E. Cort has shown how the interpretation of *anekantavada* as 'intellectual *ahimsa*' was adopted by other scholars and "has had a powerful afterlife" (Cort 2000: 328). *Anekantavada*, according to its modern interpretation, has not stayed confined to respect for other opinions in the intellectual field. In a broader context, it has become an expression

---

[16] Vegetarianism, according to the modern interpretation, is not only regarded as a more natural and healthier diet. The avoidance of non-vegetarian food, furthermore, is claimed to reduce the risk of infectious diseases and to lower the aggressive potential of an individual. See, for instance, Upadhyaya Munishree Kamakumar Nandi (n.d.: 78–111).

[17] A. B. Dhruva first used it in his "Introduction" to *Syadvadamanjari of Mallisena with the Anyayoga-Vyavaccheda of Hemacandra* (1933: lxxiv). Since this publication has not been available to me, I rely on Cort (2000: 327, 344–45).

of religious tolerance and harmony in a globalised world. It furthermore takes the role of an intellectual weapon against any kind of intolerance, fundamentalism and terrorism.

However, as John E. Cort (2000) and some other Western scholars (Dundas 2002: 229–33; Wiley 2006: 36) have argued, the interpretation of *anekantavada* as 'intellectual *ahimsa*' in form of tolerance towards the (religious) views of others has to be regarded as a "misreading" (Dundas 2002: 232) of the original doctrine. Most Jain teachers, who made use of *anekantavada* in its dual aspects as a metaphysical concept and philosophical method, although recognising a partial truth in other religious and philosophical systems, nevertheless still held the Jain doctrine and practice the only one which could lead to salvation. Furthermore, a history of Jain literature also shows instances of religious intolerance and sometimes rather harsh critical remarks against non-Jain texts and beliefs (Cort 2000: 331–36; Dundas 2002: 232–33; Wiley 2006: 36). Finally, the reinterpretation of an ancient complex doctrine as 'religious tolerance' proves to be problematic, as Paul Dundas rightly states:

> Religious tolerance, effectively a political concept born in the European Enlightenment, does not transpose itself particularly comfortably into the traditional Indian context in which Jain philosophy was located. Although there can be no doubt about the general persistence of flexible attitudes towards objects of worship in South Asia, Indian religions and philosophical movements were highly critical of the knowledge systems and ideologies of their rivals. (Dundas 2002: 232–33)

Nevertheless, the reinterpretation of *anekantavada* as religious tolerance and respect for the view of others has been widely propagated during the twentieth century and in this regard Jains have been claiming to possess the most tolerant of all religious traditions.

As this account of the reinterpretation and re-use of *ahimsa, aparigraha* and *anekantavada* in the JWOL has shown, it is based on the modern popular presentation of Jainism as it has been propagated since the beginning of the twentieth century. Though the JWOL's main message is neither completely new nor uniquely Jain (we have seen parallels to the representation of 'Neo-Hinduism' in the West), its 'framing', however, is. How then, we may ask, was this JWOL created? The answer to this question leads us back to the context of the North American Jain diaspora. The formulation of the JWOL evolved in the US through a "think tank called the Long Range Planning Committee",[18] established in recent years by the umbrella organisation JAINA. This 'think tank', a team of Jain professionals residing in the US, developed a 'Jain Vision 2020', which is introduced as follows:

---

[18] See http://www.jainlink.org/?page=vision (p. 1). The following account of the JWOL as part of the 'Jain Vision 2020' is based on this webpage.

We Jains have been on a path of Non-Violence, Non-Absolutism (Anekantvad), and Non-Absolutism (Aparigrah) for 1000's of years. And recently Science is walking with us-hand in hand on this path. For 1000's of years Jains have believed in [...] animal compassion, vegetarianism, environmentalism, equal rights for women, respect for other culture, religion, and traditions, forgiveness, and more. And now more than ever, the western world can leverage Jain philosophy. Only now North America and the rest of the world are discovering and practicing what Jains have known and practiced for 1000's of years.

Jains are sitting on a treasure and have so much to offer. Imagine if we had shared this treasure with the world 1000's of years ago, this world would have been a very different place. But it is not too late. When you plant a seed, the soil has to be right, there has to be enough light and water for a great tree to grow. The environment has to be conducive. In the same way, the North Americans are conducive to sharing the treasures which are in Jainism. (http://www.jainlink.org?page=vision, pp.1–2)

This 'vision', according to its 'architects', "is not just to LIVE a Jain Way of life, but to PROMOTE it" (http://www.jainlink.org?page=vision, p. 2). Besides the promotion of the JWOL, other catchwords included in the Jain Vision 2020, which are worth mentioning here, are the 'branding' and 'positioning' of Jainism in order to make it easy to understand and be compared to other religious traditions: "[W]hen someone asks what is Jainism- we give a short crisp response" (http://www.jainlink.org?page=vision, p. 3). The creation of the JWOL and the usage of the 'three A's' as its main pillars reflects some kind of 'branding'. Three Jain principles have been taken out of their traditional context and been given a new interpretation, which represents Jainism as a universal 'way of life' which can be practiced by anybody without the need for formal conversion. To spread the message of the JWOL, the development of strong connections with non-Jain organisations, such as humanitarian, interfaith, vegetarian or animal right associations, as well as to the media are part of the Jain Vision 2020 agenda. Furthermore, the Jain Vision 2020 aims at evolving the "traditional Jain practices by adopting the Jain Way of Life to the modern, North American lifestyle" (http://www.jainlink.org?page=vision, p. 2).

This vision is interesting, for it reflects the context in which it has been developed, namely, the religious diaspora of North America. In this regard, immigrant Jains share important similarities with other immigrant religious groups in North America: first of all, as other South Asian immigrants, Jains feel the necessity to adapt their tradition to the new surroundings. This becomes especially important regarding the second and third generation for whose members traditional languages, rituals and symbols often have lost their meaning. Parents mostly seek the assistance of organisations at the crucial point when their children begin to socialise outside of the home (Williams 1998: 189).

Furthermore, in the context of immigrant communities, the question of individual and group identity becomes more pressing in a multicultural environment.

This process of identity formation in the diaspora is closely linked to religion, as South Indian immigrants to the US, according to their own statements, "are more religiously active than they were in India or Pakistan", which "[...] reflects the power inherent in religion to provide a transcendent foundation for personal and group identity in the midst of the enormous transitions that migration entails" (Williams 1998: 188). Apart from the search for an own identity, the defining of the own religious tradition for its presentation to outsiders is considered crucial. Therefore, 'branding' and 'positioning' of the own religious tradition becomes catchwords for activists of immigrant religious groups.[19] In this regard, however, the Jains somewhat differ from other Indian immigrants, since they are not only a tiny minority in the diaspora, but also in their homeland, India. While the question of religious identity, nevertheless, seems to be more pressing in the context of the diaspora, in case of the Jains, the issue is also important in India. At this point, another difference between immigrant Jains and other Indian immigrants, especially Hindus, and, to some extent also Sikhs, has to be mentioned: Unlike the Hindutva movement and the Sikhs in their fight for an independent Sikh nation, diaspora Jains do not sponsor religious nationalism in India for the simple reason that there is no Jain nationalism comparable to the Hindutva or (Sikh) Khalistan movements. On the other hand, Hindu nationalism has its impact on Jains, especially on the question of Jain identity. While Hindutva activists claim Jains as part of the Hindu religion and culture, Jains become more aware of their separate identity. This tendency can be found in India, but also among diaspora Jains, some of whom, for instance, are very actively engaged in trying to prove the ancient and independent roots of Jainism.

In the modern presentation of Jainism to non-Jains, the Jain Vision 2020 with its focus on the JWOL resembles the modern interpretation of other religious traditions, especially of Indian origin: here, the stress is laid on the alleged compatibility with science, on non-violence, tolerance and a universal outlook. In this regard, Jain activists with their focus on the reinterpretation of the 'three A's' claim the JWOL to be perfectly suited to take a leading role in a globalised world of religious pluralism.

## CONCLUSION: COMING BACK TO INDIA AND THE YJI

In a globalised world with transnational networks, especially electronic media such as the internet, religious ideas, concepts and organisations spread, and developments among religious communities in the diaspora have their influence

---

[19] For a study of Hindu immigrants to the US and their organisations' aims at the 'codification' of an 'American Hinduism,' see Kurien (2004).

back on the Indian 'homeland' (Williams 1998: 193–94). In case of the YJI, its establishment and adoption of the JWOL has been very much influenced by Jain organisations in the US (which, again, have been influenced by organisations first founded in Britain). These transnational exchanges work in different directions. The modern interpretations of the three principles of *ahimsa*, *aparigraha* and *anekantvada*, for instance, could already be found in India decades before the YJI adopted the JWOL from North American Jain immigrants. Especially the younger generation makes increasingly use of transnational networks and there is an extensive variety in means of communication (such as internet discussion groups) which link Jains in India with Jains all over the world and brings about transformations not only in India. Some aspects of the Jain Vision 2020, when taken out of the North American background, certainly do not make too much sense in an Indian context. This, for instance, holds true for the issue of how to deal with interreligious marriages, which, though increasing in India, at present are still more common in the US. Furthermore, Indian Jains might have little reasons to "adopt the Jain Way of life to the modern North American Lifestyle" (http://www.jainlink.org?page=vision, p. 2). Nevertheless, young Jains in India also feel the need to adopt their tradition to the modern, globalised world, and the 'branding' of Jainism, symbolised in the 'three A's' of the JWOL and based on a modern re-use and reinterpretation of ancient Jain concepts, is one part of it.

## PHOTO CREDIT

All photographs reproducedin this chapter are by Sabine Scholz.

## BIBLIOGRAPHY

Banks, Marcus, 1991, "Orthodoxy and Dissent: Varieties of Religious Belief among Immigrant Gujarati Jains in Britain". In: Michael Carrithers and Caroline Humphrey (eds), *The Assembly of Listeners*: *Jains in Society*. Cambridge University Press, Cambridge, pp. 241–59.

———, 1992, *Organizing Jainism in India and England*. Clarendon Press, Oxford.

Bhattacharyya, Narendra Nath, 1999, *A Glossary of Indian Religious Terms and Concepts*. Manohar, New Delhi.

Carrithers, Michael and Caroline Humphrey (eds), 1991, *The Assembly of Listeners: Jains in Society*. Cambridge University Press, Cambridge.

Cort, John E., 2000 (July), "'Intellectual Ahimsa' Revisited: Jain Tolerance and Intolerance to Others". *Philosophy East and West*. Vol. 50, no. 3, pp. 324–47.

Dhruva, A. B., 1933, "Introduction". In: A. B. Dhruva (ed.), *Syadvadamanjari of Mallisena with the Anyayoga-Vyavaccheda of Hemacandra*. Bombay Sanskrit and Prakrit, Series 83, The Department of Public Instruction, Bombay, pp. xiii–cxxv.

Dixit, K. K., 1978, *Early Jainism*. L. D. Institute of Indology, Ahmedabad.

Dundas, Paul, 1991, "The Digambara Jain Warrior". In: Michael Carrithers and Caroline Humphrey (eds), *The Assembly of Listeners: Jains in Society*. Cambridge University Press, Cambridge, pp. 169–86.

———, 2002, *The Jains*, Second revised edition. Routledge, London and New York.

Jaini, Jagmander Lal, 1921 (November), "The Jainas of India and Dr. H. S. Gour's 'Hindu Code'". *The Jaina Gazette*. Vol. XVII, no.11, pp. 293–305.

Jaini, Padmanabh S., 1979, *The Jaina Path of Purification*. University of California Press, Berkeley, Los Angeles and London.

Kumar, Bhuvanendra, 1996, *Jainism in America*. Jain Humanities Press, Mississauga, Columbus and Tempe.

Kurien, Prema, 2004 (August), "Mulitculturalism, Immigrant Religion, and Diasporic Nationalism: The Development of an American Hinduism". *Social Problems*. Vol. 51, no. 3, pp. 362–85.

Matilal, Bimal Krishna, 1981, *The Central Philosophy of Jainism (Anekanta-Vada)*. L. D. Institute of Indology, Ahmedabad.

Mehta, J. K., 1929 (July, August and September), "Religion of Mahatma Gandhi". *The Jaina Gazette*. Vol. XXV, nos. 7, 8 and 9, pp. 199–202.

Upadhyaya Munishri Kamakumar Nandi, n.d., *Fundamental Features of Jainism*. No publisher stated, Delhi.

Wiley, Kristie L., 2006, *The A to Z of Jainism*. Vision Books, New Delhi, Mumbai and Hyderabad.

Williams, Raymond Brady, 1998 (July), "Asian Indian and Pakistani Religions in the United States". In: *Annals of the American Academy of Political and Social Science*. Vol. 558, Americans and Religions in the Twenty-First Century, pp. 178–95.

Young Jains of India (ed.), 2005, *Progress Through Jain Way of Life*. Indore Convention, 23–25 December 2005, Program Booklet.

## Internet Sources

http://www.censusindia.gov.in/Census_Data_2001/Census_Data_Online/Social_and_cultural/Religion.aspx (accessed on 04 July 2007).

http://www.guardian.co.uk/world/2002/oct/30/religion.uk16 (accessed on 29 April 2009).

http://www.jaina.org (accessed on 29 June 2008).

http://www.jainlink.org/?page=Vision (accessed on 30 June 2008).

http://www.jainology.org/?q=aboutus (accessed on 29 April 2009).

http://www.jainology.org/?q=en/resources/Jain-Organisations-In-the-UK (accessed on 29 April 2009).

http://www.yjindia.org (accessed on 09 June 2008).

http://www.yjponline.org (accessed on 26 June 2008).

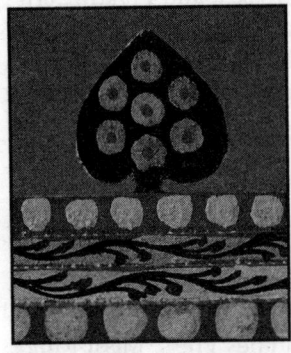

# Chapter 14

# ICONS, NATIONS AND RE-USE

## MARIANNE, FRANCE AND BHARAT MATA, INDIA

### BY SUBRATA K. MITRA AND LION KÖNIG

## INTRODUCTION

Seen through the eyes of ordinary folks, nations and states are doppelgaengers: for both take turns at nurturing and disciplining. These different and reciprocal functions require states and nations to be present visually, in concrete form even while keeping their abstract aura intact. Like the term *body politic* suggests,[1] these abstract entities must have a corpus with which ordinary people can identify, and a soul that, in some sense, will also be a collective embodiment of their individual quest for a larger, more enduring self that transcends the

---

[1] The well-known image on the title page of the first edition of Thomas Hobbes' *Leviathan*, which shows the state as being the sum of its people, underlines this point.

merely mortal.[2] In his discussion of the evolution of Marianne—icon of the French Revolution of 1789—Joseph Jurt speaks of the "bodiless Republic", which the French Revolution created (2005: 113f). Having destroyed the omnipresence of the authoritarian monarch, the new republic was dependent on community symbols and an imagery of its own to create and uphold a new identity. In a monarchic society, the sovereign has a face, the monarch *embodies* the rule. Jurt emphasises with regard to the body politic how it is immune to mortality—even if the *body personal* passes away.

Icons, like Marianne in France and Bharat Mata in India, are attempts at devising cultural symbols—*imaginaires*[3]—which offer a sense of collective identity as well as a frame of collective action. Icons are simplifying mechanisms that impart a sense of unity and coherence to an idea which is far more complex because candidates for iconisation are multiple; icon makers vary from artists and statesmen to rabble rousers and placardists. The whole process of artistic production of a national icon is deeply political and the path to the iconic status is marked with invention, fortuitous turn of circumstance and re-use[4] of revered images from the past.

On the basis of the analytic narratives of 'Marianne' in France and 'Bharat Mata' in India, we explore in this essay the general theme of icons as part of the project of nation-building. Our approach is based on the core assumption that power requires legitimacy and that legitimacy, in order to be real, has to respond

---

[2] There is a range of literature which discusses the visualisation of the modern state on the basis of Hobbes' central work. Horst Bredekamp, for example, is concerned with the core question of why Hobbes could not imagine the state without picturing it; see Bredekamp (1999, 2006). A work which specifically addresses the construction of the body politic and its role in state formation is Albrecht Koschorke. *Der fiktive Staat: Konstruktionen des politische Körpers in der Geschichte Europas* (2007). For a politically biased analysis of the role of political symbolism in Hobbes, see: Carl Schmitt, *Der Leviathan in der Staatslehre des Thomas Hobbes: Sinn und Fehlschlag eines politischen Symbols* (1938). Probably influenced by Hobbes' writing, Samuel von Pufendorf in his 1690 publication, *The Present State of Germany, or, an Account of the Extent, Rise, Form, Wealth, Strength, Weaknesses and Interests of that Empire,* describes the state as a 'body' and personifies it. Pufendorf writes that "there is nothing left for us to say but that Germany is an *Irregular body, and like some mis-shapen Monster,* if, at least, it be measured by the common Rules of Politicks [sic] and Civil Prudence [...]" (emphasis added).

[3] See *What Good are the Arts?* by John Carey (2005) for an appreciation of iconic art as neither 'high art' with its remit of beauty and spirituality nor as merely representational. Its message is directly political. "What could make it a work of art has nothing in its physical makeup but how it was regarded, how it was thought of" (Carey 2005: 17). See also Roland Barthes, *Mythologies* (1995). Roland Barthes describes mythologies in terms of social imaginaries that are anchored in social reality but have an abstract dimension that engages the imagination of people and spaces beyond the immediate context.

[4] The research on 're-use', emanating from art history, has gradually found its way into the larger field of social investigation. See Julia A. B. Hegewald & Subrata K. Mitra (2008).

to deeply seated needs for comfort, nurture, security, material ambition and the transcendence of all these in a larger purpose. Nations and states, to scale the heights they aim at, have to find a place in the 'hearts and minds' of the people. Despite their claim to a genuinely pure form of the nation, icons, themselves, carry elements of the past and as such are themselves mostly hybrid creations. Their hybridity is an attempt to overcome the contradictions inherent in the 'imagined community'[5] and dichotomy of the 'self and the other' a positive appreciation of syncretism (Fludernik 1998: 10). Successful iconisation is conditional on the creation of a 'third space' between the dominant and the oppressed.[6] The icon makers are avid re-users, shaping, borrowing and transforming the past into new forms and churning them out in large numbers for mass consumption.

We explore this theme through an analysis of the connected issues of why and how national allegories are brought into the public sphere, which social and political relevance these images have and whether or not the meaning of national allegories can change.

## VISUALISING THE NATION

Iconisation is a quintessentially political act which seeks to convey a message to a heterogeneous multitude in the most effective way possible. In a context

[5] In his concept of the 'imagined community', Benedict Anderson (1983) has anticipated the debate on the positive and constructive understandings of reality.

[6] Homi K. Bhabha defines the 'Third Space' in the following words:

The production of meaning requires that these two spaces be mobilised and the passage to a Third Space, which represents both the general conditions of language and the specific implication of the utterance in the performative and the institutional strategy of which it cannot 'in itself' be conscious [...] The meaning of the utterance is quite literally neither the one nor the other. This ambivalence is emphasised when we realise that there is no way that the contents of this proposition will reveal the structure of its positionality; no way that context can be mimetically read off from the content. (Bhabha 1994: 36)

With regard to the functional utility of the Third Space as an epistemological tool, he notes that:

[...] a politics of social difference [that] is genuinely articulatory in its understanding that to be discursively represented and socially representative—to assume an effective political identity or image—the limits and conditions of specularity have to be exceeded and erased by the inscription of otherness. To revise the problem of global space from the post-colonial perspective is to move the location of culture difference away from the space of demographic plurality to the borderline negotiations of cultural translation. (Bhabha 1994: 223, cited in Fludernik 1998: 49)

of political turmoil, a simple and powerful image can capture the attention of a mass audience more effectively than an elaborate treatise. If the intended audience happens to be divided on the lines of literacy, language, class, political idiom or geographic space, then visual publicity can immensely enhance the speed of communication. Icons are understood across language barriers because they 'function' without verbal language.[7]

Of course, icons 'work' if they are well-chosen; the icon-maker is sometimes well served in re-using past icons, or visual material susceptible to iconisation. Not surprisingly, not all icons survive and develop over the years. Regime change and the ensuing political turmoil often provide the right context for iconisation. In a revolutionary context, as we shall see below in the case of France, icons are often chosen by the people (that is, from below) and then cleverly adopted by politicians (that is, from above). This does not preclude elite chicanery where images produced above are passed on to the layers below as if they were the genuine vernacular item; the fate of the sickle and hammer and other icons of socialist realism in the successor states of the Soviet Union following the fall of communism, and the swastika in Nazi-Germany testify to the all too frequent attempts at fakery when it comes to iconisation.

Political iconography is a relatively new field at the interface of social sciences, art and cultural theory. In 2001, Sumathi Ramaswamy announced a 'visual turn' in modern Indian studies.[8] Now, as we edge towards the end of the first decade of the twenty-first century, it is widely believed that patriotic art has an important argument to make, an argument which may not necessarily repeat the one of the official verbal archive. Images now play a crucial role in understanding how the abstract nation state comes to have the presence and power to command citizens' lives to the point of death. It resonates with Martin Heidegger, who claimed that "the fundamental event of the modern age is the conquest of the world as picture."[9]

Until very recently though, political icons were "pariahs of the academic world"—ignored, even belittled by both art historians and political scientists. Political icons were seen as "inconsequential ephemera not worth noticing, let alone collecting and analyzing" (Neumayer & Schelberger 2008: vii). Political scientists have interpreted myths and political symbols as deprivations and as

---

[7] Julia Hegewald, personal communication, 21 August 2009.

[8] See Ramaswamy (2008: vii). The 'visual turn' or 'iconic turn' as formulated by Gottfried Boehm in 1994 denotes a scholarly and intellectual practice that appreciates the structural character of pictorials. Pictures, it is argued, structure the way of thinking of their observer. In a move away from the predominant logocentrism of philosophy, the American cultural theorist, William J. T. Mitchell, announced a 'pictorial turn' in 1992 with the aim of not merely thinking *about* pictures but rather thinking with the help of pictures (Mitchell 1992).

[9] This quotation has been cited in Ramaswamy (2003: 153).

a kind of a manipulative policy of compensation (Bruchhausen 1999: 1). Due to a change in perspective and increasing, albeit still little, research in the field, it is now even assumed that a new narrative might emerge, which "may be quite disjunct from the familiar stories of a non-visual history" (Pinney 2004: 8) and that myths and symbols are "important media when it comes to forging identity and national consciousness" (Bruchhausen 1999: 1). However, among the modalities deployed to cultivate love and longing for the nation, the pictorial has been least recognised or analysed. Yet, recent scholarship shows the important role played by images in understanding how the abstract nation state comes to have the enlivened presence and power to command mass allegiance. Some scholars now even claim that "political symbols or symbolic politics cannot be considered as a phenomenon of the artistic and literary domain alone but are used as effective strategies in the struggle for national consciousness and identity as well as in the political claim to power" (Bruchhausen 1999: 2). Klaus von Beyme suggests that symbolism and iconography have a definite political as well as social relevance. He speaks of an "optical integration of the people"[10] and pleads for a sound history of the effects of political symbolism.

With regard to the role of icons in nation-building, insights from the fields of cultural studies prove to be particularly helpful. Critical theory has dealt with questions which political science has not dared to ask. What the latter takes for granted, the former ponders about. One of the representatives of the critical camp, Jan Assmann, notes in an eminent analysis of the cultural memory that every culture develops something which could be referred to as its 'connective structure', which bridges and unites in two dimensions: the social and the time dimension. The 'connective structure' ties a person to their fellow human beings by functioning as a 'symbolic world of meaning'[11] which creates a common space of experience, expectation and action. Furthermore, it also ties the past to the present by shaping decisive experiences and memories and keeping them alive. It encloses, in a continuously developing present, images and stories of times long passed, and thereby is about memory of the past and hope of the future (Assmann 2007: 16). National icons, create, in a sense, an idealised past as well as a strong present through which their creators hope to be able to mould the shape of the future.

As we learn from Walter Benjamin, it is the victors who tell the story of events past as only the victorious have the power to decide what is retained and what

---

[10] See Beyme (1998: 241). The quotation provided above is a translation from the German by Lion König.

[11] Assmann here takes up what Berger and Luckmann have termed 'symbolische Sinnwelt'. See Berger and Luckmann (2007), quoted in Assmann (2007: 16).

is forgotten. Not surprisingly, political icons signify particular constructions of the past from the perspective specific to their power and time. An aura of contestation naturally trails the triumphant march of icons, endowing the past with a sense of uncertainty and the present with a veneer of anxiety. Warring factions and divided faiths might accept an icon to tide over a particularly difficult patch—Hindus and Muslims marching to the unified song of the nation in 1930s India, offering joint opposition to the English—but this contingency robs it of any claim to eternity. Icons hold ajar a trapdoor to the past (Naipaul 1977: 10).[12] They come and go, keeping pace with the changing currents of history.

Before turning to the actual cases, it needs to be established what the images under consideration technically really are—symbols or allegories? According to reference works, such as M. H. Abrams' *Glossary of Literary Terms*, a symbol is marked by its clear and definite character, while an allegory only makes an allusion; as opposed to the symbol, the meaning of the allegory is not fixed. As Samuel Taylor Coleridge put it, "an allegory is but a translation of abstract notions into a picture-language […] on the other hand a symbol [...] is characterised by a translucence of the special in the individual, or of the general in the especial" (Coleridge 1816 cited in Abrams 2005: 313). What we are dealing with in the case of Marianne and Bharat Mata are, according to Coleridge's definition, allegories. The abstract, that is, the nation (-state) is translated into the concrete picture-language of the mother figure. The meaning of allegories, as von Bruchhausen outlines using the examples of Marianne and Germania is variable. She refers to these allegories as 'projection surfaces' (Bruchhausen 1999: 2) whose meaning is not fixed and which therefore encourage political elites to interpret them and make them widely acceptable.[13]

Most Western states have a national allegory. They all came up during precarious times they had to go through. 'Germania', the national allegory of Germany, was famously painted by Philipp Veit in 1848, the year of the German Revolution (see Plate 14.1). The painting, now in the *Germanisches Nationalmuseum* in Nuernberg, shows a woman in an upright pose, freed from shackles which lie on the ground next to her right foot. She holds a sword in

---

[12] The past is remembered just as it is contested depending on the ideological angle from which one looks at it. That the past influences the present is well known. The important point here is to recognise that the present influences the past; for what we recognise in an unspecific past as definite depends on who we are and what we want to achieve throughout recounting of the past. The Indian historian Romila Thapar has put it this way: "Historical explanation [...] creates an awareness of how the past impinges on the present, as well as the reverse" (2002: xix).

[13] Compare also the approaches of Hans-Georg Gadamer (1975) and Mona Ozouf (1977), discussed in greater detail in Bruchhausen (1999: 17).

her right hand as a sign of her ability to fight and the revolutionary flag, a symbol of the longing for German unity, which was later to become the flag of the German Federal Republic, black, red, gold in her left hand. The oak leaves wreath on her head symbolizes loyalty and faithfulness, the olive branch on the sword shows the love for peace and the sun which is rising behind her is indicative of the new age that is dawning. The figure of Uncle Sam pointing with his index finger at potential new soldiers from the famous recruiting poster of World War I is widely known. Created in 1812 in the war against England, the allegory is another example of the iconisation of the nation at times of deep crisis. Similarly, John Bull, the British equivalent of Uncle Sam is depicted on recruiting posters of World War I. Wearing a waistcoat which shows the Union Jack, the British flag, he is standing in front of a line of British soldiers, pointing his finger at the spectator, in the same manner as Uncle Sam does and asks "Who's absent? Is it you?" The figure is named after John Arbuthnot's satire *The History of John Bull*, written in 1727. Britain is a rather special case in this respect as it is a nation with two allegories which are used interchangeably, namely, John Bull, and Britannia, who resembles figures of Greek mythology wearing a Greek helmet, and carrying a trident and shield, which shows the Union Jack.

## THE FRENCH REVOLUTION AND THE ICONISATION OF MARIANNE

France provides a very well researched case when it comes to the national allegory. 'Marianne' has been made manifest in numerous depictions as famous artists like Eugène Delacroix and Honoré Daumier have taken on the subject and have contributed to the popularity and fame of the image (see Plate 14.2). Delacroix's painting is often referred to as the most famous image of Marianne, as it was the first work of art that freed the allegory from her original social indifference, placed it within a revolutionary tradition and thereby gave it a sociopolitical dimension (Bruchhausen 1999: 118).

Scholars have argued over the origin of the name; why Marianne and not Françoise, Mireille or Madeleine, as the French Embassy asks on their website?[14] Some people thought it came from the sixteenth-century Jesuit Mariana; others thought it was the image of the wife of the politician Jean Reubell. According to an anecdote, in 1797 when seeking a pleasant name for the new Republic, Paul de Barras, one of the members of the *Directoire*, during an evening at Reubell's house, asked his hostess' name: 'Marie-Anne', she replied. 'Perfect', Barras

---

[14] This can be accessed at: http://ambafrance-us.org/spip.php?article619.

exclaimed. "It is a short and simple name which befits the Republic just as much as yourself, Madame."[15]

It is certain that 'Marianne' was a very common name in seventeenth-century France and it was also the name of a radically left secret society. The first written mention of the name of Marianne to designate the Republic is said to have appeared in August 1792 in Puylaurens in the Tarn department near Toulouse. At that time, people used to sing a song in the Provencal dialect by the poet Guillaume Lavabre, entitled "Garisou de Mariano" or "La guerison de Marianne", Marianne's recovery, in which the female figure represents the French Republic.[16]

There has also been an extensive discussion of why the national allegory of France, like most national allegories with the exception of the one of the United States, is female. Again, various explanations are given: the female body, it is claimed, is closest to Plato's idea of beauty. Also, in Indo-Germanic languages, most virtues are feminine. It is further suggested by some scholars that the male is always part of the political action; the female on the other hand symbolises the detachment from real conflicts and therefore has a potential to unite. A very convincing argument is that the nation, which is perceived as having existed ever since requires some kind of 'naturalisation'. If the nation is seen as natural, not as constructed, then it is possible to visualise the nation as female. Feminists on the other hand suggest that the conception of the nation as female enables a 'masculinist' relationship to take place.[17] It encourages the male citizen to "view the national territory as a vulnerable woman who needs their protection and as a mother who had to be rescued through heroism and sacrifice" (Ramaswamy 2001: 109, 97–114)—this will be particularly visible in the Indian case.

The history of Marianne dates back to the thirteenth century: in 1274 there is a reference to a 'Domina Franca' in the medieval manual *Grandes chroniques*. Nearly 300 years later, in 1558, the French cardinal, diplomat and poet Jean du Bellay personifies France as a mother. He writes: "France, mère des arts, des armes et des lois, tu m'as nourri longtemps du lait de ta mamelle."[18] On 25 September 1792, the seal of the new state was created and the image of the monarch was replaced by the one of Marianne.[19] One year later, in 1793, the

---

[15] See the webpage of the French embassy: http://ambafrance-us.org/spip.php?article619.

[16] See the webpage of the French embassy: http://ambafrance-us.org/spip.php?article619.

[17] Sumathi Ramaswamy (2001) provides a list of feminist geographers who have put that claim forward. These include: Catherine Nash (1993: 39–51), Gilian Rose (1993), Alison Blunt and Gilian Rose (1994).

[18] See du Bellay cited in Bruchhausen (1999: 104). The phrase can be translated as: "France, mother of arts, of arms, and of laws. You have nourished me for a long time with milk from your breast."

[19] The description of the new seal was as follows: "la France sous les traits d'une femme vetue à l'antique, debout, tenant de la main droite une pique surmontée du bonnet Phrygian ou bonnet de la liberté" (Agulhon & Bonte 1992: 17, cited in Jurt 2005: 119).

city council of Paris suggested to use Marianne as a tool in the battle against Catholicism and as a worldly counterweight to Godmother Mary. Marianne was increasingly depicted as a mother nurturing the young Republic. Honoré Daumier painted a corpulent Marianne with muscular arms and androgynous build who is suckling two children on her heavy breasts (see Plate 14.3). A third child is sitting in front of her, reading a book. The Republic thus is presented as nourishing and instructing her children. This painting has been used as an example of the motherly type of Marianne (as opposed to the forceful, martial type created by Delacroix) (Jurt 2005: 122).[20]

Despite these two alternatives from which the Republic could choose according to the occasion, Marianne had to assert herself against rival images. The figure of the Greek demigod Hercules was one of them and was favoured by those who demanded a more radical interpretation of the Republic—a similarity to the Indian case as will be shown below.[21]

Daumier's painting adds, according to Bruchhausen a third variant, a liberal-civic Marianne to the two then already existing ones, the popular revolutionary and the official *déesse* (Bruchhausen 1999: 128), the goddess.

The three children are meant to represent the three core values on which the French Republic is founded—liberty, equality and fraternity.[22] The image of the nursing mother is also a reference to Rousseau as it implies care, equality in nature, free individuals, a denial of the corporative state and a renewal of nature (Bruchhausen 1999: 129). But Marianne is not only depicted in these paintings, she is virtually omnipresent; she can be found on stamps, coins, on the former Franc banknotes and as busts in official buildings.[23] Her silhouette also forms the central part of the official government logo, which the French Embassy to the United States refers to as a:

> ... new 'identifier' created by the French government. [...] It will appear on all material—brochures, internal and external publications, publicity campaigns, letter headings, business cards—emanating from the government, starting with the various ministries [...] and the Préfectures, the decentralised government departments in the regions and Départements.

---

[20] For a more detailed analysis of the political art of the French Republic with a specific discussion of Daumier and Delacroix, see Clark (1999).

[21] A term which has been used in the German literature to refer to these complementary symbols is 'Erinnerungskonkurrenzen', which is best translated as 'competition of memories' (Knabel 2005: 12).

[22] See also Bruchhausen (1999: 129) where she claims that the three children represent the secularised Trinity of the revolutionary parole as well as the enlightenment.

[23] See Winfried Speitkamp (1997). The author distinguishes between three types of carriers of symbolic meaning ('Symboltraeger'): those of the first degree like monuments, national anthems and flags, which make a direct statement, those of the second degree like coins, notes, stamps and street names that demand an own symbolic building up and those of the third type: objects which do not explicitly make a claim for symbolic meaning but which become a symbol, like in the French case the Bastille (cited in Jurt 2005: 115 f).

The French Embassy on their homepage reports that this is done to unify government public relations, but it is also designed "to give a more accessible image to a State currently seen as abstract, remote and archaic, all the more essential in that French citizens express high expectations of the State. The logo chosen, 'federating and mobilising', offers security and optimism, not forgetting patriotic pride."[24] "Blue-white-red, Marianne, Liberté–Egalité–Fraternité, the Republic: these powerful symbols represent France and its values,"[25] as the authors continue to stress.

The omnipresence of the image is furthered not only by the fact that a bronze sculpture of Marianne overlooks the Place de la Nation in Paris symbolising the 'Triumph of the Republic'; her portrait is modelled after French celebrities like Brigitte Bardot, Catherine Deneuve, Laetita Casta—the celebrity from France's rebel province of Corsica. In 2002, however, a new Marianne was born. She does not have the features of a famous French woman but those of an anonymous 'beurette', a female of North African descent. She was discovered by a scouting agent looking for a model who would symbolise a modern, multiethnic France with a place in it for the more than five million French citizens of Muslim faith. One year later, in 2003, the high-profile association Ni Putes Ni Soumises[26] (NPNS) organised an exhibition to ethnicize France's female symbol. On the columns of the Palais Bourbon, the home of the French National Assembly, a series of fourteen photographs was displayed. In an "orchestrated performance of ethnicity" (Winter 2009: 240), the pictures showed young women, a third of which were of North African background, all of them artistically posing in head or head-and-shoulder shots, draped in Republican imagery: the Phrygian cap with a miniature version of the French flag or a *cocarde* in an attempt to officially acknowledge the changed and changing citizenry of France (Winter 2009).

## BHARAT MATA AND INDIA'S STRUGGLE FOR INDEPENDENCE

The Indian case is different from the French counterpart in many ways. The French Revolution of 1789 was led by the dissident Parisian bourgeoisie, elements of the aristocracy and the mob against the church and the King. It spread from Paris to the provinces and eventually led the French emblem beyond the

---

[24] The wording has been taken from the website of the French Embassy (http://ambafrance-us.org/spip.php?article619).
[25] See: http://ambafrance-us.org/spip.php?article619.
[26] The name of the association can be translated as 'Neither Whores Nor Submissives' to stress the aspect of women's empowerment and as a countermove to the earlier Mariannes who contributed to the sexualisation of the allegory.

frontiers of France, proclaiming the Rights of Man[27] as the symbol of a new age. The Indian struggle for independence from colonial rule drew on the religiosity of the masses, first in the worship of Ganesh and Kali as figures of power and collective identity, and eventually, under Gandhi's leadership, reaching its peak in the identification of the anti-colonial movement with *satyagraha*—a personal quest for truth and purity of purpose. The revolutionary mobs in France held religion and politics apart; in India, their close links were never denied. The French drew on revolutionary terror as the ultimate argument of politics; Indians were told to abjure violence, even at the risk of delaying the coming of Independence.[28]

In contrast to the implication of Marianne for revolution and nation-building in France, the significance of Bharat Mata in India's national struggle for independence is under-researched and remains sketchy. It is not clear when the concept of presenting India as a goddess appeared for the first time (Plate 14.4). However:

> ... the cult of the mother goddess in India[29] existed before the introduction of the Western model of the modern nation-state and the elaboration of an infrastructure for visual mass media around 1900. (Brosius 2005: 242)

Then, with the rise of nationalism and the spread of the popular media in around 1900, "mother goddesses and warrior saints were reinterpreted and married to each other in the dynamic narrative of national sovereignty" (Brosius 2005: 242). Because of this 'career', it is claimed that they would later acquire "a new relevance for post-colonial Hindu nationalism" (Brosius 2005: 242). The few scholars who have dealt with the topic of political iconography in India,[30] most of them with a background in anthropology, have argued that "Bharat Mata came to be particularly attributed with the efficacy of a war-goddess that was consequently related to both patriotic self-empowerment and sacred rituals of human sacrifice" (Brosius 2005: 244).

---

[27] Thomas Paine's *The Rights of Man: Being an Answer to Mr. Burke's Attack on the French Revolution* was published in two parts in 1791 and 1792, and is one of the most famous vindications of the events of 1789. It and shows how quickly the ideals of the French Revolution travelled to other parts of the world.

[28] Mahatma Gandhi is credited with having cancelled the national struggle after the Chaurichaura incident in 1922 where the mob set fire to a police station, burning to death twenty-two policemen. Although some, like Jawaharlal Nehru, had reservations about the wisdom of his decision, the Congress party formally approved of it (Brown 1989: 167).

[29] The tradition of mother goddesses dates back several millennia. Simple terracotta figures from the third millennium BCE Indus Valley culture represent mother—or fertility goddesses. These have an unbroken continuity via particularly well-known pieces from the Maurya and Sunga dynasties to modern day village art. Julia Hegewald, personal communication, 18 September 2009.

[30] Sumathi Ramaswamy, Christiane Brosius, Erwin Neumayer and Christine Schelberger certainly range among the most cited scholars in this field.

Today, we are witnessing a re-use of Bharat Mata by the Hindutva move-ment as a powerful 'wish-image', especially in her association with Hindu god-desses like Kali or Durga (see Plate 14.5)—this derived from the time of British colonisation (Brosius 2005: 243). Hindu nationalists like Golwalkar dedicated homage to the mother, suggesting that love for the nation could transform the weak into firm, iron men (Brosius 2005: 243f). Indeed, Bharat Mata has become a popular fetish object in the present-day Hindu nationalist movement. From the 1920s onwards, the map of 'Akhanda Bharat', the undivided India has become a regular feature of Bharat Mata's iconography. It is argued that this facilitates her representation as a "goddess of territory and polity" (Ramaswamy 2001). The photograph reprinted below (Plate 14.6) was taken in the central office of the Bharatiya Janata Party in New Delhi in March 2009. They show Hindu New Year greetings and the depiction of Bharat Mata in front of a map of Akhanda Bharat on the left—a piece of evidence for the frequent use of the image in the Hindu nationalist context.[31]

Taking up the term 'scapes' introduced into the field of media studies by Arjun Appadurai,[32] it was Sumathi Ramaswamy who spoke of 'bodyscapes', of personalised maps[33] and a replacement of maps by icons and human bodies in the shape of the allegory. In almost all bodyscapes, Bharat Mata's apparel and especially her sari plays a crucial role in producing and claiming national space. It invariably extends to cover pre-Partition India, even in the 'bodyscapes' pro-duced after 1947, and also in recent years in Hindu-nationalist cartography. In this context, a word should also be said as to the colour-coding: Bharat Mata generally wears red, the colour of auspiciousness in Hindu ritual symbolism. Also in the literature by Indian thinkers and politicians, India is referred to as a nurturing mother as the following two excerpts from writings of Jawaharlal Nehru and V. D. Savarkar will illustrate. In his major work, *Hindutva: Who Is a Hindu?*, Savarkar praises India as follows:

She is the richly endowed daughter of God—This is our Motherland. Her rivers are deep and perennial. Her land is yielding to the plough and her fields loaded

---

[31] McKean (1996), Brosius (1997, 2005, 2006), Ahmed-Ghosh (2003), Kovacs (2004) provide further valuable insights into the topic of the Hindu nationalist use of the Bharat Mata imagery.

[32] What Arjun Appadurai referred to as 'scapes' are 'dynamic landscapes' which he defines as "deeply perspectival constructs, inflected by the historical, linguistic and political situated-ness of different sorts of actors" (Appadurai 1997: 17).

[33] The veneration of a map as a sacred image is evocative of sacred space in Hindu mythology. In a way, there are some earlier examples of this in religious maps of cities, which, at times, show a goddess below the city map, often with the main temple of a town located above her womb. There are examples of such maps from several south Indian cities (for example, Shrirangam) and also in connection with Lhasa in Tibet (where it is a demoness). Here, the ground is perceived as sacred, as the body of a goddess or demoness and the geography of the city is imbued with sacred meanings, the city is alive and divine. Julia Hegewald, personal communication, 18 September 2009.

with golden harvests. Her necessaries of life are few and a genial nature yields them all almost for the asking. Rich in her fauna, rich in her flora, she knows she owes it all to the immediate source of light and heat—The Sun. […] Verily Hind is the richly endowed daughter of God. (Savarkar 1949: 109)

In his *Discovery of India*, Nehru writes:

Sometimes as I reached a gathering, a great roar of welcome would greet me: *Bharat Mata ki Jai*—Victory to Mother India. I would ask them unexpectedly what they meant by this cry, who was this Bharat Mata, […] whose victory they wanted? My question would amuse them and surprise them, and then, not knowing what exactly to answer, they would look at each other and at me. I persisted in my questioning. At last a vigorous Jat, […] would say that it was the *dharti*, the good earth of India that they meant. What earth? Their particular village patch or all the patches in the district or province, or in the whole of India? And so question and answer went on, till they would impatiently ask me to tell them all about it. I would endeavour to do so and explain that India was all this that they had thought, but it was much more. The mountains and the rivers of India, and the forests and the broad fields, which gave us food were all dear to us, but what counted ultimately were the people of India, people like them and me, who were spread out all over this vast land. Bharat Mata, Mother India, was essentially these millions of people, and victory to her meant victory to these people. You are parts of this Bharat Mata I told them, you are in a manner yourselves Bharat Mata, and as this idea slowly soaked into their brains, their eyes would light up as if they had made a great discovery. (Nehru 1946: 58–61)

Below is an episode of the time around 1905 when the Indian lawyer and politician K. M. Munshi met Aurobindo Ghosh and asked him:

'How can one become patriotic?' With a disarming smile, Aurobindo pointed at a wall map of India and said: 'Do you see this map? It is not a map, but the portrait of *Bharat-mata*: its cities and mountains, rivers and jungles form her physical body. All her children are her nerves, large and small ... Concentrate on Bharat as a living mother, worship her with the nine-fold *bhakti*.'[34]

Rabindranath Tagore in his work *Ghare Bhaire* (The Home and the World) written in the years of 1915 and 1916 underlines the importance of political icons for the nation. Sandip, one of the male protagonists addresses Bimala, the heroine, with the following words:

Have I not told you that, in you, I visualise the *Shakti* [the power] of our country? The geography of a country is not the whole truth. No one can give up his life for a map! When I see you before me, then only do I realise how lovely my country is.

---

[34] This quotation has been taken from J. H. Dave et al. (n.d.), cited in Ramaswamy (2001: 97–114).

By the time Tagore wrote these lines, the practice of imagining India as a female entity had become a habit among patriotic Indians. Sandip tells his beloved that if he fell fighting:

> It shall not be on the dust of some map-made land, but on a lovingly spread skirt [...] like that of the earthen-red *sari* you wore the other day, with a broad blood-red border. Can I ever forget it? Such are the visions which give vigour to life, and joy to death!

As already indicated above, the history of Bharat Mata does not date back too long. The origin of the icon lies in a related figure, Banga Mata, Mother Bengal. In 1905, the undivided Bengal was painted by Abanindranath Tagore as the Goddess Banga Mata to symbolise the unity of the country against the dissection. In the goddess' four hands the four symbols, a sheet of cloth, a sheaf of rice, a book and a rosary signify agricultural, industrial, as well as religious and intellectual well-being. Although the development cannot be traced in great detail, it can be said that when Bengal was divided into several new states, the painted deity took on the mantle of Bharat Mata, which stood for the self-sufficiency of the Indian nation in the making. What is problematic with this image is that it works through a religious symbolism, and the early nationalist pictures, for example, the Holy Cow prints sometimes served to exclude or even antagonise non-Hindu Indian communities. Some such prints were even banned for fear of inciting communal passion along the volatile Hindu–Muslim divide (Neumayer & Schelberger 2008: 38).

In the course of the nationalist movement, different depictions of Bharat Mata flourished. A 1937 image from Coimbatore shows:

> Bharat Mata wrapped in the tricolour of India. Her sari border is embroidered with the *charkha*, the spinning wheel, the symbol of the Congress Party. The deity encompasses the contours of the Indian map. Under her blessing hand are the multitude of Indian people, and in the foreground are assembled many of the famous leaders of the Independence movement. (Neumayer & Schelberger 2008: 47)

Among them, Mahatma Gandhi, Jawaharlal Nehru, and Rabindranath Tagore.

An undated photograph which is exposed at the Nehru Memorial Museum and Library in New Delhi shows a group of women and a young boy in Pune during the Civil Disobedience Movement holding a piece of cloth in front of them. Painted on it is Bharat Mata holding a trident in one of her hands. The picture is reprinted in *Visualizing Indian Women, 1875–1947* (Karlekar 2006). The editor has added the line: "Devotion to the nationalist cause was equal to serving one's mother, a filial duty" (Karlekar 2006: 90).

In the wake of drastic events, the new Republic had to face, Bharat Mata was again visualised. A painting by Sobha Singh from 1947 shows Mother India clad in the Indian flag and with a halo, which makes her appear holy and mystical, with the trident in her hand and with a roaring lion kicking the fairly large British crown into an abyss. The Ashoka pillar stands in the background. A similar imagery is again visible in a painting by an unknown artist from 1962, the year of the Indo-China War. The centre of the picture is occupied by the Ashoka pillar and Bharat Mata with a flag in her left hand and a sword in her right one leads four roaring lions against the Chinese dragon crawling in over the Himalayan border. Another category of Bharat Mata paintings are the 'martyr pictures'. A painting entitled *Subhash's Sacrifice* shows Subhas Chandra Bose offering his severed and still heavily bleeding head to 'the Mother'. To Bose's knees flow the equally severed heads of other prominent Indians who died for the nationalist cause, among them Bhagat Singh. Dated to circa 1950, Bharat Mata and her lion have subdued the 'British beast', depicted here in the form of a crocodile. Another painting from 1966 with the title *The Call of the Mother* shows Bharat Mata in the upper middle in front of the contours of the map of undivided India with Bhagat Singh and Subhas Chandra Bose kneeling on either side. Singh is offering her his severed head and Bose is saluting her. In the bottom part of the picture are two young soldiers, one male, one female, ready for combat. The Indian flag is planted on the snowy mountains of the Himalaya behind them.

According to Neumayer and Schelberger, such depictions of self-inflicted pain and sacrifice have a long tradition in Indian religious iconography. Similar themes were also known in European expressionist art at the turn of the nineteenth century (Neumayer & Schelberger 2008: 51). In India, the worship of terrorist martyrs was a singular strain in the political iconography of the early 1930s, fostered by the trial and hanging of Bhagat Singh and his comrades. Because of the popularity of these nationalists, their deeds are, from time to time, recalled by different political groups to emphasise their own patriotic credibility (Neumayer & Schelberger 2008: 49).

However, apart from the fierce and martial Bharat Mata there is also the loving, caring and nurturing one. A painting from 1948 by an unknown artist shows a smiling, four-armed Bharat Mata with the Indian flag in one hand and with a shell and a lotus flower in the other ones. A little Gandhi is sitting on her lap and she kindly caresses him with her hand. The question, whether there is such a thing as 'the real' Bharat Mata continues to be open. As Neumayer and Schelberger point out:

> … the diverse pictorial traditions of India made it difficult to find a symbol of national integrity acceptable to all. To worship a geographical map of India seemed to be a way out of the dilemma of finding a symbol for the motherland

without antagonising the religious sentiments averse to the idea of bowing before an image of an anthropomorphic god or goddess. One of the earliest and largest temples of Bharat Mata was established in 1936 in the city of Varanasi, where a large relief map of *Akhanda Bharat* […] lies enshrined. By this time, the practice of using a contour map of India to deify Bharat Mata had already gained popularity. (Neumayer & Schelberger 2008: 129)

However, the popularity seems to have declined rapidly. According to Ramaswamy, the temple (see Plate 14.7) is largely ignored by pilgrims to Varanasi:

> Today, the Bharat Mata Mandir wears an air of dismal abandon as it stands amidst the hustle and bustle of down-town Banares. The typical visitor to the temple to-day is more likely to be a foreign tourist rather than the Indian patriot, although local schools occasionally bring the young citizen to view the map and learn the country. (Ramaswamy 2006: 181)

Ramaswamy also reports a conversation with Shyam Das Singh, the manager of the temple, who claims that "if only there had been an anthropomorphic *murti* [image] in the temple, and not a mere map, then millions of Indians would come through its doors" (Ramaswamy 2006: 181). This, Ramaswamy goes on to conclude, offers a:

> … very telling lesson about the dilemmas of colonial and national modernity in India. This is a modernity where older practices of reverence [such as idola-try] have been rendered increasingly problematic, even an embarrassment, but new ones wrought to replace these ancient ways have proven to be inadequate. (Ramaswamy 2006: 182)

This would be an example for a failed attempt at the re-use of the concept of sacred geography. While the Bharat Mata iconography is an example of a heav-ily contested allegory and certainly inadequate to represent the whole of India in its religious diversity, it cannot be said to have been completely unused in the recent past. It has been used by the Hindu right to assemble their followers (see Plate 14.6).

Bharat Mata was challenged in the Tamil speaking parts of the subcontinent from the 1890s onwards by another goddess of polity, Tamilttay, Mother Tamil, which was a personification of the Tamil language, personified as goddess and mother. Bodyscapes of Mother Tamil have been circulated through various Tamil nationalist publications since the mid-1930s and have been, according to Ramaswamy (2001: 108), occasionally included in Tamil schoolbooks. Interest-ingly enough, "Mother Tamil cartographically lays claim to the entire subcon-tinent as she occupies the map of India, thereby challenging Mother India's hegemonic presence" (Ramaswamy 2001: 108f).

A development in Bharat Mata iconography was the painting by the Indian painter, Maqbool Fida Husain. The *Times of India* reports that in February 2006, Husain received much criticism after his painting entitled *Bharat Mata* became known to the public.[35] Husain then decided to withdraw the painting from the auction where the painting was up for sale and he made a public apology. Despite this apology, Husain faced censorship from the Government of India. Indian bureaucrats refused to allow his *Bharat Mata* to be publicly displayed because they feared public outroar if the painting was exhibited. Several nationalist groups vocally protested against Husain's work. This was, however, not the first time that a work of art by an Indian artist was seen as offensive by his fellow countrymen. A decade earlier, Husain produced a series of paintings depicting Hindu goddesses Saraswati and Draupadi in nude. The works attracted violent outrage and an angry mob ransacked his home in Mumbai. His work of art has been defended by politicians, 'progressive' Hindus and artists, who have pointed out the presence of nude sculptures and imagery in ancient Indian art and even on temples.

This reveals that India's national allegory has become part of the collective memory, which groups on the right guard and violently defend. The Sangh Parivar, a genuine term used to depict the broad spectrum of Hindu nationalist forces, attempt to formulate a specific India and a specific Indian culture, and by censoring what they perceive as subversive art, they set the limits in which this art can exist. As an insightful interview with an artist affiliated to the Sangh Parivar reveals, an expression of Hindu nationalist ideology in the artwork is preferred over artistic imagination and creativity.[36]

## COMPARING FRANCE AND INDIA: UNCERTAIN PRESENT, UNEASY PASTS

This chapter has shown that 'bodyscapes' and national allegories serve to enliven an abstract idea and transform the nation into an intensely human place, a homeland and a motherland. They facilitate the filial attachment of the

---

[35] The painting shows a nude female figure whose body marks the contours of Akhand Bharat.

[36] Satyanarayan Maurya who paints New Year Cards and cartoons for Hindu nationalist organisations is quoted with the words:

> When I do work for the nation, I think that I am worshipping Ram, Hanuman, and Shiva, and Bharat Mata [...] I am inspired by my ideology. I became an artist later on. I can't forget my ideology [...] My ideology means that I worship my country [...] as my Motherland [...] *I am a national artist* [...]. (Emphasis in original) See Brosius (2007: 178)

citizen to national territory, producing sentiments of longing and belonging that a geographical map cannot possibly generate. Therefore, symbolic politics cannot be considered as a phenomenon of the artistic and literary domain alone but as something that is used as an effective strategy in the struggle for national consciousness and identity as well as in the political claim to power.

In comparison, it can be said that the developments of both 'Marianne' and 'Bharat Mata' were neither linear nor free from controversy. Where Marianne appears solidly ensconced in the French soil, the political stock of Bharat Mata rises and falls depending on the temporal context, bringing back memories of lost battles for unity and continuing strife over the ownership of the high moral ground of India's unfolding nationhood. There are more differentiating factors than uniting ones between the two allegories. While Bharat Mata is often depicted as a deity and has after all emerged from a religious background of the cults of mother goddesses,[37] Marianne is a strictly secular image, albeit one that has replaced Mother Mary and has transferred some of her duties to a worldly context. Also as far as the national reach is concerned, the Indian allegory is restricted to the north of the country while her French counterpart has a nationwide reach. Still, the question whether Marianne is equally esteemed in parts of the country which like to stress their particular identity, like Corsica and Brittany, remains open. What can be said though is that Marianne does not have to cope with any antagonists comparable to the ones Mother India has to cope with. The pre-independence rivals of Mother India, namely, 'Mother Bengal' (Banga Mata) and 'Mother Tamil' (Tamilttay) continue to have a surreptitious existence, in the form of linguistic and cultural boundaries which facilitated the strengthening of regional identity and consciousness after the reorganisation of Indian states in the 1950s.

In her discussion of the effects of semantic ambiguities that national allegories inevitably bring with them, von Bruchhausen makes the point that in the case of Marianne, the variety of different meanings which she describes as typical for the French allegory was decided on a governmental level. The government passed laws, decreed the expression and manifestation of the allegory, and consequently, the code of the French allegory was rather rigid. Turning to the more ambiguous case of the German allegory 'Germania', Bruchhausen goes on to conclude that "semantic ambiguities offer the advantage to integrate people with different political convictions" (Bruchhausen 1999: 2). The Indian case clearly shows that this is an assumption which can hardly be upheld. The

---

[37] The cultural link between the mother figure and Indian society has been often celebrated in mass culture and cinema, for example, in Mehboob Khan's film *Bharat Mata* of 1957. It is not uninteresting to note here that the director of the film was an Indian Muslim.

lack of clarity of what Bharat Mata actually stands has not contributed to her mass appeal. Von Bruchhausen's second assumption that "semantic ambiguities are not very useful to initiate political mobilisations" (Bruchhausen 1999: 2) is more justifiable against the background of the Indian experience. The representation of Marianne may have initiated "strong political conflicts because of her rigid code" (Bruchhausen 1999: 2), as Bruchhausen claims, but the absence of a coding for Bharat Mata has led to her use and abuse and has eventually transformed her into a historical myth rather than a social fact in India in as well as outside the country.

With regard to the key questions underlying the chapters of this volume, it can be said that images were re-used and modified according to the needs of their times. Both Marianne and Bharat Mata created integration as well as disintegration and anxiety. In India, pre-modern myths of mother goddesses and in the French case, early personifications of the nation were re-used and brought to new life as icons of the modern nation. This was a non-linear process and the icons were—and in the Indian case still are—heavily contested. Despite this contestation, the French and Indian cases serve to falsify Eric Hobsbawm's hypothesis that female symbols and allegories are doomed to vanish from the public sphere and the political imagery (Hobsbawm 2001: 127–48).[38] They are there and they are probably there to stay—perhaps in a different context, and with a different outlook, but still as signs of the nation. However, there are voices claiming that Bharat Mata has fulfilled her purpose of uniting citizens under a Hindu nationalist message and is now no longer of topical interest. Anja Kovacs (2004: 376) speaks of an "emptying out of the Bharat Mata imagery" and notes:

> [...] the RSS's Bharat Mata is a chaste mother, victimized by Muslims and in need of the protection of her virile sons [...] it was the sons of Bharat Mata who were held responsible for restoring the mother to her earlier glorious state. The responsibility of the mother was limited to rousing her sons. Once that mission was accomplished, her role became secondary. (Kovacs 2004: 375 f)

Yet, Kovacs also gives an example of the re-use of Bharat Mata in the Hindu nationalist context. While the Rashtriya Swayamsevak Sangh does not emphasise Bharat Mata very strongly, the women's organisation of the Sangh Parivar, the Rashtra Sevika Samiti, "frequently refers explicitly to Bharat Mata as *Durgadevi* (goddess Durga) [...] Therefore, in the Samiti's representation of Bharat Mata, there is recognition of the agency of the goddess often lacking elsewhere" (Kovacs 2004: 376). Kovacs also demonstrates how the Rashtra Sevika Samiti has given

---

[38] See also Klaudia Knabel (2005) who shows that the great potential for interpreting and reinterpreting a national myth enables it to survive and to uphold its topicality in contemporary nationalist discourse.

Bharat Mata a character distinct from the one the Rashtriya Swayamsevak Sangh had attributed to the image. Unlike the parent organisation, the women's wing gives "ample attention to the warrior qualities of the goddess Durga and recognizes fierceness as an important aspect of Bharat Mata" (Kovacs 2004: 376).

## CONCLUSION: THE PARTING OF WAYS

The history and politics of iconisation carry the footprints of the long march of the nation. The successful transition from the ancient regime to the modern world requires a cluster of forces at work, re-using the past, justifying the present, anticipating the future and folding the contradictory elements into a single, composite image—an icon of the nation. Bhabha's third space is the legitimate home of the successful icon, one more congenial to the 'cunning of reason'[39] and resistant to artful fakery.

The difference between France and India may not be as radical as one might think because even in France, Marianne is not a supra-political image but a partisan political figure.[40]

Both in France and in India, the collective urge to form a nation found expression in the visual form of an iconic image that conflated contradictory impulses—of desire for power, possession and dominance, its sublimation in love of an ideal, and the spirit of noble sacrifice that accompanies it. A new genre—between the religious and the representative—eminently amenable to poster art and mass consumption, these iconic images gave vent to a widely shared sentiment of *l'amour de la patrie* and *deshabhakti*—a hybrid space beyond the merely carnal and the conventionally religious.

---

[39] The juxtaposition of structure and agency accounts for the grand march of history—the 'unfolding of reason'—as Hegel saw it. Contrary to the claim of the icon maker to exclusive authorship of history, one needs to only point out the assertion of Sartre: "Men make their history upon the basis of prior conditions." (Hazel Barnes paraphrasing Marx, Engels and Sartre, in: *Search for a Method*, p. xviii). Similarly, Hegel, according to Jivanta Schoettli, implies that:

... providence realizes its intent through the history that men make by their actions. Men are free to act, but the desires that motivate them (as social beings) are part of a cosmic plan ... Men are free to act but the desires that motivate them stem from a larger, overarching structural context. (Schoettli 2009: 53–54)

[40] In the 1980s, the right-wing French party Front National, under the leadership of Jean-Marie Le Pen designed election posters that showed a veiled Marianne with the sentence: "20 years from now, France will be an Islamic Republic." In 1985, also the *Figaro Magazine* displayed a Marianne with a veil on its cover in order to make a statement on the issue of immigration. See Bernhard Schmid's "Debatte um 'Islamphobie': Wer hat Angst vor Differenz?" (http://www.hagalil.com/archiv/2003/12/islamophobie.htm).

In art historical terms, one can argue that content invents form, but form can also inspire content through its conceptual flow from one political context to another. More detailed historical investigation is needed to discover why and how the iconic image first appeared in India and what element of conceptual flow from outside the country might have inspired it. What we already know is the amount of conceptual borrowing there was within India and how much the appearance of the Banga Mata inspired other regions to come up with their own variations on the general theme, and how the Bharat Mata—in its composite form—encompassed these sisters without, as we saw in the 1950s outpouring of regional identities and subnational movements, their historical memories.

In contrast to India, France has been more successful in establishing its national allegory, giving it an institutional form and policing its use. The Marianne 'industry', as we have seen above, has successfully kept in step with changing times, drafting in a Moroccan model in its effort to find a unifying symbol for a nation where substantial immigrant minorities do not identify with the revolutionary myth. The French success also derives from the fact that it is a much more homogenous nation and because it has institutionalised the allegory by making it omnipresent. France has responded to changes in the structure of the population and has thereby managed to keep the allegory 'alive'. Bharat Mata, on the other hand, a figure of nostalgia and a deity, one like many others of its ilk, has died in the hearts of a majority of the Indian people.

The issue of why Marianne and Bharat Mata—two iconic figures with striking similarities, leading their nascent nations into hope and glory, reusing local material and memory, feeding into local artistic imagination—have nevertheless had such widely different careers is best left to future research. Beginning with her revolutionary origin, Marianne has been through myriad reincarnations, has survived restoration of monarchy, conservative backlashes and the transition to multicultural democracy. It has become, simultaneously, a self-sustaining historical myth and political presence, adorning stamps, seals, monuments and public buildings. Mother India, on the other hand, has been bypassed by the post-independence Republic which has chosen the more ancient—and less political Ashoka Chakra and the four addorsed lions—as its icon, while Bharat Mata has receded from the public arena into the shadow land of partisan politics.

The best one can conclude from this comparison is that historical events make re-use possible and necessary, but re-use by itself does not make history. Context matters, as do a cluster of other factors. At the height of the anti-colonial struggle, "Bharat Mata ki jay"—victory to Mother India—had been a slogan of unity. The departure of the British robbed it of its specific unifying function. In their solicitude to differentiate themselves from the Hindu right, the centrist Congress leadership promoted the *charkha*—the spinning wheel popularised by

Gandhi—as their icon. After Independence, the *charkha* gave way to the Ashoka Chakra, as the state sought to distance itself from the competing partisan icons.[41] On the French side, the adversaries of the valiant Marianne—the Church and the *ancien régime*—stayed on in the background, making her continuous presence and intergenerational renewal through re-use—both necessary and possible. That said, even when it does not 'work', re-use does not just disappear into nothingness, but bides its time in the entrails of collective memory, re-emerging when the context makes space for it. The re-induction of Bharat Mata into the public arena at the height of the 1962 Indo-China war is a case in point.

## PHOTO CREDIT

All photographs reproduced in this chapter are by Lion König.

## BIBLIOGRAPHY

### Secondary Sources

Abrams, Meyer H., 1999, *A Glossary of Literary Terms*. Harcourt Brace College, Fort Worth.

Abrams, Meyer H. & Stephen Greenblatt (eds), 1979, *The Norton Anthology of English Literature in Two Volumes* (4th edition). Norton, New York.

Agulhon, Maurice & Pierre Bonte, 1992, *Marianne: Les visages de la République*. Gallimard-Jeunesse, Paris.

Ahmed-Ghosh, Huma, 2003, "Writing the Nation on the Beauty Queen's Body: Implications for a 'Hindu' Nation". *Meridians: Feminism, Race, Transnationalism*. Vol. 4, no. 1, pp. 205–27.

Anderson, Benedict, 1983, *Imagined Communities: Reflections on the Origin and Spread of Nationalism*. Verso, London.

Appadurai, Arjun, 1997, *Modernity at Large: Cultural Dimensions of Globalization*. Oxford University Press, New Delhi.

---

[41] The *charkha* survived as a party political icon of the Indian National Congress. Increasingly, there is a new genre of memorialisation where partisan icons are making their way to the public sphere by finding a niche for themselves in the parliament—the most important public building of the Indian Republic. Rohini Mohan (2009) makes the point that statues of national leaders erected on the premises of the Indian parliament today—over 50, together with 45 portraits—are not there to salute nation builders but to score easy political points.

Arbuthnot, John, 1976 [1712]. In: Bower and Robert A. Erickson (eds), *The History of John Bull*. Alan W. Clarendon Press, Oxford.

Assmann, Jan, 2007, *Das kulturelle Gedächtnis: Schrift, Erinnerung und politische Identität in frühen Hochkulturen*. C. H. Beck, München.

Bachmann-Medick, Doris, 2009, *Cultural Turns: Neuorientierungen in den Kulturwissenschaften*. Rowohlt, Reinbeck.

Berger, Peter L. & Thomas Luckmann, 2007, *Die Gesellschaftliche Konstruktion der Wirklichkeit: Eine Theorie der Wissenssoziologie*. Fischer, Frankfurt am Main. (Translated from the English in 1967, *The Social Construction of Reality: A Treatise in the Sociology of Knowledge*. Doubleday, New York.)

Barnes, Hazel E., 1963, "Introduction". In: Jean-Paul Sartre (ed.), *Search for a Method* (translated from the French by Hazel Barnes). Vintage Books, New York, pp. vii–xxxi.

Barthes, Roland, 1995, *Mythologies*. Seuil, Paris.

Beyme, Klaus von, 1998, *Die Kunst der Macht und die Gegenmacht der Kunst: Studien zum Spannungsverhältnis von Kunst und Politik*. Suhrkamp, Frankfurt a.M.

Bhabha, Homi K., 1994, *The Location of Culture*. Routledge, London.

Blunt, Alison and Gilian Rose (eds), 1994, *Writing Women and Space: Colonial and Postcolonial Geographies*. Guilford Press, New York.

Boehm, Gottfried, 1994, "Die Wiederkehr der Bilder". In: Gottfried Boehm (ed.), *Was ist ein Bild?*. Fink, München, pp. 11–38.

Bredekamp, Horst, 1999, *Thomas Hobbes' Visuelle Strategien. Der Leviathan: Das Urbild des modernen Staates; Werkillustrationen und Portraits*. Akademie Verlag, Berlin.

———, 2006, *Der Leviathan: Das Urbild des modernen Staates und seine Gegenbilder 1651–2001*. Akademie Verlag, Berlin.

Brosius, Christiane, 1997, "Motherland in Hindutva Iconography". *India Magazine*. Vol. 17, no. 12, pp. 22–29.

———, 2005, *Empowering Visions: The Politics of Representation in Hindu Nationalism*. Anthem Press, London.

———, 2007, "'I Am a National Artist': Popular Art in the Sphere of Hindutva". In: Richard Davis (ed.), *Picturing the Nation: Iconographies of Modern India*. Orient Longman, Hyderabad, pp. 171–205.

Brown, Judith, 1989, *Gandhi: Prisoner of Hope*. Yale University Press, New Haven.

Bruchhausen, Esther-Beatrice Christiane von, 1999, "Das Zeichen im Kostümball: Marianne und Germania in der politischen Ikonographie", PhD thesis. University of Halle-Wittenberg.

Carey, John, 2005, *What Good are the Arts?* Faber and Faber, London.

Clark, Timothy J. 1999, *The Absolute Bourgeois: Artists and Politics in France 1848–1851*. Thames and Hudson, London.

Coleridge, Samuel Taylor, 1816, "The Statesman's Manual". In: M. H. Abrams (eds), 2005, *A Glossary of Literary Terms*. Thomson Wadsworth, Boston.

Dave, J. H. et al., n.d., *Munshi: His Art and Work*, Volume I. Shri Munshi Seventieth Birthday Citizens' Celebration Committee, Bombay.

Fludernik, Monika (ed.), 1998, *Hybridity and Postcolonialism: Twentieth-Century Indian Literature*. Stauffenburg-Verlag, Tuebingen.

Gadamer, Hans-Georg, 1975, *Wahrheit und Methode: Grundzüge einer Philosophischen Hermeneutik*. Mohr, Tuebingen.

Hegewald, Julia A. B. & Subrata K. Mitra, 2008, "Jagannatha Compared: The Politics of Appropriation, Re-use and Regional Traditions in India". *Heidelberg Papers in South Asian and Comparative Politics (HPSACP)*. No. 36, pp. 1–37. Available at http://archiv.ub.uniheidelberg.de/volltextserver/frontdoor.php?source_opus=8015 (accessed on 20 July 2011).

Hobbes, Thomas (ed.), 1960 [1651], *Leviathan: Or the Matter, Forme and Power of a Commonwealth Ecclesiasticall and Civil* (with an introduction by Michael Oakeshott). Blackwell, Oxford.

Hobsbawm, Eric J., 2001, "Mann und Frau: Bilder der Politischen Linken". In: Eric J. Hobsbawm (ed.), *Ungewöhnliche Menschen: Über Widerstand, Rebellion und Jazz*. Hanser, München, pp. 127–48 (translated from the English, 1998, *Uncommon People: Resistance, Rebellion and Jazz*. Weidenfeld & Nicholson, London).

Jurt, Joseph, 2005, "Die Allegorie der Freiheit in der Französischen Tradition". In: Klaudia Knabel, Dietmar Rieger and Stephanie Wodianka (eds), *Nationale Mythen—Kollektive Symbole: Funktionen, Konstruktionen und Medien der Erinnerung*. Vandenhoeck & Ruprecht, Göttingen, pp. 113–26.

Karlekar, Malavika (ed.), 2006, *Visualizing Indian Women, 1875–1947*. Oxford University Press, New Delhi.

Knabel, Klaudia, 2005, "Der Import einer nationalen Ikone: Jeanne d'Arc in Deutschland". In: Klaudia Knabel, Dietmar Rieger and Stephanie Wodianka (eds), *Nationale Mythen-kollektive Symbole: Funktionen, Konstruktionen und Medien der Erinnerung*. Vandenhoeck & Ruprecht, Göttingen, pp. 101–10.

Koschorke, Albrecht, 2007, *Der fiktive Staat: Konstruktionen des politischen Körpers in der Geschichte Europas*. Fischer Taschenbuch Verlag, Frankfurt.

Kovacs, Anja, 2004, "You Don't Understand We are at War! Refashioning Durga in the Service of Hindu Nationalism". *Contemporary South Asia*. Vol. 13, no. 4, pp. 373–88.

McKean, Lise, 1996, "Mother India and her Militant Matriots". In: John S. Hawley and Donna M. Wulff (eds), *Devi: Goddesses of India*. University of California Press, Berkeley, pp. 250–80.

Mitchell, William J. T., 1992 (March), "The Pictorial Turn". *Artforum*. Vol. 30, no. 7 (March), pp. 89–94. Reprinted in: William J. T. Mitchell (ed.), *Picture Theory: Essays on Verbal and Visual Representation*, The University of Chicago Press, Chicago, pp. 33–34.)

Mohan, Rohini, 2009, "A Cheque in Stone". *Tehelka*. Vol. 6, no. 9, pp. 18–19.

Naipaul, V. S., 1977, *India: A Wounded Civilisation*. Penguin, Harmondsworth.

Nash, Catherine, 1993 (Summer), "Remapping and Renaming: New Cartographies of Identity, Gender and Landscape in Ireland". *Feminist Review*. Vol. 44 (Summer), pp. 39–51.

Nehru, Jawaharlal, 1946, *The Discovery of India*. Oxford University Press, New Delhi.

Neumayer, Erwin & Christine Schelberger, 2003, *Popular Indian Art: Raja Ravi Varma and the Printed Gods of India*. Oxford University Press, New Delhi.

———, 2008, *Bharat Mata: India's Freedom Movement in Popular Art*. Oxford University Press, New Delhi.

Nora, Pierre, 1996, *Realms of Memory: Rethinking the French Past/The Construction of the French Past*, Vol. I: *Conflicts and Divisions*, Vol. II: *Traditions*, Vol. III: *Symbols*. Columbia University Press, New York.

Ozouf, Mona, 1977, "Le Simulacre et la Fête révolutionnaire". In: Jean Ehrard and Paul Viallaneix (eds), *Les Fêtes de la Révolution: Colloque de Clermont-Ferrand, (Juin 1974)*. Société des Études Robespierristes, Paris, pp. 323–53.

Paine, Thomas, 1969 [1791/92], *Rights of Man: Being an Answer to Mr. Burke's Attack on the French Revolution*. Penguin, Harmondsworth. (Edited by Henry Collins.)

Plessen, Marie Louise von, 1996, "Germania aus dem Fundus". In (ed.), *Marianne und Germania 1789–1889: Frankreich und Deutschland Zwei Welten-Eine Revue*. Argon, Berlin, pp. 31–36.

Pinney, Christopher, 2004, *Photos of the Gods: The Printed Image and Political Struggle in India*. Oxford University Press, New Delhi.

Pufendorf, Samuel von, 1690, *The Present State of Germany, or, an Account of the Extent, Rise, Form, Wealth, Strength, Weaknesses and Interests of that Empire*. Richard Chiswell, London.

Ramaswamy, Sumathi, 2001, "Maps and Mother Goddesses in Modern India". *Imago Mundi*. Vol. 53, pp. 97–114.

——— (ed.), 2003, *Beyond Appearances? Visual Practices and Ideologies in Modern India*. SAGE Publications, New Delhi.

———, 2006, "Enshrining the Map of India: Cartography, Nationalism, and the Politics of Deity in Varanasi". In: Martin Gaenszle and Jörg Gengnagel (eds), *Visualizing Space in Banares: Images, Maps and the Practice of Representation*. Harrassowitz, Wiesbaden, pp. 165–88.

———, 2008, "Foreword". In: Erwin Neumayer and Christine Schelberger (eds), *Bharat Mata: India's Freedom Movement in Popular Art*. Oxford University Press, New Delhi, pp. vii–xii.

Rose, Gilian, 1993, *Feminism and Geography: The Limits of Geographical Knowledge*. University of Minnesota Press, Minneapolis.

Sartre, Jean-Paul, 1963, *Search for a Method* (translated from the French and with an Introdction by Hazel E. Barnes). Vintage Books, New York.

Savarkar, Vinayak Damodar, 1949, *Hindutva: Who is a Hindu?*. Gokhale, Poona.

Schmitt, Carl, 1938, *Der Leviathan in der Staatslehre des Thomas Hobbes: Sinn und Fehlschlag eines politischen Symbols*. Hanseatische Verlagsanstalt, Hamburg.

Schoettli, Jivanta, 2009, "Strategy and Vision in Politics: Jawaharlal Nehru's Policy Choices and the Designing of Political Institutions, PhD thesis, Heidelberg University. Published at http://archiv.ub.uni-heidelberg.de/volltextserver/volltexte/2009/9977 (accessed on: 8 June 2010).

Speitkamp, Winfried, 1997, "Denkmalsturz und Symbolkonflikt in der modernen Geschichte: Eine Einleitung". In: Winfried Speitkamp (ed.), *Denkmalsturz: Zur Konfliktgeschichte politischer Symbolik*. Vandenhoeck & Ruprecht, Göttingen, pp. 5–21.

Tagore, Rabindranath, 1919, *The Home and the World*. Macmillan, London. (Translated by Surendranath Tagore.)

Thapar, Romila, *Early India: From the Origins to AD 1300*. University of California Press, Berkeley and Los Angeles.

Winter, Bronwyn, 2009, "Marianne goes Multicultural: *Ni putes ni soumises* and the Republicanisation of Ethnic Minority Women in France". In: Vesna Drapac and André Lambelet (eds), *French History and Civilization*. Papers from the George Rudé Seminar, Vol. II, pp. 228–40. Available at http://www.h-france.net/rude/rude%20volume%20ii/Winter%20Final%20Version.pdf.

## Internet Sources

"Marianne." Available at http://ambafrance-us.org/spip.php?article619 (accessed on: 13 March 2009).

Schmid, Bernhard, 2003, "Debatte um 'Islamphobie': Wer hat Angst vor Differenz?". Available at http://www.hagalil.com/archiv/2003/12/islamophobie.htm (accessed on: 03 September 2009).

## Film Sources

Khan, Mehboob, 1957, *Bharat Mata*. Mehboob Productions, Bombay.

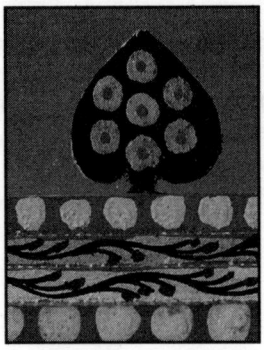

# GLOSSARY

| | |
|---|---|
| *acharya* / Acharya | title given to a male Jaina ascetic, often used at start of his name; leader of a group of ascetics, mendicant scholar and teacher |
| *adhishthana* | basement sequences of mouldings |
| Aesthetic Movement | nineteenth-century European artistic movement in which aesthetic values were considered more important than moral or social issues |
| *ahimsa* | non-harming, non-violence, non-injury; the primary moral precept of all Jainas |
| AICC | All India Congress Committee; general meeting and the highest decision-making body of the Indian National Congress |
| Akhand Hindustan | irredentist Hindu nationalist 1940s project in favour of a Greater India including Afghanistan, Nepal, Ceylon, Bhutan, Burma, the Princely States and British India |
| Aligarh University | originally named 'Muslim Anglo-Oriental College' and founded in 1875, was subsequently renamed 'Aligarh University' in 1920 and currently known as AMU, Aligarh Muslim University |
| All India Congress (AIC) | central organisation of the Indian National Congress founded in 1885 in Bombay |
| All India Muslim League (AIML) | central organisation of the Muslim League founded in 1906 in Dhaka |

| | |
|---|---|
| Ambedkar | Bhimrao Ramji Ambedkar (1891–1956); social reformer and leader of the Dalit Movement in India |
| *anekantavada* | the theory of the many-sided nature of reality, non-onesidedness |
| *antarala* | vestibule, space or intermediate compartment between shrine and hall |
| *aparigraha* | non-possession, non-possessiveness |
| aquatints | an intaglio printmaking technique and a variant of etching, where an acid resistant resin is applied to a metal plate |
| *arhat* | 'worthy of worship', a title for someone who has reached enlightenment; same as: Jina, Tirthankara and *kevalin* |
| *ardha-mandapa* | pillared hall, usually at the entrance to a temple structure |
| *Arthashastra* | an ancient Indian Hindu treatise on statecraft, economic policy and military strategy, which is usually compared with Machiavelli's *The Prince*. The author, Kautilya, is identified as Chanakya (c. 350–283 BCE), a scholar and prime ministerial figure under the rule of Chandragupta Maurya |
| Arya Samaj | Hindu Reform Movement founded by Svami Dayananda in 1875. Alternatively: Association of Moderate Hindu Nationalists (*Aryan Society*) created in 1875 by Saraswati (1824–1883) |
| *Ashvamedha-parvan* | (also *Ashvamedhika-parvan*.) Book fourteen out of eighteen in the *Mahabharata* epic; describing the horse sacrifice (*ashvamedha*) performed by the victorious Pandavas upon their return to the throne in Hastinapura. As part of the ritual, the sacrificial horse is allowed to roam freely followed by an army that claims all territories for the sacrificer king |
| *ata* | Kannada term used to refer to a theatre play |
| avatar | 'descent'; incarnation, manifestation |
| *babul* work | technique in which tiny gold or silver cones cover the surface of a hollow dome or teardrop shape out of which the ornament is formed. It is named after its similarity in appearance to the flowers of the acacia tree. Also called *kikar* (in the Punjab) or *khardar* ('work of thorns') |
| Bahiskrut Sabha | association founded by Ambedkar on 20 July 1924 |

| | |
|---|---|
| Bahubali | ascetic par excellence; according to the Digamba-ras, the first person to attain full enlightenment in the present time cycle; born as the son of the first Tirthankara Adinatha (Rishabhanatha); also known as Gommata or Gommateshvara |
| Bangistan | Muslim territory of east India planned by Rahmat Ali as an outpost of Pakistan. The sound nearly echoes the name of 'Pakistan', phonetically |
| *bayalata* | Kannada term used for a play performed in the open air |
| Bengal Pact | agreement signed at the local level in Calcutta be-tween both Hindu and Muslim supporters of con-stitutional methods opposed to Gandhian boycott techniques. It is considered to be the first instance of an all-Bengali nationalism by some |
| Bengalistan | 'country' of the Bengali; a recent invention and a rather ambiguous ending in '–stan'. |
| Bengsam | a pre-Partition name for eastern Pakistan (Bengal and Assam united) |
| Besant, Annie | born in London, 1847, and died in India in 1933. She was a prominent figure in the Theosophical Society and campaigned actively for women's rights as well as Irish and Indian self-rule. She joined the INC, helped launch the Home Rule League and became the first female president of the INC in 1917 |
| *bhagavata* | the singer, performing songs and poems in the Yak-shagana dance drama |
| *bhagavatike* | Kannada term for 'singing' |
| *bhajan* | religious hymn; the chanting of religious hymns |
| *bhamini(-shatpadi)* | Kannada verse form with six feet or lines counted in morae. The first two lines have fourteen morae each, subdivided into two 3 + 4 groups. The third line has one additional group of 3 + 4 = 7 morae and, by definition, ends in a long vowel (2 morae), thus this line counts a total of twenty-one morae. As in all *shatpadi*s, the second set of three feet or lines is identical to the first |
| Bharat | Hindi term for the Republic of India. |
| *bhikku* | Buddhist monk |
| *bhoga* | sacred temple offerings |
| *bindu* | 'drop'; the primordial point, the source of the uni-verse |

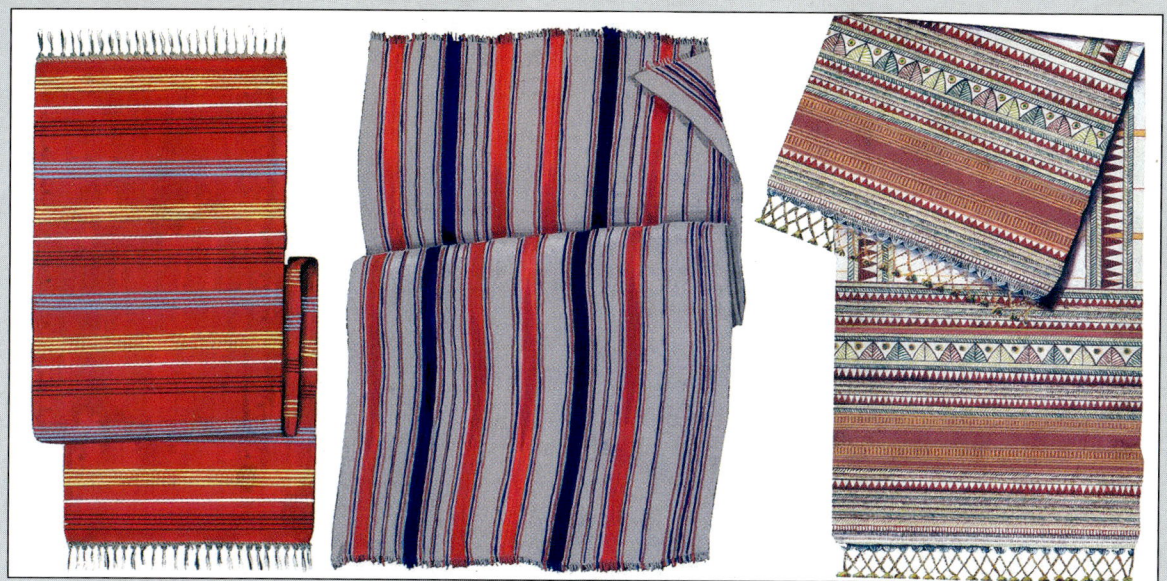

**Plate 8.5**

Woven crafts (from left to right): Bondo, Gadaba and Dongria Kondh.

**Plate 8.6**

Saora paintings at a gate at VIP Road in Bhubaneswar 2008.

**Plate 8.7**

Sculptures (hybridised tribal stone art) at VIP Road in Bhubaneswar, 2008.

**Plate 8.8**

Saora paintings at a highway bridge in Bhubaneswar, 2008.

**Plate 8.9**
Saora Anital, Ritual Art (a modern variation sold in the market).

**Plate 8.10**
Chief Minister of Orissa Naveen Pattnaik inaugurating the Museum of Tribal Arts in the presence of Godoba ladies in Bhubaneswar, 2001. See Saora paintings at the Museum of Tribal Art, Bhubaneswar.

**Plate 8.11**
Bonda house pattern.

**Plate 13.1**
Digambara Jain monk at Shedbal,
North Karnataka, begging for food
(December 2006).

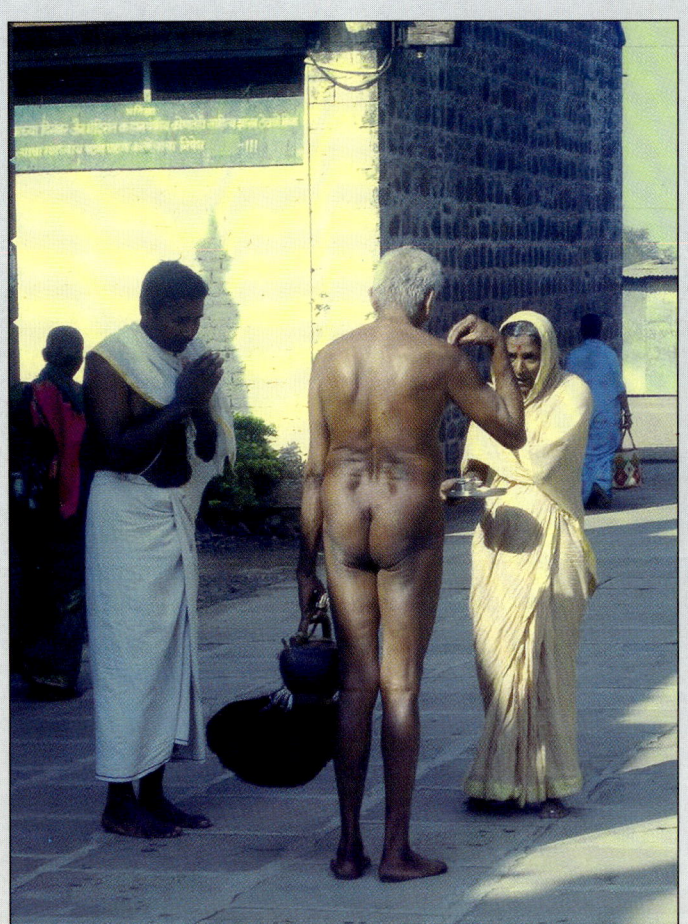

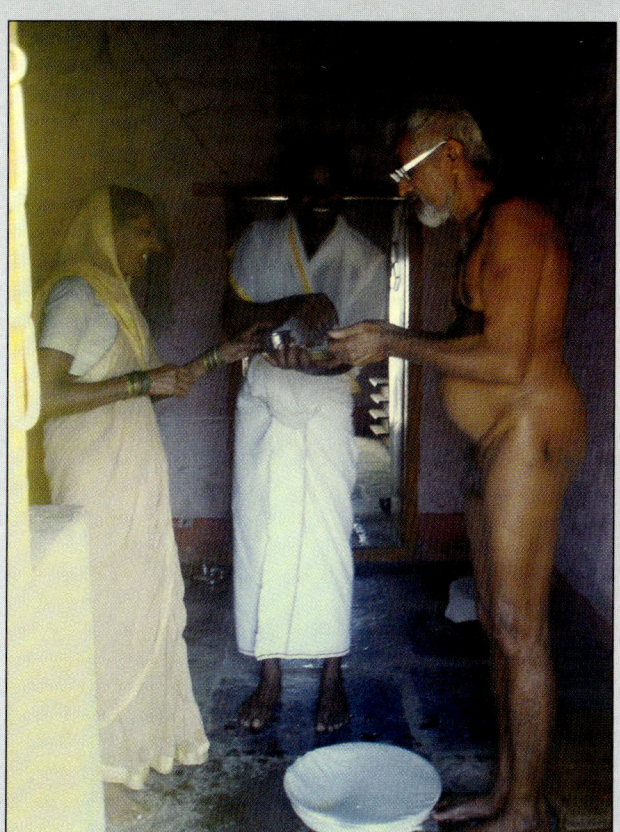

**Plate 13.2**
Digambara Jain monk being fed
by lay followers at Shedbal, north
Karnataka (December 2006).

**Plate 14.1**
Germania (1848) by Philip Veit.

**Plate 14.2**

Marianne by Delacroix.

**Plate 14.3**

Marianne by Honoré Daumier.

**Plate 14.4**

Bharat Mata, a current poster art.

**Plate 14.5**

Depiction of Goddess Durga as Bharat Mata.

**Plate 14.6**
Hindu New Year's greetings alongside a depiction of Bharat Mata; BJP Central Office, Ashoka Road, New Delhi.

**Plate 14.7**
The relief map inside the Bharat Mata Temple.

| | |
|---|---|
| *badagu-tittu* | the northern style of the Yakshagana dance-drama |
| *basadi* | south Indian term for a Jaina temple; alternative version: *basti* |
| *bodhisattva* | an enlightened being, motivated to help others to attain liberation; a Buddha to be |
| Brahmadeva | *yaksha* of the tenth Jina, Shitalnatha; usually portrayed riding a horse |
| brahman/Brahmin | a member of the priestly and highest class of the Hindu caste system |
| Britannia | one of the two national allegories of Britain; the second one is John Bull |
| Cabinet Mission | the 1946 Cabinet Mission was made up of three members of the immediate post-war Labour cabinet, set up to talk to nationalist leaders in view of establishing a devolution process for a united India |
| Calanti Vishnu | the moving Vishnu |
| *cannetille* work | in jewellery, a style where curled gold wires are covered with trails of tiny gold granules, named after a style of metal embroidery done in Napoleonic France. It was popular in Europe from about 1820 to 1850 |
| *caturmukha* | four-faced icon, or shrine with doors on all four sides; same as *sarvatobhadra*; Sanskrit version of the Gujarati term: *caumukha/i* |
| *chakra* | wheel; in Buddhist art of the Mauryan period, commonly encountered as a symbol on pillars and edicts and associated with Ashoka's unified empire; in Hindu art, closely associated with the god Vishnu |
| *charkha* | spinning wheel; popularised by Mahatma Gandhi |
| caste system | refers to the Hindu social system of stratification in which *jatis* are the basic social units that govern marriages, social networks, food taboos and rituals. More than 2,000 *jatis* are divided into four broad hierarchical levels known as *varnas* that are associated with particular functions: the priests, the warriors and rulers, the mercantile groups and the service groups |
| *chaturvarna* | the four *varnas* (colours); division of Hindu society into the four social classes of *brahmans*, *kshatriyas*, *vaishyas* and *shudras*. The so-called untouchables remain outside of this order |
| Chaudhury Rahmat Ali (1895–1951) | a Sunni intellectual living in Europe, designed a more precise idea of what a modern Muslim nation in South Asia could be |

| | |
|---|---|
| claw setting | method of setting a gemstone in which metal claws worked up from the ornament are used to hold the stone in place |
| closed setting | style of setting a gemstone in which it may only be seen from the front of the ornament, the back of the stone being enclosed. Traditional Indian jewellery employed setting methods of this type and in order to increase the light in the gemstones and enhance their colour, foil was often inserted behind the stone |
| consociational theory | a theory developed by political scientist Arend Lijphart, which suggests a form of government for managing conflict in deeply divided societies based on guaranteed group representation. Its main characteristics are a grand coalition government, a mutual (minority) veto, proportionality and segmental (cultural) autonomy |
| Constituent Assembly Debates | Documentation of the proceedings of the Constituent Assembly of India |
| Cripps Mission | Richard Stafford Cripps (1882–1952) was a British Labour politician and senior member of Prime Minister Churchill's war cabinet. He was the head of a mission sent to India by the British War Cabinet in order to negotiate support from imprisoned Congress nationalists |
| Dalits | mixed population group of numerous castes and groups who were traditionally considered as 'untouchables' |
| *dastu* | mnemonics used to define tala patterns and dance steps |
| *dharma* (*dhamma*) | 'religion', 'law', and so on |
| Dharmapala | Anagarika Dharmapala, founder of the Maha Boddhi Society in Sri Lanka in 1891 |
| *darshan* | the sacred rite of viewing an icon |
| Digambara | 'sky clad', the group of Jainas whose male mendicants reject clothing and go naked |
| *dvaita* | dualist school of Indian philosophy in contrast to the monistic (*advaita*) teachings. For the historical context in which Kannada Yakshagana developed, the dualist school of Madhvacarya (thirteenth century), its Vaishnava theism and the revival of |

Vaishnava *bhakti* movements is of particular importance

**Emergency** — a twenty-one-month period, when President Fakhruddin Ali Ahmed, upon advice by Prime Minister Indira Gandhi, declared a state of emergency under Article 352 of the Constitution of India, effectively bestowing on her the power to rule by decree, suspending elections and civil liberties

**Fabianism** — an intellectual tradition that originated in late nineteenth-century Britain, which was best known for its ideas of social democracy and the need for change to be gradual and reformist as opposed to revolutionary

**Fazlul Haq** — Abul Kasem Fazlul Haq (1873–1962) is from the eastern part of Bengal and considered one of the most formidable inter-war politicians of Bengal. He is said to be very much opposed to the *zamindari* system

*gada* — mace, club; one of the main weapons and attributes of Vishnu

*gana* — dwarfish imp; semidivine, usually potbellied dwarfs

**Gandhi, Mohandas** — born on 2 October 1869, was a key figure in negotiations with the British. Drawing upon Christian thought as well as Hinduism, Mahatma Gandhi developed alternative methods of resistance to colonial oppression through mass civil disobedience, non-violence and the pursuit of truth

*garbha-griha* — 'womb chamber'; sanctum or image chamber of a temple

**Germania** — national allegory of Germany

*gokhru* — traditional earrings using a form of babul work, sometimes with larger spikes, worn in the Punjab, Rajasthan and Himachal Pradesh

**Gommata/ Gommateshvara** — ascetic par excellence, according to the Digambaras, the first person to attain full enlightenment in the present time cycle; born as the son of the first Tirthankara Adinatha (Rishabhanatha); also known as Bahubali

*gopura* — towered gateway of a South Indian temple complex

Government of India Act 1935
: the last pre-independence constitutional reform under British rule and became one of the main pillars of independent India's constitution. Among many provisions, it introduced direct elections on the basis of an expanded electorate and ended the principle of diarchy in favour of granting more autonomy to the Indian provinces

Great Calcutta Killing
: a widespread massacre of the Calcutta Muslim community organised by local Hindu extremist militias opposed to the whole of Bengal becoming a part of a separate Pakistan

Greater Bengal
: ethnic Bengali project in favour of a territory comprising Assam and Bengal

*harake*
: vow (Kannada language)

*harake-ata*
: a theatrical performance commissioned in fulfilment of a vow (*harake*)

Harijan
: 'Son of God'; term given by Mahatma Gandhi to the Dalits or untouchables

Harikatha (Kalakshepam)
: Vaishnava storytelling genre particularly in south India in which a single person relates and comments on mythological stories through singing, recitation, prose and rudimentary acting. Performers are known as Haridasas

Hindu Code Bill
: controversial Bills, including the Hindu Marriage Act (1955), the Hindu Succession Act (1956), the Hindu Minority and Guardianship Act (1956) and the Hindu Adoptions and Maintenance Act (1956), passed by the post-colonial government of India under Jawaharlal Nehru in order to codify and reform Hindu Personal Law

*himsa*
: injury, harming, violence

Hindu Mahasabha
: also known as Akhil Bharatiya Hindu Mahasabha, founded by V. D. Sarvarkar in 1915, is a Hindu nationalist party. It saw itself as an alternative for Hindus to the secular Congress party

Hindu Nationalism
: Hindu Nationalism is in favour of a strictly Hindu India where Muslim and other religious communities would have to submit to an official religion

Hindu Nationalist
: see Rashtriya Swayamsevak Sangh (RSS) militias

Indian Councils Act
: a piece of legislation passed by the Parliament of Great Britain in 1861 that transformed the Viceroy

|                                     | of India's executive council into a cabinet run on the portfolio system |
| ----------------------------------- | --- |
| Indian Imperial Provinces           | there were eleven British Provinces in British India and about eight main Princely States, all grouped in the Indian British Empire |
| Indian Muslim community             | a quarter of the Indian British Empire's population was Muslim, more than 40 per cent of them living in the province of Bengal |
| Indian National Congress (INC)      | the first and foremost political party of India, founded in 1885 by Allan Octavian Hume, spearheading the Indian Independence movement and dominating Indian party politics in the first two decades after Independence and thereafter |
| Iqbal                               | Muhammad Iqbal (1876–1938) became the Muslim League president in 1930 and demanded the grouping of Muslim-majority provinces in north-west British India into one single Muslim state |
| Islamistan                          | synonymous of a nation for all the Muslims of the British Empire or for the entire world population of Muslims |
| Jamat                               | any radical Islamic political party |
| Jamat-e-Islami (JI)                 | Islamic political party opposed to the Muslim League that was created in 1941 by Abul Ala Maududi (1903–1979), a former collaborator of Iqbal |
| Jamat-ul-Ulama-e-Hind (JUH)         | Islamic political party created in 1919 in order to support the Congress and regrouping reformists and mass re-Islamisation movements like the Tabligh |
| Jamat-ul-Ulama-e-Islam (JUI)        | part of the JUH that broke up from the Congress in 1945 and joined the Muslim League |
| *jana-jati*s                        | Scheduled Tribes |
| *jali*                              | perforated screen |
| *jati*                              | 'birth'; social status dependant on the family one has been born into; sub-caste |
| Jihadist                            | holy warrior of the Islamic kind |
| Jina                                | 'conqueror', 'spiritual victor', the twenty-four enlightened teachers of each world age; same as Tirthankara, *arhat* and *kevalin* |
| Jinnah                              | Muhammad Ali Jinnah (1876–1948), initially a member of the Indian National Congress, joined the Muslim League in the 1930s and became the Father of Pakistan in 1947 |

| | |
|---|---|
| *kalasha* | pot-like finial |
| Kalighat | suburb of Calcutta (Ghat of Kali) with the famous Kali Temple and its associated painting style, which flourished at the place particularly during the nineteenth and early twentieth centuries |
| Kannada (Hari) Dasas | devotees of Hari (Vishnu); itinerant saint-singers who left a considerable number of religious poems and songs in *shatpadi*s and similar metres. The *Dasa* tradition continues today but flourished in the late fifteenth and sixteenth centuries |
| *karma* | 'action'; the good and bad actions of an individual which influence his or her rebirth; fate |
| Kashmiri Brahmin | refers to people belonging to a particular sect of Hindu Pandits who originate from the Kashmir region. Nehru's father, Motilal Nehru and mother, Swarupa Rani, came from Kashmiri Brahmin families |
| *kevalin* | a person who has attained spiritual liberation; same as: Jina, Tirthankara or *arhat* |
| Keynes, John Maynard | born in 1883 and died in 1946, Keynes was a British economist whose ideas are considered to be the foundation stones for modern macroeconomics |
| Khaksar | Muslim militia created by Allama Mashriqi (1888–1983) that did not depend on the Muslim League directly. One of his militants tried to assassinate Jinnah |
| *kikar* work | see *babul* work |
| *kisan* | can be translated as farmer or peasant. The 1920s Kisan Movements were an important precursor to the nationwide Independence movement led by Mahatma Gandhi in the 1930s |
| *khardar* work | 'work of thorns', see *babul* work |
| *kshetrapala* | guardian of the sacred temple complex |
| *kuftkari* | steel decorated with overlaid gold or silver wires. Traditionally used for arms and armour in the Punjab and Rajasthan. Sometimes known in English as 'koftgari' |
| *kundan* work | uniquely Indian technique of using hyper-purified gold, in the form of foil, to set gemstones into ornaments of gold, jade or other materials. Its purity enables the gold to be welded through |

| | |
|---|---|
| | pressure alone at room temperature. This allows the jeweller considerable flexibility in setting the stones, although a closed setting is always used |
| Koh-i-Noor | 'mountain of light'; once the largest diamond in the world which passed from Hindu into Islamic, Sikh and later into British hands |
| *kshatriya* | member of the second or warrior caste of the Hindu caste system |
| *kudu* | horseshoe-shaped blind arch |
| *kuta* | square roof form |
| Lahore Resolution | voted in Lahore at the annual Muslim League session of March 1940 by the All-India Muslim League, it provided a new meaning and use for the word 'Pakistan', quite different from Rahmat Ali's version: all of India's Muslim-majority provinces (and not just the Muslim West) were to form several entities gathered into a Muslim Confederated State affiliated to a united India |
| *lakh* | Indian measure denoting 100,000 |
| *lalata-bimba* | central symbol on door lintel, generally indicative of the presiding deity |
| *lanchana* | symbol of cognisance, characterising sign, emblem |
| League of Muslim Nations | Rahmat Ali wanted to replace the All-India Muslim League with a League of Muslim Nations projecting the union of Pakistan, Bengal and Usmanistan (Princely State of Hyderabad) |
| Licence permit Raj | this term refers to the elaborate licenses, regulations and accompanying red tape that were required to set up and run businesses in India between 1947 and 1990, before the onset of liberalisation |
| *linga* | phallic emblem of the god Shiva |
| Lingayat | reformed religious group centring on the worship of the *linga*; same as Vira-Shaiva |
| lithography | print method in which a drawing is made with a greasy substance on a limestone or zinc plate. Subsequently, ink is applied, which only holds on to the shapes drawn in ink. The image is printed onto dampened paper with a special press |
| Lok Sabha | the lower house of the Indian parliament |
| *Mahabharata* | one of the two major Sanskrit epics of ancient India, the other being the *Ramayana* |

| | |
|---|---|
| Mahad Satyagraha | a mass meeting organised by Ambedkar on 25 December 1927, which led to the demanding of Dalit access to water tanks |
| *mahaprasad* | offerings to Lord Jagannatha |
| Mahar | largest scheduled caste group in Maharashtra; B. R. Ambedkar was born into this caste |
| Mahasabha | cf. Hindu Mahasabha |
| *makara* | mythical crocodile-like sea creature |
| *mandala* | 'circle'; circular diagram, delimiting a sacred area; map of the cosmos |
| *mandapa* | columned temple hall |
| Marathi | official language of the state of Maharahstra |
| Marianne | national allegory of France |
| *matte-tala* | a rhythmic pattern; in Kannada, Yakshagana, *matte-tala* has ten beats. It is largely obsolete in performance practice today, but common in Yakshagana manuscripts |
| Menon, Krishna | freedom fighter, close confidante of Nehru, diplomat for independent India and Defense Minister from 1957–1962 |
| *millat* | an Islamic term designating the religion of the Elect |
| *milli* | an Islamic term designating the Elect, the chosen people of God |
| Mohajir | Muslims from inner India who became refugees in Pakistan after the 1947 Partition |
| Mohajiristan | a separate state claimed by Mohajir refugees in modern day Pakistan, probably situated in and around Karachi, thus very much anti-Sindi |
| Montague-Chelmsford Reforms | the Government of India Act of 1919, commonly known as Montagu-Chelmsford reforms, established a Council of State and an Imperial Legislative Assembly and expanded the franchise. Two important provisions of the Act were the introduction of diarchy, a dual form of government dividing areas of governance between British officials and elected Indian representatives and the creation of reserved seats for Muslim and non-Brahmin categories |
| mora (Pl. morae) | (Sanskrit: *matra*); technical term in prosody; describing a sound unit based on the length of vowels and their position. Short vowels are counted as a single mora, long vowels as double morae. A group of two |

| | or more consonants following the vowel 'lengthens' the vowel 'by position'; an already long vowel is counted as three morae in this case |
|---|---|
| Morley-Minto Reforms | the Government of India Act of 1909, commonly known as the Mrley-Minto reforms, set up legislative councils with elected representatives on the basis of a limited Indian franchise and separate electorates for Hindus and Muslims |
| Mughalstan | nostalgic supporters of the Mughal Empire fantasize the re-establishment of a Mughal-inspired territory in northern India based on Muslim-majority districts being linked together |
| *mujahid* | militiaman fighting for an Islamic State in South Asia |
| *muktaya* | concluding sequence of a tala defined by a separate set of mnemonics and dance steps; while used in the rendering of songs at the end of verse (parts), there is no text sung over the *muktaya* pattern |
| *munshi* | Indians who acted as language teachers, translators and occasionally cultural advisors for missionaries and colonial officials |
| *murti* | sacred image |
| Muslim League | association founded in 1907 to safeguard the rights of Muslims which later became the political group campaigning for a separate Pakistan |
| Muslim National Guard | a Muslim militia faithful to the Muslim League, cf. *khaksar* |
| nabob | English colonial expression for British merchants or administrators of high status; corruption of the Bengali pronunciation of *navab* (provincial governor; Muslim nobleman) |
| Nandi | bull, vehicle of the god Shiva and closely associated with Basavanna, the founder of the Vira-Shaiva movement in Karnataka |
| Navoyana Buddhism | form of Buddhism created by B. R. Ambedkar |
| Nehru, Kamala | born in 1899, was the wife of Jawaharlal Nehru whom she married in 1916 in an arranged and traditional marriage. Imprisoned during the civil disobedience movement, Kamala became a freedom fighter in her own right |
| Noakhali massacres | in the Noakhali district of Eastern Bengal, a series of massacres conducted by Muslim Nationalist |

|  | Militias occurred in October 1946 as a retaliation of the August 'Great Calcutta Killing' |
| North West Frontier Province (NFWP) | a province of British India bordering Afghanistan, whose inhabitants are Pashtos (or Pathans) |
| open setting | style of setting a gemstone so that it is visible from both sides of the ornament and light shines through the stone. This type of setting was popular in Europe and tiny metal claws were often used to hold the stone in place. It began to be used in India during the nineteenth century |
| *pachchikam* work | style of setting gemstones in a metal ornament in which the stones are surrounded by raised pieces of metal recalling the claws often used in European gem setting, which however here have no function. The stones are secured by traditional Indian methods and are in a closed setting with a back of gold or silver gilt |
| *padma* | lotus, closely associated with the god Vishnu as one of his attributes |
| *padmasana* | lotus posture |
| *paduka* | sacred foot imprint |
| *paddanas* | Kannada term for oral epics connected with local deities (*butas* or *daivas*) |
| Pak-stan | there are several theories on the origin of the word 'Pakistan'. The *Star of India* daily, only ever mentioned one origin: 'Pak' (meaning 'pure' in Farsi) and '-stan' meaning 'country'. The added 'i' is supposed to be part of the Punjabi pronunciation of Rahmat Ali and his fellow students who popularised the concept |
| Pali | a South Asian, Middle Indo-Aryan language; language of the earliest Buddhist texts, collected in the so-called Pali Canon |
| pan-Islamism | ideology aiming at uniting all Muslims living on earth under one single and same banner |
| *Pandas* | priestly order of Puri |
| *pandit* | learned man |
| *paricha* | keeper of temple records |
| Pashto (fr., Pashtu) | an ethnic group speaking an Iranian language and living in NWFP, that is very close to the Afghans |
| *pushpapottika* | curved bracket with pendant lotus bud |
| *parivraja* | renunciation |

| | |
|---|---|
| Parshvanatha | the twenty-third of the group of twenty-four enlightened Jain teachers or Jinas; usually identified by a sheltering cobra hood behind his head |
| *pattacitra* | paintings on cloth (generally cotton) treated with natural glue; common in the region of Bengal and Bihar |
| *pradakshina-patha* | circumambulation path, ambulatory |
| *prana* | 'breath'; rhythmical life energy |
| *prasanga* | literally 'subject', 'topic', 'event', 'episode'; the play-text underlying a Yakshagana performance, consisting of songs and poems |
| *pratima* | sacred statue |
| Punjabistan | an exclusively Muslim Punjab |
| *puranas* | 'old', 'of ancient times'; proper name of a genre of authoritative scriptures on the universe and Hindu gods |
| *qalamdan* | ox or case for storing pens in Persia and India, usually made of metal, lacquered or painted wood or papier mache (papier mâché); also spelled *kalamdan* |
| Quaid/Quaid-e-azam | names used by many Muslim Leaguers to refer to Jinnah; 'Quaid' is an abbreviation of 'Quaid-e-Azam' or 'Great Leader' in Urdu language, the projected official language for Pakistan |
| *raga* | 'modes' in Indian music; each *raga* is defined by the particular combination of notes and their specific intervals in ascending and descending scales; for example, *saurashtra raga, bhairavi raga, purvi raga* |
| Rashtriya Swayamsevak Sangh (RSS) | in English: 'Organisation of the Volunteers fighting for the Motherland', a radical Hindu Nationalist militia resorting to violence |
| *repoussé*-work | technique of working sheet metal into three-dimensional forms by hammering it up from the back. Details may be chased in from the front |
| Romanticism | an artistic, literary and intellectual movement that gained momentum in eighteenth and nineteenth century Europe |
| Round Table Conferences (RTCs) | these were a series of meetings held in London between 1930 and 1932. Various Indian interests were represented there in consultation with British Members of Parliament of all shades. The Government of India Act of 1935, the last colonial constitution for India, was a product of the RTCs |

| | |
|---|---|
| *rudraksha-mala* | prayer beads or rosary used by followers of Shiva and made of seeds from a particular shrub |
| Sabha | cf. Hindu Mahasabha |
| *samaj* | association or organisation |
| *sangha* | Buddhist community of monks and nuns |
| *satyagraha* | the philosophy of non-violence as articulated by Mahatma Gandhi |
| Scheduled Castes | Dalits; in the past also known as 'Depressed Classes'; are an Indian population grouping recognised by the Constitution of India |
| *sevak* | temple servant |
| *shala* | barrel-vaulted roof form |
| *sankha/shankha* | shell, conch; attribute of Vishnu |
| *shatpadi* | class of Kannada metres characterised by six (*shat*) metrical feet (*pada/padi*). A verse-foot roughly corresponds to a 'line' in Western poetry. All *shatpadis* can be halved, and the two halves follow exactly the same metrical pattern. The first two feet always have the same number of morae |
| *shramanic* tradition | ascetic tradition of wandering monks and nuns |
| *shudra/sundra* | member of the lowest caste of the Hindu caste system, associated with the professions of framers, craftsmen and labourers |
| Shvetambara | 'white (cotton) clad', group of Jaina ascetics of whom also the male mendicants wear simple white robes |
| Seringapatam | anglicised term used during the British Raj for a settlement and fort on an island in the Kaveri River close to Mysore; today known as Srirangapatnam; site of the 'Battle of Seringapatam' (14 May 1799) in which the East India Company subdued the Kingdom of Mysore and killed Tipu Sultan |
| Shi'a Islam | most Indian Muslims were of Sunni background. However, most Muslim League leaders like Jinnah were wealthy Shi'a Muslim merchants originally from Kathiawar, in the Kutch region of Gujarat |
| Sindis | an ethnic group of British India living in the Sind province, with Karachi as its main city. Today, Karachi's population is mainly of Mohajir origin |
| *sthala-purana/ sthala-mahatme* | myths relating the 'history' of a place, usually a temple and its relationship with its presiding deity |

| | |
|---|---|
| Sthanakavasi | a non-image worshipping sectarian branch of the Shvetambaras |
| social imaginary | the set of values, institutions, laws and symbols associated with a particular social group. It has been used extensively by the Canadian philosopher, Charles Taylor to discuss the specific features of modernity and, in particular, Western modernity |
| Subhas Chandra Bose | Subhas Chandra Bose (1897–1945) was a member of the Congress who joined the Japanese in fighting the British in Burma |
| Suhrawardy | Husain Shahid Suhrawardy (1893–1963), major architect of the Muslim League victory in Bengal in the 1937 elections, was also the League's financier for the 1946 elections. He was in favour of a united Bengal and migrated to Pakistan in the 1950s only to join the opposition. Together with Fazlul Haq, he is considered one of the founding fathers of the Bangladesh nation today |
| *Sukraniti* | a manual of politics that is claimed to have been written by Vaisampayana, the narrator of the *Mahabharata* |
| *swami*-work | high-relief depictions of Hindu deities ('*Swamis*') in gold and silver were worked on ornaments and vessels, typically of European-inspired shape, that were made in southern India for sale primarily to European customers in India and abroad |
| *tala* | denotes both hand-held cymbals and rhythmic patterns in Kannada Yakshagana. The rhythmic patterns are characterised by their number of counts (steady beat, *laya*) over which emphasised and unemphasised beats are distributed. A full *tala* structure consists of several repetitions of its base pattern in a cycle (*avarta*) |
| Taylor, Charles | Canadian philosopher from Montreal, Quebec best known for his contributions to political philosophy, the philosophy of social science and the history of philosophy |
| *tenku-tittu* | the southern style of the Yakshagana dance drama |
| Terapanthis | term used to describe a non-image worshipping sectarian branch of the Shvetambaras as well as a sectarian division within the Digambara tradition |

| | |
|---|---|
| *theva* work | known in Britain as 'Pertabgarh work', this technique probably originated in Pratapgarh in Rajasthan in the late eighteenth or nineteenth century and was also practised in Indore and Ratlam. It continues to be employed today. An open-work design in a sheet of gold is cut out and fused to coloured glass, and the resulting plaque enclosed in a silver gilt surround |
| *tilaka* | mark applied with paste or powder which is worn on the forehead |
| Tipu Sultan | son of Hyder Ali and ruler of the Kingdom of Mysore, also known as the 'Tiger of Mysore'; was defeated in the third Anglo-Mysore War at Seringapatam in 1799 |
| Tirthankara | 'ford-maker', the twenty-four enlightened teachers; same as: Jina, *arhat* and *kevalin* |
| *trivude-tala* | a rhythmic pattern; in Kannada Yakshagana, *trivude* (*triputa*) tala has seven beats. The first, fourth and sixth are emphasised |
| Tulu | Dravidian language spoken in the southern parts of coastal Karnataka; associated with particular cultural practices such as matrilocal lines of inheritance and particular religious cults of local deities (*buta*) involving impersonation and possession as well as a body of oral literature associated with these deities |
| Uncle Sam | national allegory of the United States of America |
| Urdustan | a Mohajir vision of Pakistan where the only official language would be Urdu and where all regional cultures would be repressed. For many Mohajirs, Urdustan would be the real idea of Pakistan, a country created for Indian Muslims, above all |
| Utilitarianism | a political theory and philosophy which argues that the moral worth of an action can be judged according to its utility in providing happiness or pleasure for the greatest number. The key thinkers associated with this doctrine were Jeremy Bentham and John Stuart Mill |
| *vahana* | vehicle, mount; emblem of a divinity, usually in animal form |

| | |
|---|---|
| *vaishya* | member of the third caste of the Hindu caste system, associated with trade, cattle herding and arts and crafts |
| *vardhika(-shatpadi)* | Kannada verse form with six feet or lines counted in morae. The first two lines have twenty morae subdivided into groups of five morae each. The third line has two additional groups (5 + 5 = 10 morae), and, like *bhamini*, ends in a long vowel by definition (2 morae), thus the third line has a total of thirty-two morae. As in all *shatpadis*, the second set of three feet or lines is identical to the first |
| *vihara* | monastery |
| *vimana* | term used to describe the main temple part containing the shrine, as well as the temple tower of the south Indian temple tradition |
| Vira-Shaiva | Hindu religious group centring around the worship of the *linga*; same as Lingayat |
| Webb, Sidney and Beatrice | were amongst the founding members of Britain's Fabian Society in 1884. Together they became influential political figures, impacting intellectual society as well as Labour party policymaking |
| Westminster model | a democratic parliamentary system of government modelled after the politics of the United Kingdom. Among its main features are the concentration of executive power in the prime minister and cabinet, fusion of the legislature and the executive, separate roles for the head of state and head of government, cabinet responsibility to parliament, an asymmetric bicameralism and a first-past-the-post electoral system |
| *yaksha* | male divinity, associated with the Jinas as guardian deity |
| Yaksha Brahmadeva | see Brahmadeva |
| *yakshi* | female divinity associated with the Jinas as guardian deity |
| Yakshagana | dance drama performed in the coastal districts of Karnataka |
| *yali* | fantastic, leonine beast with a lion face; also known as: *vyala* |

| | |
|---|---|
| *yantra* | 'instrument', 'tool'; geometrical diagram said to be filled with magical powers and used as a meditation prop |
| *yavana* | foreigner |
| *yoni* | receptacle or female sexual organ; usually shown in union with the *linga* and creating a kind of support for it |
| *zamindar* | landowner or collector of taxes |

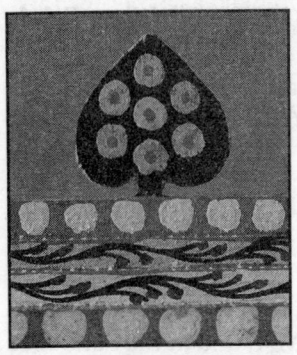

# ABOUT THE EDITORS AND CONTRIBUTORS

## THE EDITORS

**Julia A. B. Hegewald** is Professor and Head of Department of Asian and Islamic Art History, in the Institute for Oriental and Asian Studies (IOA) at the University of Bonn, Germany. She is Director of the Emmy Noether Research Project on Jainism in Karnataka, funded by the German Research Foundation (DFG). She has been a Reader in Art History and Visual Studies at the University of Manchester (2007–10), a postdoctoral Fellow at the South Asia Institute at Heidelberg University (2005–07) and a Research Fellow at University College Oxford (1998–2005). She graduated from the School of Oriental and African Studies (SOAS), University of London, from where she also holds a PhD. She is the author of *Water Architecture in South Asia: A Study of Types, Developments and Meanings* (2002), *Jaina Temple Architecture in India: The Development of a Distinct Language in Space and Ritual* (2009) and the editor of *The Jaina Heritage: Distinction, Decline and Resilience* (2010).

**Subrata K. Mitra** was trained as a political scientist at the University of Delhi and Jawaharlal Nehru University, both in India, as well as at the University of Rochester, New York, USA. He is currently Professor and Head, Department of Political Science at the South Asia Institute, Heidelberg University and was the coordinator, Area A (Governance and Administration), Cluster of Excellence—Asia and Europe in a Global Context: Shifting Asymmetries in

Cultural Flows (2008–2010). His publications include *The Puzzle of India's Governance: Culture, Context and Comparative Theory* (2005) and *When Rebels become Stakeholders* (2009). He is the academic editor of *Advances in South Asian Studies*, Heidelberg Series in South Asian and Comparative Studies and editor of *Critical Issues in the Modern Politics of South Asia (2009)*.

## THE CONTRIBUTORS

**Nick Barnard** was educated at Oxford University, UK, where he read Philosophy, Politics and Economics (1986–1989, BA Hons and MA) and at the School of Oriental and African Studies, London University (1996–99) where he completed an MA in South Asian Area Studies. He is a Curator of South Asian art in the Asian Department of the Victoria and Albert Museum, London. His principal interests are Indian jewellery, sculpture and architecture, and the Museum's Jaina collections. His book *Indian Jewellery: The V&A Collection*, was published in 2008. He has also published essays, reviews and catalogue entries on diverse subjects including "Hastings, Jones and the European Interest in Hindu Traditions", Indian jewellery, painting, architectural models and gardens and an internet resource on Jainism.

**Katrin Binder** (b. Fischer) lectures part-time at the chair of Indology, University of Wuerzburg, Germany. She graduated with a Master's degree in Indology and Comparative Religious Studies from Tuebingen University, Germany. She has recently completed her PhD on the Yakshagana theatre of coastal Karnataka at this University. She has worked on this performing art since 2001 while also training as a performer at the Udupi Yakshagana Kendra. She has also published on the work of the Basel mission in south India and translated literary texts from Kannada into German. She currently lectures part time at the Chair of Indology, University of Wuezburg, Germany.

**Thierry DiCostanzo** once worked for two years in Bangladesh at the University of Chittagong, as part of a French government programme. He also taught in different countries around the world. He currently teaches Indian colonial history at the University of Strasbourg, France, where he is part of a research programme at the Maison Interuniversitaire des Sciences de l'Homme, Alsace. His research interests are closely connected with Global History and Indian Nationalism. He regularly conducts research visits and gives guest lectures in Indian universities. His study on religious nationalism is to be published in French in the Anglo American Studies Series.

**Lion König** studied Political Science of South Asia and English Philology at Heidelberg University, Germany, and at the University of Edinburgh, UK. His research interests include citizenship, identity politics, cultural policy and political iconography in the Indian context. Currently, he is a Doctoral Fellow of the Cluster of Excellence: *Asia and Europe in a Global Context: Shifting Asymmetries in Cultural Flows* at Heidelberg University. He is, together with Harihar Bhattacharyya and Anja Kluge, co-editor of and contributor to *The Politics of Citizenship, Identity and the State in South Asia* (forthcoming).

**Tiziana Lorenzetti** graduated from the University of Roma 'La Sapienza' in 1985 and received her PhD in History of Indian Art in 1996. After this, she completed her postdoctoral studies at the 'National Museum Institute of History of Art' of New Delhi. She has carried out a number of surveys in many states of India, also collaborating on scientific missions. She has published a book (*Il tempio induista, struttura e simboli*, 2007) as well as several articles on various problems and periods of Indian art. She teaches at the University of Rome and is Research Associate at The University of Manchester. Her main fields of interest are Indian temple architecture, religious symbolism and Hindu painting.

**George Michell** was trained as an architect in Melbourne, Australia, and then studied Indian archaeology at the School of Oriental and African Studies (SOAS), University of London. He has carried out numerous research projects in India, including a survey of Hampi-Vijayanagara. His major publications are *The New Cambridge History of India I:6, Architecture and Art of Southern India, Vijayanagara and the Successor States* (1995) and *Encyclopaedia of Indian Temple Architecture: South India, Dravidadesa, Later Phase, c. A.D. 1289–1798* (2001).

**Prasanna K. Nayak** (b. 1951) has taught anthropology at Utkal University, Bhubaneswar, Orissa, for about 36 years and superannuated in June 2011 as Professor and Head of the Department of Anthropology at the same university. He has been an Alexander von Humboldt Fellow at the Freie University Berlin and Baden Wuertemberg Fellow at University of Heidelberg. He has also conducted and guided field researches in tribal areas of Orissa and published several articles based on intensive fieldwork in tribal Orissa. His books are *Blood, Women and Territory: An Analysis of Clan Feuds of the Dongia Kondhs* and *From Bondage to Rural Enterprise: A Situational Analysis and Participatory Strategies with the Bondo Highlanders*.

**Edward A. Rodrigues** studied his BA sociology from St Xaviers College Mumbai, MA and MPhil in sociology from Jawaharlal Nehru University, New

Delhi and PhD in Sociology from University of Pune. He has taught Sociology and Anthropology at St Xaviers College, Mumbai for the last twenty-two years. Since January 2009, he is Associate Professor in Sociology at the Department of Sociology, University of Mumbai. Dr Rodrigues specialises in Dalit Studies, human rights and the cultural politics of non-Western modernity. He has written on these themes in several journals, edited volumes as well as in the mainstream press in India. His work *Modernity and the Project of Dalit Emancipation in Western India* is due for publication shortly. In 2007, he was British Academy Fellow at the Department of Religious Studies, University of Manchester, UK.

**Sabine Scholz** studied Religious Studies and Indology at the University of Leipzig, Germnay, from where she holds an MA (2005). From 2005 to 2009, she was a member of the Emmy Noether Research Group on Jainism in Karnataka, at first at the University of Heidelberg, Germany, and then at the University of Manchester, UK. As a member of this interdisciplinary research team, she worked on a doctoral dissertation on Digambara Jaina identity in south India. She completed her thesis under the supervision of Professor Julia A. B. Hegewald and received her doctoral degree from the University of Manchester in 2010.

**Jivanta Schöttli** completed her PhD (summa cum laude) in political science at the South Asia Institute (SAI), University of Heidelberg, Germany in 2009. Her thesis entitled, *Strategy and Vision in Politics: Jawaharlal Nehru's Policy Choices and the Designing of Political Institutions* and has been published as a book. A graduate from the London School of Economics in International Relations (BSc) and Economic History (MSc), she is now a lecturer at the SAI where she teaches comparative politics and international relations with a focus on South Asia. Her current research interests include Indian contemporary politics and political theory, especially in its application to non-Western contexts.

**Clemens Spiess** studied Political Science and Anthropology at Heidelberg University, Germany. After his MA, he joined Heidelberg University's South Asia Institute (SAI) as a Lecturer and, in 2004, completed his doctorate on *One-party-dominance in changing societies: The African National Congress and the Indian National Congress in comparative perspective*. From 2004 to 2007, he was the Director of Heinrich-Böll-Foundation's India Office in New Delhi before returning to the Department of Political Science at Heidelberg University's SAI. Currently, he heads the South Asia Office of AWO International in Kathmandu. For more than ten years, he has been dealing extensively with political processes in South Asia and completed numerous research trips to India. His noteworthy publications are: *Political Parties in South Asia* (2004), *Democracy and Party Systems in Developing Countries* (2008) and *State and Society in South Asia* (2010).

# INDEX

53